Contents

Stephen Bygrave is Senior Lecturer in English at the
University of Southampton

Graham Allen is Lecturer in English at University College Cork, Ireland

Richard Allen is Staff Tutor in Arts at The Open University

Amanda Gilroy is Lecturer in English at the University of Groningen,
The Netherlands

Nigel Leask is Fellow and Director of Studies in English at Queens'
College, Cambridge, and a University Lecturer in English

Susan Matthews is Lecturer in English at Roehampton Institute, London

Preface

This book is one of a four-volume series. Each volume is designed as an introduction to a different aspect of literary study. The three other books in this series focus respectively on a genre (the realist novel), a concept (gender) and on the idea of the canon and the single author.

Romantic Writings focuses on works produced in a particular historical period. It is intended to show what is to be gained by studying texts in relation to the contexts in which they were produced. The period considered here is roughly that between 1780 and 1830. This is sometimes called the Romantic period and the book considers how appropriate a description this is. It does so by considering texts by canonical authors (Blake, Wordsworth, Coleridge, Byron, Keats and Shelley) alongside some by less well-known writers such as Mary Robinson, Maria Edgeworth and Letitia Elizabeth Landon.

The book is mainly concerned with the poetry of the period, which accounts for what may seem rather sketchy discussion of Jane Austen, Mary Shelley, and others. (These two are treated in more depth in the companion volume to this book, *The Realist Novel.*)

Romantic Writings has been designed to prepare readers for higher levels of study in literature. The text begins at a very accessible level and gradually increases in sophistication, refining the process of reading and learning through the book. Exercises in reading and studying literature with sample discussions are included in each chapter.

Tim Benton's intervention was crucial in completing this volume. I would like to thank all the contributors to the book and all my colleagues on the course team for their comments on its drafts. Among the latter I should single out in particular Ellie Chambers, who showed us all how to write distance-teaching material, and Julie Dickens, whose unflagging efficiency and good humour throughout the project qualifies her as its 'onlie begetter'. Thanks also to the editors at the Open University: Clive Baldwin, Kate Clements, Rachel Crease, and Abigail Croydon.

Stephen Bygrave

Note on texts

Quotations of poetry and prose writing in this book are taken from a variety of sources, full details of which are given in the Bibliography at the end of the book. In almost all cases, we have provided line numbers – or, in the case of William Blake, plate numbers – to assist readers in locating material in any edition of the texts discussed. There are several convenient anthologies of Romantic writings, but one that may be particularly recommended, and from which some material here is quoted, is Duncan Wu (ed.) *Romanticism: An Anthology* (Blackwell, 1994).

Introduction

The title of this book is 'Romantic Writings'. Why should we call some writing 'Romantic' with a capital 'R'? Nowadays the word is often used to refer to a popular form of the novel which explores aspects of romantic love through its own special conventions and vocabulary ('His strong brown arms enfolded her softly yielding body'). The sense of 'romantic' as in romantic love is relevant to the use of 'Romantic' that we shall be considering. So too are the associations of the word romantic with yearning, the mysterious, the irrational, and with transcending everyday reality; but the word 'Romantic' has a specialized as well as a colloquial sense. The medieval or Renaissance 'romance' was a literary form which had as its subject exotic or far-fetched stories of knights and ladies and adventures. An example of this form in English is the stories of King Arthur and the Knights of the Round Table in their search for the 'Holy Grail' – stories of questing for an ideal. So the adjective 'romantic' also denoted a character or action suited to such tales. The term 'romantic' began to be used in English in the early nineteenth century to refer to a belief that life could be lived by ideals rather than rules. 'Romantic' also came to be used to describe a group of writers from around the turn of the eighteenth century whose work demonstrated such a belief and who were thought in retrospect to have other characteristics in common. Since then 'Romantic' has been used as an academic category within the English Literature curriculum.

In this book we shall be examining this more specialized use of the term 'Romantic' in relation to writings produced in the period from about 1780 to 1830. We shall look at a range of writings to see how much they have in common and how suitable is their retrospective categorization as 'Romantic'. The question will arise whether 'Romantic writing' as an academic category excludes or marginalizes some types of writing by valuing certain characteristics above others.

Romanticism has been described as a European movement which came to affect all the arts in the first half of the nineteenth century. It is a very generalized way of claiming coherence for a vast range of cultural practices; nevertheless, in retrospect resemblances can be seen between what different writers, artists and musicians were producing in different parts of Europe and many have seen these resemblances as strong enough to amount to a movement. We will be restricting ourselves to Romantic writing, which has been defined in a number of ways: for example, as a response to the political revolutions of the last decade of the eighteenth century, or as a reaction to Classicism (that is to rules of writing drawn from the example of ancient Greek and Latin texts). The first is a definition which relates the writing to its historical context; the second is a formal or aesthetic definition. As a formal or aesthetic movement, the tendencies of Romanticism were generalized in the following terms by René Wellek in 1963:

> we find throughout Europe the same conceptions of poetry and of the
> workings and nature of poetic imagination, the same conception of
> nature and its relation to man, and basically the same poetic style, with
> a use of imagery, symbolism and myth which is clearly distinct from

that of eighteenth-century neoclassicism ... [each of] the following three criteria ... is central for one aspect of the practice of literature: imagination for the view of poetry, nature for the view of the world, and symbol and myth for poetic style.

(Part Two, p.326)

Wellek's is a useful account of what Romantic literature as a European movement has usually been held to consist of. However, in this book we are primarily concerned with British Romantic writing (we will return to Wellek in the Conclusion).

So how is British 'Romantic writing' to be identified? When Jerome McGann was commissioned to edit an anthology of Romantic verse for Oxford University Press, he thought it would be possible to read *all* the poetry published in the period, but this is not realistic for most of us. Choices have to be made, and we don't have an infinite range of choices. Nevertheless, there was until recently a kind of academic consensus about what British Romanticism is.

First of all, with the occasional exception of a Gothic novel and the more common exception of *Frankenstein*, British Romanticism was defined as poetry – not prose, and only very rarely non-fictional prose. What is more, 'Romantic poetry' was regarded as mostly having been written by just six male English poets: William Blake, William Wordsworth, Samuel Taylor Coleridge, Lord Byron, Percy Bysshe Shelley and John Keats. Writers whose publishers or whose audience were not based in London might have been represented by Walter Scott (though probably only as a novelist), John Clare and Robert Burns. Poetry by women in the period was more or less ignored. Romantic poetry was discussed in relation to broad, ambitious terms like 'Imagination' and 'Nature'. This sketch is of course a caricature – I don't think you would find a teacher of Romantic writing who would defend such a course. Nevertheless, many students came away with an impression that Romantic writing comprised something like the above.

We shall be asking whether writings of the time did share characteristics which would justify our categorizing them as Romantic. Wordsworth and Coleridge didn't think of themselves as Romantics and wouldn't have thought of themselves as sharing characteristics with, say, Keats. None of these was at all as widely read at the time as the poets Samuel Rogers, Thomas Campbell, or Thomas Moore. (The bestselling poet of the nineteenth century as a whole was not Scott or Byron or Tennyson, and certainly not Wordsworth, but Felicia Dorothea Hemans, now remembered only as the author of 'The Boy Stood on the Burning Deck'.) Neither Percy Shelley's *A Defence of Poetry* nor William Wordsworth's *The Prelude*, both of which we will be looking at as central Romantic texts, were even published during their authors' lifetimes.

When we come on to examine in more detail, say, what the British Romantics meant by 'Imagination', we may find that things are not as clear-cut as writers such as Wellek have claimed. Although many contemporary writers would have agreed on the importance of 'Imagination', there would have been little agreement on what it was or on who did and did not possess it. The differences between writers can seem almost as strong as the resemblances. Establishing a single definition may not be a practicable aim. It is by looking at the circumstances in which their writing was produced – who was it for? what was the reaction to it? and so on – that we can arrive at a more satisfactory understanding. That would then be to understand Romantic texts in historical rather than in formal terms. In this instance the texts are from the period between about 1780 and 1830, which was a period of great social and cultural change. I hope to show you why the writing produced within this period had a coherence which may justify treating it as distinct from the writing of other periods.

Such distinctions are not easy to make. There may be disagreement about the characteristics of, say, 'Victorianism', but there is not much disagreement about the historical period that the term designates. 'Romanticism' is much more slippery. While the term is still with us in some ways, the movement that has been given that name was current about two hundred years ago. An anthology of verse from this period published in 1928 was called *The Oxford Book of Regency Verse*. The Regency is a period with clear boundaries: it is the period from February 1811 to January 1820 during which the Prince of Wales (the future George IV) acted as regent for his father. 'Romanticism' seems to be a term for a movement not necessarily confined to one period, and the 'Romantic period' has no clear chronological boundaries.

The anthology compiled by Jerome McGann mentioned above was a successor to *The Oxford Book of Romantic Verse*, but he chose to call it *The New Oxford Book of Romantic Period Verse* because, as he notes in his introduction, 'the romantic period and … the romantic movement are not the same thing' (p.xx). What he means is that a writer such as Jane Austen lived through the Romantic *period* without belonging to the Romantic *movement* – indeed she seems mostly to be *anti*-Romantic. She was against most sorts of innovation, against extravagant displays of feeling, and so on. I will discuss Austen briefly in Chapter Two, but she illustrates the obvious fact that not all writers living at the same time (in any period of history) share the same attitudes, approaches and characteristics. If Romantic writing is to be treated as a distinct kind of writing, then we need to be able to say what it is distinct *from*, which will involve us in looking at the history of the period in which it was written and at the other kinds of writing available within the period. These questions about which texts from the past are selected for attention and how they are described, explain why this book is called 'Romantic Writings'. To have called it, say, 'Romantic Literature' would have begged these questions. 'Literature' can mean anything that is written, but it now implies a specially privileged body of writing (indeed, it can be argued that such a notion was an invention of this period).

In the first two chapters we will be looking mainly at *lyric* poetry – that is at poems in which, by and large, our interest is with the first-person speaker of a poem and the thoughts and feelings of the moment it records. But it is important to remember that Romantic writing includes a great many *narrative* works, that is, works in which we have an interest in the story they tell. Many of these narratives are in prose – Mary Shelley's *Frankenstein* is one of the most famous – but many too are in verse. If you have any prior associations with Romantic writing they will probably be to do with lyric poems written about extreme, but private, feelings. Probably the term 'Romantic' connotes to us a sense of disengagement, of remoteness from actual social conditions. This is partly a result of the influence of Victorian anthologies such as *Palgrave's Golden Treasury*, in which the selections created a view of the Romantic writers as lyric poets alone and as lovers, even priests, of nature. This takes them outside the history in which they wrote. This book will attempt to show something of what such a selection leaves out. We will try to understand Romantic texts by reading them in relation to the history within which they were produced. In the first two chapters I'll suggest that to answer the question 'what was Romanticism?' we need to ask another – '*when* was Romanticism?'

Stephen Bygrave

Part One

Romantic poems and contexts

by Stephen Bygrave

This chapter has two aims. The first is to introduce you to a variety of Romantic writings, which will allow you to start building your own sense of their common tendencies. All these texts were produced in the last decades of the eighteenth century or in the first half of the nineteenth century, so the second aim is to begin explaining the context in which they were written. These texts were part of a historical period with its own particular habits, events, concerns, and so on. It has been common to label this 'the Romantic period', and I hope in what follows to enable you to think about what that description means.

We will be looking at two main topics: (1) at what it might mean to read historically, the advantages of such a way of reading and how we might do it; and (2) at the novelty of Romantic writing, by looking at the figure of the child as it appears in Wordsworth and, in more detail, in Blake's *Songs of Innocence and Experience*.

Writing in history

I want to begin by looking at two Romantic poems. First we will look at the poems individually, then see whether we can identify any features they have in common. The first is by William Wordsworth and was written in 1798. Please read it two or three times, thinking first about what *kind* of poem you think it is. Is it a lyric or a narrative? (That is to say, does it record the feelings of a particular moment or does it tell a story?)

> She dwelt among th' untrodden ways
> Beside the springs of Dove,
> A maid whom there were none to praise
> And very few to love.
>
> A violet by a mossy stone   5
> Half-hidden from the eye!
> Fair as a star when only one
> Is shining in the sky!
>
> She *lived* unknown, and few could know
> When Lucy ceased to be;   10
> But she is in her grave, and oh!
> The difference to me.

(Wu, *Romanticism*, 1994, p.245)

The poem looks as though it is going to be a narrative – as though it is going to tell a story. We expect to find out what happens to this girl or woman, but all that we learn, from the last stanza, is her name and that she dies. So the poem is actually a lyric. Specifically, by the end it seems to be an elegy, or perhaps a love poem.

Now read the poem again, thinking about the following questions: (1) What is the point of the comparisons in the middle stanza? What do they suggest about the 'she' of the poem? (2) Who is the subject of this poem? Who is it actually *about*?

Discussion

1 Instead of giving a literal description of the girl or woman the middle stanza substitutes for her a violet and a star. These, we infer, stand for her being beautiful ('fair') but also obscure ('half-hidden'). The violet and the star are *symbols* for her beauty and obscurity. We are not told her story, nor even what she looks like. She is represented by symbols drawn from the natural world rather than described as a person. The girl or woman is seen to be extraordinary – as extraordinary in her private way as a single star visible in the night sky.

2 'Me' is the last word of the poem, and comes as something of a surprise. Finally, the focus is not upon the girl, now named as Lucy, but upon the speaker (or narrator), who has not appeared until this point. It seems that the poem is not about Lucy, but about the effect her absence has on the speaker. The poem comes to rest on a wholly individual feeling. As readers we are flattered to find ourselves amongst the 'few' who know about this and for whom it is significant. ■

The second poem is by John Clare and was written some time after 1842. This poem too changes course in its final stanza. Read the poem right through but concentrate here on the first two stanzas, noting any difficulties you have with them.

1

I am — yet what I am none cares or knows;
   My friends forsake me like a memory lost: —
I am the self-consumer of my woes; —
   They rise and vanish in oblivion's host,
Like shadows in love's frenzied stifled throes: —   5
And yet I am, and live — like vapours tost

2

Into the nothingness of scorn and noise, —
   Into the living sea of waking dreams,
Where there is neither sense of life or joys,
   But the vast shipwreck of my lifes esteems;   10
Even the dearest, that I love the best
Are strange — nay, rather stranger than the rest.

3

I long for scenes, where man hath never trod
   A place where woman never smiled or wept
There to abide with my Creator, God;   15
   And sleep as I in childhood, sweetly slept,
Untroubling, and untroubled where I lie,
The grass below — above the vaulted sky.

(Wu, *Romanticism*, 1994, p.1001)

4

Lines 3–5 are quite difficult here. If 'woes' have to be 'self-consumed' they have no outlet. In these stanzas, everything that might confirm the speaker's identity – even his 'woes' – is strange and insubstantial like shadows, vapour or dreams. The poem begins strikingly: 'I am'. At first this seems to be an assertion of identity as striking as the one which ended the Wordsworth poem. Yet this is at once seen to be impossible – just as to say simply 'I am' is grammatically impossible, or at least incomplete, since the verb 'to be' needs a complement. That is to say, nothing can just *be*; it has to *be* something. And what follows in the first two stanzas does not elaborate on an assertion of identity, but takes it away – together with all the people and things that might confirm it.

Now read the poem again, thinking about the following questions: (1) Do you notice anything about the punctuation? (2) How does the poem change course in the last stanza?

D i s c u s s i o n

1   There seems to be a possessive apostrophe missing from the word 'lifes' in line 10. You probably also noticed all the dashes, which are often added on to the other punctuation marks. Their effect is to break the poem up into a series of exclamations. All the same, these two stanzas constitute a single sentence, which continues across the break between the first two stanzas, a sentence which reads as 'tost/Into the nothingness … Into the living sea …', and so on.

2   In the final stanza the speaker (or narrator) does not describe his state as he has in the first two. Instead he 'longs' for a change of 'scene'. Yet what he longs for is somewhere 'man hath never trod/A place where woman never smiled or wept'. He yearns for what is impossible. The speaker longs to return to something like his childhood, to a lost paradise in which he was close to God. He wants to 'abide' in a 'scene' or 'place' which is natural, between 'the grass … [and] the vaulted sky', and in which he can be free and secure. There is a desire for escape – or even for death. He wants to be free not just from constraint but from human society. ■

Now read the two poems again and think about what, if anything, they have in common.

D i s c u s s i o n

Both poems are introspective – perhaps even self-pitying in the case of the Clare – and both look upon private experience as suitable material for poetry. Everything referred to in the Clare poem seems to be used as a way of finding an equivalent for the speaker's psychological state. Ending as it does, the Wordsworth poem might be seen to be claiming that individual feeling is valid in itself. In the case of the Clare poem, to write about suffering is different from merely suffering. The poem was unpublished in his lifetime, but nevertheless Clare put private experience into words and into poetic form. In both poems then, private experience is made public. To publish something is to make it public. Publication after all *means* making public. It might be said also that both poems look upon private experience as it were from the outside. This assertion of the self and what it wishes, feels, fears, and so on, is a characteristic of Romantic writing.

Both poems draw on natural objects as a source of comparisons. Nature provides Wordsworth with symbols for the 'unknown' beauty of Lucy. There are several references in the Clare poem to natural objects and phenomena: there are 'vapours' (line 6), the sea (line 8) and the grass and sky (line 18). However, in both cases this is succeeded, as we have seen, by longing for a state that does not exist. In neither poem is nature looked at from the outside and described. In both cases it is used to find an equivalent for a state of the self, so that the external is, as it were, internalized.

The Wordsworth poem at first stresses Lucy's ordinariness before claiming her to be extraordinary. Her death makes a 'difference'. And the difference Lucy's death makes cannot be explained or rationalized but only stated. The Clare poem ends with a desire to be transfigured, or to have transcended the state in which it begins. In both poems the 'real' or material is succeeded by the ideal or, we might say, the natural by the supernatural. The two poems share a desire to transfigure or transcend the ordinary. This desire to transcend particular circumstances, or the claim to have done so, is a second characteristic of Romantic writing. ■

We have noted two tendencies that these poems share: an insistence that private experience (and private opinion) is publicly valid, and a desire for transcendence. We will see both these tendencies again and again in Romantic texts. These tendencies are to do with the content of poems which may not seem to have much in common formally.

If we find the poems difficult, the difficulties can mostly be resolved by attention to their language. That is to say, neither poem seems to rely heavily on references to people, things, or events outside itself. All the same, we might feel that additional information would be helpful. For instance, the punctuation of the Clare poem seemed to hamper our understanding at first. The punctuation is not Clare's – the poem was transcribed by a warder in the Northampton madhouse in which he was kept. This information about Clare's circumstances might also lead us to speculate about the references to the fantasy of release that the poem contains. In his 'Note on the texts' Duncan Wu explains why he has not regularized (that is, tidied up) the punctuation of the Clare texts for his edition (*Romanticism*, p.xxxi); nevertheless, he does alter the text, as do the editors of the standard edition of Clare's works, by substituting the word 'tost' for the word 'lost', which is what actually appears in the transcript (Robinson and Powell, *The Later Poems of John Clare*, 1984, pp.396–7). Such a substitution would have been made because 'tost' made more sense to the editors, or was more in line with how they understood Clare's intentions.

The Wordsworth poem, which is untitled, was sent with another, beginning 'Strange fits of passion I have known', in a joint letter from William Wordsworth and his sister Dorothy to Coleridge from Goslar in Germany in December 1798. It was published in Volume II of the second edition of the *Lyrical Ballads* collection in 1800. *Lyrical Ballads* was a collection of poems by Wordsworth and Coleridge which was first published in 1798. We will come back to Wordsworth's Preface to an 1802 edition later in this chapter. This poem of Wordsworth's is often seen as belonging to a group of four poems written around the same time, all of which refer to 'Lucy'. We don't know the identity of this 'Lucy', although Coleridge was first in attempting to identify her by speculating about another poem in this group, 'Most probably in some gloomier moment he [Wordsworth] had fancied the moment in which his Sister might die' (letter of 6 April, 1799; Griggs (ed.), *Collected Letters of Coleridge*, 1956, Vol. 1, p.479). Other critics have suggested that the absence with which the poem grapples is the absence of the poet from his homeland. It is not because of our inability to identify Lucy that the poem is enigmatic, but because of the feeling which it seems to express – a loss which is felt powerfully by the speaker, but only by him. It makes no general or public difference, but a difference to him which is made public by the poem.

We read these two poems first of all as words on the page, without reference to the context in which they were written. Once we had some additional information our perspective on the poems changed. The information I gave you may have prompted new questions and I hope that these were interesting questions. From the poems we were also able to describe two tendencies of Romantic poems. But that description was very general. It would not enable us to identify as 'Romantic' any other poem. It was so general it could apply to many other poems which might not generally be regarded as Romantic poems. Romantic writings share a broadly similar historical context and our reading gains from knowledge of this context. I hope I can demonstrate this by looking at a poem by Percy Bysshe Shelley. **As you read it, I would like you to consider two questions. (1) Does there seem to be a dominant mood or feeling to the poem? (2) What part is played by form, especially grammar and rhyme, in the poem?**

England in 1819

An old mad, blind, despised, and dying King;
Princes, the dregs of their dull race, who flow
Through public scorn – mud from a muddy spring;
Rulers who neither see, nor feel, nor know,
But leech-like to their fainting country cling   5
Till they drop, blind in blood, without a blow.
A people starved and stabbed in th' untilled field;
An army, whom liberticide and prey
Makes as a two-edged sword to all who wield;
Golden and sanguine laws which tempt and slay;   10
Religion Christless, Godless – a book sealed;
A senate, time's worst statute, unrepealed –
Are graves, from which a glorious phantom may
Burst, to illumine our tempestuous day.

(Wu, *Romanticism*, 1994, p.876)

Discussion

1   The poem is *angry*, isn't it? That anger is clear whether or not you understand the details, and is communicated by the poem's uncompromising vocabulary – for example 'mad', 'despised', 'dregs' and 'scorn', all in the first two-and-a-half lines.

2   The anger is contained within a very strict form – there are only four rhymes. The poem is a sonnet – a poem of fourteen lines usually divided between a group of eight lines (the octet), and a second group of six lines (the sestet). Despite the punctuation – which is Shelley's – you may have felt that the poem was actually a single sentence. There is no real division between octet and sestet. It is not until right at the end that the sentence completes itself (all these things 'are graves'). And right at the end the poem also changes course.

   Up to that point it's been a list of pretty grievous symptoms. They are also *public* symptoms, symptoms of public sickness or corruption. All the great institutions of the state – the monarchy, the army, religion – are sick or corrupted. The king is 'dying', the rulers 'drop', and so on. These are symptoms of a fatal illness. Then right at the end it is revealed that they are symptoms of *change*. Death may be followed by a rebirth. After death there may rise a new order. We cannot say who or what the 'glorious phantom' *is* – the poem is a lot more specific about the disease than the cure. But it finally escapes its catalogue of exploitation and violence by a move into an ideal future. It moves from negative to positive, and from diagnosis to prophecy, suggesting the possibility at least of a dazzling transformation. ■

Beyond these points you may have had difficulties with the poem's references to historical events you may not know about. The very title of the poem advertises its relation to a particular time in history, and it does refer to things, events or people outside itself much more than the Wordsworth and Clare poems did. Did we need a context for it before we started?

   1819 was the fifty-ninth year of the reign of George III, who was indeed adjudged mad by the clinicians of the day. He died the following year and was succeeded by his son who had reigned as regent since 1810. The sons of George III are the 'princes' of line 2. The 'senate ... unrepealed' (line 12) refers to the British Parliament, whose electoral system was regarded as corrupt by those who advocated its reform. In particular, the poem alludes (in line 7) to violence against the people. In August 1819 troops were sent in to dispel a large but peaceful demonstration for parliamentary reform on St Peter's Fields in Manchester. Eleven people were killed and more than four hundred injured in an event which came to be known as the 'Peterloo Massacre'. St Peter's Fields might have been cultivated to save the demonstrators from starvation, but was where they were cut down instead. Fields would remain 'untilled' when they were unprofitable to their landlords, and this turned them into battlefields when hungry families protested. The poem sees economic exploitation and violence as interrelated – it yokes them together in the phrase 'starved and stabbed'. Blood and money are linked again in the later phrase 'golden and sanguine laws' (line 10). They 'tempt and slay' because the government had used *agents provocateurs* to incite uprisings.

   The anger at the government and the monarchy evident in this sonnet explains why it was withheld from publication until 1839, after Shelley's death. The poem takes the part of the 'people' against the powers of the state. But although it may be in part written *about* a 'people', who are largely illiterate, it surely is not written *to* them. The arresting opening of the poem may seem quite like that of speech. After that its vocabulary is much more varied: 'sanguine' and 'slay' (line 10) are versions of the much blunter terms 'blood' and 'stabbed' in lines 6 and 7. The later terms seem though to be more like euphemisms than synonyms. The start of the poem gets its effect from monosyllables; later these are set against longer, Latinate words: 'liberticide', 'unrepealed', 'illumine', 'tempestuous'. How many people in the England of 1819 would have had the classical learning to understand 'A senate' (line 12) as a synonym for the British Parliament? This raises the question of whether the poem in fact depends on a version of the élitism it seems to attack. This kind of question arises out of knowledge about the context in which the poem was written, so I would say that we do need this kind of knowledge.

We looked at the Wordsworth and Clare poems first of all in terms of the internal workings of their language, and then in terms of how they might be re-read within a certain context. Students are still commonly taught to read literary texts in a way which assumes that meaning is always located in the text itself. If the text is read carefully and sensitively, the argument goes, it will answer all the questions we could possibly have about it. We do not need anything but the text itself. I have suggested by contrast that our reading of a poem is sharpened and deepened by reading it in context. I will be giving you such contexts for the other poems we go on to look at. Once we know about these contexts we tend to read the poems in a different way. We see each poem as a response to a particular situation. This does not mean that the poem only functions within that particular situation, for then we would have very little hope of ever understanding it. In the case of the first two poems we have looked at, the contexts I offered you were not connected with great public events. But we could not really understand Shelley's poem without some additional knowledge of the history about which, and within which, he was writing. There is no substitute for reading the poems carefully, but to read them fully requires that we keep in mind the history within which they were produced.

I have suggested that Romantic writing is best understood as the writing of a particular historical period. For British writing, the Romantic period is usually agreed to be between roughly 1780 and 1830. But 'Romanticism' is a term that is convenient rather than precise. It is convenient because it gives us a label for some tendencies current around the same time and which we recognize to be similar. These tendencies became apparent not only in writing and in the other arts but in science and technology, politics, religion, and eventually in all areas of daily life throughout Europe. This period encompasses the American Revolution (independence having been declared in 1776), the French Revolution (from 1789), and wars of national independence in Poland, Spain, Greece, and elsewhere. (However, the dates would be different if we were to think of Romantic writing in continental Europe rather than in Britain, in which case we would have to extend the period at least as far as the European revolutions of 1848, or different again if we were to think of fields other than writing.) This, then, was a period of revolutions. Within it, the outbreak of war between Britain and revolutionary France in 1793, and the final defeat of Napoleon at Waterloo in 1815 are important landmarks.

The French Revolution itself was not a single event but a series of events which together marked a break from the past. A system of government that had existed for hundreds of years was swept away, classes that had previously held no vote and had no voice took power, and a king was executed. These enormous and apparently sudden changes raised the possibility of all sorts of other changes, some of which were to be hoped for and some to be feared. The example of events in France raised the hopes of some in Britain for reform of the franchise, for religious toleration, for a change in the legal status of women, and so on. Perhaps the most influential British defender of the French Revolution was Thomas Paine (1737–1809). He had been in America during the War of Independence and his *Rights of Man* (1791 and 1792) was the manifesto of those who were pressing for reforms. Others saw such reforms as examples of 'Jacobinism', that is, as innovations that threatened the British constitution with the anarchy, blood-letting, and eventual tyranny to which the French Revolution had led. Such views led to the prosecution of the publishers of *Rights of Man* and to Paine fleeing from England. So events in France became part of British history. The history of Romanticism in British writing is often written as the history of responses and counter-responses to the French Revolution.

In this period Britain became the first industrial nation and secured its status as the great colonial power it only ceased to be after the Second World War. Cynthia Chase claims that the period saw the invention of democracy, the invention of revolution, and the invention of a reading public (Chase, *Romanticism*, 1993, p.1). Most of the writers we will be considering participated in debates about the Revolution in the war years which followed – debates which have been called a 'war of ideas'. When the government instituted trials for treason in 1794 it put three *writers* in the dock: Thomas Hardy (the radical, not the later novelist), founding member of the London Corresponding Society, which met to discuss the democratic ideas of Thomas Paine and William Godwin; John Horne Tooke, the grammarian; and the poet and orator John Thelwall, who was, as we shall see, a friend of Wordsworth and Coleridge.

Such events are often spoken of as the optional 'background' to reading literary texts which are the 'foreground' and which can, by implication, be focused without any reference to the background. I want to argue that these events are more than just a background which we can ignore while we get on with the real job of reading literary texts.

Reading in history

Before looking at some specific poems, I want to talk more generally about the problems we have in reading a poem from the past – and the problems we encounter in reading any text historically. Our knowledge of the past, what is called 'history', comes through 'reading' the texts of the past, whether that text is a manuscript, a book, someone's spoken or recorded reminiscences ('oral history'), or an artefact such as a building or a piece of broken pottery dug up on an archaeological site. What we know about history may come from reading a book or article by a professional historian, or from television, radio, magazines or historical novels. Faced with any of these, what we are doing is interpreting texts – observing, asking questions, comparing what we see or infer with what we already know, organizing our observations or inferences to certain ends. A piece of broken pot has to be fitted into our understanding of – or our construction of – a whole society or civilization.

When we read texts, we often feel we should be looking for some 'hidden' or 'deeper' meaning, as though the words that comprise a text are like the soil lying on top of the piece of pottery that the archaeologist has to clean away from it. Yet we can see that this is obviously not so – it is not the case that the words which comprise, say, Shakespeare's Othello or Desdemona somehow get in the way of their 'secret' meaning – a meaning that the English Literature taught at school encourages us to call the 'character' of each. The words are all they are: there is literally nothing to Othello or Desdemona but the words by which they are constructed – those that are given to those figures in the play and to others. We can then bring other words to bear. Just as we might bring to bear on our piece of broken pot knowledge of the kitchen arrangements of a past civilization, so we might bring to bear on the words that make up 'Othello' or 'Desdemona' other words, words from other texts by Shakespeare, by his contemporaries, and by subsequent interpreters. This is what I have called the context of a text. I have suggested that a context is necessary fully to understand any text. We find out about a context by asking questions. Who wrote a text? When was it written? Who was it written for? How did they read it? and so on. Answers to these questions will give us a way of placing the text in its historical context.

This context is complex. A poem is written within a larger historical context. From its publication it will have a history of who read it and how it was received. It will also have what we might call a prehistory. The text may have a prehistory in its earlier drafts and revisions, in other works by its author (if we know who he or she is) and by her or his contemporaries. It also has a prehistory in its formal models. For example, we have looked at a sonnet in this chapter (Shelley's 'England in 1819'). The sonnet is a form which originated in Italy and was brought to Britain by Tudor courtiers. It is a form with its own strict conventions and is particularly associated with two earlier English poets, Shakespeare and Milton. A Romantic sonnet may bear the traces of such earlier sonnets.

This is not to turn the past into a set of texts – we can only know the past through texts, whether these texts are written down or are artefacts, like bits of pottery, but this does not mean that the past itself is a text. The past is fixed, but even if we consider a bit of the past that we ourselves remember, we remember it differently from other people, or we may find that things we overlooked at the time are what we now see as important. So we turn the past into history, and we rewrite history, or even remember differently because of our present needs. Once, the pot would have been used for something, and not regarded as an object to be interpreted. You treated the cup you drank your coffee from this morning differently from the way you would treat a piece of the Elgin Marbles (at least I hope so); but in 2000 years' time, or even a hundred, your own coffee cup may have a different status, for someone else, than it did for you this morning.

Things are written in different contexts, as we have seen, but we all read in different contexts too. For instance, you may be reading this book because you are required to as part of an academic course, because (misled by the cover) you thought it contained lethal cocktail recipes, or because you are my proud mother. Whichever of these descriptions most nearly fits you, you are reading for certain purposes and reading in a particular context. Though it may sound grandiose, you too are reading in history, like it or not. What this means is that in reading a text two histories come together – that of the text and that of its reader. There are two histories involved in reading a text from the past. At least two. I have suggested already that one way we understand texts is by what has been said about them in the past, so that what Dr Johnson said about Othello or Desdemona is one of the things that has contributed to our understanding of Othello or Desdemona. (For the record, Johnson thought the play a dreadful warning of the dangers of a mixed marriage.) We can try to find out who read a poem written in the sixteenth century and what they might have made of it, but we cannot become that reader, nor is there any point in trying. How a poem was read in the past becomes part of what we know about that poem, but we know it *now*, and when we read a poem that knowledge competes for our mental attention with all the other things that we know now.

These two histories, that of the text and of who we are in history, are of course complicated matters, but we can make two summary points.

1   As readers we bring to the text certain assumptions drawn from our previous reading experiences, from the way we have been taught, as well as equally important factors like our race, our gender, our class.

2   The text is embedded in various kinds of history. It is part of the larger historical situation in which it was produced. It also has a prehistory, and a subsequent history which will include how it was received.

By means of this last point we can see that we treat a text with more attention, or even reverence, if it has been highly valued historically. Shakespeare's work was not rated any more highly than that of his fellow dramatists in his lifetime, but there has been a whole history of praise for it since. Now if a text comes to us for the first time with the name 'William Shakespeare' attached to it we regard it rather differently from one by a contemporary best-selling novelist. The second point we can draw out of this is that 'meaning' is not the property of an author.

People often ask 'What does the author mean?', 'What is the author trying to say?' The question is fair enough in the sense that we may initially be struggling to make sense of an unfamiliar text. Look back at the Clare poem for instance. Does 'they' in line 4 refer back to 'my friends' or 'my woes'? What is going 'into' what (line 7)? The answers come from attention to the language of the poem and to the context(s) we can reconstruct for it. Attention to the language of the poem suggests that the answer to the first question is probably the latter ('woes') and the answer to the second question is that the phrase ran 'I am ... tost/Into the nothingness ...'. Contextual information about the way the poem has come down to us also revealed that modern editors substituted the word 'tost' for the word 'lost'. The fact that this decision affects the text we read raises a question of where contexts begin and end. Are they limited to the time when a text was produced?

And what role does author's intention play? These are questions we shall consider in the next section.

However, asking 'What does the *author* mean?' or 'What is the *author* trying to say?' is looking in the wrong place for the answer. We find the 'meaning' of the piece of pottery in the pot and in the way we think it functioned within a civilization, not by asking the potter. Besides, try finding a 2000-year-old potter willing to answer your questions, or give Shakespeare a ring and ask him what he meant by *Othello*. What an author planned to do, or thought they were doing in producing a text is one kind of information we can gather about a text, but it is often unreliable, and it is only one kind of information amongst others. We make our own judgements about people, and do not simply accept that they are what they think themselves to be. Or we might say that the relation of a text to its author is like that of a child to its parents. If you wanted to know the child's opinion about something, you would not ask the parents.

In the case of Shakespeare, we know almost nothing about his intentions in writing a text. In the case of the Romantic writers, we know a great deal. As we shall see in Chapter Three, they left a good deal of evidence as to what they intended both in general and in relation to specific texts. They produced a great many prefaces, manifestos and theoretical treatises, as well as less formal comments in conversations, letters and notebooks, which may provide a helpful context for reading their work. If, however, the effect of your reading of their texts does not accord with their descriptions, that does not mean your reading is 'wrong'; it may mean that the difference in time between the writing and the reading leads to different results.

The relation of a poem to history is not necessarily evident or straightforward. In Chapter Two we will be looking at some of the great public events that occurred during the Romantic period. Then, as now, it may be that such events did not impinge directly on the daily life of most people. Some of the poems we will be looking at in this chapter seem entirely to do with such ordinary daily life. I would make two points about this though. First, that daily life itself happened (and happens) in history: it too has a history of its own. Second, that the growth of the press in the years we are considering meant that people knew more about what was going on beyond the boundaries of their parishes. Public events came to have more currency in daily life than had been possible before.

The analogy I offered above assumes that our interest in a text is comparable with the interest an archaeologist might have in an artefact, but this is not necessarily so. To compare literary texts with bits of pottery is not to compare like with like. I have also spoken in rather abstract theoretical terms. I wanted to suggest something that might be true for reading all texts of the past, not only the texts of Romanticism. How then does this relate to the specifics of reading Romantic texts?

Well, it goes right down to the level of the single word. Even single words in Romantic texts can be charged in a way we may not notice. For example, the term 'democracy' is fairly uncontroversially used as the name for a good and desirable state of affairs in modern western societies, though definitions vary greatly. In the late eighteenth century, however, to be a 'democrat' was to be a supporter of the French Revolution – hence a report by a Home Office spy on Coleridge, the Wordsworths and their friend John Thelwall, called them 'a Sett of Violent Democrats'. The term carried a special charge; the opposite of a 'democrat' would be a supporter of the existing constitution, a 'patriot'. The single word then has connotations we may miss if we assume that words have always meant the same. In Shelley's 'England in 1819' we saw an appeal to 'the people'. Words such as 'rights', 'liberty' and 'the people' also carried a political charge: to use those words would imply radical political beliefs, while to use terms like 'law' and 'the mob' would imply conservative ones. 'For God and King' was the cry of those who attacked supporters of the Revolution.

The word revolution itself in its original sense means simply a rotation or complete cycle. Where the word was applied to the overturning of a state it was applied at first in a consciously metaphorical sense – a sense that we have perhaps lost, so that 'revolution' has become a dead metaphor. Similar examples could be taken from the works of any period, but my argument here is that Romantic texts are more than usually highly politically charged. Reading them in context, you become aware of the charges they carry.

In general, then, Romantic texts need to be understood with some sense of the historical circumstances within which they were produced. In putting a stress on 'history' you might think that I am saying that you cannot possibly understand a text until you know a whole lot of facts that are separate from it. Now of course I am not suggesting that you should be able to go from a single poem to being able to talk about a whole civilization. To read texts historically does not mean putting aside all our present assumptions, worries and desires and trying to put on those of some past era. We move from the known into the previously unknown, from what we already know to some new knowledge.

In the three poems we have already looked at we began by seeing how far we could get simply by reading carefully the poems themselves. Such careful reading is indispensable. Then I suggested contexts for the poems that might have led us to read them differently. But does this mean that there are two kinds of reading? Are these two activities really separate? In the following quotation, Cynthia Chase refers to these two activities as, respectively, focusing 'on the text's linguistic mode of production' and 'recovering [its] historical particularity'. Chase poses these two activities as alternative ways of reading. (In the quotation, by 'discourses' she means what was said and written as opposed to what happened, by 'reception' how texts were first read, and by 'rhetorical structures' the way their language is organized.)

> One [approach] is to place literary works in a historical context made up of social and political events and discourses (not, as in an earlier history of ideas, in the context of philosophical or other literary works), in the interest of recovering their historical particularity through the details of their reception. [...] The other is to focus on the text's linguistic mode of production and examine its 'inner' workings: the relationships among its themes and statements and its rhetorical structures.

> (Chase, *Romanticism*, 1993, p.4)

Chase calls these two modes respectively 'New Historicism' and 'rhetorical reading'. Though the quotation is from a book about Romanticism, she does imply that these modes of reading hold good for all literary works. I hope that you find that these two modes are not opposed at all. Attention to the linguistic detail of a text need not at all be opposed to an awareness of the way it works within and upon history. We cannot put ourselves outside of history any more than we can put ourselves outside of language. To talk about the '"inner" workings' of a poem sounds suspiciously like the way we might worry about 'a deeper meaning'. And there is surely no inside and outside in this way. That is a difficult point, but perhaps it can be demonstrated as we look at more poems.

Three poems about London

Romantic writing might be described as a set of different and often competing voices. One characteristic of Romantic texts is not only that they differ from each other, but that they may explicitly or implicitly debate with each other. This can be seen when we compare texts. You will find such comparisons as you read on through the book; here we will start by comparing three poems about London. The first was published posthumously in 1806 in the *Poetical Works* of Mary Robinson. **Read it now thinking about the following two questions: (1) What can we say about the language of this poem? (2) It is a descriptive poem in blank verse, but is there a method to its description? In all three poems we have looked at so far there was a change of direction at the end. Is that also true here? Or does it end in the same way it began?**

London's Summer Morning

Who has not waked to list the busy sounds
Of summer's morning, in the sultry smoke
Of noisy London? On the pavement hot
The sooty chimney-boy, with dingy face
And tattered covering, shrilly bawls his trade,   5
Rousing the sleepy housemaid. At the door
The milk-pail rattles, and the tinkling bell
Proclaims the dustman's office; while the street
Is lost in clouds impervious. Now begins
The din of hackney-coaches, waggons, carts;   10
While tinmen's shops, and noisy trunk-makers,
Knife-grinders, coopers, squeaking cork-cutters,
Fruit barrows, and the hunger-giving cries
Of vegetable-vendors, fill the air.
Now every shop displays its varied trade,   15
And the fresh-sprinkled pavement cools the feet
Of early walkers. At the private door
The ruddy housemaid twirls the busy mop,
Annoying the smart girl 'prentice, or neat girl,
Tripping with band-box lightly. Now the sun   20
Darts burning splendour on the glittering pane,
Save where the canvas awning throws a shade
On the gay merchandise. Now, spruce and trim,
In shops (where beauty smiles with industry)
Sits the smart damsel; while the passenger   25

Peeps through the window, watching every charm.
Now pastry dainties catch the eye minute
Of humming insects, while the limy snare
Waits to enthral them. Now the lamp-lighter
Mounts the tall ladder, nimbly venturous,   30
To trim the half-filled lamps, while at his feet
The pot-boy yells discordant! All along
The sultry pavement, the old-clothes-man cries
In tone monotonous, while sidelong views
The area for his traffic: now the bag   35
Is slyly opened, and the half-worn suit
(Sometimes the pilfered treasures of the base
Domestic spoiler), for one half its worth,
Sinks in the green abyss. The porter now
Bears his huge load along the burning way;   40
And the poor poet wakes from busy dreams,
To paint the summer morning.

(Lonsdale, *Eighteenth-Century Women Poets*, 1989, pp.472–3)

Discussion

1   In this poem there are several examples of a specialized poetic language. There are some inversions of the word order of speech – for example 'clouds impervious' (line 9), 'eye minute' (line 27), 'tone monotonous' (line 34). Some words have gone, or changed their meaning: so a 'band-box' (line 20) is a hatbox, ''prentice' (line 19) is short for 'apprentice' and 'the dustman's office' (line 8) means his job, not his place of work. Other words were archaic even at the time of writing: 'list' for 'listen' in the first line for example. There are also several examples of calling things by elaborately roundabout names (technically known as *periphrasis*) – for example the 'green abyss' of the old clothes man's sack (line 39) or the 'limy snare' of the flytrap (line 28). This gives us some difficulty with the phrase in brackets at lines 37–8. A 'base domestic spoiler' is a thief or burglar: sometimes the old-clothes-man sells stolen goods – the booty (or 'spoils') of the thief. Lastly, hardly a noun here is without a complementary adjective (in the first sentence for example we have 'busy sounds', 'sultry smoke' and 'noisy London'). Specialized poetic diction, periphrasis, and an over-reliance on adjectives: all these are characteristics of the language of eighteenth-century poetry attacked by Wordsworth and Coleridge.

2   In a later chapter we will see Wordsworth employing a very similar technique of listing an unsorted series of perceptions to represent a nightmarish London in the seventh book of *The Prelude*. But there is nothing nightmarish here. Although most of the street trades mentioned in this poem have vanished, it is, I think, still recognizable as a description of what city life is like. The poem's method is basically to list what is seen and heard: the only organizing principle is of following what takes the eye and ear of the speaker. So there is no argument, and unlike the poems we looked at earlier, this one does not change course at the end. ■

Now read the poem again. Pay special attention to the question that opens the poem. (1) What is its effect? (2) Look at the reference to the poet herself at the end. What is her role?

D i s c u s s i o n

1   The poem opens with a question ('Who has not waked to list ...?'). This is a rhetorical question – that is, the answer expected is something like 'Yes, we all recognize this'.

2   Rather than claiming a special, visionary way of seeing for the poet the poem claims that it records common sights. Although it ends with a reference to 'the poet', hers seems to be a trade not unlike the others: her job is 'to paint the summer morning'. ■

Our second poem about London was published a year after Mary Robinson's, in Volume I of William Wordsworth's *Poems in Two Volumes*, 1807. Wordsworth has a reputation as a 'Nature poet' so it may be a surprise to read this celebration of a city. The term 'point of view' is one that you will have encountered in talking about the novel and it is also useful here. **What is Wordsworth's point of view in this poem?**

Composed upon Westminster Bridge, 3 September 1803

Earth has not anything to shew more fair:
Dull would he be of soul who could pass by
A sight so touching in its majesty.
This city now doth like a garment wear
The beauty of the morning – silent, bare,   5
Ships, towers, domes, theatres and temples lie
Open unto the fields, and to the sky,
All bright and glittering in the smokeless air.
Never did sun more beautifully steep
In his first splendour valley, rock, or hill;   10
Ne'er saw I, never felt, a calm so deep.
The river glideth at his own sweet will –
Dear God! the very houses seem asleep;
And all that mighty heart is lying still.

(Wu, *Romanticism*, 1994, p.276)

D i s c u s s i o n

Well, literally he is above the city – looking down from the bridge of the title – so that the city is spread out before him like a natural panorama. In fact Wordsworth insists that as such it is *superior* to any natural scene. But this is because of the moment in which it is seen – the poem comes with a date attached, as though it records, or is recorded at, a particular moment. It is an untypical moment – the buildings are 'silent, bare', and the air is 'smokeless'. That negative was – and is – an unusual word, and of course makes us think of the opposite, positive term. 'Smokeless' reminds us that normally the air would be 'smoky'. But this is not a normal moment. The city is unpeopled.

Without its inhabitants, the city itself is personified – it is people not places who wear garments, who sleep, and who have will and hearts. It is as though Wordsworth gives the city itself human characteristics in order to

17

populate a city he sees as depopulated. And this leads to an apparent contradiction: surely a heart that is 'lying still' belongs to someone who is not asleep but dead.

Wordsworth also seems to be a privileged spectator of this better than natural scene: privileged because of his viewpoint, because he is the sole spectator, and also because the 'majestic' scene therefore yields a moral or psychological lesson to him alone ('Ne'er saw I, never felt a calm so deep'). ■

The third poem is from William Blake's *Songs of Innocence and of Experience*, first published in 1794, and from the section entitled *Songs of Experience*. **What is the point of view here? Can it be compared to the Wordsworth poem in other ways?**

London

I wander through each chartered street
Near where the chartered Thames does flow,
And mark in every face I meet
Marks of weakness, marks of woe.

In every cry of every man,   5
In every infant's cry of fear,
In every voice, in every ban,
The mind-forged manacles I hear.

How the chimney-sweeper's cry
Every black'ning church appals.   10
And the hapless soldier's sigh
Runs in blood down palace walls.

But most through midnight streets I hear
How the youthful harlot's curse
Blasts the new born infant's tear,   15
And blights with plagues the marriage hearse.

(Wu, *Romanticism*, 1994, p.73)

Discussion

Blake is at street level, face to face with the inhabitants of the city Wordsworth does not see. This poem too is a kind of list, but it is not at all a random list. The speaker here sees and hears something of all the great institutions of the state – the church, the army, the monarchy and, lastly, the family; and the street-cries here are cries, sighs and curses. I don't know whether you got a sense, on first reading the Blake poem, of a power that was, at least at first, separate from meaning. That is to say, I think you may have found the poem impressive without being able to say, for example, what is going on in the last stanza.

I hope that you will have noticed that the Wordsworth poem was another sonnet. As we saw, the sonnet as a form originated in Italy and was brought to Britain by Renaissance courtiers. Thus it is an aristocratic form, in keeping perhaps with the *superiority* of the narrator on which Wordsworth's poem depends. Wordsworth's use of the aristocratic form of the sonnet contrasts with Blake's use of what could be argued to be a more popular form, perhaps like the form of a ballad or a hymn.

18

Figure 1   William Blake, 'London', *Songs of Experience*, from *Songs of Innocence and Experience*, Plate 36, designed 1789–94, relief etching, finished in pen and watercolour on paper, 10.8 x 6.8 cm. Reproduced by permission of the Syndics of the Fitzwilliam Museum, Cambridge, P.125-1950.

19

We might say that where there was a sense of *exclusion* in the Wordsworth (an insistence on the untypicality of the moment, a repeated 'Never ... Never'), there is an opposite sense here, a sense of *inclusion* ('In every... In every ...' – actually the word 'every' occurs six times in the poem – and the other repetitions, notably 'mark' in the first stanza, first as a verb then twice as a noun, beat the bounds of this chartered, manacled routine). There is an insistence on absolute freedom in the Wordsworth as against a more determined sense in the Blake, a sense of freedom only within strict, 'chartered' limits which almost extend to a 'ban'. You will see a telling example of this if you look at their respective attitudes to the River Thames. Wordsworth's river moves gracefully at its own pace, and *chooses* to do so, as though it were human (line 12). Blake's Thames is, like the London streets, 'chartered' (line 2).

A charter was a document granted by the sovereign establishing a corporation (such as the corporation of London) and giving it certain rights and privileges. A charter might also reward a political friend of the king by granting a monopoly in the import or sale of certain goods. Charters then were meant to confer rights, but, as Thomas Paine wrote in 1791 in Part II of *The Rights of Man*, 'charters, by annulling those rights in the majority, leave the right by exclusion in the hands of the few' (*The Thomas Paine Reader*, 1987, p.317). Blake, like Mary Robinson, sees a commercial city; but unlike her he sees it as thoroughly exploitative.

Hence that difficult last stanza. This is usually paraphrased as suggesting that the harlot is a carrier of venereal disease. The harlot on the 'midnight streets' represents desires which cannot be satisfied or even acknowledged within the respectable, daylight world. Though 'youthful' she is corrupted and that corruption infects the new-born and returns to the world as 'plagues'. A 'marriage hearse' is almost an oxymoron (a contradiction in terms), since a hearse is to do with death not marriage, so the phrase brings together love and death. The last stanza, then, represents one basic function of any society – the way it reproduces itself – as a sordid commercial exchange which is inevitably corrupt and corrupting. ∎

There are immediate contexts to be considered in the cases of all three poems. In the case of the Mary Robinson poem there is a context which may at first sound like mere gossip. Robinson had been notorious as 'Perdita', the actress who became mistress of the Prince of Wales and subsequently of other men. She does not here try to cash in on her notorious persona as, we shall see, did Byron. And, remembering her reference to the job rather than the vocation of writing, it is worth pointing out that Robinson, who wrote novels and plays as well as poems, was the only one of these three writers to have earned a living largely from her writing. (Indeed, Robinson, despite illness later in her life, was also able to support her mother and daughter.)

Blake's poem was published as an illuminated text, its words hand-engraved and incorporated within a border and an illustration in which a young boy apparently guides an old man. An earlier entry in Blake's notebook, probably from 1791 or 1792, runs as follows:

An Ancient Proverb

Remove away that blackening church,
Remove away that marriage hearse,
Remove away that —— of blood –
You'll quite remove the ancient curse.

(Bentley, *William Blake's Writings*, 1978, Vol. II, p.969)

Other drafts have the words 'man' or 'place' for the blank in the third line. Here the 'ancient curse' is clearly the power of the state through its institutions. There is also a draft of 'London' in the notebook in which the phrase 'mind-forg'd manacles' (line 8) appears as 'german manacles'. The British royal family was originally from Germany and the particular reference is to fears that King George III might raise troops against the reformers in Britain. This is succeeded by a reference to a general and inevitable enslavement.

In the case of the Wordsworth sonnet there is an apparent origin (as there is for several of his poems, including the famous 'I wandered lonely as a cloud') in an entry in the journal of his sister Dorothy:

> After various troubles and disasters we left London on Saturday morning at ½ past 5 or 6, the 31st July (I have forgot which). We mounted the Dover Coach at Charing Cross. It was a beautiful morning. The City, St Paul's, with the River and a multitude of little Boats, made a most beautiful sight as we crossed Westminster Bridge. The houses were not overhung by their cloud of smoke and they were spread out endlessly, yet the sun shone so brightly with such a pure light that there was even something like the purity of one of nature's own grand spectacles.

> (Moorman (ed.), *Journal of Dorothy Wordsworth*, 1971, pp.150–1)

Look back at the poem. What, if anything, does it add to this prose account?

D i s c u s s i o n

There is only one substantial difference, I think, but it is a crucial one. William rewrote Dorothy's account *as a poem*. I have suggested that any kind of writing is a sort of making public, but a poem is a public form in a very obvious sense. When published a poem is sold and has potentially hundreds or thousands of readers while the only reader of a journal may be its author. The Westminster Bridge sonnet is one of Wordworth's most famous poems – probably after 'I wandered lonely as a cloud' the *most* famous – and if you have read any of his work before, you may well have come across this poem, whereas you are unlikely to have read Dorothy's journal entry. Poems have a prestige that by and large entries in a journal do not. We might want to argue that here there is actually a kind of plagiarism on William's part. At any rate, the use that William Wordsworth makes of his sister's experience and of her writing raises issues about the prestige of poetry and the relations between male and female writing that we will start to consider later. ∎

There is another important context here. In some notes on his poems, dictated many years later to his friend Isabella Fenwick, Wordsworth says that the poem was 'Composed on the roof of a coach on my way to France Sept. 1802'. Actually, on 3 September Wordsworth had just returned from France. In 1838 when Wordsworth included the poem in another collected volume he corrected the date from '1803' to '1802'. The date is important. William and Dorothy Wordsworth were visiting France at the first opportunity they had to do so in a brief respite from the war following the Peace of Amiens in 1802. They were going to Calais to meet Annette Vallon and the child she had borne ten years earlier. William Wordsworth was the father, and had never met his daughter Caroline. He was to marry another woman, Mary Hutchinson, at the beginning of October that year. The poem is one of several sonnets written around this time, often located by giving a date and place of composition – Dover, Calais, and the French and English coasts as well as London – and often too using the location to reflect on recent personal and public history.

In terms of my earlier analogy, which of these three poems do you think would be most useful to a historian?

Discussion

On the face of it, it would be the Mary Robinson. In terms of information about city life it is full of details wholly absent from the other two poems. On the other hand, Wordsworth's very insistence on the uniqueness of the view he sees of the city implies something about the new commercial city. The Blake poem subverts such a hopeful view by seeing the city as the capital and thus as the headquarters of all the chief institutions of the state. That's to say, once we allow that *attitudes* are a part of history as well, then we can see that texts do not simply 'reflect' what is outside them, they can also quite literally make history. Such texts may act upon, or 'make', the present in which they were written. And, irrespective of how representative or not are the attitudes of Blake or Wordsworth or Mary Robinson, they are part of what we know about the period in which they were written. ■

Thinking back to all three poems, what, if anything, do they have in common?

Discussion

All three poems are representations of the great commercial city written around the same time. But they do not seem to have much in common which would justify our calling them all 'Romantic': each treats its subject in a different way. In each case the poem is presented as the special view of an individual – special if only in the sense in the Robinson and Wordsworth poems that this is a particular moment in time and space. Blake and Wordsworth, I think, both try to draw a conclusion from, or to moralize on, the things they have seen. The Mary Robinson poem, on the other hand, has no pretensions about transcending the familiar world that it sees. Also, where the Wordsworth poem ignores women and the Blake sees them only in sexual or childbearing terms, the Mary Robinson poem sees women and their ordinary activities as worthy of record. ■

As all this suggests, Romanticism is not a single thing. If we are to retain the term, Romantic writing may be best thought of as a set of different and often competing voices. Nevertheless, those voices may argue over an agenda set by political and social circumstances that were experienced in common. As Shelley asserts in the 'Preface' to his poem *Laon and Cythna*, published in 1817:

> There must be a resemblance, which does not depend upon their own will, between all the writers of any particular age. They cannot escape from subjection to a common influence which arises out of an infinite combination of circumstances belonging to the times in which they live; though each is in a degree the author of the very influence by which his being is thus pervaded.
>
> (Webb, *Percy Bysshe Shelley: Poems and Prose*, 1995, p.57)

Shelley suggests that among *any* group of writers there is inescapably a 'common influence ... belonging to the times in which they live'. Many in the early nineteenth century recognized this common influence. William Hazlitt called it a 'spirit of the age'. There is a sense in much Romantic writing that, whatever the differences between individual writers, they were all confronted with a new world coming into being. 'We have it in our power to begin the world over again,' wrote the radical Tom Paine of the American Revolution. 'A situation, similar to the present, hath not happened since the days of Noah until now' (*The Thomas Paine Reader*, 1987, p.109). This new world seemed to demand new ways of representing it.

Novelty and nature

One of the most famous claims for the novelty of Romantic writing comes in a document we shall be considering more fully in Chapter Three, Wordsworth's 'Preface' to the *Lyrical Ballads* of 1802. We saw how Robinson, much more than Blake and Wordsworth in the poems we looked at, seemed to rely on earlier conventions and specialized language. Wordsworth challenges the reliance on such conventions, arguing in the Preface that the language of poetry ought to be the 'language of men'. The Preface defends his choice of language and subject-matter for the poems in the volume. Both are drawn, he says, from the rural poor. In the following passage there is a claim that 'ordinary' experience and language should be revalued. **Read it now, thinking about this question: Why does Wordsworth claim that the lives and language of the rural poor are suitable for poetry?**

> Low and rustic life was generally chosen because in that situation the essential passions of the heart find a better soil in which they can attain their maturity, are less under restraint, and speak a plainer and more emphatic language; because in that condition of life our elementary feelings coexist in a state of greater simplicity, and consequently may be more accurately contemplated and more forcibly communicated; because the manners of rural life germinate from those elementary feelings, and (from the necessary character of rural occupations) are more easily comprehended and are more durable;

and lastly, because in that condition the passions of men are incorporated with the beautiful and permanent forms of nature.

The language too of these men is adopted [...] because such men hourly communicate with the best objects from which the best part of language is originally derived, and because, from their rank in society and the sameness and narrow circle of their intercourse being less under the influence of social vanity they convey their feelings and notions in simple and unelaborated expressions.

(Wu, *Romanticism*, 1994, p.252)

Discussion

The rural poor are fit to provide poetry with a subject-matter and a language because of their fundamental human feelings ('passions') which their language is capable of expressing simply and forcefully. Their feelings and their language are so influenced by the 'beautiful and permanent forms of nature' as to be 'incorporated with' them. Wordsworth's language slips between the natural and the human world: small rural communities provide 'a better soil', behaviour 'germinates', and so on. Perhaps it is natural objects which Wordsworth refers to again near the end of the passage as 'the best objects from which the best part of language is originally derived'. The feelings and language of the rural poor are uncorrupted rather than unsophisticated. They are unaffected by fashion so their habits do not change. ■

Now look at the passage again, thinking about Wordsworth's own language in it. What words does he use to make a claim for the superiority of the lives and language of the rural poor?

Discussion

Some of the words he uses to make the claim are 'passions', 'the heart', 'essential', 'plain', 'emphatic', 'sincerity', 'simple', and 'elementary'. Most of all perhaps the claim is founded on 'nature'. All these are to do with a state which is close to nature, with a state which Wordsworth sees as being fundamentally human. ■

Wordsworth's Preface has a reputation as a document that proclaimed a literary revolution and that could be seen as socially radical too; but it has some reactionary tendencies to its argument. To some extent we can see both even from this brief extract. For example, it could be argued that Wordsworth idealizes rural life, asserting its unchanging value at just the time when it was undergoing great changes because of industrialization, enclosure of agricultural land and movement into the cities. Wordsworth has an alternative to the present trends he opposes. His version of rural life is of a simpler state having a more sincere language. Wordsworth seems in fact to be proclaiming a conservative revolution, a return to certain 'essential' truths from which modern urban society has deviated, as is evident from the decadent literature which feeds it.

On the other hand, the Preface as a whole seems to have a radical agenda, justifying the poems that follow by distinguishing them from what Wordsworth sees as their corrupt predecessors. He attacks the dominant poetic language of the previous century and opposes the cultural trends of the society to which the poems were addressed. The Preface was read as a claim for a kind of literary version of extension of the franchise. The rural poor were to be allowed a voice – so, as we shall see, were children. The claim made in the Preface for a more democratic literature could be seen as an implicit call for more democracy in the state: it could be seen to have what Wordsworth's younger contemporary William Hazlitt later called a 'levelling tendency'.

Children and the Romantic lyric

According to Wordsworth, the novelty of the poems from *Lyrical Ballads* was to come from their concentration on the way of life and on the language of the rural poor. Among them Wordsworth claims to find the 'permanent forms' of experience and the simple eloquence that eighteenth-century writers claimed to find in the literature of ancient Greece and Rome. Literary novelty would come from something that in social and historical terms was not new at all. Poems could not in themselves change the social and political circumstances attacked in the Preface, but they might take the first step towards changing them. They could do so by changing attitudes. Fundamental change would require a fundamental change of attitudes. It might require ridding literature (and ridding oneself) of the preconceptions and prejudices laid on by education and social custom, in order to wipe the slate clean and begin from the viewpoint of a child. If you look again at the list of terms I quoted from the Wordsworth extract you might notice that many could apply equally to children. Children could be said to speak in 'simple and unelaborated expressions' and in the eighteenth century children were often seen as truly uncorrupted and as closer to nature.

In a sense, as children we have to do what Tom Paine recommended and 'begin the world over again'. Children appear again and again in Romantic poems. For example, both poems we looked at first, Wordsworth's 'She dwelt among th' untrodden ways' and John Clare's 'I am ...', refer to children. Clare yearns nostalgically for the security and innocence of his childhood and the Wordsworth poem concerns a child. (From the poem itself it is only evident that Lucy is 'a maid', but another of the 'Lucy' poems, 'Three years she grew in sun and shower', says that Lucy dies at the age of three.) In this section we will look at some other telling examples of the way children are used in Romantic poems by Wordsworth and Blake. For a poet to explore the child's point of view offered the possibility of seeing the world anew. This was particularly valuable when, as we have seen, many believed they were witnessing the start of a new world.

For our first example of the way children are used in Romantic poetry, I want to look at a poem first published in the 1798 edition of *Lyrical Ballads,* Wordsworth's 'Anecdote for Fathers'. **Read the poem first of all, and consider the following questions: What does the title lead us to expect? Are these expectations borne out by the poem?**

Anecdote for Fathers, Showing how the Art of Lying may be Taught

I have a boy of five years old,
His face is fair and fresh to see,
His limbs are cast in beauty's mould,
And dearly he loves me.

One morn we strolled on our dry walk,   5
Our quiet house all full in view,
And held such intermitted talk
As we are wont to do.

My thoughts on former pleasures ran;
I thought of Kilve's delightful shore –   10
Our pleasant home, when spring began
A long long year before.

A day it was when I could bear
To think, and think, and think again;
With so much happiness to spare   15
I could not feel a pain.

My boy was by my side, so slim
And graceful in his rustic dress!
And oftentimes I talked to him
In very idleness.   20

The young lambs ran a pretty race,
The morning sun shone bright and warm;
'Kilve', said I, 'was a pleasant place,
And so is Liswyn farm.

My little boy, which like you more?'   25
I said, and took him by the arm,
'Our home by Kilve's delightful shore,
Or here at Liswyn farm?

And tell me, had you rather be
(I said, and held him by the arm)   30
At Kilve's smooth shore by the green sea
Or here at Liswyn farm?'

In careless mood he looked at me
While still I held him by the arm
And said, 'At Kilve I'd rather be   35
Than here at Liswyn farm.'

'Now, little Edward, say why so,
My little Edward, tell me why.'
'I cannot tell, I do not know.'
'Why, this is strange!' said I.   40

'For, here are woods, and green hills warm;
There surely must some reason be
Why you would change sweet Liswyn farm
For Kilve by the green sea.'

At this, my boy, so fair and slim,   45
Hung down his head, nor made reply,
And five times did I say to him,
'Why, Edward, tell me why?'

His head he raised; there was in sight –
It caught his eye, he saw it plain –   50
Upon the house-top, glittering bright,
A broad and gilded vane.

Then did the boy his tongue unlock
And thus to me he made reply;
'At Kilve there was no weather-cock,   55
And that's the reason why.'

O dearest, dearest boy! my heart
For better lore would seldom yearn,
Could I but teach the hundredth part
Of what from thee I learn.   60

(Wu, *Romanticism*, 1994, pp.204–6)

Discussion

In the Introduction to the book I made a very basic distinction between *lyric* and *narrative*. A lyric is usually a first-person expression of emotion while a narrative poem is usually in the third person and tells a story. Like the term 'lyrical ballad' itself – the title of the collection in which this poem first appeared – this poem seems to be a hybrid of lyric and narrative. An anecdote after all is a little narrative. We have a narrator and another character with a speaking part, the narrator's son. Things happen in the course of the poem. And the sub-title suggests that this is not a poem that is going to remain satisfied with the representation of feeling – as 'She dwelt among th' untrodden ways' was – but one which has a didactic purpose. However, Wordsworth dropped the sub-title from editions of his poems after 1845.

Actually, I find it quite difficult to see how the sub-title relates to the poem. The poem is didactic in that the narrator does 'learn' something from the child, though it is not clear what that is. The sub-title leads us to expect something rather moralizing. And we do not not get this. Presumably the child could learn to lie out of wanting to please the adult, to tell him what he wants to hear. But this would be a rather reductive way of reading the poem. We cannot draw a moral from it – certainly not the moral that this is how lying can be taught. It just is not conclusive in that way. ∎

I said that things happen in the course of this poem. These though are not so much actions as events in speech or psychological events. **Read the poem again. What is the difference between the narrator and the child?**

In pressing his son for rational answers to his questions the narrator cannot bridge the gulf between the viewpoint of the adult and the child. The child simply does not speak the language of reason spoken by the adult. The narrator therefore cannot prompt his son to give an answer that will satisfy his rational expectations. He does not however try to bully or coerce or even to persuade the child to do so. You may disagree about this. You may find that the repetition of the adult's question is not just insistent but coercive. (In later versions of the poem Wordsworth softened the 'five times' (line 47) to 'three times'.) 'Anecdote for Fathers' looks like a dialogue, but is actually a sort of catechism (a form of religious instruction in which the person receiving instruction repeats answers they have memorized). The child in the poem was meant to give the reasons for his preference – that is, to give reasons satisfactory to an adult – unable to do this, he desperately improvises, ending up as teacher to the adult. We are left with two viewpoints which are not opposed but simply different. The two sides may not comprehend each other, but they are not hostile to each other. ■

I wanted to look at the Wordsworth poem for two reasons. First, because, like the better known poem usually printed alongside it, 'We Are Seven', the poem gives a voice to a marginal figure, a child. Other poems by Wordsworth in *Lyrical Ballads* concern discharged soldiers, mad mothers, idiot boys, forsaken women, and so on. Wordsworth makes the marginal central, in ways which seemed to have the aim of political as well as literary reform. The adult authority figure can be seen as failing to understand the child's point of view – a point of view which is neither superior nor inferior to his own but simply different. Second, the dialogue between adult and child recurs in Blake's *Songs of Innocence and Experience*, which we shall be looking at soon. I have been suggesting that the apparently greater wisdom of the adult in the dialogue represents reason – the limitations as well as the strengths of reason – and the child represents an irrational or extra-rational capacity that we might call imagination. In the Wordsworth poem the two sides are not reconciled but neither are they at war. Adult and child agree to differ. The difference between them is a difference and not a conflict; certainly it is not presented as a political conflict.

However, Wordsworth draws out an implicit political context in another of his notes dictated to Isabella Fenwick. **Do you find this later account surprising? Does it affect the way we read the poem?**

> This ['Anecdote for Fathers'] was suggested in front of Alfoxden [the house in Somerset the Wordsworths leased in 1798]. The boy was a son of my friend Basil Montagu, who had been two or three years under our care. The name of Kilve is from a village on the Bristol Channel, about a mile from Alfoxden; and the name of Liswyn Farm was taken from a beautiful spot on the Wye. When Mr Coleridge, my Sister, and I, had been visiting the famous John Thelwall, who had taken refuge from politics, after a trial for high treason, with a view to bring up his family by the profits of agriculture, which proved as

unfortunate a speculation as that he had fled from, Coleridge and he had both been public lecturers: Coleridge mingling, with his politics, theology; from which the other elocutionist abstained, unless it were for the sake of a sneer. This quondam community of public employment induced Thelwall to visit Coleridge at Nether Stowey, where he fell in my way. He really was a man of extraordinary talent, an affectionate husband, and a good father. Though brought up in the city on a tailor's board, he was truly sensible of the beauty of natural objects. I remember once when Coleridge, he, and I were seated together upon the turf on the brink of a stream in the most beautiful part of the most beautiful glen of Alfoxden, Coleridge exclaimed, 'This is a place to reconcile one to all the jarrings and conflicts of the wide world.' – 'Nay,' said Thelwall, 'to make one forget them altogether.' The visit of this man to Coleridge was, as I believe Coleridge has related, the occasion of a spy being sent by Government to relate our proceedings, which were, I can say with truth, such as the world at large would have thought ludicrously harmless.

(Mason, *Lyrical Ballads*, 1992 edn., p.346–7)

D i s c u s s i o n

I think it *is* surprising to find the poem given this context. I hope you felt it was worth my giving the note in full. Only the first three sentences here give a 'background' to the poem in the way we have been reading it. They are factual. They might correct the impression that this was the poem of a proud parent. If we had seen this as a cutely moralizing poem – as we might have been led to do by the title, or still more by the sub-title – this account suggests another way of reading it. The context for Wordsworth's poem is not moral, as the title of the poem suggests it might be. Rather, it is to do with events of the time at which it was written. Wordsworth relates his own involvement in radical politics. He calls this involvement 'ludicrously harmless', but he was indeed spied upon, and John Thelwall had recently been on trial for his life. Wordsworth's poem, which might seem 'to reconcile one to all the jarrings and conflicts of the wide world', is revealed to be shot through with the conflicts of the 1790s. His report of the exchange between Thelwall and Coleridge suggests that those conflicts *should* not be forgotten even if they *can* be.

I am not suggesting that the adult and the child in this poem should stand for the government and the radicals or anything like that. However, Wordsworth's anecdote about the poem shows the extent to which politics necessarily impinge on the writing of texts (or did so at the time Wordsworth recalls). ■

So far, I have given you certain contexts for poems after you had read them. I want now to take a slightly different approach and look in some detail at a single collection of poems. William Blake's *Songs of Innocence and of Experience, Shewing the Two Contrary States of the Human Soul* is a collection in which poems about children predominate. The conflict between different kinds of authority represented by the Wordsworth poem we have just looked at is much more explicit in Blake's work.

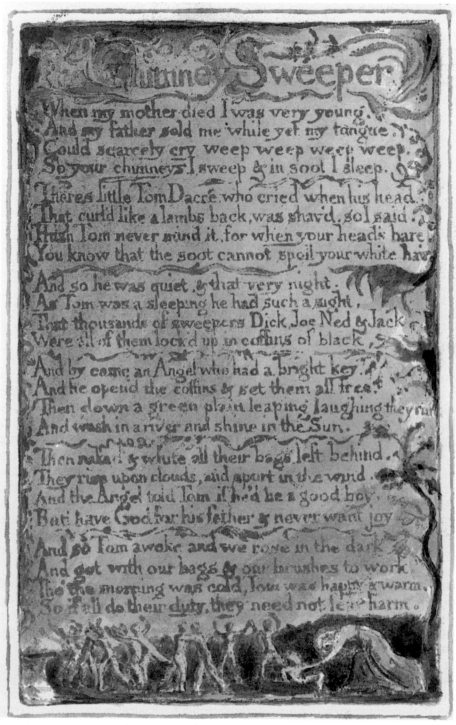

Figure 2   William Blake, 'The Chimney Sweeper', *Songs of Innocence*,
from *Songs of Innocence and Experience*, Plate 23, designed 1789–94, relief
etching, finished in pen and watercolour on paper, 11 x 6.8 cm. Reproduced
by permission of the Syndics of the Fitzwilliam Museum, Cambridge,
P.125-1950.

Blake's Songs of Innocence and of Experience

We will start by looking at 'The Chimney Sweeper' from *Songs of Innocence*. This is a poem in which the speaker reaches a conclusion. **Read the poem through and consider whether this conclusion is justified. In other words, do we take the final line 'straight' or ironically?**

The Chimney Sweeper

When my mother died I was very young,
And my father sold me while yet my tongue
Could scarcely cry 'weep weep weep weep!'
So your chimneys I sweep, and in soot I sleep.

There's little Tom Dacre, who cried when his head,   5
That curled like a lamb's back, was shaved; so I said
'Hush, Tom! Never mind it, for when your head's bare
You know that the soot cannot spoil your white hair.'

And so he was quiet, and that very night,
As Tom was a-sleeping, he had such a sight!   10
That thousands of sweepers – Dick, Joe, Ned and Jack,
Were all of them locked up in coffins of black.

And by came an angel who had a bright key,
And he opened the coffins and set them all free;
Then down a green plain leaping, laughing they run   15
And wash in a river, and shine in the sun.

Then naked and white, all their bags left behind,
They rise upon clouds and sport in the wind;
And the angel told Tom, if he'd be a good boy,
He'd have God for his father, and never want joy.   20

And so Tom awoke, and we rose in the dark,
And got with our bags and our brushes to work;
Though the morning was cold, Tom was happy and warm –
So if all do their duty they need not fear harm.

(Wu, *Romanticism*, 1994, pp.57–8)

Discussion

Perhaps there does not seem much warrant for taking the final line ironically. We might not agree with the speaker's conclusion, but then he is a naive child. Perhaps it is only when we read more of Blake that we realize that it is extremely unlikely that we would find him recommending the consolations offered by the Established Church in this way. Perhaps if I had not put the suspicion in your mind you would not have thought of reading this line ironically. But once we are given the suspicion then we can look again at, for example, the bizarre version of the resurrection that we are offered in stanzas three to five. Then we might start to question why there should be two sweeps – the speaker who offers us a brief autobiography in the first stanza and 'little Tom Dacre'. Is it not the case that the speaker is trying not only to console Tom Dacre but to convince him of something? The consolation he offers Tom in lines 6–8 does not seem to be much of a consolation. At the end the speaker tries to convince Tom broadly that exploitation in this life does not matter because what counts is an afterlife in which we will all be equal. This is meant to send Tom happily back up his chimney, and it seems to work. ■

This is a poem from *Songs of Innocence*, but experience certainly casts shadows here. **What makes the poem 'innocent'?**

D i s c u s s i o n

What makes it innocent is the speaker's lack of awareness of these sinister shadows. He too is exploited. On first reading the metre probably carried you past a detail that on re-reading might stop you short: the word 'sold' in the first stanza: 'When my mother died I was very young/And my father *sold* me ... '. The child exists at once within an exploitative economic context. With hindsight it is shocking that this should seem to the speaker of the poem to be a normal state of affairs. If we do take the last line 'straight' then Blake is suggesting that it is also a state of affairs which cannot be changed. All we could do would be to accept our earthly fate and expect our reward in the afterlife. This is clearly an argument that is useful to the employers of sweeps, but it is made by a sweep. Is this not an example of the way we may be enslaved without there needing to be a slave driver? Might not the speaker of the poem be said to be enslaving himself (and Tom Dacre)? Is he not locked in the 'mind-forged manacles' we have already seen in 'London'? ■

Now you may have wondered whether this poem is typical of the *Songs of Innocence*. Whether it is or not, on this evidence it seems that the state of innocence may be dangerously close to ignorance. In *The Book of Thel* (1789), a brief, illuminated work written at the same time as the *Songs of Innocence*, Thel, a young girl, is shown visions of death and sexuality from which, finally, she retreats. She fails to move from 'innocence' to 'experience'. *The Book of Thel* suggests that innocence is not the same as ignorance: innocence is good but ignorance is bad. There is a higher kind of innocence to be achieved, which may be an innocence in the midst of corruption.

Blake first printed *Songs of Innocence* as a free-standing collection in 1789. He published *Songs of Innocence and of Experience* in 1794, though *Songs of Innocence* continued to be produced separately. The poems of the *Songs of Innocence* draw on the conventions of pastoral, an ancient literary mode. In pastoral the sun always shines and little work gets done. Shepherds make music, write poems and fall in love rather than tending their sheep. The pastoral world exists alongside the actual world, from which it is a temporary escape. In Christian terms, it is then a kind of unfallen world. It is appropriate therefore that children also feature largely within it. ('Anecdote for Fathers' too has a kind of pastoral setting, with lambs and with the child in 'rustic dress'.)

On first reading the poems of Blake's collection, the reader may react with a kind of embarrassment. The *Songs of Innocence* seem naïve, employing forms such as the ballad or the hymn. These are the forms of popular not high culture. Also it is not clear whether the poems are written *for* children, or are merely *about* children. We are encouraged to value complexity, and where we find a childlike simplicity, that is what we are embarrassed by: we want to find irony in it. To some extent we do find irony when we read some of the *Songs of Innocence* alongside the parallel poems from *Songs of Experience* – a tiger to go with a lamb, 'Infant Sorrow' to go with 'Infant Joy', and so on. We should bear in mind though that such a perspective was not available to the initial audience for the work. As I have said, *Songs of Innocence* continued to be published separately even after the production of *Songs of Innocence and Experience*. How do the poems from *Innocence* look standing alone? Are they ironic? If they are, surely it is a rather different sort of irony from the irony of, say, Jane Austen.

Innocence and Experience

Let's consider a pair of poems, the two versions of 'Nurse's Song'. We will look first at the *Innocence* version of the poem. This is a narrative poem: things happen and it has a narrator; the poem's speaker is the nurse of the title. As you read the poem think about these two questions. **First of all, what is significant about these events? Secondly, do we make a judgement upon the nurse?**

Nurse's Song

When the voices of children are heard on the green
And laughing is heard on the hill,
My heart is at rest within my breast
And everything else is still.

'Then come home my children, the sun is gone down   5
And the dews of night arise;
Come, come, leave off play, and let us away
Till the morning appears in the skies.'

'No, no! Let us play, for it is yet day
And we cannot go to sleep;   10
Besides, in the sky, the little birds fly
And the hills are all covered with sheep.'

'Well, well, go and play, till the light fades away
And then go home to bed.'
The little ones leaped and shouted and laughed   15
And all the hills echoed.

(Wu, *Romanticism*, 1994, pp.62–3)

D i s c u s s i o n

The disagreement between the children and the nurse is over whether or not her command should be obeyed. It is not, but she relents and the children play on. The word 'play' occurs three times in the poem. Here play becomes recreation becomes re-creation. The 'echo' from the hills confirms the liberty they have won. The poem is 'symbolic', if only in the sense that it is not ultimately about children's bedtimes.

We are not told what to think and there is no reason to associate the speaker (who in the opening stanza speaks in the first person) with the

33

poet. The nurse seems to surrender her authority here, but what is Blake's authority? The verbs are almost all passive, leading to the nurse's apparent relinquishment of her authority. Perhaps she even joins in with the hand-over of authority. (Her command to 'come home' in line 5 has changed to 'go home' in line 14.) Either way, the nurse surrenders her authority as soon it is challenged. She does not try to impose it on the children. The sense of secure well-being she expressed in the first stanza is made general by the end. And it is important to notice that this benign and ideal figure of authority is female, where the actively malign figures in the collection are male. Or maybe that sense of well-being has been transferred rather than made general. That is to say, the nurse apparently continues to watch the children rather than, say, joining in with their games. In the illumination the nurse sits outside the circle in which the children are playing, reading a book. ■

We will go on to look at the 'Nurse's Song' from *Experience*. But there is another comparison we could draw first, with Wordsworth. **Look back at his 'Anecdote for Fathers', if you need to remind yourself of it. How does 'Nurse's Song' compare?**

D i s c u s s i o n

Both poems are dialogues between an adult and a child or children. The children of 'Nurse's Song' possess a pre-rational or maybe extra-rational understanding. As with 'Anecdote for Fathers' they seem to have some wisdom which is overlooked by the adult. And as with 'Anecdote for Fathers' the issue is not really whether they are right or wrong (here either it is night or it is day, but either way birds and sheep do not have much to do with it). In their extra-rational sense the children of 'Nurse's Song' are not unlike the child in the Wordsworth poem, but there is a big difference in the significance claimed for their way of understanding.

We see in this poem from *Songs of Innocence* what we found in Wordsworth's poem: that children have a viewpoint distinct from that of adults. This viewpoint may reveal the limitation of adult reason. Blake though pursues the implications of the distinction. He goes on to question its moral, institutional and economic bases. We might say that what in Wordsworth is a difference of viewpoints is in Blake a conflict of interests. The Wordsworth poem ends with the two speakers merely repeating their points of view, the Blake ends with a change from the initial situation – and, we might say, a change in the power relationship. Here a new social relation is established. ■

When we looked at the extract from the Preface to *Lyrical Ballads* we also noticed the importance given to 'nature'. **How does nature figure in Blake's poem?**

D i s c u s s i o n

At the end, as the children celebrate, the hills echo their shouts. The poem turns from society to nature. Nature confirms what has been won (albeit without much of a struggle) in human society, through dialogue. Book VIII of Wordsworth's *Prelude* is sub-titled 'Love of Nature Leading to Love of

Mankind'. At the end of Blake's 'Nurse's Song' we move outwards from the human to the natural; perhaps this movement is the reverse of the move in Wordsworth. And there does not seem to be anything particularly wonderful about nature here. Harmony among the children is made literal by the hills echoing their celebrations, but there are no self-evidently restorative benefits in nature itself. What could be more natural than to sleep when it is dark? The nurse had wanted the children to obey a 'natural' rhythm that they reject. ■

Blake felt that, over time, priests, monarchs and their apologists had perverted words from their true meanings. We should therefore question the received values implied even within single words. 'Innocence' and 'experience' then are likely to be problematic terms. As for the child in Wordsworth's poem, there may be in innocence a knowledge which is unavailable in the corrupted experience of the adult.

Look now at the 'Nurse's Song' from *Experience*. How does it compare with the version in *Innocence*?

Nurse's Song

When the voices of children are heard on the green
And whisp'rings are in the dale,
The days of my youth rise fresh in my mind,
My face turns green and pale.

Then come home my children, the sun is gone down,   5
And the dews of night arise;
Your spring and your day are wasted in play,
And your winter and night in disguise.

(Wu, *Romanticism*, 1994, p.70)

D i s c u s s i o n

The *Experience* 'Nurse's Song' is much shorter, and there is no narrative progression. It has the same opening line as the *Innocence* version, but it contains only one voice, that of the nurse. Like most of the *Songs of Experience* the poem is a monologue rather than a dialogue. So we never get the children's reply, and the power relationship remains frozen.

Looking at the children the nurse sees only herself and her own lost youth. She is green with envy (line 4). She moralizes upon their environment – 'spring' and 'day' look like synonyms for 'youth'. Their 'play' will be succeeded by their ageing, and in age they will play a part rather than playing games. They will assume a social role. (That at least is how I understand the last word of the poem, 'disguise'.) Childhood and age will both be 'wasted' (line 7).

Here then from the start the nurse interprets childhood rather than merely responding to the children. There is an anxiety that was not present in the *Innocence* version, or even paranoia ('whisp'rings are in the dale'). On this evidence it would be difficult to see experience as anything other than a negative state. ■

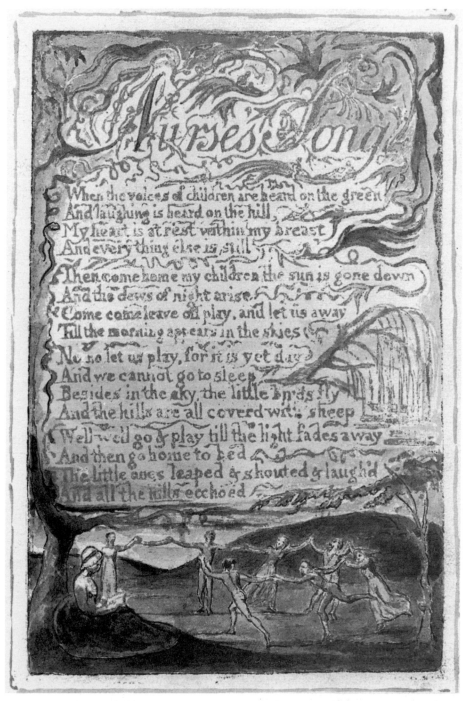

Figure 3   William Blake, 'Nurse's Song', *Songs of Innocence*, from *Songs of Innocence and Experience*, Plate 13, designed 1789–94, relief etching, finished in pen and watercolour on paper, 11.5 x 7.7 cm. Reproduced by permission of the Syndics of the Fitzwilliam Museum, Cambridge, P.125-1950.

Figure 4 William Blake, 'Nurse's Song', *Songs of Experience*, from *Songs of Innocence and Experience*, Plate 50, designed 1789–94, relief etching, finished in pen and watercolour on paper, 10.7 x 6.7 cm. Reproduced by permission of the Syndics of the Fitzwilliam Museum, Cambridge, P.125-1950.

For an example of negativity, we could do worse than consider 'A Poison Tree' from *Experience*. There is a strong, clear and rather dramatic narrative to this poem. Read the poem through and try to paraphrase its main point in a couple of sentences.

A Poison Tree

I was angry with my friend;
I told my wrath, my wrath did end.
I was angry with my foe;
I told it not, my wrath did grow.

And I watered it in fears,   5
Night and morning with my tears;
And I sunned it with smiles,
And with soft deceitful wiles.

And it grew both day and night
And it bore an apple bright;   10
And my foe beheld it shine,
And he knew that it was mine.

And into my garden stole
When the night had veiled the pole –
In the morning glad I see   15
My foe outstretched beneath the tree.

(Wu, *Romanticism*, 1994, p.75)

My own attempt at a paraphrase would be as follows. The free and immediate expression of emotion (even of anger) is healthy; its suppression or repression has far worse consequences.

The form of the poem strikes me as very economical. Its development might even seem logical. **Does the form of the poem remind you of anything? What logic does it follow?**

D i s c u s s i o n

The formal models for the poem seem to be hymns or nursery rhymes. Each line is a self-contained semantic unit. We have sixteen clauses in sixteen lines, though not one to each line. The poem is obedient to its initial logic.

That logic is extraordinarily negative: a 'positive' alternative exists only in the first two lines. One feeling of anger is expressed and so 'ends', but it takes the whole of the rest of the poem for the unexpressed anger of the third line to find an outlet. There is a metaphoric 'growth' from the verb 'grow' itself (line 4). Drama plays itself out with inexorable logic. The poem progresses simply by the repeated use of the word 'and'. The tree the speaker nurses to fruition is a perversion, but remains 'natural'. 'Positive' terms ('sunned', 'bright') exist only within the context of the speaker's deceit and lust for revenge. This infects both protagonists: the speaker propagates the 'poison' and tempts his (or her) 'foe' but the foe 'steals' into the garden (that is to say, it is theft as well as stealth) having succumbed to temptation. The foe falls, literally, but the speaker has also fallen, though he or she is unaware of this. ■

In Blake's notebook the poem was entitled 'Christian Forbearance'. The object of his irony is the teaching of the contemporary Established Church. Even in its published version the poem might be read as saying something like *this is* where your so-called Christian forbearance gets you'. But Blake does so by returning to fundamentals, by going back to origins and rewriting the myths. The tree bearing a single apple would undoubtedly have reminded contemporary readers of the Tree of Knowledge in the Garden of Eden, the tempting of Eve by Satan and God's subsequent expulsion of Adam and Eve from the Garden. In Christian mythology these events are described as the Fall and are regarded as the origin of sin in human life.

It is often said that the history of wars is written by the victors. To find the 'truth' of history then it might have to be rewritten from the opposite point of view. As we shall see in the next chapter, the great precedent for such an ambition was Milton's seventeenth-century epic *Paradise Lost*. There Milton had rewritten Genesis, retelling the stories of the war in heaven, the Fall of Man and the Creation itself. Blake too wanted to go back to origins, to re-examine the myths upon which society was founded. By rewriting those fundamental stories he believed it should be possible to put right an original misrepresentation. Myths of origin (such as the myths of the Creation and the Fall) could function as a justification of revolutionary ideas. This is what Blake does in his own epics, but it is something we can see too in *Songs of Experience*. Even in the tiny space of 'A Poison Tree' we can see Blake going back to the primary myths of his society (here the myth of the Fall) in order to reinterpret and revise them. It might be said to compress the whole of *Paradise Lost* into sixteen lines.

My paraphrase of the poem overlooked something crucial. It did not account for the speaker being 'glad' to see the destruction of his or her 'foe'. Some of the *Songs of Innocence* could be said to be 'innocent' only because their narrator is; but here, within a narrative about corruption and guilt, the narrator too is guilty. If Blake is saying that the expression of emotion is healthy, then anger will be a test case, particularly because anger has theological implications. After all, the God of the Old Testament is an angry God.

Discussing Blake only as a poet is doing him less than justice. He was author, printer, illustrator, engraver, publisher, and bookseller of all his own works. Each of them is unique, hand-produced by Blake by a method of printing he devised himself. This is why references to Blake's writings usually include the number of the plate on which they were illuminated. Blake's only conventionally published volume was *Poetical Sketches* (1783). Each of his subsequent works is an integrated whole comprising poem and illumination together. You cannot really discuss Blake as a poet without considering the illuminations too. When we do consider the illumination to 'A Poison Tree' something else is suggested. It shows the 'foe outstretched beneath the tree' in a pose of crucifixion, as though he is a Christ who is sacrificed for the narrator's sins (see Figure 5).

In these poems we have seen innocence shadowed by experience. Blake's subtitle for *Songs of Innocence and Experience* is *Shewing the Two Contrary States of the Human Soul*. Four *Songs of Innocence* became *Songs of Experience* when the poems were published together: 'Little Girl Lost', 'Little Girl Found', 'The Schoolboy', and 'The Voice of the Ancient Bard'. If

Figure 5   William Blake, 'A Poison Tree', *Songs of Experience*, from *Songs of Innocence and Experience*, Plate 48, designed 1789–94, relief etching, finished in pen and watercolour on paper, 10.8 x 6.5 cm. Reproduced by permission of the Syndics of the Fitzwilliam Museum, Cambridge, P.125-1950.

they are interchangeable in this way, how can they be 'contrary'? The answer I think comes in one of the proverbs from *The Marriage of Heaven and Hell,* 'Without contraries is no progression'. Both qualities are necessary. And we cannot understand the one without the other.

In a sense then the problem of the *Songs of Innocence is* the problem of 'innocence' itself. That is to say, we are usually more confident about identifying what we take to be lies than in defining 'truth', better at saying something is a fantasy than in giving a definition of reality. The problem of innocence is like that. We often overlook the fact that the word is actually negative because the positive term has dropped out of the language. To be innocent is to be not nocent, to be not guilty. It would seem then that innocence, rather than being a positive quality signifies the absence of certain negative qualities. With this in mind, I want to return now to the *Songs of Innocence* and to look at the 'Introduction' to that work.

Remember the shadows of exploitation and corruption we discovered in 'The Chimney Sweeper'. **Does the following poem seem wholly innocent?**

Introduction

Piping down the valleys wild,
Piping songs of pleasant glee,
On a cloud I saw a child
And he laughing said to me:

'Pipe a song about a lamb!'   5
So I piped with a merry cheer;
'Piper, pipe that song again!'
So I piped – he wept to hear.

'Drop thy pipe, thy happy pipe,
Sing thy songs of happy cheer!'   10
So I sung the same again
While he wept with joy to hear.

'Piper sit thee down and write
In a book, that all may read.'
So he vanished from my sight   15
And I plucked a hollow reed.

And I made a rural pen,
And I stained the water clear,
And I wrote my happy songs
Every child may joy to hear.   20

(Wu, *Romanticism,* 1994, p.54)

D i s c u s s i o n

Now the poem is certainly happy and easy in some ways – there are no difficulties of diction or syntax. It seems to draw on the conventions of the pastoral – the unfallen world of shepherds and children. The poem is again a dialogue, but there does not seem to be any kind of power-play between the piper and the child: the child requests rather then commanding. We do notice though a kind of chronological progression from piping to singing to

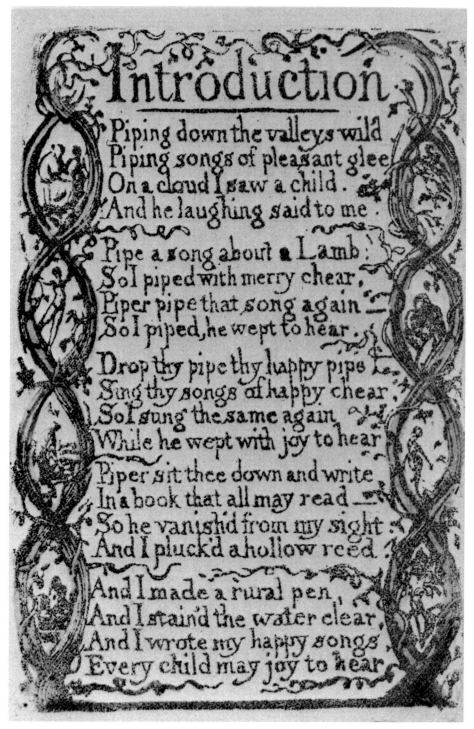

Figure 6   William Blake, 'Introduction', *Songs of Innocence*, from *Songs of Innocence and Experience*, Plate 4, designed 1789–94, relief etching, finished in pen and watercolour on paper, 11.1 x 7.8 cm. Reproduced by permission of the Syndics of the Fitzwilliam Museum, Cambridge, P.125-1950.

writing. And the poem does not entirely follow the conventions of the pastoral. The 'hollow reed' for example is not used to make a flute as is usual in pastoral, but a pen. And that verb 'stain' in the last stanza doesn't seem to fit with such a world at all. The poem, then, cannot be seen as wholly innocent. How can we account for this ambiguity? ■

You may have noticed that both these slightly discordant elements refer to writing. The growth of literacy and the availability of printed matter of all kinds made writing into a mass medium. As such, it was a medium that a government conducting a controversial war was anxious to keep under control. You may remember that the government put three writers on trial for treason in 1794. So the references to writing were quite pointed for Blake's first readers. The act of writing itself is not neutral during a period of censorship.

Blake's reference to writing may also allude to a more specific controversy during the decade following the French Revolution. There was a debate in Britain about the nature of its constitution. In France the National Assembly published its *Declaration of the Rights of Man* in 1789, the year of the French Revolution and the same year *Songs of Innocence* was illuminated. British radicals wanted the French example imitated in Britain, which did not – and does not – have a written constitution. For the Tory Edmund Burke the essence of the British constitution was that it was a set of national customs and traditions which were not written down: 'the constitution on paper is one thing, and in fact and experience is another'. Burke believed that we could trust the constitution because it was invisible. The radical Tom Paine replied in his *Rights of Man* that a constitution had to be visible, to be written down: 'A constitution is not a thing in name only, but in fact. It has not an ideal but a real existence; and wherever it cannot be produced in visible form, there is none' (*The Thomas Paine Reader*, 1987, p.220). For Paine and some of the radicals, then, speaking was conservative, writing was radical. Despite their own earlier radicalism, Wordsworth and Coleridge were supporting censorship of the press by 1817. Printing had become a political tool, and it was always a tool that was available to Blake.

In *The Marriage of Heaven and Hell*, Blake called his own underground print shop the 'printing house in hell'. There he called his method of printing 'the infernal method', giving it a symbolic significance:

> But first the notion that man has a body distinct from his soul is to be
> expunged. This I shall do by printing in the infernal method, by
> corrosives, which in hell are salutary and medicinal, melting apparent
> surfaces away, and displaying the infinite which was hid.

> (Wu, *Romanticism*, 1994, p.83)

This describes Blake's engraving technique – using acid to burn off the surface of the plate to reveal the text and design incised on it. But the description is used to symbolize the effect he intended his work to have as well as the means by which it was produced. He wanted to burn away the 'apparent surfaces' and reveal the 'infinite' beneath. In this quotation

Blake's language seems very different from that of, say, Wordsworth or Clare in the poems we looked at first. But it does describe impulses similar to ones we noticed there: a dissatisfaction with the ordinary world and a desire to transcend it. Blake saw all around him the 'infinite' he wanted to reveal. This is the way that religious visionaries claim to see but, just as Blake does not separate body from soul, he does not separate religion from politics.

Maybe there is a historical irony to the 'Introduction' to the *Songs of Innocence*. The inspiring child vanishes at the moment of writing. The pen 'stains the water clear'. In the illumination for 'Nurse's Song' the nurse is reading. In *The Marriage of Heaven and Hell*, begun in 1790 and completed in 1792–3, Blake had promised or threatened a 'Bible of Hell', and in *The Book of Urizen*, printed in 1794, he provided a kind of Genesis, an alternative creation. Urizen is a figure who stands for the violent repression and envy that Blake associates with figures in authority. His name is perhaps pronounced 'your reason'. His first act in the newly created cosmos is to produce a 'Book of Brass'. This book is a repressive instrument. Written on it are the words 'One king, one God, one law'. The origin of tyranny was simultaneous with the origin of writing. So – was Blake for or against writing? Well, he was not as wholly committed to writing as he would have been if he had been only a poet, and the point is that what he calls the 'single vision' of Urizen is repressive. We need always a different perspective, sometimes a radically different perspective. And that is what Blake always provides.

E.P. Thompson described Blake as 'the authentic voice of a long popular tradition', a tradition of religious and political dissent (Thompson, *The Making of the English Working Class*, 1968, p.56). Blake was working class, the son of a haberdasher. His only formal education was in art. He went as a student to the Royal Academy, and was apprenticed to an engraver at the age of 14. With the exception of a three-year stay at Felpham on the south coast, he lived almost all his life in London, making his living as an engraver. In London he had contacts with radical groups such as the London Corresponding Society. Thompson sees Blake as a hero of popular radicalism, the Jacobin artist-engraver who before 1794 wore a red revolutionary bonnet in the streets of London and who just escaped a charge of sedition at Felpham in 1803. (Blake had thrown a drunken soldier named Schofield out of his garden at Felpham and Schofield accused Blake of high treason, an offence which carried a sentence of death.)

In this section I have tried to sketch a context for reading Blake. We began by comparing his use of the viewpoint of the child with Wordsworth's. Interest in this viewpoint is a common element in Romantic writing, but the way in which it is explored by these two differs, as we have seen. We went on to look at a very radical revision of a myth of origins in 'A Poison Tree'. It is often said that, with Shelley, Blake is the most politically radical of all the Romantic poets, and I have implied that his writing is much more radical than Wordsworth's. I just want to end this section with a qualifying comment.

Perhaps the notion of a 'radical' Blake versus a 'reactionary' Wordsworth is insufficient, as David Simpson suggests:

It is not enough to say that Blake is 'radical' because his text is so, while Wordsworth is somehow reactionary because he writes a language more nearly approximating to that of ordinary social intercourse; [...] in our myth of Blake's aesthetic wholeness there may be something we should suspect. Because his text is radical [...] we move [...] to a radical Blake. The radical text was very possibly written on the assumption that it would not be read. [...] Even today we seldom read Blake but have to make do with variously inadequate facsimiles. [...] The real Blake is locked away in museums, a prey to the very social tendencies we assume that he opposed. Or did he? For Blake was never 'there' for the taking. [...] Most of his books were incapable of being mass-produced, given the coloring process, and they were too expensive for most potential readers.

(Simpson, 'Reading Blake and Derrida', 1986, pp.22–3)

Simpson suggests that we need to be careful about what we assume is radical and what conservative. We have already seen how reading a text is modified by knowledge of its context. Some apparently radical texts may come to seem less radical when we take into account *who* they were written for, *who* they were read by, and *how* they were read. The reverse may also be true. That is, texts may appear conservative because we expect from them things which are no part of their context. We are liable to misread texts written by women in the period if we read them in terms appropriate to male Romantic poets. I will be dealing with an important example of this in Chapter Two.

Simpson's comments may remind us of how easy it is to romanticize the Romantics. They remind us too of the central importance of the first audience for a work. They also remind us that in some ways Romantic writers use their texts to argue with each other. For many British writers the figure to be argued with was Wordsworth. The reasons for this are to do with factors in the politics and history of the time during which they wrote, and in Chapter Two we shall look at those factors in a bit more detail.

Conclusion

We began by making two observations about Romantic poems. The first was their assertion of the powers of the self; the second was their assertion of the validity of strong feeling. We saw an extreme version of this second tendency in Blake's 'A Poison Tree'. In Blake we also found a claim that the self may be deluded if it thinks itself to be free. We have seen these tendencies recur in different forms in many of the texts we have looked at. Such tendencies are identified by the term 'Romanticism'. But such a bland definition is too general to identify a piece of writing as 'Romantic'. And in fact the examples of Romantic lyric that we have looked at have shown some variety.

So we considered whether Romantic writing is a certain kind of writing or the writing of a particular period. I have suggested that what allows us to see many of these writings as similar in retrospect is their participation in and reaction to the same historical events. I have been arguing that we find the coherence of a literary period in its history. However, no literary period (and no historical period) has an intrinsic, cut-and-dried coherence; it is something which we discover (or construct) in looking back. (Did you notice that the second poem we looked at, John Clare's 'I Am ...', was written beyond the time usually given as the end-point of Romanticism?)

Seeing Romantic writing as writing in history allows us to take account of how it takes part in the events and responds to the pressures of the turbulent period in which it was written. We saw a clear example of this in Shelley's 'England in 1819'. We couldn't really have appreciated what was going on in that poem without knowing about the events it referred to. The historical context was helpful too in seeing how three writers tackled what was apparently the same subject: London. We saw also that poems that do not actually mention historical events may still depend upon them. A poem may conceal what it depends upon. We can see this from Wordsworth's 'Composed upon Westminster Bridge' which concealed its history in the sense that the poem represented the city as something which it was not (nature, or a person), and that it depended on Dorothy but did not acknowledge her.

In Chapter Two we will look more closely at the history of the period and consider further the diversity of Romantic writings and their relationship to history.

Versions of British Romantic writing

by Stephen Bygrave

Chapter One showed the benefits of reading Romantic texts in terms of the history within which they were produced. In this chapter we will continue to look mainly at lyric poems, although here my discussion will broaden to consider briefly fiction by Mary Shelley and Jane Austen and will conclude by introducing you to two longer poems by P. B. Shelley and William Wordsworth which will be discussed more fully in Chapter Five.

In this chapter we will be looking at three main topics: (1) the history of the period of British Romanticism and the position of writers in that period; (2) the changed conditions for authorship in the period and in particular what these meant for women writers; and (3) the figure of the Romantic artist.

When was Romanticism?

It is common to divide a 'first generation' of Romantic writers, which includes Blake, Wordsworth and Coleridge, from a 'second generation' including Shelley, Keats, and Byron. One difference between the two generations was that the second generation died relatively young. We would do well also to consider the social backgrounds of the two groups. Of the first generation, only Blake, a Londoner, was brought up in a city. He was working class, the son of a hosier. Wordsworth's father was a Cumberland solicitor and Coleridge's a Devonshire vicar. Both Wordsworth and Coleridge went to Cambridge University (although they did not meet while they were there) and both eventually lived off annuities from rich patrons. All three had contact with radical groups who met to discuss the revolutionary ideas of Godwin and Paine. Although Blake did not attend school, he was trained as an engraver at the Royal Academy and was an artisan, a professional tradesman. Of the second generation, while Keats was attacked in class terms as 'Cockney Keats' by right-wing reviewers, Byron inherited a title and estate at the age of 10 and Shelley was heir to a baronetcy. Byron and Shelley both lived in exile, from which they criticized the reactionary character of English society. If there was a difference in social class between the two generations of writers, there was also a difference in historical experience. The Europe inhabited by the second generation was very different from Europe in the 1790s, the decade during which Wordsworth and Coleridge began to publish.

Romantic literature of the first generation was wartime literature. Apart from a period of fourteen months after the peace of Amiens in March 1802 and a few months at the end of 1814, Britain was continuously at war from February 1793 until the Battle of Waterloo in June 1815. There were revolutions across Europe in the 1790s. Britain led a series of shifting alliances involving, amongst others, Russia, Prussia and Austria in attempting to contain an increasingly expansionist France. There continued to be a real danger of French invasion into the early 1800s. After war broke out between

Britain and France in February 1793 sympathy for Revolutionary ideals was not just unpopular, it was treasonable. In Britain there were the treason trials of Thelwall and others in 1794. The Seditious Meetings Act and the Treasonable Practices Act of 1795 (known as the 'Gagging Acts') restricted public meetings and what could be said at them. So fear of revolution and the conditions of war led to suppression of public meetings and censorship of the press. (The need to speak in an oblique or guarded way, in a kind of code, may account for the difficulty of some Romantic texts – for example, the elliptical, visionary character of the language of Blake's prophecies.) Pitt, the Prime Minister up to 1801, developed a domestic spy system – as we have seen, Blake was indicted for sedition (which was a capital offence) and Wordsworth and Coleridge were spied upon. However, the attitude of some in Britain who were enthusiastic about the Revolution changed as events unfolded in France. Robespierre and the Jacobins took over from the more moderate Girondins, leading to the 'Terror' of 1793–4 – the period of the guillotine and of the trial and execution of Louis XVI and Marie Antoinette amongst others. Napoleon assumed absolute power as First Consul in November 1799. These were the crucial events in turning many, including Wordsworth and Coleridge, away from their initial sympathy with the aims of the French Revolution to opposition to it.

The historical situation was different in the decade during which Shelley, Keats and Byron began to publish. The war had ended at Waterloo in 1815, but divisions and tensions came back to the surface in Britain. The war had affected Britain's sources of supply and the effects of this were worsened by a series of bad harvests in the 1810s. Organized breaking of the machines that were replacing the workforce in the weaving and lace industries had occurred in Nottinghamshire and Yorkshire in 1811 and these 'Luddite' riots continued. In December 1816 leaders of the Spa Fields Riot were arraigned for high treason. In 1817 three Derbyshire men were executed for their part in a rebellion probably instigated by a government spy. The government had suspended Habeas Corpus (the right in English law to freedom from imprisonment without trial) between 1794 and 1801 and suspended it again in March 1817, driving democratic societies underground with its Seditious Meetings Act the same year. As we have seen from Shelley's 'England in 1819', the 'Peterloo Massacre' was in some ways the climax of the economic and political discontent of the immediate postwar years (see p.8 above); Shelley's poem 'The Mask of Anarchy', was a direct response. Following Peterloo, the government introduced legislation ('The Six Acts') further restricting the right to hold meetings and the freedom of the press.

Wordsworth had been a sympathizer with the early ideals of the Revolution but his change of mind and his eventual acceptance of government employment was seen as a retreat into conservatism and as a betrayal of the democratic ideals of the Revolution to the reactionary forces of the British Establishment. Shelley, Keats and Byron all accused Coleridge and Wordsworth of 'apostasy', that is of having changed sides. (The original apostate was Lucifer, who was an angel but who fell and became Satan.) Byron, Shelley and Keats were themselves all too young to have lived either through the Revolution itself or the reaction. Wordsworth has some famous lines on the early days of the Revolution:

Bliss was it in that dawn to be alive,
But to be young was very heaven!

(*The Prelude*, 1799–1806, Book X, ll.692–3; Wu, *Romanticism*, 1994, p.438)

The second generation never saw that 'dawn'. Their world was largely the reactionary Europe of the post-war alliances.

Leaders from Austria, Britain, Prussia and Russia met at the Congress of Vienna in 1815. In order to surround the defeated France with 'buffer states' the four powers had redrawn European borders. For example, Poland came under Russian control and the Italian territory of Lombardy-Venetia became part of the Austrian Empire. It was in such circumstances that nationalist movements sprang up across Europe. Byron and Shelley both had links with such radical groups. Both chose to live in exile for personal and economic reasons, and exile became an element in the stereotype figure of the alienated, withdrawn, brooding hero of Byron's writings. We shall be looking later at the figure of the poet as it appears in Wordsworth and Shelley. Byron and Shelley represent two influential stances towards post-war Europe. One we have already seen in Shelley's poem 'England in 1819': a kind of utopianism, projecting everything forward into a hopeful future. The second we shall be considering in Chapter Seven: the apparent cynicism of Byron, revelling in the superficiality of the world.

So the difference between the first and second generations of Romantic writers can be seen as the difference between the point of view of wartime and post-war writers. We can examine this difference by looking at a pair of poems. Both these poems are sonnets and I think they both attempt to put the phenomena of war and conquest into a different, longer perspective, whether natural, mythological or historical. The first is Wordsworth's 'Composed by the Side of Grasmere Lake'.

This poem was, Wordsworth says, written in 1807. It was published, slightly revised, as the fifth of the *Sonnets on National Independence and Liberty* in his volume *Benjamin the Waggoner* in 1819. I should say at the start that this is quite a difficult poem – it does not seem to follow the recommendations we saw Wordsworth making about literary language in the Preface to the *Lyrical Ballads* of 1802. There are for example several mythological references: Jove is the Roman name for Jupiter, the ruler of the gods; Mars is the Roman god of war; Venus the goddess of beauty (all these of course are also planets); and Pan is the god of nature. 'Eve' in the first line here means 'evening', not the first woman.

Read the poem through first of all. **Are there ways in which it could be compared with Wordsworth's sonnet on Westminster Bridge (see pp.17–22 above)?**

Composed by the Side of Grasmere Lake

Eve's lingering clouds extend in solid bars
Through the grey west; and lo! these waters, steeled
By breezeless air to smoothest polish, yield
A vivid repetition of the stars;
Jove – Venus – and the ruddy crest of Mars,   5
Amid his fellows beauteously revealed

49

At happy distance from earth's groaning field,
Where ruthless mortals wage incessant wars.
Is it a mirror? – or the nether sphere
Opening its vast abyss, while fancy feeds 10
On the rich show! – But list! a voice is near;
Great Pan himself low-whispering through the reeds,
'Be thankful thou; for, if unholy deeds
Ravage the world, tranquillity is here!'

(Ketcham, *Shorter Poems, 1807–1820, by William Wordsworth*,
1989, p.43)

Discussion

Like the sonnet on Westminster Bridge this is a poem from which people
are absent. Here we don't even get the 'I' that surfaces in that earlier poem
('Ne'er saw I, never felt, a calm so deep'). This poem also shares with the
earlier sonnet a technique of personifying that which is inanimate – the
stars, and Nature itself in the final lines. I have mentioned the variety of
voices in Romantic writing. Here the voice of Pan from the reeds seems to
be a consoling voice, soothing rather than answering the restless questioning of the sestet of the poem. Perhaps the title might lead us to expect a
poem of natural description, but what happens is that the landscape seems
continually to reflect worldly events, specifically war. ■

What suggests that this is a poem which is *about* war?

Discussion

The poem refers to 'incessant wars' (l.8) and there is, as I have said, the reference to Mars (lines 5–7). Mars is particularly noticeable because of its
beauty. It has always been called 'the red planet', and here its 'ruddy crest'
may also suggest blood. But Mars seems to be serenely beautiful, and happily sharing the heavens with Jove and Venus. There is another single word
which suggests the presence of war.

I am thinking of the word 'steeled' in line 2. The *Oxford English Dictionary* defines the verb 'to steel' primarily as to cause to resemble steel
and, figuratively, to make hard, unbending, or strong as steel. These definitions of course imply the presence or the threat of some powerfully negative force. You might steel yourself for battle, or to withstand something
else unpleasant. So the normal associations of the word would be to do
with things less pleasant than a Lake District landscape. As a noun of
course 'steel' might mean weaponry (as in the phrase 'cold steel'). The OED
gives a secondary figurative meaning for the verb: 'to make like steel *in
appearance*'. It does not cite an authority for this usage, but calls it 'rare'
and gives a date: 1807, the year this poem was written. ■

In the poem Wordsworth uses the phrase 'incessant wars'. As I have said,
Britain had been almost continuously at war since 1793 and, despite Napoleon's defeat by the British navy at Trafalgar in 1805, he had gone on to win
a famous victory against Austria at Austerlitz – 'incessant wars' seemed
likely. In the year that the poem was written the French provoked the

Peninsular Wars by invading Spain and Portugal, where relatives of Napoleon were eventually installed as a new royal family. War continued uninterrupted until after Waterloo in 1815. So the new visual sense of 'steeled' (made like steel in appearance) carries with it the sense of grim, stoical resignation.

Landscape at this point of the poem seems to be an emblem or reflection of war. Does this change?

Discussion

At first the heavens seem distant from the earth. It's there that Jove, Venus and Mars are visible. So we glimpse a mythic world 'at happy distance from earth's groaning field' (line 7). The lake reflects the stars in 'a vivid repetition' (line 4). In Wordsworth's best-known poem, clouds are humanized: 'I wandered lonely *as a cloud*'. Here, clouds are hard objects. They 'extend in solid bars' (line 1), just as the lake waters are 'steeled'. The clouds are also 'lingering', just as wars are 'incessant'. And 'breezeless' (line 3) suggests 'breezy' (just as 'smokeless' earlier suggested 'smoky'). In the opening lines then there is no movement and no energy in nature to set against the 'ruthless' activities of the human world.

You might have noticed oppositions in the octet of the sonnet – air and stars versus water, the ethereal versus the solid, the original versus its reflection, the gods versus the earth. But these are then reversed or at least complicated by the sestet, in which it is less easy to see which is which. The question in lines 9–11 is difficult and Wordsworth seems to have recognized this in making alterations in later editions. So in a collected edition of 1827 the question runs:

> Is it a mirror? – or the nether sphere
> Opening to view the abyss in which it feeds
> Its own calm fires?

In later editions 'the nether sphere' becomes female, and 'feeds/*Her* own calm fires' (Ketcham, *Shorter Poems*, 1989, p.43; my emphasis). Do the heavens also reflect the earth? Is it heaven up there or a reflection of hell ('the nether sphere', line 9)? The syntax is not clear (does 'it' in line 9 refer to the earth or the heavens?), but it is apparent how easily this scene has opened onto the 'abyss' (line 10). Natural phenomena – the water, the stars and planets – have been made into symptoms and portents of a world at war. It's not clear whether what we are seeing is hell or a reflection of our own world at war. Which is the original and which the reflection? There is now a mutual reflection. ■

The last word of the poem, 'here', is what linguists call a *deictic*, from a Greek verb meaning 'to show'. A deictic is a word which shows something or points it out. Other deictics are such words as 'there', 'this', and 'that'.

1   **Read the poem aloud, and try putting a stress on the last word, 'here'. What difference does this make?**

2   **Does the ending of the poem take us off in a different direction?**

1   If we stressed 'here', the last word of the poem, we would be stressing the particular location we are told about in the title. And saying 'here' is a way of saying 'not there'. So 'here' would be opposed to 'the world' in the previous line. The opposition of 'the world' and nature, or of world-liness and retirement, is a poetic convention going back hundreds of years before this poem. In this case though the opposition does not really seem to work. The poem has come down to earth, but not to a world of secular reason, nor to a conventionally Christian world either.

2   At any rate, a poem which began as a more or less 'realistic' description of a scene claims to have transcended this scene by the end. In the final lines the gods come down to earth. The poem proceeds to a final conso-lation – in the voice of Nature itself. A god appears to speak and settle matters. Mortals commit 'unholy deeds' (line 13), but the immortals guarantee 'tranquillity' by the side of Grasmere lake. Having asked ques-tions which are unanswerable, it is not surprising that Wordsworth does not answer them. Rather, he escapes from such questions into a different realm altogether. The ending then is another claim for transcendence. ∎

We will come back to this ending in a moment, but for our second poem I want to look at Shelley's 'Ozymandias', another sonnet, written in 1817. (There is, by the way, no consensus on whether the title is pronounced with the stress on the third or the fourth syllable.) I have referred to Romantic writing as a set of different voices. **Are there noticeably differ-ent voices within this poem?**

Ozymandias

I met a traveller from an antique land
Who said, 'Two vast and trunkless legs of stone
Stand in the desert. Near them, on the sand
Half-sunk, a shattered visage lies, whose frown
And wrinkled lip, and sneer of cold command,   5
Tell that its sculptor well those passions read
Which yet survive, stamped on these lifeless things,
The hand that mocked them, and the heart that fed;
And on the pedestal, these words appear:
"My name is Ozymandias, King of Kings,   10
Look on my works, ye mighty, and despair!"
Nothing beside remains. Round the decay
Of that colossal wreck, boundless and bare
The lone and level sands stretch far away.'

(Wu, *Romanticism*, 1994, p.860)

D i s c u s s i o n

Even in this short poem there are three voices: the initial narrator, the trav-eller whose tale takes up most of the poem, and the quoted words of Ozymandias. In each of the poems about London everything could be seen to be unified as the perceptions of their narrator, but that is not the case here. Perhaps we should consider the relationships between these view-points, as we do in reading fiction. ∎

Now read the poem again. **What is the relationship between the sculptor and Ozymandias? Why is it important to the poem?**

Discussion

In the past, we infer, the relationship has been that of artist and patron. Ozymandias presumably commissioned his own monument from the sculptor. It is possible to read the poem as being to do with the ultimate superiority of artistic to political power: Ozymandias's boast (lines 10–11) is revealed as empty because his power has vanished almost without trace, while the work of the anonymous sculptor lives on. Such a reading would see the poem as making what we might call a classical statement, along the lines of *ars longa, vita brevis* ('art is long, life is short'). Such a statement could of course have been made in almost any period. How then does the poem relate to the historical period in which it was written? Once again, to explain I will have to try and sketch a context which is not given by the poem itself. ■

This is a poem which is 'about' history in one obvious sense. Ozymandias is the name Greek travellers gave to the Egyptian Pharaoh Rameses II, who died in 1234 BC, and the poem is concerned with his fabled power. It is also about the time in which it was written – it has been my case that this is true of all texts. The poem is not set at any particular time: it does not carry with it any dates as Wordsworth's Westminster Bridge poem did. However it is set clearly at some point in the modern world: the traveller is from 'an antique land' and Ozymandias is long dead. There is actually a more than accidental relationship to the modern world. Shelley could only have known about Ozymandias/Rameses II after the looting of Egyptian treasures that followed the invasion of Egypt by a French army in 1798.

Some statues and other relics were brought to Britain. The memorial to Rameses at Thebes stood near the remains of another memorial. This was to the Pharaoh Amenhotep III whom the Greeks knew as Memnon, and Shelley could have seen the head of 'Young Memnon' in 1817 in the British Museum. (Incidentally, there is not much sign on that head of 'the wrinkled lip/And sneer of cold command' of the poem.) Probably Shelley and his friend Horace Smith agreed to each write a poem on the theme of Egyptian ruins as they had earlier each written a sonnet on the Nile. The inscriptions on such sculpture were in hieroglyphics, which could not be translated until after 1822 (when the Rosetta Stone was deciphered), so the inscription Shelley quotes is from a literary source.

As I have said, this is a context that does not come with the poem itself. The poem does however allude to the contemporary world in its claim that the 'passions' for conquest and for power 'yet survive'. They survived notably in the figure who made it possible for Shelley to know about Ozymandias. The French army that invaded Egypt in 1798 was under the command of Napoleon Bonaparte. 'Ozymandias' concerns a tyrant, as many Romantic poems do – Coleridge's 'Kubla Khan' for instance had been published in 1816. The poem is not necessarily 'about' Napoleon but his career is a relevant context for it. By 1817, when this poem was written, Napoleon was a prisoner of war on the island of St Helena and he had come to stand for the fallen Romantic hero. The seemingly infinite power of Napoleon proved finite, and Shelley has shown ironically the insufficiency of Ozymandias' boast merely by citing it.

He also resists the temptation to offer a moralizing inscription to his own poem which would be similarly false. The close of 'England in 1819' pointed towards a hopeful future, but the close of this poem moves out in space rather than forward in time. This is noted by Anne Janowitz in some very interesting comments on the form of the poem:

> The sonnet structure itself is curiously wrought. The octave and sestet are not strictly set apart from one another, as the 'things/kings' rhyme links the two halves of the poem. Indeed, there is no substantial break in perspective between octave and sestet. The shift, if there is one, comes between lines 11 and 12. But rather than 'clinching' or summing up or aphorizing the octave, as we expect in the sonnet genre, the final lines of 'Ozymandias' open up upon a scene which awaits further interpretation.
>
> (Janowitz, 'Shelley's monument to Ozymandias', 1984, p.488)

The two poems we have looked at were written within a few years of each other. Both employ the same form, though as we have seen they do very different things with it. Janowitz's comments on the final lines of 'Ozymandias' seem to invite us to compare this ending with the clinching aphorism that ends the Wordsworth sonnet. **Look at the two endings. Is there a contrast to be made between them? Do they tell us something about the contrast between the 'two generations' of Romantic poets?**

D i s c u s s i o n

One way in which we might contrast the poems is by noticing that the Wordsworth poem moves from the vast to the personal (from the sky above to a whispered reassurance), and that there is the reverse movement in the Shelley poem (from the anecdotal 'I met a traveller' to that final 'opening up', as Janowitz describes it). The close of 'Composed by the Side of Grasmere Lake' introduces another voice. It offers a solution to the problems of 'restless mortals' in a god-given 'tranquillity'. This ending might be seen as a rather dishonest way out of problems that could not be resolved. Alternatively, it might be seen as an access of energy that checks the energy of the questions: sooner the energy of Pan than of Mars. This move from the political world into the unchanging 'tranquillity' of nature is what seemed to many of Wordsworth's radical contemporaries to be a retreat. The Shelley poem zooms out from the boastful inscription and pans across deserts of 'lone and level sands'. Though tyranny might remain, it could be placed in a long historical perspective. Wordsworth resolves his unease about historical events only by escaping from them into the consolations of nature, while Shelley finds consolation in the historical process itself.

These poems are different then, and the difference between them is not due to an explicit disagreement over the same issue. They do though let us see the way contemporary history may have a bearing on poems which do not directly take it as their subject. They also let us see the differences between poems by writers of the first and second generations.

Wordsworth wrote his poem in wartime, Shelley his after the war was over. I think that a difference in historical experience is discernible in these two poems. ■

Whatever the contrasts between these poems by Wordsworth and Shelley, they are both poems by male authors confidently employing a prestigious poetic form. Let's now look at the situation of female writers in the period.

Gender and authorship

The period of Romantic writing is also the period in which Britain became an industrial nation. There were changes in the technology and commerce of publishing and in what it meant to be an author as a result. Romantic writing is often said to have extended the readership and the subject-matter of writing. Conditions of authorship changed too. In the eighteenth century many writers had depended financially on a patron, usually an aristocrat, to whom their books would then be dedicated. Books were often sold by subscription – that is, by raising money from subscribers who agreed to pay for a book before it was published, or sometimes even before it was written. Throughout most of the eighteenth century the bookseller was responsible for the whole process of raising subscriptions and printing and selling books. In the years with which we are concerned all this fell away. The structure of publisher or wholesaler, printer, and retail bookseller came into being – this is the structure we still have.

In this section I want to consider what some of these changes meant for women writers and readers. We will be looking briefly at two novels, Jane Austen's *Pride and Prejudice* and Mary Shelley's *Frankenstein*, and at poetry by women. We have looked at male writers in terms of the historical and social circumstances in which they produced their work and seen how these circumstances differed according to individuals. Here I want to consider circumstances which were to an extent common to women writers. These affected both what they wrote and the way it was received.

Professional authors were still mostly male. There is a good reason why this was so. Women still had no independent economic status. Married women had no right to own property or to keep any money they earned. In law only widows and single women whose parents were dead could own their own property. And social custom as well as law tended to confine women to the roles of wife and mother. Published women writers were mostly wealthy and well connected, having access to publishers and to other writers and artists. Women outside the traditional literary classes needed a patron to help find subscribers if they were to break into print.

By the late eighteenth century there were examples for female writers to follow. In the 1750s and 1760s a circle of female intellectuals had met on a regular basis in London. These were the so-called 'Bluestockings', many of whom had managed to learn Greek and Latin (the prerogative of a male education) as well as modern European languages. In their salons they would debate moral questions, translate the classics and engage in literary criticism – the kind of intellectual activities hitherto restricted to men.

However, the role of woman as author threatened to subvert gender divisions and to transgress boundaries which confined her to the private sphere of domesticity and motherhood. In Chapter One we noted that publication *means* making public. As the profession of authorship began to open for women, the division of private from public became blurred. Reviewers discussing fiction and poetry which had been written by women often took the short step from moralizing about the text to moralizing about the writer. In the past women dramatists such as Aphra Behn had in this way been compromised by the notorious moral laxity of the theatre. Women would be praised for their role as mothers, but told that this role excluded the role of author.

Where there was transgression of these roles it had to be imagined in remote locations or fantastic forms, as it is in Mary Shelley's *Frankenstein*. Like the creature, the novel had no name attached to it. It was first published, in 1818, anonymously. Most of the early reviews assumed it had been written by a man. In the Gothic novel the villains were figures of legitimate social authority: fathers, judges, priests, aristocrats. There was thus a subversive thrill about reading them. The text of *Frankenstein* scandalized middle-class propriety by representing to it its deepest fears and desires. Amongst other things, the novel is about the murder of an entire family.

In the introduction to the revised edition of the novel published in 1831 Mary Shelley wrote of her novel: 'And now, once again, I bid my hideous progeny go forth and prosper. I have affection for it' (1994 edn, p.197). For a novel so concerned with production and birth there seems to be a kind of maternal repugnance. As many influential feminist readings of the novel have pointed out, Mary Shelley herself was both a mother and the author of *Frankenstein* before she was twenty. Her child, a girl born on 22 February 1815, survived only a few days and died without being given a name. Her own famous mother, Mary Wollstonecraft, had died after giving birth to her; and three of her own four children died in infancy.

In the novel itself, it may be that Victor Frankenstein's real blasphemy lies not in supplanting God but in supplanting woman, producing from the laboratory instead of from the womb. There is an interesting sidelight on this in Percy Shelley's review of *Frankenstein*, written in 1817 but not published until 1832. Shelley pretends that he doesn't know who the author is. The creature's crimes, Shelley writes, are not 'the offspring of an unaccountable propensity to evil', but nor are they Victor Frankenstein's fault; rather they are 'the children, as it were, of Necessity and Human Nature' (Ingpen and Peck (eds.) *The Complete Works of P.B. Shelley*, 1926–30, vol. 6, p.264). Shelley is suggesting the roots of revolutionary action, but, applied to a novel whose subject bypasses the normal processes of reproduction, the metaphor of childbearing is striking. The creature's actions are excused and generalized.

Another important way in which *Frankenstein* can be read in terms of gender is in its treatment of education, and we will go on to look at this. Education was strictly gendered. In *A Vindication of the Rights of Woman* (1792) Mary Wollstonecraft attacked a situation in which women's education fitted them only to get husbands. Women were taught a set of 'feminine' accomplishments, constituting an ideology of 'sensibility', which, as she saw it, enslaved them:

Their senses are inflamed, and their understandings neglected,
consequently they become the prey of their senses, delicately termed
sensibility, and are blown about by every momentary gust of feeling. [...]
    Novels, music, poetry, and gallantry, all tend to make women the
creatures of sensation, and their character is thus formed in the mould
of folly during the time they are acquiring accomplishments, the only
improvement they are excited, by their station in society, to acquire.

(Wollstonecraft, *A Vindication of the Rights of Woman*, 1975
edn, p.152)

We will see in Chapters Four and Eight that sensibility is explicitly equated
with femininity. Here it is clear that sensibility is a product of the education
of women.

For Wollstonecraft the gendering of education is primary: education
enforces and sustains the gender distinctions in society. And education
forms an important concern of her daughter's novel *Frankenstein*. Critics
have seen the creature's situation as analogous to a slave, a colonial subject, or a woman. In such a reading the gendering of education is seen as
destructive.

Frankenstein *and education*

In *Frankenstein* the creature has to learn about the lack of a family that distinguishes it from its maker, as it has to learn about everything else. In fact
a central concern of the novel is education. The creature's narrative is about
education – a humane education which contrasts with that of Victor Frankenstein. In the course of the novel Victor's education takes him from the
near magic and alchemy of medieval and Renaissance science to the experimental science of the Enlightenment. This has been read from a gendered
perspective, seeing the creature's education as feminine, and Victor's education as masculine.

Though it is produced rather than born, the creature is a kind of feminine 'child of nature'. Seeing the moon, it doesn't know what to call it. It
calls it 'a gentle light', 'a radiant form', and finally 'the orb of night': thus it
goes from not knowing its name to a kind of eighteenth-century periphrasis. It discovers fire, and also discovers what we recognize to be snow: 'I
found my feet chilled by the cold damp substance that covered the
ground'. Finally, in learning what it calls the 'godlike science' of language, it
learns that it is separate. The De Laceys inhabit a 'cottage', it lives in a
'kennel'. Repulsed by them, it still helps them. The creature acquires
knowledge through voyeurism and through eavesdropping. Felix reads
aloud to Safie from Volney's *Ruins of Empire* where the creature learns for
the first time about economic and sexual divisions.

In Volume II, Chapter VII, of the novel we are given the creature's
reading list: *Paradise Lost*, Plutarch's *Lives* and Goethe's *The Sorrows of
Young Werther*. These books are not randomly chosen; the books that the
creature reads are those that Mary Shelley read herself. Through them the
creature is able to question its own identity, its own origins, and to become
humanized. The creature reads Milton's *Paradise Lost* as a 'true history'
rather than as a myth of origins. Plutarch's *Lives* are biographies of great

men, so the creature reads of the public virtue of Plutarch's heroes, and becomes, in effect, a republican. And Goethe's *Werther* is about a young man, an artist who, hopelessly in love with a woman who is unattainable, eventually commits suicide. It became a classic of sensibility because of its concern with passionate and obsessive feeling, with the attempt of the imagination to conquer 'reality'. Through reading, the creature ceases to be an outsider, it enters into sentiment. In considering fictional origins it discovers its own, by purloining Frankenstein's journal. Knowledge is to say the least a mixed blessing, as it was for Adam and Eve: 'sorrow only increased with knowledge'. Reading gives the creature expectations that cannot be fulfilled in the social world.

In the novel, the ambassador of that world is the narrator, Walton. We tend to be attracted by what seem the subversive possibilities of the novel: its narrative encourages us to care less about the innocent victims (Justine, Elizabeth, Clerval) than on those whose freedom of imagination has brought about their deaths. As we become involved with the events of the novel, we may forget that Walton is there, and that Mrs Elizabeth Saville is there behind him as the supposed first reader of this narrative, but none of it could happen without him. It is Walton who has taken us over the threshold from a world we recognize as being much like our own into the world of the fantastic, and finally it is Walton who is able to salvage something from the wreck by avoiding another wreck.

Near the end of the novel, when Walton's ship is surrounded by ice, his situation is that of Frankenstein in the narrative: 'the lives of all these men are endangered through me. If we are lost, my mad schemes are the cause'. Unlike Frankenstein however, he turns back from what would have been the disastrous consequences of his actions. He turns around and goes back home to his family. There is finally a movement of reconciliation, of comedy. Now this may be an action we morally approve of, but we tend to be interested in the figures who transgress rather than in those who behave in morally acceptable ways. The novel as a whole seems to recommend sentiment and moral relativism – most of the values in fact metaphorically represented in the flat country of Geneva rather than in the extreme landscapes of the Alps and northern seas in which the pursuit is conducted. If though the novel does recommend those values, it does so largely by showing the effects of their absence or by describing their opposites. We need not argue that Walton is the hero to see it (especially in the later version) as ultimately conservative, urging us not to meddle, to stay at home and obey the law. However, the creature is excluded by both law and custom from education, companionship and from human society itself. Its actions are seen to be motivated, if not justified, in a way that Victor Frankenstein's are not.

The creature is rejected because of its appearance rather than for its behaviour, and it is unaware of an appearance that is frightening and loathsome to others until it looks at itself in a pool in Volume II, Chapter IV. Just at the point where the creature has acquired an image of a society which it could join, it recognizes that it is separate from the 'perfect forms' of a society which it has yet to learn must reject it. What it does see is that it will only be allowed to be what others see it as, recognizing 'that I was in reality the monster that I am' (p.90).

Women and the novel

The position of female authors was different in terms of what could be written as well as how it was received. Only certain forms and kinds of content were held to be appropriate for women authors. The term 'romance' included most of what would later be called the novel, often seen as a female form both in terms of its readers and its authorship. Well over half of the novels written during the eighteenth century were written by women. Though the novel did not have the scandalous potential of drama it was well down in a hierarchy of genres of which the twin peaks were tragedy and the epic. Reading novels was sometimes regarded as sinful, but more often simply as a trivial pastime. Certainly the novel did not have the privileged status which many Romantic writers claimed for poetry.

The first tendencies of Romantic poems we noticed were a dwelling on the private experience of the self and a desire to transcend the social world. Jane Austen seems to display the opposite tendencies to these. She seems in many ways to be the antithesis of the Romantic poets. Wordsworth called the *Lyrical Ballads* 'experiments' and Shelley called his poem *The Revolt of Islam* 'an experiment on the temper of the public mind', but Austen does not seem experimental in her forms, nor to experiment with the content of her fictions, which is primarily ethical. She is not concerned, as the Romantic poets are, with transcending the social world through language, but rather with discriminating among the various languages of a social world she accepts. Her values seem to be those of the professional classes and of the landowning gentry; her high Anglicanism contrasts with the low church backgrounds of the first generation of poets and the atheism of the second, and so on.

Pride and Prejudice, for example, is a novel which obeys the expectations of the romance genre in that Elizabeth Bennet is finally rewarded by marriage to the right man. It endorses basically conservative values: you pass on what you own, but not what you feel – the values of property and propriety. Those values, however, need to be reasserted precisely because they are under threat. And they are embodied not by any of the variously inadequate male characters but by Elizabeth. Throughout the novel the heroine comes to speak for virtues in which nearly all the male characters are deficient.

Jane Austen seems conservative then. But her novels suggest that gender divisions hindered the achievement of those conservative virtues. Austen insists, as Wollstonecraft does, that 'reason' is not a gendered faculty. Women are not mere creatures of sensation and may possess 'reason' at least as much as men. There is a similar insistence among the writings of Austen's female contemporaries and immediate predecessors. It may therefore be an oversimplification to dismiss women writers of the period as conservative.

I would like you to consider a passage defending women's writing. It comes from Maria Edgeworth's first published work, *Letters for Literary Ladies* (1795). **What is women's writing being defended *against*?**

Edgeworth has one of her male correspondents write to the other:

> Even if literature were no other use to the fair sex than to supply them with employment, I should think the time dedicated to the cultivation of their minds well bestowed: they are surely better occupied when they are reading and writing than when coqueting or gaming, losing their fortunes or their characters. You despise the writings of women:– you think that they might have made a better use of the pen, than to write plays, and poetry, and romances. Considering that the pen was to women a new instrument, I think that they have made at least as good a use of it as learned men did of the needle some centuries ago, when they set themselves to determine how many spirits could stand upon its point, and were ready to tear one another to pieces in the discussion of this sublime question. Let the sexes mutually forgive each other their follies; or, what is much better, let them combine their talents for their general advantage.

> (Edgeworth, *Letters for Literary Ladies*, 1993 edn, p.25)

Discussion

Maria Edgeworth defends women's writing only against the charge that it is an idle pursuit. She is careful not to imply that acceptance of women's writing might lead to their taking of political power. Even if she had wanted to be more forthright in making her claim for women's writing there were factors which would have inhibited her. She was writing in the 1790s in the decade after the French Revolution when, despite the expansion of publishing and the press, control was strict, and when the very fact of female authorship was associated with demands for female equality. These demands in turn were seen as revolutionary. These are reasons why Edgeworth's claims for women's writing are much more conservative than the claims made for poetry by male poets. ∎

Women and poetry

In some ways prose fiction offered women writers a form whose boundaries were not finally fixed and which, because it was not always taken seriously, was allowed to develop its own audience and its own conventions. Poetry, as we have noted, had a prestige which assumed it to be masculine. None of the multi-volume anthologies or smaller compilations of English poets published from the second half of the eighteenth century contained more than a single woman poet: Queen Elizabeth. Women did of course function as subjects for poems by male writers, in ways which we can see by looking back at the poems we have looked at so far.

Earlier we considered the similarity between William Wordsworth's Westminster Bridge sonnet and Dorothy's journal account (p.21 above). William's making public what Dorothy had noticed by casting it in the privileged form of poetry wins him applause that would be denied the private, feminine utterance. In 'She dwelt among th' untrodden ways' Lucy exists for the masculine speaker as an image or emblem of a femininity which is associated both with nature and with death. In later versions of 'Composed by the Side of Grasmere Lake' the 'nether sphere' is female. In Blake, women may be represented as sexual victims (as in 'London' for example), or as the benevolent ideal of teachers and guardians (as in the first 'Nurse's Song' for example); but in both cases they fulfil fairly conventional roles.

A list of the supposed characteristics of Romantic poetry – emotional, intuitive, spontaneous – would look rather like a list of the preconceptions about femininity addressed in Mary Wollstonecraft's *Vindication of the Rights of Woman*. They are not terms which could be applied to Mary Robinson's poem, 'London's Summer Morning': Robinson there refers to herself *as* a poet (p.16 above). She represents herself neither as a passive emblem of nature nor as an outsider who is prophetic or specially gifted. To be a poet in Robinson's terms is to have a job, not a vocation. Women were under 'pressure to conform to certain patterns of ideal womanhood, none of which included the possibility of a poet's vocation. It was considered scandalous in the early nineteenth century for a woman to write publicly; if she did, she was judged not as a writer but as a woman' (Homans, *Women Writers and Poetic Identity*, 1980, p.5). This was certainly true of Wollstonecraft: opponents tried to discredit her arguments by referring instead to her private relationships. And as Homans suggests, for a woman to be not just a writer but a poet was especially to transgress the boundaries of gender.

As a way of focusing these issues, I want to consider a poem written in about 1795 by the Bluestocking poet, essayist and writer for children, Anna Letitia Barbauld (1743–1825). The poem is entitled 'The Rights of Woman'. Now that title would have triggered particular associations. The French revolutionaries had published their *Declaration of the Rights of Man* in 1789. Thomas Paine's polemic *Rights of Man*, had been published in two parts in 1791 and 1792. The first part had sold 50,000 in a few weeks and a cheap reprint sold 32,000 copies in a month. Paine was prosecuted for seditious libel and fled the country. His Victorian biographer claimed that by the following year 200,000 copies of *Rights of Man* were in circulation. Mary Wollstonecraft's *Vindication of the Rights of Woman* was also published in 1792. The book, dedicated to the French revolutionary politician Talleyrand and asserting female rights by analogy with the rights demanded by the revolutionaries, caused a furore. So the associations of Barbauld's title would be with 'Jacobinism' – with the democratic programme of Paine and with Wollstonecraft's call for 'a revolution in female manners'. **The title of the poem then leads us to expect that it will be a call for revolution, or at least for political emancipation. Is this what we find?**

The Rights of Woman

Yes, injured woman – rise, assert thy right!
Woman! too long degraded, scorned, oppressed;
Oh born to rule in partial law's despite,
Resume thy native empire o'er the breast!

Go forth arrayed in panoply divine,   5
That angel pureness which admits no stain;
Go, bid proud man his boasted rule resign
And kiss the golden sceptre of thy reign.

Go, gird thyself with grace, collect thy store
Of bright artillery glancing from afar –   10
Soft melting tones thy thundering cannon's roar,
Blushes and fears thy magazine of war.

Thy rights are empire: urge no meaner claim –
Felt, not defined, and if debated, lost;
Like sacred mysteries which withheld from fame,   15
Shunning discussion, are revered the most.

Try all that wit and art suggest to bend
Of thy imperial foe the stubborn knee;
Make treacherous Man thy subject, not thy friend –
Thou mayst command but never canst be free.   20

Awe the licentious and restrain the rude;
Soften the sullen, clear the cloudy brow;
Be more than princes' gifts, thy favours sued –
She hazards all, who will the least allow.

But hope not, courted idol of mankind,   25
On this proud eminence secure to stay;
Subduing and subdued, thou soon shalt find
Thy coldness soften, and thy pride give way.

Then, then, abandon each ambitious thought,
Conquest or rule thy heart shall feebly move,   30
In Nature's school, by her soft maxims taught
That separate rights are lost in mutual love.

(Wu, *Romanticism*, 1994, p.23)

D i s c u s s i o n

The poem is much more lighthearted than we might have expected. The word 'rights' *is* important: it occurs in the first and last lines of the poem. In line 13 these are said to be the rights to an empire. The poem adjures women to reverse a situation in which they have been 'degraded, scorned, oppressed' by men (line 2). Until the end that is. The last couple of stanzas reveal that this has been mockery, or at least that it would be impossible. The strident opening of the poem – all those exclamation marks! – is revealed as mock stridency. This probably happens as early as the second stanza, where the flattery of feminine attributes ('arrayed in panoply divine/That angel pureness which admits no stain') is wholly conventional. Throughout women are associated with 'grace', 'soft melting tones', 'blushes and fears', and so on. By the end of the poem any insistence on '*separate* rights' has disappeared. Instead there is a reassertion of the conventional relationship between the sexes. At the end they live in peaceful equality, and woman returns to her conventional role. ∎

In Wordsworth's 'Composed by the Side of Grasmere Lake' we noticed the way martial imagery crept into natural description. The distant presence of war provided a threat to the 'tranquillity' the poem asserted. Barbauld's poem too was written in wartime. **How is war present in it? And does this poem similarly assert a 'tranquillity' at a distance from war?**

D i s c u s s i o n

War provides a metaphor for the relationship between the sexes. Barbauld employs martial imagery but in a context which deprives it of any threat. In the third stanza for example, feminine charms are figured as weapons of war: a woman's glances are 'bright artillery', her voice a cannon and her 'blushes and fears' a magazine of ammunition. It is a common technique of irony for vocabulary from something so weighty to be applied to something so trivial as flirtation. In this case I think the technique – which is known as mock-heroic – derives from Alexander Pope's poem *The Rape of the Lock* (the final version of which was produced in 1714). In Chapter Seven we will see Byron employing a similar technique in *Don Juan*. Barbauld's poem as a whole moves from the weighty to the trivial and from the public to the private. At first the relationship between the sexes is likened to a struggle between empires – a struggle in which women's 'native empire [is] o'er the breast' (line 4) and man is 'the imperial foe' (line 18). But this is succeeded by a return to the sphere of the private and personal. It is within that sphere that the sexes may have a relationship. The conclusion of the poem is justified by the example (and the teaching) of Nature (line 31), as it was in Wordsworth's 'Composed by the Side of Grasmere Lake'. ■

The title of the poem pointed us towards a political context for it. We saw that the politics that we may have been led to expect by the title was wittily deflected. **But does that mean that a political reading is inappropriate? What view of gender does the poem take?**

D i s c u s s i o n

The poem raises gender as a political problem. However, it asserts that the problem is to be solved in the private sphere, and not in the contentious world of power politics. Barbauld's poem, like 'The Chimney Sweeper' from Blake's *Songs of Innocence*, is a poem that reaches a conclusion. And we might feel that the speaker here reaches a conclusion similar to that in the Blake poem, that she connives in her own oppression. There is for example no sense that women might have a role which is not in relation to men. We cannot say that the speaker is ignorant of the charge that women are 'degraded, scorned, oppressed', since she makes it herself. Rather, she rejects the charge. The ideal of 'mutual love' she upholds is like the notion of equality upheld in the passage from Maria Edgeworth. ■

I said that Barbauld's poem is ironic and that like Blake's 'The Chimney Sweeper' it reached a conclusion. It may have occurred to you to ask why then we should not read the conclusion of Barbauld's poem as ironic as we did Blake's. My justification for finding irony in 'The Chimney Sweeper' was in reference to a context – to Blake's opposition to the Established Church, for instance. When we look at contexts for Barbauld's poem we find that there may be a context more specific than the celebrity of Wollstonecraft's *Vindication*. Wollstonecraft had quoted another poem by Barbauld in the

Vindication as an instance of how 'even women of superior sense' reproduce male views of women, allowing them beauty but not reason (Wollstonecraft, *A Vindication of the Rights of Woman*, p.143). Barbauld's poem may then be a specific riposte to Wollstonecraft aimed at reasserting her own view of gender roles. This suggests motives for the poem which may support the reading offered here.

The women writers we have considered in this section all seem content with received literary forms and we have noted the importance that Romantic writers gave to novelty. These writers tend to be conservative and represent a challenge to generalizations about Romantic writing.

However, in considering Austen I suggested that her treatment of gender was a great deal less conservative than of other issues. Among Austen's contemporaries too there is often this questioning of gender roles. In conversational novels by Maria Edgeworth and others, there is a critique of the male artist and male Romanticism, an assertion of feminine rationality through dialogue, and a struggle against the ideology of sensibility. As we have seen, for women to write and publish may itself have been regarded as a subversive act. These issues will be explored further in Chapter Four.

If we read poetry by women in the period expecting it to have the same tendencies as Romantic poetry by men, then we may misread it. We looked earlier at a poem by Mary Robinson which sat oddly with the two better known poems we considered alongside it. The two initial tendencies we identified in Romantic poems were a stress on the self and a dissatisfaction with the actual world. Just as neither was true of Jane Austen, neither is true of the Mary Robinson poem, nor of the poem by Anna Barbauld.

Of course there are women poets who write in an idiom like that of Milton or Wordsworth, but one reason for the relative neglect of poetry by women in these years is because much of it cannot be read in the same way as we read these male poets. Only in recent years has poetry by women in the period begun to be widely available. Its publication is causing us to revise an older view of what Romantic writing consists of. If the Barbauld poem does not accord with received ideas of what Romantic writing is, then perhaps the category should be expanded. This returns us to the notion of selection I broached in the Introduction to this book. If the writing of the period is not a single, fixed thing, then the category 'Romanticism' must be the product of a certain selection. And it is not only texts which are selected, but a whole range of literary practices and preoccupations which are deemed to be more important or more worthy of study than others.

The figure of the poet

We have seen that many regarded the French Revolution as marking a sudden and decisive break with the past. However, in Britain there was a precedent. Three phenomena of the French Revolution I mentioned were the sweeping away of a long-established system of government, the emergence to power of classes which had previously held no vote and had no voice, and the execution of a king (p.10 above). All these had occurred in Britain in the mid-seventeenth century – a period which some describe as 'the English Revolution'. Many in the 1790s drew a parallel with this earlier period. The Commonwealth established in the 1650s was eventually to fail and the monarchy to be restored. But the radicals in the later revolutionary period were part of a British radical tradition.

The earlier period proved that republicanism had a history. It also had its poet, John Milton. Milton had been employed as a propagandist by Cromwell and had supported the execution of the king. In his epics *Paradise Lost* and *Paradise Regained* Milton retold the Bible stories of the Fall and of the temptation of Jesus Christ. Both epics had been written after the failure of the hopes for that earlier revolution. *Paradise Lost* in particular could be seen to be relevant to Milton himself and to have lessons for the Romantic writers a century and a half later. Like them, Milton was writing after the failure of a revolution. *Paradise Lost* retold a familiar story of the rebellion of the angels and the Fall of Man. But as we have seen from Blake's lyrics, Milton's poem furnished an example of how history could be reinterpreted. For Blake, the rebel Satan might be the 'true hero' of *Paradise Lost* and Milton might be 'of the devil's party without knowing it'. His work demonstrated how the propaganda of the winning side could be questioned and might be turned around. Milton's great literary authority provided the Romantic writers with an example of opposition to political authority. He stood as a massive example of commitment not only to poetry but also to republicanism.

Milton is the example by which the Romantic writers constantly try to define their role. And a specific view of the role of the poet is built into their theory. For example, in the extract from the Preface to the *Lyrical Ballads* which we looked at in Chapter One, Wordsworth insists that ordinary experience and ordinary language for its expression are valuable. Yet he assumes this experience still depends for its expression on the poet – a poet who is far from ordinary. At the same time as a mass reading public is emerging, comes the idea of the inspired artist who is different from that public. This idea of the poet (or artist in general) is an important part of what we inherit from Romanticism. For example, one aspect of this is the myth of the doomed Romantic poet. (One qualification for the job of second-generation Romantic poet seems to have been an early death.) Indirectly, the figure of the poet appears again and again in Romantic poems, in various guises: as a prophet in all the Romantic rewritings of the Bible and of Milton, most obviously in Blake and Shelley; as rebel or outlaw in such figures as Cain or Prometheus, the Wandering Jew and the Ancient Mariner; and as hero, whether in the shape of Napoleon or of an autobiographical protagonist. Often the poet is represented as someone who is specially gifted and who may be outside the everyday constraints of society, even outside the law.

As an example of such a view we will now look at some very high claims for the role of the poet, in an extract from Shelley's *A Defence of Poetry* (1821), a text we shall return to in the next chapter. It is important because it suggests that the poet is not merely a commentator upon society but plays a central part. You will need to know that the word 'Elysian' in the second paragraph below refers to Elysium, which is the abode of the blessed after death in Greek mythology, and that a 'hierophant' in the third paragraph is another ancient Greek term, meaning the person who expounds the sacred mysteries or ceremonies. **Read the quotation carefully, paragraph by paragraph. (1) In the first paragraph Shelley claims that poetry is the most important of the arts. On what basis does he claim this? (2) The second paragraph describes what poetry can do. What is this? Does Shelley's description suggest any of the other texts we have looked at so far? (3) The third paragraph refers to the functions of poetry and of the poet. What are they? In what sense were these functions particularly important at the time when Shelley was writing?**

> For language is arbitrarily produced by the imagination and has relation to thoughts alone; but all other materials, instruments and conditions of art have relations among each other which limit and interpose between conception and expression. [...]
>
> Poetry lifts the veil from the hidden beauty of the world, and makes familiar objects be as if they were not familiar; it re-produces all that it represents, and the impersonations clothed in its Elysian light stand thenceforward in the minds of those who have once contemplated them as memorials of that gentle and exalted content which extends itself over all thoughts and actions with which it coexists. [...]
>
> For the literature of England [...] has arisen, as it were, from a new birth. [...] The most unfailing herald, companion, or follower of the awakening of a great people to work a beneficial change in opinion or institution, is poetry. At such periods there is an accumulation of the power of communicating and receiving intense and impassioned conceptions respecting man and nature. The persons in whom this power resides may often (as far as regards many portions of their nature) have little apparent correspondence with that spirit of good of which they are the ministers. But even whilst they deny and abjure, they are yet compelled to serve the power which is seated upon the throne of their own soul. It is impossible to read the compositions of the most celebrated writers of the present day without being startled with the electric life which burns within their words. They measure the circumference and sound the depths of human nature with a comprehensive and all-penetrating spirit, and they are themselves perhaps the most sincerely astonished at its manifestations, for it is less their own spirit than the spirit of the age. Poets are the hierophants of an unapprehended inspiration, the mirrors of the gigantic shadows which futurity casts upon the present, the words which express what they understand not; the trumpets which sing to battle, and feel not what they inspire; the influence which is moved not, but moves. Poets are the unacknowledged legislators of the world.
>
> (Wu, *Romanticism*, 1994, pp.958, 961 and 969)

Discussion

1 The first paragraph quoted here speaks of the superiority of poetry as the art that employs language. Language has a more immediate relation to 'thoughts alone' than the media of any of the other arts. The high status claimed for poetry is because of this immediacy.

66

2   The second paragraph speaks of the way that we can be made to see familiar things anew, as though for the first time. This defamiliarization, as it might be called, an uncovering and discovering of what had seemed familiar, is an important concern in many Romantic texts. That's why recovering and exploring the viewpoint of a child was so important in many of them. Perhaps Shelley's claim here may have made us think again of the importance of children in some of the early lyrics of Blake and Wordsworth we have looked at.

3   The third paragraph relates specifically to the function of poetry at the time at which Shelley is writing, making a claim for the social power of poetry. This power is self-consciously modern, an 'electric life'. Like electricity this power may not be visible but nonetheless it operates publicly, upon society, rather than merely privately upon the individual reader. And it becomes vital at a period of change. There is an apocalyptic sense to Shelley's claims: there has been a renaissance, a 'new birth', and poets are the prophets of this Second Coming. Poets themselves are disinterested but they are 'unacknowledged legislators'. They may be prophets without honour, but they *are* prophets. I use the religious language deliberately, because it seems to me that Shelley's language here *is* religious, though not Christian. ∎

Shelley speaks of 'poetry' rather than of 'poems'. He sees poetry not as the aggregate of poems but as a mode of behaviour and as a way of thinking: poetry is a mode of ethics and knowledge as well as a literary mode. Though many eighteenth-century poets imitated or alluded to the language of Milton's poems, many Romantic writers attempted also to reinterpret them so as to release their radical potential.

So far in this chapter we have looked only at lyric poems, but Milton's example is as a writer of epic. So I want to end by looking briefly at an extract from each of two much longer poems by Wordsworth and Shelley that will be considered in some detail later. Both these extracts are concerned with the figure of the poet. Wordsworth's *Prelude* as a whole is an epic on 'the growth of a poet's mind'. Shelley's *Prometheus Unbound* is concerned with the liberation of Prometheus from his enslavement by the tyrant Jupiter. Thus Jupiter and Prometheus occupy roughly the roles respectively of God and Satan in Milton's epic *Paradise Lost*, and Shelley makes the association explicit in his preface.

These two passages have a couple of important words in common. First of all, read both passages through and see if you can notice what those words are. The extract from *The Prelude* follows an incident described by Wordsworth in which as a boy he stole a rowing boat for a moonlight trip across Lake Ullswater. He feels as though he has been admonished and pursued then abandoned by Nature:

                [...] after I had seen
    That spectacle, for many days my brain
    Worked with a dim and undetermined sense   420
    Of unknown modes of being. In my thoughts
    There was a darkness – call it solitude
    Or blank desertion; no familiar shapes
    Of hourly objects, images of trees,

Of sea or sky, no colours of green fields,
But huge and mighty forms that do not live
Like living men moved slowly through my mind
By day and were the trouble of my dreams.

(Book I, ll.418–28; Wu, *Romanticism*, 1994, p.293)

The second passage is spoken by a character in Shelley's *Prometheus Unbound*. *Prometheus Unbound* is a drama, but because of its vast geographical and cosmic sweep it is a drama that could never be staged. By the way, a 'nursling' in line 749 just means an infant that is being nursed – Shelley got the word from Milton.

On a poet's lips I slept
Dreaming like a love-adept
In the sound his breathing kept;
Nor seeks nor finds he mortal blisses,   740
But feeds on the aerial kisses
Of shapes that haunt thought's wildernesses.
He will watch from dawn to gloom
The lake-reflected sun illume
The yellow bees in the ivy-bloom,   745
Nor heed nor see, what things they be;
But from these create he can
Forms more real than living man,
Nurslings of immortality!

(Act I, ll.737–49; ibid., pp.897–8)

I hope you have noticed that the words 'shapes' and 'forms' occur in both passages. **What do they refer to in each case? Are they used in the same way?**

Discussion

Wordsworth's 'forms' are threatening emanations *of* Nature, Shelley's are constructed *from* Nature. Wordsworth's 'huge and mighty forms that do not live/Like living men' contrast with Shelley's 'Forms more real than living man'. Wordsworth locates an external reality in Nature, Shelley uses Nature to create an ideal and separate reality. While for the poet of the first passage 'desertion' by the 'images' of Nature is a terrible punishment, for the poet of the second passage it is necessary not to see or even notice Nature. Actually there is rarely very much in the way of natural description in Wordsworth. Rather, Nature functions as a moral force. And though it may not be apparent from this short passage alone, this power is derived from Nature, not 'created' from it as in the passage from Shelley. Wordsworth's concern is with laws derived from a Nature the Shelleyan poet will 'neither heed nor see'. ■

I hope you noticed too that the second passage is about a poet, and describes the poet's special way of seeing. This is a poet who doesn't seem actually to do any *writing*. These passages then are about the poet's imagination. They are to do with the possibility of transcendence, of something which is beyond words. For both Wordsworth and Shelley objects are charged with some significance beyond their physical qualities. But the verbal similarities between these two well-known passages seem to conceal what are almost opposite tendencies. On the one hand, there is a tendency in Wordsworth to find 'reality' *within* nature; on the other, in Shelley there is a tendency to want to go *through* the natural world to find a separate, higher reality.

Conclusion

We began this chapter by looking at some Romantic poets in terms of the broader history within which their work was produced. We looked specifically at the way the six canonical male Romantic poets are usually divided into 'two generations'. We saw that the difference in generations did have consequences for their poetry. Wordsworth was from a generation who had lived through the Revolutionary period and its subsequent dissipation in a long war; Shelley was from a generation who saw only the betrayal of those early ideals. For him, those ideals remained viable and Wordsworth represented their betrayal. We looked at sonnets by Wordsworth and by Shelley which could be seen respectively to represent wartime and post-war perspectives. (In Chapter Five we will be looking further at the ways in which Wordsworth's poetry draws away from historical circumstances in asserting the value of an ahistorical 'Nature'.) So we have found important differences between the six male poets whose work is conventionally taken to define or represent Romantic poetry.

When we moved on to look at some of the other writing produced in the same period, we saw what concentration on the six male poets and their work may exclude. Recent work on women writers is allowing us to consider, maybe for the first time, writers such as Anna Barbauld and Mary Robinson whose work is more concerned with a communal, social world than with transcending that world through 'imagination'. Likewise, we have seen that whereas male Romantic writers insist on the novelty of their work, the work of women writers may often be concerned with exploiting more conventional forms. This may lead us to reconsider what is meant by Romanticism, which, we need to remember, is a retrospective construction.

There are definitions of Romanticism; in the Introduction to the book we considered one by René Wellek, which we will return to in the Conclusion. However, once we consider some works which are described as being Romantic, we find almost as many differences as similarities between them. We may allow that there was something that we can classify as Romantic writing, but by no means all of the writing produced in the period could be so described. Romanticism may then be a distorting lens through which to read the texts of the period.

Alternatively, we may want to say that what these writings have in common is that they were produced in the same period – the 'Romantic period', whose characteristics we can identify. What binds them together is not that they are formally similar, or that they consistently demonstrate the same interests, but that their historical juxtaposition means that they all argue over a similar agenda and sometimes they argue with each other. (As we have seen, much of the debate arose around the French Revolution.)

This seems to be what Shelley had in mind when he wrote about the 'resemblance' between writers of a 'particular age' (p.23 above). Such a historically based definition of Romanticism might allow us to extend it to include such writers as Barbauld and Robinson who formally and politically seem so different from Blake, Wordsworth and the others.

The chapters that follow continue this debate. We will be looking at some Romantic poems and prose and at some of the other kinds of writing available in the period. In the last section of this chapter we looked at the figure of the Romantic artist and at the importance of 'imagination' and these will be the concern of Chapter Three in which we will look at the theories of art (the aesthetics) of some of the Romantic writers. Then in Chapter Four we will turn to a discussion of some of the women writers whose work was produced in the Revolutionary period.

Defences of poetry

by Graham Allen

Introduction

In this chapter we will be looking at various theories of poetry produced during the Romantic period. The title of this chapter, 'Defences of poetry', refers to the theories and criticism of the Romantic poets and their need to defend their positions in the various critical conflicts of the period. One of the questions we need to ask is, from what did poets and critics feel that poetry needed defending? I will be referring to various critical texts during the discussion. You will notice that these texts are all by male authors. This chapter does not attempt to develop the re-definition of Romanticism in the context of writing by female authors which was discussed in Chapter Two. In this chapter, then, our focus is on the aesthetics of the six canonical male Romantic poets. It should be noted, however, that whilst some male authors of the period (Wordsworth, for example) use the masculine gender to refer to poets and readers, my own writing does not repeat such assumptions about the gender of authors and readers.

Before you begin the chapter you should have already read the following: Wordsworth's 1802 'Preface' to *Lyrical Ballads*, extracts from Coleridge's *Biographia Literaria*, and Shelley's *A Defence of Poetry*. These texts will be the main focus of the following discussion.

Romantic poetic criticism and theory is a very large subject. However, as might be expected, a great many of the debates about poetry during the period centred on the question of the politics of its language. This fact allows us to structure our examination of this subject around three principal issues:

1 Arguments concerning the appropriate kind of language for poetry. I will call this area the 'levelling of language'; you will see why I use that phrase in a moment.

2 Arguments concerning the poetic imagination and its relation to language. This, as we will see later, involves an examination of what is often called 'the expressive theory of poetry'.

3 Arguments concerning the relationship between poetic language and politics. As we make our way through this chapter it will become clear how closely tied to ideological conflict poetry was during the Romantic period.

The levelling of language

In Chapter One we looked at a passage from Wordsworth's 1802 Preface to *Lyrical Ballads* and noted how controversial its claims were for many of its contemporary readers. As we saw, the Preface was interpreted by some as 'a call for more democracy in the state' and it was seen as representing a 'levelling tendency' by William Hazlitt. If poetic language had traditionally been viewed as a language reserved for those with the best education (society's élite), then the argument Wordsworth makes in the Preface can seem to argue for what in Chapter One was styled a 'literary version of extension of the [political] franchise'. Wordsworth makes central those forms of 'low' or 'common' language traditionally excluded from and contrasted to the 'high' language of poetry. Would you now please read the section from near the beginning of the Preface which begins 'The principal object ... ' and ends with '... and his affections ameliorated'. These five paragraphs contain the section you looked at in Chapter One, so as you read them, think back to that earlier discussion. **Why were Wordsworth's views considered so controversial?**

D i s c u s s i o n

It is this section, above all others, which gave Wordsworth's 1802 Preface its reputation as a radical, even revolutionary, document. This revolutionary character was thought to reside not merely in the claims made about the language of 'low and rustic' people but also in the social and political implications of such assertions. Wordsworth argued against the received idea of poetic language as a refined, perfected mode of eloquence available only to those with an education in previous literary models. The Preface provoked controversy largely because of what I have called Wordsworth's levelling of poetic language. ■

The 1802 Preface provoked strong responses, but in retrospect one of the most interesting came fifteen years after its publication. Rather surprisingly perhaps, this critical response came from the co-author of the volume, namely S.T. Coleridge. Coleridge and Wordsworth had started off as friends and collaborators, a friendship which resulted in the *Lyrical Ballads* project. However, in the years that followed they became estranged. By the time of his *Biographia Literaria* ('literary autobiography') not only Coleridge but the political situation in Europe had changed considerably. In the summer of the year 1815, the same year which saw the final defeat of Napoleon at Waterloo, Coleridge sat down to begin his 'literary autobiography' keen to distance himself from the more radical opinions of the Preface and the 'school' of poetry thought to have been inaugurated by it. In *Biographia Literaria*, Coleridge attacked opinions he and Wordsworth had once shared, including some Coleridge himself had suggested.

Coleridge argued that the fundamental elements of language can be found, not in one specific, unsophisticated class of language users, the rural poor, but in that apparently classless concept, grammar. Coleridge means by this that the most 'truthful' form of language is that which most thoroughly escapes from the constantly changing attitudes and presuppositions of the social world. Another way of saying this would be that the best language for poetry is the most logical, the universal rather than the socially and politically specific. Coleridge also argued that the language capable of expressing true insights inevitably belongs to those socially privileged classes for whom the exercise of philosophical and spiritual meditation is a daily occurrence. Wordsworth asserts that the poet, in order to draw close to 'truth', should strip him – or her – self of the excess baggage of civilized, upper-class life. Coleridge, on the other hand, asserts that it is only in the meditative opportunities provided by a socially privileged life that such values and the appropriate language in which to express them can be attained.

There are, however, similarities as well as differences between Wordsworth's and Coleridge's theories of poetic language. For example, they seem to agree that the poet is in many ways distinguished from and, linguistically speaking, superior to the 'low and rustic' people who are amongst the subjects of the *Lyrical Ballads*. If you re-read the section we have been discussing from Wordsworth's Preface you will see that this idea of the special position of the poet qualifies Wordsworth's statements about the language of 'low and rustic' people. **Re-read the section and note down signs of Wordsworth's tampering with the 'real language of men'.**

Discussion

They are everywhere! Wordsworth talks in various places of a 'selection' process. Who is making this selection from the language of Wordsworth's poetic subjects, his 'ordinary' rural men and women? Clearly it is Wordsworth himself. Just as clearly, such a selection process suggests a gap between the actual language of Wordsworth's subjects and the language of his poems in the *Lyrical Ballads*. Wordsworth also speaks of throwing over the language of such people 'a certain colouring of imagination, whereby ordinary things should be presented to the mind in an unusual way'. Again, we need to ask whose imagination is performing this process of covering and colouring. And again the answer is the poet, distinguished, once more, from his subjects. Later in the book we will look at the assumptions about gender in Wordsworth's approach. The selection process involved in Wordsworth's art implies that the poet is a 'man speaking to men'; women can be the 'subjects' of Wordsworth's poetic art, but they do not seem to be able to fill the role of speaker or hearer. ■

The argument about whether the language of poetry should be drawn from the 'low' or the 'high' stratas of society continued throughout the Romantic period. The debate illustrates the way in which discussions of poetry and of poetic language were never far from discussions of social and political issues. In fact the period provides a dramatic demonstration of the conflictual nature of language – the fact that language is a phenomenon which foregrounds and embodies social and class divisions. A common assumption about language, even literary language, is that it is a neutral medium. However, it does not take much effort to recognize that the way in which people speak and write reflects social, particularly class, prejudices and presumptions. You might think here, for example, of accent or of vocabulary, the use of 'simple', or 'difficult', or 'technical' words. Language, as used by particular people in particular circumstances, reflects social divisions and demarcations, but it is also received in terms of those divisions and demarcations. In the Romantic period there was a widespread interest in poets from the lower orders of society (Robert Burns is a famous example). This interest in 'peasant poets', amongst other kinds of lower-class writers, reflects a social phenomenon: the influence of democratic ideas. We have just looked at a major expression of such a social extension of the language of poetry in Wordsworth's Preface. However, there were many in this period who retained the notion that poetry was a literary language suited only to the more educated and thus, in terms of class, 'higher' members of society. To employ in poetry the language of the 'low and rustic', as Wordsworth does, would have been to break society's and literature's rigid class divisions. For many people, to hear of 'low and rustic' people actually writing and publishing poetry themselves would seem scandalous, even revolutionary. Poetic language, for such people, was the property of the 'high', educated classes.

A good example of this point is John Gibson Lockhart's critical piece of 1818, 'The Cockney School of Poetry' from *Blackwood's Edinburgh Magazine*. Before you read it, some context may be helpful. A 'Cockney' is someone from the East End of London, and Lockhart was employing here a contemporary distinction between the poor, unfashionable east side of London and the west side, associated with London's fashionable society and, traditionally, with the monarchical court. To have been trained as an 'apothecary' (a doctor) was not to have joined such a socially respectable group as the medical profession of today. **On what grounds does Lockhart decide to attack Keats?**

Discussion

Lockhart attacks Keats's poetry by foregrounding, in a negative manner, Keats's lower-class origins. He draws attention to Keats's training as an apothecary. For Lockhart there was a similarity between Keats's profession and the poetic language of Wordsworth's 'low and rustic' subjects; both being regarded as inappropriate to the 'high' art of poetry. Lockhart has great fun in playing around with Keats's name, 'Mr John Keats', 'Mr Keats', and 'Mr John'. He argues that Keats is an ignorant, uncultured Cockney 'poetaster' (a writer of trashy verse; a pretender) whose work is being championed and thrust into the public domain by a mafia-like band of fellow Cockney patrons, headed by Leigh Hunt. ■

Leigh Hunt, along with his brother John, edited *The Examiner*, a weekly paper which was directed at a radical and reformist readership. *Blackwood's Edinburgh Magazine*, from which Lockhart's review comes, was established in 1817 and quickly gained a reputation for satirical and even libellous reviews. It had a more conservative readership than *The Examiner*. It is clear from the review of Keats that the poet's actual work is less important to Lockhart than the scoring of points against his rivals in the world of journalism, a world itself dominated by the wider world of national politics. There is precious little analysis of Keats's poetry in the review. Instead, the reviewer arranges a series of quotations around attacks of a quite personal and clearly political nature. Lockhart seems to believe that citing the social inferiority of Keats is sufficient to prove that the poetry is bad. So he simply condemns Keats's *Endymion* as 'calm, settled, imperturbable drivelling' and characterizes Hunt's writing as 'loose, nerveless versification and Cockney rhymes'. The ultimate point of the review seems to be that people from the lower classes have no business mixing in the refined world of poetry.

Lockhart's critical position can be said to confuse an analysis of Keats's poetry with a discussion of Keats himself. He sees no problem in criticizing the poetry by attacking the author of that poetry. This conflation of poetry with its author is not a process unique to critics such as Lockhart. Wordsworth and Coleridge both suggest that the poet's individual imaginative capacity is the decisive element in good poetry. Having connected the issue of the 'levelling of language' with the poetic imagination, we need now to consider the poetic imagination in more detail.

Imagination and the figure of the poet

Wordsworth and Coleridge did not only argue over the nature of poetic language; they also conducted a continuing debate over the precise nature and the correct definition of two terms, fancy and the imagination. Coleridge's *Biographia Literaria* can be said to have many subjects, but two of the most important are his 'critique of Wordsworth', as it is often styled, and his attempt to provide a philosophical and aesthetically rigorous definition of poetry by defining the creative imagination. In his thirteenth chapter Coleridge condenses his main thesis about the nature of poetry. Read the passage from this chapter in which Coleridge discusses 'fancy' and 'imagination'. As you read, ask yourself what Coleridge means by 'imagination'.

The initial distinction between 'primary' and 'secondary' imagination seems rather abstract doesn't it? 'I AM' is an abbreviation of the words God says to Moses, 'I AM THAT I AM' and is, then, being used as a name for God. Coleridge is specifically referring here to the notion of God as the first principle of the universe. God does not need to find proof of his existence or pre-eminence, he simply knows himself to be God.

For Coleridge, then, God is absolute self-consciousness. Coleridge's point is that there is an element of this God-like quality in all human beings. On this basis, what Coleridge means by the 'primary imagination' is our 'God-like' knowledge of our existence – our self-consciousness – whilst by the 'secondary imagination' Coleridge refers to the manner in which he believed we can recreate that self-consciousness in art.

I want you now to look at the oppositional relationship Coleridge sets up between 'fancy' and 'imagination'. **Does Coleridge really define what these terms mean?**

Discussion

The definition of fancy seems largely to be serve as a clarifying opposition to the major term of this passage, that of the imagination. The passage sets up a list of oppositions collected around the two terms: 'imagination' (that is, the plastic, or shaping, creative power) and 'fancy' (that is, artifice, as in the diction of much eighteenth-century poetry). The imagination, Coleridge asserts, 'dissolves, diffuses, dissipates, in order to re-create', it is also said to 'idealize and to unify'. It is a 'vital' (living, positive, transforming) principle directed at a world which is described as 'essentially fixed and dead'. Opposed to this definition of the imagination, 'the fancy' is represented as a faculty which merely shuffles the 'fixed and dead' elements of the material universe around. It 'has no other counters to play with but fixities and definites'. Significantly, Coleridge also associates the 'fancy' with 'memory' and, by implication, associates the 'imagination' with a 'vital' response to the present.

Coleridge's analysis is characterized by an attempt to transform what he saw as the conventional and unprincipled tradition of literary criticism into a truly philosophical mode of discourse. In other words, literary criticism was lacking in philosophically valid first principles, that is, a basis in logic. It is, in fact, precisely this lack of coherent principles which Coleridge points to as the major flaw of Wordsworth's Preface. Although the oppositions contained in this passage are extremely suggestive, whether they provide us with a first principle (the 'imagination') upon which we can build a truly rigorous theory of poetry is another question. Many would argue that there's too much abstract philosophizing here and not enough attention to 'poetry'. ■

The *Biographia Literaria* is divided into two parts: the first deals amongst other things with the definition of the imagination; the second contains Coleridge's 'critique of Wordsworth'. The definition of 'the creative imagination' we have just been looking at is supposed to function as a link between these two parts. In the next part, which begins with Chapter 14, Coleridge embarks on his 'critique of Wordsworth'. However, instead of using his theory of the 'creative imagination' to commence his 'critique of Wordsworth', Coleridge ends Chapter 14 with a rousing description of what we called in Chapter Two 'the figure of the poet'. Please read the conclusion of Chapter 14. **How does Coleridge connect his theory of the imagination with his description of 'the figure of the poet'?**

D i s c u s s i o n

What we find in this central section of the *Biographia Literaria* is a movement from a definition of the nature of poetry to a definition of the nature of the 'figure of the poet'. And in this section a description of the ideal poet becomes a description of the imagination. The nature of the ideal poet and the nature of the imagination seem to be one and the same. It is possible to say, in fact, that these two things are necessarily connected. It seems difficult to speak of the imagination without also speaking of the figure who is thought to possess and to exercise that faculty or power. Poets are defined in terms of their possession of imagination. The imagination, it seems, is dependent on the 'figure of the poet' and to describe or define imagination is to describe or define the 'person' of the poet who possesses it. By the 'person' of the poet we would mean the poet's unique character, personality and consciousness (or psychological make-up). The true poet is someone Coleridge would describe as possessing creative imagination, but imagination itself is defined in terms of the 'person' of the poet.

There is a certain circularity in Coleridge's argument here, isn't there? Coleridge seems to be moving away from the establishment of philosophically legitimate first principles (from 'logic') back to a rhetorical argument, to an expression of his own beliefs rather than of 'the truth'. ■

It is useful to recognize this movement from logic to rhetoric in Coleridge, since it is repeated often in Romantic literary theory. An attempt to define the nature of poetry seems constantly to shift into a description and definition of the ideal figure of the poet, not a definition of the essential formal characteristics of poetry. This connects with a long history of defining Romantic writing in terms of the personality of its authors. We have already noted the way in which, in John Gibson Lockhart's review of Keats, an attack on the 'person' of the poet is substituted for a critique of the poetry itself. Coleridge's mixing of a philosophical theory of poetry with an idealized representation of 'the figure of the poet' might be said to repeat Lockhart's substitution (of description or definition for what we might call 'personalism') on a higher level. What is the reason for this constant recourse to the 'figure of the poet' in Romantic criticism and theory?

To answer this question we need to look at what I called at the beginning of this chapter the 'expressive theory' of poetry and art. In his influential book *The Mirror and the Lamp* the Romantic scholar M.H. Abrams defines Romanticism in terms of an interplay between two views of art: the mimetic view (symbolized by the mirror) and the expressive view (symbolized by the lamp). By mimesis Abrams means that view of art which defines it in terms of how effectively it imitates the world. Art, on the model of mimesis, is a form of copying, a kind of mirror. Eighteenth-century theories of art were largely mimetic.

If authors work solely with the mimetic model they may well see their role *as authors* as relatively passive. If art is essentially imitative of the universe, then the significance of a work of art, along with all judgments concerning its effectiveness, will depend on how well it copies its object or objects of representation. When Wordsworth states in the 1802 Preface that he has 'at all times endeavoured to look steadily at my subject', he is asking his readers to judge the poems he collected in the *Lyrical Ballads* on the mimetic model. In mimetic art and theory the 'meaning' of an artwork, be it a painting or a poem, is presumed to lie *outside* of that work. The artist's function, on this model, is to faithfully imitate a 'meaning' which is presumed to pre-exist the artwork itself. Such artists may view themselves as skilled crafts-workers. However, in the fourteenth chapter of the *Biographia Literaria*, Coleridge, instead of suggesting that the ideal poet imitates or copies what he calls 'the whole soul of man', states, rather, that the poet brings it 'into activity'. **What does Coleridge mean by this? We might answer this question by considering how such a statement reverses some implications of the mimetic view of art.**

Discussion

What Coleridge means is that the poet in some way *embodies* the 'whole soul of man'. Coleridge's poet does not simply copy the world, in some way the activity of the poet's whole soul is able to transform the world, for example bringing a 'sense of novelty and freshness' to old and familiar objects. Indeed, the subject of this ideal poet's work is no longer something that could be described as *outside* the poet (the universe, nature, and so on) but is actually 'the whole soul of man', and includes the poet's own 'soul'. The Coleridgean poet is, in an important sense, the creator of the work's meaning. The meaning of the work, for Coleridge, originates from *within* the poet. Such a poet-figure functions rather like a lamp, shedding a light into the world, rather than like a mirror, which can only reflect a light already in existence. This distinction, between imitating and creating, seems to be what Coleridge has in mind in his opposition between fancy and imagination. Coleridge may seem to return to a mimetic view when he states that the imagination ('this power') 'still subordinates art to nature', but this is not in fact the case. The poet's imagination is part of nature, and the expression of imagination, moving from within the poet out into the world, is a natural phenomenon, like the singing of birds. The poet's subordination to nature is not because the poet must copy nature, but because the imagination is itself a 'natural' power. ∎

How do Wordsworth and Coleridge define the creative imagination and the figure of the poet; how do they relate the two?

D i s c u s s i o n

The poet, in the literary theory of Wordsworth and Coleridge, and in much Romantic criticism and theory generally, seems to share in or even to rival the creative powers once wholly attributed to God. The theory of the creative imagination seems to lead them to a view of poets as exceptional, even God-like figures. The theory also seems to sideline their attempts to define the formal characteristics of poetry. ∎

To summarize the position as we have done above is a good start in coming to understand Romantic theories of poetry. However, it is not the end of the story. We also need to ask ourselves why these particular theories developed during the period. When we ask this question we begin to move into an analysis of the 'defences of poetry', an analysis of the reasons why poets and poetic theorists believed poetry needed defending. In asking these questions we also have to begin to look at the contexts within which they wrote.

Poetic language and politics

Some poets and critics held the view that established literary conventions, rules and expectations were being broken by the 'new' modes of poetry we have come to call Romantic. Many Romantic defences of poetry were motivated by a need to challenge that view. When a piece of art seems to flout all recognized rules and conventions, we sometimes label it as tasteless. The issue of 'taste', of what good poetry should be, of how to distinguish between 'good' and 'bad' poetry, was a hotly contested one in the period. We have discussed Wordsworth's poetic theories in terms of a literary and social 'revolution' of a sort, and we have also reminded ourselves of the socially conflictual nature of all language, and particularly literary language. That the question of 'taste' is important in the criticism of the period is, then, hardly surprising. We saw in Chapter One how Wordsworth and Coleridge attacked various 'features of the language of eighteenth-century poetry'. In the following passage from his 'Essay, supplementary to the Preface' (1815), Wordsworth delivers his response to the question of taste in no unguarded terms. Note that this supplementary 'Preface' was written in the same year that Coleridge began his *Biographia Literaria*. Are there signs within it of a move away from the radicalism of the *Lyrical Ballads* period similar to the one we have noted in Coleridge's later work?

The passage is a heavily stylized one in which the dominant figure of speech is the rhetorical question (that is, a question for which an answer is not expected). Read through this series of rhetorical questions and try to establish what you think are Wordsworth's own answers to them. **Do these implicit answers tell us anything about Wordsworth's attitude to the views set out in his Preface over fifteen years earlier? Do they tell us anything about Wordsworth's political allegiances in the year of Waterloo, 1815?**

> And where lies the real difficulty of creating that taste by which a truly original poet is to be relished? Is it in breaking the bonds of custom, in overcoming the prejudices of false refinement, and displacing the aversions of inexperience? Or, if he labour for an object which here and elsewhere I have proposed to myself, does it consist in divesting the reader of the pride that induces him to dwell upon those points wherein men differ from each other, to the exclusion of those in which all men are alike, or the same; and in making him ashamed of the vanity that renders him insensible of the appropriate excellence which civil arrangements, less unjust than might appear, and Nature illimitable in her bounty, have conferred on men who may stand below him in the scale of society? Finally, does it lie in establishing that dominion over the spirits of readers by which they are to be humbled and humanized, in order that they may be purified and exalted?
>
> (Bromwich, *Romantic Critical Essays*, 1987, pp.46–7)

Discussion

Wordsworth is clearly arguing that great poetry can have an extremely important, even decisive, effect on its readers. The answers which are suggested by Wordsworth's rhetorical questions seem to suggest that poetry can break 'the bonds of custom', overcome 'the prejudices of false refinement', and displace 'the aversions of inexperience'. The third sentence is rather convoluted. In the first half of it (up to 'or the same') we can see Wordsworth covering familiar ground and arguing that poetry can demonstrate the essential equality of all people – the poet is, as he says in the 1802 Preface, 'a man speaking to men'. But the second half of the sentence qualifies this view: humans may have common experiences but differences in social status are 'less unjust than might appear'. Individual excellence is 'appropriate' to the level each person occupies in the 'scale of society'. The tensions within this sentence demonstrate how politically conservative Wordsworth had become by this period. The 'levelling of language' is still there, but its political implications are purposefully played down by their author. In the final sentence poetry's radical disturbance of conventional modes of taste is distinguished from radical political positions. Here poetry is said to be able to 'humble and humanize', 'purify and exalt' – this is the language of individual experience not that of social change.

Wordsworth presents here a vision of what poetry *can* do, not what it actually does. The whole passage works on an opposition between the potential of poetry to instil what we might call 'true taste' and the resistance of what we might call culturally dominant 'false taste'. Poetry, in this passage, is presented as being perpetually at war with society. Indeed, Wordsworth seems to regard poetry as a reforming power which is constantly attempting to break through the barriers of dominant modes of taste, conventional codes, or what we would nowadays call ideology.

There remains, then, an apparently reformist aspect to Wordsworth's view of the function of poetry in society. Poetry is a force which reforms and is even at variance with society. And yet Wordsworth's actual view of society ('less unjust than might appear') seems to be that it is pretty well organized. Isn't this a contradiction in his argument? One answer might be that whilst Wordsworth has retained a radical social description of poetry, his actual view of society has become less radical. Wordsworth's views on poetry were fashioned in the revolutionary period at the end of the eighteenth century. By 1815 he no longer believed in revolution, but the traces of that earlier period still remained in his views about poetry. These revolutionary aspects seem now to be directed at moral, even religious, imbalances: 'pride', 'vanity', 'that domain over the spirits of readers by which they are to be humbled and humanized, in order that they may be purified and exalted'. We seem, in fact, to have moved from social reform in the 1802 Preface to spiritual reform in the 1815 'Essay, supplementary to the Preface'. This movement reflects Wordsworth's growing conservatism during the intervening period. ∎

If this is Wordsworth's definition of poetry, what then is his view of the reader? Here's another passage from the 'Essay, supplementary to the Preface'. **Read it through and consider how Wordsworth sees the respective roles of reader and poet.**

> Of genius the only proof is, the act of doing well what is worthy to be done, and what was never done before: Of genius, in the fine arts, the only infallible sign is the widening the sphere of human sensibility, for the delight, honour, and benefit of human nature. Genius is the introduction of a new element into the intellectual universe: or, if that be not allowed, it is the application of powers to objects on which they had not before been exercised, or the employment of them in such a manner as to produce effects hitherto unknown. What is all this but an advance, or a conquest, made by the soul of the poet? Is it to be supposed that the reader can make progress of this kind, like an Indian prince or general – stretched on his palanquin [portable couch], and borne by his slaves? No; he is invigorated and inspirited by his leader, in order that he may exert himself; for he cannot proceed in quiescence, he cannot be carried like a dead weight. Therefore to create taste is to call forth and bestow power, of which knowledge is the effect; and *there* lies the true difficulty.
>
> (Ibid., p.48)

Discussion

This passage encapsulates much of what we have already discussed, both here and in Chapter Two, concerning the figure of the poet and the imagination. Wordsworth here makes astonishingly large claims for poetry and for the poet, whose function now is to widen 'the sphere of human sensibility' and the dimensions of the human 'soul'. Poetry, for Wordsworth, is no longer something that can be defined or understood in formal terms, it is, on the contrary, a mode of 'power'. Good readers respond to this 'power' and find it within themselves. Poetry can 'call forth and bestow power'. The reader's role seems to be to answer the call. Once again, Wordsworth's arguments hinge on the notion of the poet as a kind of social and spiritual leader, a special, imaginative, inspired figure whom others should follow. The poet in this passage is a 'genius', possessing originality, in the sense that the true poet can do 'what was never done before'. ■

Wordsworth's use of the word 'power' is, however, rather abstract. Is there a more concrete way of understanding what he means by it? We might be able to answer this question by looking at the readers of literature during this period.

The reader in the Romantic period

In the second chapter of his important study *Culture and Society, 1780–1950*, a chapter entitled 'The Romantic artist', Raymond Williams argues that many of the major changes in literary and cultural thinking – changes we now describe as Romantic innovations – were a response to changes in the nature of the reading public. Williams writes that 'From the third and fourth decades of the eighteenth century there had been growing up a large new middle-class reading public, the rise in which corresponds very closely with the rise to influence and power of the same class' (Williams, *Culture and Society*, 1958, p.50). The emergence of this large new 'reading public' created important changes in the way in which writers defined themselves and their relationship to their 'public'; in the manner in which the 'reading public' was imagined; and in definitions of the nature of art itself.

Romantic authors were in some ways more distant from their audience than previous authors had been. Writing for a mass, anonymous 'reading public', is different to writing for the kind of small group of subscribers referred to in Chapter Two of this book, or for a patron and his or her social and familial 'circle', or for a known set of friends and supporters. That kind of 'patronage' system, Williams argues, was gradually being replaced in the eighteenth century by the modern system of publishing with which we are all familiar and which Williams defines in terms of 'the market'. In that 'modern' situation, authors often have their most direct contact with publishers, literary agents and other members of the literary 'market', and are left to imagine for themselves the intended audience of their work. There are, of course, the reviewers, but how many authors write *for* their reviewers?

This 'market' system presented new possibilities for groups previously excluded from literary production, notably women writers and writers from the 'lower' classes. But what is crucial for us here is that this growing 'reading public' needed to be imagined by the Romantic writer. The

Romantic writer was in a position to reach quantities of readers undreamt of by earlier writers. Such a situation offered up a vision to the writer of the possibility of influencing a large section of society. Poets such as Sir Walter Scott and Lord Byron, for example, can be said to have gained a kind of popularity and fame unmatched in previous ages. So, if the rapidly increasing 'reading public' offered the Romantic artist a vision of influence on a grand scale, it also offered a vision of society as a community of readers, all influenced by the same work, all defining themselves in terms of the same set of influences. This vision of a society of readers is close to what we would nowadays call *culture*. The two words which Williams chose for the title of his book, *culture* and *society*, did not begin to take on their modern definitions until the eighteenth and nineteenth centuries (see Williams, *Keywords*, 1976). The changes in the reading public, therefore, can be said to have inspired the writers of the Romantic period with the possibility of influencing what we would nowadays call 'culture' and 'society'.

The intensity with which poetry was discussed, defined, re-defined, and generally fought over during the period clearly has much to do with attempts to imagine (to represent and define) the large, new 'reading public', and, by implication, culture and society. Questions such as 'who are my readers?', 'what are their tastes and expectations about poetry?', become very important in this new anonymous, 'market' system. And writers tend to answer such questions by imagining themselves as connected to kinds or groups of readers, and other writers. These groupings will obviously reflect the poet's particular views about society, class distinctions, and so on. Such imagined groups or communities of readers and writers are often implied within a work. If writers are successful and influential enough, their readers will begin to identify with these imagined groups and communities. As Jon Klancher puts it:

> The English Romantics were the first to become radically uncertain of their readers, and they faced the task Wordsworth called '*creating* the taste' by which the writer is comprehended. [...] This inchoate cultural moment compelled a great many writers to shape the interpretative and ideological frameworks of audiences they would speak to. They carved out new readerships and transformed old ones.
>
> (Klancher, *The Making of English Reading Audiences, 1790–1832*, 1987, p.3)

Klancher and Williams show us how definitions of poetry and definitions of society were inter-related during this period. In many Romantic critical texts we can note that what begins as a description of the recent history of British poetry frequently turns into a commentary on the nature of political life over that period.

Poetry and society

William Hazlitt's *The Spirit of the Age* (1825) contained an essay entitled 'Mr Coleridge'. The final paragraphs read as follows:

> It was a misfortune to any man of talent to be born in the latter end of the last century. Genius stopped the way of Legitimacy, and therefore it

was to be abated, crushed, or set aside as a nuisance. The spirit of the monarchy was at variance with the spirit of the age. The flame of liberty, the light of the intellect was to be extinguished with the sword – or with slander, whose edge is sharper than the sword. The war between power and reason was carried on by the first of these abroad – by the last at home. No quarter was given (then or now) by the Government-critics, the authorized censors of the press, to those who followed the dictates of independence, who listened to the voice of the tempter, Fancy. Instead of gathering fruits and flowers, immortal fruits and amaranthine flowers, they soon found themselves beset not only by a host of prejudices, but assailed with all the engines of power, by nicknames, by lies, by all the arts of malice, interest and hypocrisy, without the possibility of their defending themselves 'from the pelting of the pitiless storm', that poured down upon them from the strongholds of corruption and authority. The philosphers, the dry abstract reasoners, submitted to this reverse pretty well, and armed themselves with patience, 'as with triple steel' to bear discomfiture, persecution, and disgrace. But the poets, the creatures of sympathy, could not stand the frowns both of king and people. They did not like to be shut out when places and pensions, when the critic's praises, and the laurel-wreath were about to be distributed. They did not stomach being *sent to Coventry*, and Mr Coleridge sounded a retreat for them by the help of casuistry, and a musical voice. – 'His words were hollow, but they pleased the ear' of his friends of the Lake School, who turned backed disgusted and panic-struck from the dry desert of unpopularity, like Hassan the camel driver,

> And curs'd the hour, and curs'd the luckless day,
> When first from Shiraz' walls they bent their way.

[Collins, *Persian Ecologues*, II, 29]

They are safely inclosed there, but Mr Coleridge did not enter with them; pitching his tent upon the barren waste without, and having no abiding place nor city of refuge.

(Bromwich, *Romantic Critical Essays*, 1987, pp.119–20)

Hazlitt is describing the history of the contemporary 'school' of poetry (the 'Lake School') which some critics believed to have been set up by Wordsworth, Coleridge and Southey. Notice that Hazlitt seems to make no distinction between the political history of the period, the Lake poets' reaction to these social and political events, and the development of their poetry. Poets like Wordsworth and Coleridge assert that poetry can have a decisive influence (can exert a 'power') upon contemporary society. It was equally possible in the period, however, to assert that the history of poetry in some way mirrored or even embodied political history. In his *A Defence of Poetry* Shelley attempted to unite these two elements into a single theory or definition of poetry. If you read the last paragraph of his *A Defence of Poetry*, a passage we have already looked at briefly in the previous chapter, you will see perhaps the most famous expression of this idea in all Romantic writing. The immediate subject of this paragraph is, as it was with Hazlitt, the history of contemporary British poetry.

In what ways does Shelley, in that paragraph, describe poetry as a social and political force?

Shelley argues that the spirit of truth and liberty, which manifests itself at certain moments of history, is always accompanied by a rebirth of the 'poetic' spirit. He begins by arguing that 'the literature of England' has 'ever preceded or accompanied a great and free development of the national will'. Freedom of a material and political nature, is, for Shelley, intimately tied to freedom of creative expression. Shelley goes on: 'The most unfailing herald, companion, or follower of the awakening of a great people to work a beneficial change in opinion or institution, is poetry'. Notice how Shelley's prose makes it difficult to determine whether it is historical movements of reform which foster great 'poetry', or whether it is actually 'poetry' itself which is the dynamic force in the relationship between literature and history. Poetry is a 'herald', a 'companion', and 'a follower'. As a 'herald' it seems to be in advance of historical and social changes. Yet, Shelley also calls 'poetry' a 'follower' of those changes. The ambiguities of this argument can be highlighted by comparing it to Williams's argument, in which history is unquestionably the dynamic force. ■

This blurring of the relationship between historical reform and poetic history, so that we cannot tell which is leading the other, might suggest why Shelley goes on in this paragraph to describe poets in the manner he does. He writes: 'The persons in whom this power resides, may often (as far as regards many portions of their nature) have little apparent correspondence with that spirit of good of which they are the ministers. But even whilst they deny and abjure, they are yet compelled to serve the power which is seated upon the throne of their own soul.' **How does Shelley's description of the 'figure of the poet' relate to the descriptions we have already looked at in the work of Wordsworth and Coleridge?**

Like Coleridge and Wordsworth, Shelley sees the 'figure of the poet' as someone who embodies 'truth'. He also shares their sense that the poet is a kind of prophet, or a member of the social and cultural avant-garde, someone who can, in a sense, see the future. This idea is what stands behind perhaps Shelley's most famous sentence of all, the final sentence of the *Defence*: 'Poets are the unacknowledged legislators of the world'. One obvious answer to the question why they are 'unacknowledged' is that they possess a 'power' and a 'truth' to which the society in which they exist remains blind. This, of course, makes poets into prophet-like figures. However, given what Shelley says a little earlier in this same paragraph, it seems that poets themselves do not always recognize or live up to the 'power' ('truth') that they express in their work. As Shelley says, 'even whilst they deny and abjure, they are yet compelled to serve the power which is seated upon the throne of their own soul'. It seems that Shelley is arguing that poets embody a 'power' ('truth') which they themselves might not acknowledge. This refines and develops the descriptions of the social and cultural effect of the 'figure of the poet' we have seen in Wordsworth and Coleridge. ■

Why does Shelley need to say that a poet can embody 'power' ('truth') without necessarily recognizing the fact? I want to try and answer this question by turning directly to the issue of Romantic 'defences of poetry'.

Defending Romantic poetry

You may have noticed in the previous discussions that the words 'poetry' and 'literature' have often been used interchangeably. You may also have noticed that in their definitions of poetry and their claims for its moral and social functions, the authors we have been looking at so far seem at times to use the term poetry in rather broad and metaphorical ways. As you read Wordsworth's Preface you may have also noted how much space is devoted to what seems a rather trivial debate about the relationship between poetry and prose. In fact, this section is one which readers often skip. It is, however, important to consider the way in which the concept 'poetry' was discussed in the period, since it is an issue which connects with various issues already referred to in this chapter. Think back over your reading of Shelley's *A Defence of Poetry.* **How does Shelley conceive of poetry in that essay?**

Discussion

The word 'poetry' is used by Shelley in a far broader way than we would generally use it nowadays. He uses it to cover all imaginative forms of linguistic expression. Shelley states: 'A poem is the image of life expressed in its eternal truth'. Such a definition allows Shelley to find poetry in any piece of writing in which such a representation of 'life' appears to him to have been produced. It allows him, in fact, to see 'poetry' in kinds of writing (philosophy, history, theology, amongst others) that are not normally defined as 'poetic'. ∎

Shelley's definition of poetry is, as we can see, extremely broad. He states that: 'Poetry is the record of the best and happiest moments of the happiest and best minds'. I'm sure that you'll agree that there are many other passages from the *Defence* which we could select to illustrate how broadly Shelley defines the word 'poetry'. When we read through *A Defence of Poetry* we begin to note that 'poetry' seems less a distinct mode of writing than a powerful effect produced by many different kinds of written texts and by many different kinds of authors. We have already noticed the way in which Shelley talks about 'the poet's' embodying of 'power', a word I have been relating to the word 'truth'. Poetry, in Shelley's essay, is something which has to do with a 'power', something which has effects, on individual thought, on public opinion generally, thus on society, and, finally, on history.

Such a definition of poetry clearly involves a rejection of purely formal definitions which would categorize poetry as dependent on such technical aspects as rhyme and metre. What seems important in Shelley's *Defence*, and in much Romantic criticism, is the influence or effect (the 'affective power') that poetry has upon its readers.

This point is related to the theory of the sublime, and we need to consider definitions of poetry within the context of the sublime. Edmund Burke was mentioned in Chapter One in relation to his views on the British constitution, and he will recur in later chapters as an important conservative thinker. However, Burke was also a philosopher, whose analysis of aesthetic effects was widely influential. His *Philosophical Enquiry into the Origins of Our Ideas of the Sublime and the Beautiful* (1756) has been credited with marking a turning point in aesthetic taste in Britain in the eighteenth century. Burke argued against the neo-Classicist elevation of clarity as a quality of great art, by arguing that what is noblest in art is the infinite, which by its nature cannot be clear and distinct. The imagination is most strongly affected, in his view, by what is suggested or hinted at rather than plainly stated. For him the sublime was a category in many ways superior to the beautiful: the sublime related to phenomena that inspired awe, and fear played a large part in its appreciation; the beautiful was a category related to quieter and more pacific effects.

The sublime was observable, according to writers like Burke, in the natural world. But the feelings produced by such natural phenomena as vast mountain ranges, crevasses and ravines, also had their parallel in the effects produced by certain kinds of literature. The shift we are considering here, from formal definitions of poetry to a recognition of its affective power was certainly influenced by notions of the sublime in literature. It is also important to notice that the idea of the sublime and the importance of imagination are recurrent themes in the canonical version of Romantic writings.

Given the above, it is still legitimate to ask the following question: if we cannot refer to formal rules in order to explain the nature of poetic texts or to judge whether they are successful or not, if poetry is something felt (a power 'experienced') rather than analytically evaluated, how can we be sure that what we are reading at any specific time is or isn't 'good' poetry? How do I know, when experiencing what I think is a powerful response to a poem, that my reactions are legitimate? How do I know, in such an instance, whether I am correct or merely fooled about the power of the poem I am reading?

The answer which Wordsworth and other Romantic defenders of poetry give to this question is that we know when we are experiencing authentic poetic power because authentic poetry speaks to what is essentially 'human' within us rather than to what is artificial or conventional. Leigh Hunt in an essay entitled 'On the realities of the imagination' expresses this approach very clearly in the following remarks:

> There is not a more unthinking way of talking, than to say such and such pains and pleasures are only imaginary, and therefore to be got rid of or undervalued accordingly. There is nothing imaginary, in the common acceptation of the word. [...] Whatever touches us, whatever moves us, does touch us and does move us. We recognize the reality of it, as we do that of a hand in the dark. We might as well say that a sight which makes us laugh, or a blow which brings tears to our eyes, is imaginary, as that anything else is imaginary which makes us laugh or weep. We can only judge of things by their effects.
>
> (Bromwich, *Romantic Critical Essays*, 1987, p.136)

William Hazlitt seems to agree with such sentiments in his essay 'On Gusto' and elsewhere in his criticism. There can be no formal definition of what Hazlitt calls gusto, and which, from the strength of the first sentence of his essay, we can translate as the power of strong emotion. We simply know it when we confront it. (We should perhaps note, however, that 'gusto' is the Spanish word for taste.) Hazlitt in his criticism is concerned to separate what he calls 'poetic power', which is natural and timeless, from 'social power'. Great art, Hazlitt argues, reflects back to us our essential human nature, and in that sense it is understood in terms of the powerful effect it has upon us. However, Hazlitt argues that it is a great mistake to confuse 'poetic power' with the social energies active in the contemporary world. In his essay 'Why the arts are not progressive' he argues that society progresses, or at least should seek to progress. Hazlitt was a critic firmly on the side of the radical and reformist parties of the period. However, because the power embodied within great art is timeless, 'poetic power' is not part of this socially progressive movement. Hazlitt defines socially progressive power in terms of science. His argument can, in fact, help us understand somewhat better Wordsworth's distinction between science and art in the 1802 Preface. Hazlitt writes: 'we judge of science by the number of effects produced – of art by the energy which produces them. The one is knowledge – the other power'. He goes on: 'the depths and soundings of the human heart were as well understood three thousand years ago, as they are at present; the face of nature and "the human face divine" shone as bright then as they have ever done' (Bromwich, *Romantic Critical Essays*, p.87).

Hazlitt seems to realize that there is a potential danger in defining poetry in terms of its affective power. If that power is understood in terms of poetry's influence upon what Shelley calls 'the public mind' (that is, society), then poetry becomes an indistinguishable part of the ideological conflicts which define any period of history. When poets claim a vital social role for poetry, they necessarily have to begin to defend it against the other faculties, disciplines and channels of human endeavour which claim for themselves a productive function in society and history.

We have already seen that changes in the reading public and in the material production of literary texts offered the Romantic artist the possibility of affecting public opinion. Wordsworth's Preface and Shelley's *A Defence of Poetry* both argue that poetry can have an important influence on society and history. Poets, as we have seen, were extremely aware, during the period, of a counter-influence to their own, namely the influence of critics. Shelley wrote an elegy for Keats entitled *Adonais* in which he accused Keats's reviewers, especially an anonymous reviewer of *Endymion*, of having literally caused the young poet's death. Might we not consider the various descriptions of the ideal figure of the Romantic poet as a kind of wish-fulfilment on the part of the poets? We might consider them the product of a desire for the kind of social influence enjoyed by the most widely read reviewers. It is certainly useful to consider the growth of literary magazines, quarterlies and weeklies as one important context for Romantic defences of poetry and, indeed, for some of the major poems of the period.

In his essay 'The four ages of poetry', Thomas Love Peacock has great fun in deflating the kind of arguments about poetry's social power we have been discussing. Peacock uses a similar distinction, between poetic power and social progress, to the one we have observed in the work of Hazlitt. However, unlike Hazlitt, Peacock argues that it is not timeless truths and passions which poetry expresses but truths and passions appropriate to early states of human civilization. As civilization progresses, under the direction of science, rationality and the various socially useful arts, Peacock argues that poetry grows ever more inappropriate, irrelevant and distracting.

Possibly because it is difficult to ascertain whether Peacock wrote his 'The four ages of poetry' with an ironic or a serious intent, it is an essay which is sometimes overlooked in discussions of Romantic literary criticism and theory. However, our discussion of the contexts within which poetry was produced and read has given us enough suggestions to be able to recognize that, playful or not, the thesis of the essay touches a very serious and important issue. The question of the place of poetry in the modern, increasingly technological and utilitarian world of nineteenth-century Britain, was one that Romantic defenders of poetry felt the need to engage with seriously. Certainly, the essay was treated seriously enough by Shelley to prompt him to compose perhaps the most famous, most influential and, in many ways, most brilliantly written defence of poetry of the whole period, his *A Defence of Poetry: or Remarks Suggested by an Essay Entitled 'The Four Ages of Poetry'*, to give it its full title.

Shelley responds to Peacock by turning 'poetry' into any form of expression which has the effect of promoting what Shelley, from his radical political position, considered the 'truth', the values encapsulated in the revolutionary slogan 'Liberty, Equality, Fraternity'. In this way Shelley does not need to defend poetry against rival modes of discourse; he simply identifies as 'poetry' whatever has a revolutionary social effect. We asked a question at the end of the last section concerning Shelley's description of the 'figure of the poet'. Shelley argues that the poet can be ignorant of his or her embodiment and promotion of 'power'. He can argue this because, for him, poetry is equivalent to whatever helps the progress of society towards the values of 'Liberty, Equality, Fraternity'. A poet may not actually realize that she or he is doing so, but may still forward the cause of 'true' human values. Indeed, for Shelley, every 'great' poet is defined by their performance of such an act.

Shelley's *A Defence of Poetry* combines two dominant strains in Romantic poetic theory and criticism: an idealized vision of poetry as a timeless resource of fundamental human values; and a view of poetry as positioned within the ideological conflicts of the present moment. Poetry's purpose is to produce social change, and is thus ideological; yet, because of Shelley's belief in the values of radical humanism, this very ideological characteristic means also that 'great poetry' is timeless.

We began this chapter by looking at what we called the 'levelling of language' in Wordsworth's Preface. This subject opened up various major themes in Romantic poetic theory and criticism: the notion of the 'creative imagination' and the 'expressive' view of poetry; the attempts to produce a properly philosophical 'theory' of poetry; arguments concerning the relation between poetry, poetic language and politics; changes in the reading public and the critical climate; arguments over the social 'power' or 'effect' of poetry. Shelley's *A Defence of Poetry* represents only the first part of a planned, two-part 'defence'. The second part, which he did not live to write, would have dealt with how the 'principles' presented in the first part applied to the state of contemporary poetry. This second part would surely have dealt with issues of poetic style and the appropriate 'level' of poetic language. However, the essay that we have, *A Defence of Poetry*, can be said to bring to a culmination many of the themes we have discussed in this chapter. It is an essay, as I have said, that at one and the same time idealizes poetry and places it firmly in its social and cultural contexts. In doing so, *A Defence of Poetry*, has, rightly, gained the status of *the* definitive defence of the Romantic view of poetry.

Women writers and readers

by Susan Matthews

Until the late 1970s, most university courses on Romantic writing would have focused almost exclusively on six male poets. Yet throughout the time known as the Romantic period, women were prolific writers and readers of novels, poems, and other kinds of writing including fiction and non-fiction for children. The scale of women's involvement in the arts during this time is only now being realized with many of their works being reread and often reprinted. As you have seen in Chapter Two, the study of this writing lays down a considerable challenge to the conventional view of Romanticism as a movement. And to date there is no academic consensus on where women's writing stands in relation to that view or if the period saw opportunities for women increase or decline. It may be that, as Stephen Bygrave suggests in Chapter Two, previous assumptions about Romantic writing should be revised (see p.64 above). This chapter aims to characterize the challenge offered by this body of work by women. To do this we must look at what women wrote and read during the Romantic period and whether some kinds of literature were especially associated with women. The chapter will also look at some of the ways women writers of the period were subsequently eclipsed by men. It will consider some commonly held anxieties of the period about the status and power of women's writing and suggest that these anxieties may have affected the way we came to think about Romantic writing.

The public identity

In 1795, at the age of twenty-seven, Maria Edgeworth published her first work, *Letters for Literary Ladies*. Edgeworth came from a highly literate family and her father, Richard Lovell Edgeworth, was particularly interested in educational theory and practice. She herself read very widely, in political theory and philosophy as well as fiction. At the age of fifteen Edgeworth was encouraged by her father to work on a translation of a French text for publication. But before the work was completed, her father was persuaded by a friend, Thomas Day, that it was quite inappropriate for his daughter to become an author. Edgeworth was forbidden to publish and the ban was only lifted upon Day's death in 1789. In *Letters for Literary Ladies*, Edgeworth provides a fictional account of this disagreement between her father and Day in the form of letters between two gentlemen. The first gentleman argues against offering too much education to a daughter because of the perceived danger that she will turn into a 'literary lady', a woman who, he thinks, will not make a good wife and mother. Edgeworth offers her own defence of educated women, both as writers and readers, in the fictional reply. However both men agree that there are increasing numbers of female readers and writers. Even the gentleman who opposes female education grudgingly admits:

Chapter Four

> Women of literature are much more numerous of late than they were a
> few years ago. They make a class in society, they fill the public eye,
> and have acquired a degree of consequence and an appropriate
> character.
>
> (Edgeworth, *Letters for Literary Ladies*, 1993 edn, p.8)

By 'women of literature', the gentleman means both women readers and
women writers. Recent scholars have begun to discover the truth of this
statement. Janet Todd argues that the professional female author was
becoming established by the late 1790s and she estimates that at least three
to four hundred women published during that decade:

> By the end of the 1790s, whether preaching independence, duty or
> submission, women were assuming a remarkable authority for
> themselves as authors. Women had been involved in political
> controversy before and had penned much moral advice, but they had
> rarely done either so assertively as they would do in this unsettled
> time.
>
> (Todd, *The Sign of Angellica*, 1989, p.218)

Stuart Curran has discovered hundreds of female poets published in the
Romantic period. An extract from his essay 'Romantic poetry: The I altered'
appears in Part Two of this book (p.279) and you should read this now.

Curran points to the high standing and influence of some of these
writers and he quotes the poet Mary Robinson's assessment of the achievement of women poets:

> Poetry has unquestionably risen high in British literature from the
> productions of female pens: for many English women have produced
> such original and beautiful compositions, that the first critics and
> scholars of the age have wondered, while they applauded.
>
> (Part Two, p.280)

But although Curran and Todd emphasize the number of women writers in
the Romantic period and their status and influence, others such as Roger
Lonsdale portray the place of women writers and readers differently. He
suggests that women poets such as Anna Seward, Charlotte Smith and Anna
Barbauld achieved a remarkable dominance of the literary scene in the
early Romantic period:

> in the 1780s women virtually took over, as writers and readers, the
> territories most readily conceded to them, of popular fiction and
> fashionable poetry. The emergence early in the decade of Anna
> Seward, Helen Maria Williams, and Charlotte Smith, each of whom for
> a time enjoyed high reputation, consolidated the advances made by
> women poets in the 1770s.
>
> (Lonsdale, *Eighteenth-Century Women Poets*, 1989, p.xxxv)

Yet Lonsdale sees the Romantic period develop as a time in which women
lost their accepted position as writers. Indeed he sees the male Romantic
poets as attempting to wrest the ground of poetry away from women writers and readers. Lonsdale notes that women writers were absent from influential poetry anthologies of the Romantic period:

The cause of the women writers was not helped by the fact that none were included in the huge multi-volume compilations of the works of the English poets assembled by Robert Anderson (1792–5) and Alexander Chalmers (1810), which [...] have always had a remarkable influence on subsequent views of eighteenth-century verse. A partial explanation is that no living authors were included by Anderson and Chalmers and many of the best known women poets were still alive in 1810. Alexander Dyce, who attempted to remedy this situation in his *Specimens of the British Poetesses* (1825), nevertheless believed that 'the productions of women had been carefully excluded' by the earlier editors. A diligent explorer of 'the chaos of our past Poetry', Dyce had space to give only brief and where possible, lyrical examples of his poets (including some forty from the eighteenth century) so that the cumulative effect of his representations remains slight. And, as if conscious of increasingly elevated expectations of what true poetry should be, he finally admitted to some lack of conviction about what he had assembled: 'It is true that the grander inspirations of the Muse have not often breathed into the softer frame.'

(Ibid., p.xlii)

Whereas Lonsdale sees women writers as losing ground to men in the Romantic period – ground that was not regained for a long time – Curran's narrative of women's poetry seems basically optimistic. Certainly it seems as if women writers and readers faced pressures and produced anxieties in the Romantic period which were not faced in the same way by male authors and readers.

The argument is clearly complex, for we need to consider how many women published, how their work was viewed at the time, and by whom it was read. We need to investigate what women were encouraged to read and what they actually read. As Edgeworth's experience indicates, women could face particular pressures and constraints as readers and as writers. There were anxieties about the kinds of reading that should be encouraged for women, and the effects of education on them. The learned woman, some thought, would not be a good wife and mother. It was often feared that the imagination of the woman who immersed herself in fiction, particularly in novels and romances, might develop to a dangerous extent. There were also anxieties about women as writers. Publication seemed to many a dangerous move outside the private, domestic sphere, while the very success of women as writers caused further fears about their impact on culture, which to some they seemed increasingly to influence.

The public identity that publication gave a writer could bring with it special anxieties for a woman. Prefaces to novels by women are often very revealing in this regard. Frances Burney published *Evelina*, her first novel, anonymously in 1778; even her father did not know she was the author. Her Preface reveals all kinds of anxieties, not least in the pretence that she is the editor rather than the author of the letters that make up her novel. Not only does Burney conceal her name but also her gender, and she imagines herself as 'wrapped in a mantle of impenetrable obscurity':

The following letters are presented to the public – for such by novel writers, novel readers will be called, – with a very singular mixture of timidity and confidence, resulting from the peculiar situation of the editor; who, though trembling for their success from a consciousness of their imperfections, yet fears not being involved in their disgrace, while happily wrapped up in a mantle of impenetrable obscurity.

(Burney, Evelina, 1982 edn, p.7)

Burney is particularly anxious, it seems, because she is aware of the common assumption that novels are dangerous to women readers:

> Perhaps were it possible to effect the total extirpation of novels, our young ladies in general, and boarding-school damsels in particular, might profit from their annihilation: but since the distemper they have spread seems incurable, since their contagion bids defiance to the medicine of advice or reprehension, and since they are found to baffle all the mental art of physic, save what is prescribed by the slow regimen of Time, and bitter diet of Experience, surely all attempts to contribute to the number of those which may be read, if not with advantage, at least without injury, ought rather to be encouraged than contemned.

(Ibid., p.8)

Burney here uses the colourful language of disease and infection that was favoured by moralists who attacked the novel. She writes of 'distemper', 'contagion' which is 'incurable', of the 'medicine of advice' and the 'mental art of physic'. The claims she makes for her novel seem to be minimal, of producing a work which 'may be read, if not with advantage, at least without injury'. Yet it is clear that her apparent embarrassment at being the author of a novel is counterbalanced by a sense of pride in the form. It is significant, I think, that the novelists she admires in this Preface are all male:

> Yet, while in the annals of those few of our predecessors, to whom this species of writing is indebted for being saved from contempt, and rescued from depravity, we can trace such names as Rousseau, Johnson, Marivaux, Fielding, Richardson, and Smollett, no man need blush at starting from the same post, though many, nay, most men, may sigh at finding themselves distanced.

(Ibid., p.7)

Burney's Preface to her successful first novel reveals all sorts of anxieties about publication, about the status of the novel, and about writing for and as a woman. These anxieties may have been heightened by the particular circumstances of her own family (for her father, like Edgeworth's, was a writer) but nevertheless they tell us something of women's anxieties as writers and readers.

Burney's anxious explanations can be paralleled in the Prefaces of other women writers, not least the 1831 Preface to *Frankenstein*, which Mary Shelley wrote:

> [to] give a general answer to the question, so very frequently asked me – 'How I, then a young girl, came to think of and to dilate upon so very hideous an idea?'

(Shelley, Frankenstein, 1994 edn, p.192)

Shelley, it seems, needs to justify and explain how 'a young girl' could be the author of such a story. Her explanation in part puts the blame on the male poets, Shelley and Byron, who set up the story writing competition that gave rise to her novel, though, as she puts it: 'The illustrious poets [...] annoyed by the platitude of prose, speedily relinquished their uncongenial task' (Ibid., p.194).

The concerns of these women writers may be related to attacks on the novel in the many conduct books (books of advice for women) which were published or republished around this time. For instance, the conservative moralist Hannah More writes of the danger of developing women's imagination rather than their reason and she seems particularly horrified by the work of female novelists:

> Who are those ever multiplying authors, that with unparalleled
> fecundity are overstocking the world with their quick-succeeding
> progeny? They are NOVEL-WRITERS; the easiness of whose
> productions is at once the cause of their own fruitfulness, and of the
> almost infinitely numerous race of imitators to whom they give birth.
> Such is the frightful facility of this species of composition, that every
> raw girl, while she reads is tempted to fancy that she can also write [...]
> The glutted imagination soon overflows with the redundance of cheap
> sentiment and plentiful incident, and by a sort of arithmetical
> proportion, is enabled by the perusal of any three novels, to produce a
> fourth; till every fresh production, like the prolific progeny of Banquo,
> is followed by
> Another, and another, and another!
> Is a lady, however destitute of talents, education, or knowledge
> of the world, whose studies have been completed by a circulating
> library, in any distress of mind? The writing of a novel suggests itself as
> the best soother of her sorrows!
>
> (More, *Works*, vol. 7, 1801, p.219)

The novel seems to be a particular source of anxiety to moralists. The imagery More uses suggests a horror of prolific motherhood; she imagines novels reproducing without check, overrunning and destroying culture.

The cult of separate spheres

More's colourful fears about the production of novels by women, especially her concern that readers could become writers with an ease she clearly dislikes, are shared by other cultural commentators at the time. There seem to have been widespread fears about cultural decline, often linked to a perception that the role of women in the cultural life of the nation was increasing.

In a lecture of 1801, 'On the Present State of the Art, and the Causes which check its Progress', Henry Fuseli, the President of the Royal Academy in London, worries about such a decline. The problem, Fuseli believes, is widespread and deeply ingrained, not only in England, but in other countries as well:

> The efficient cause, therefore, why higher Art at present is sunk to
> such a state of inactivity and languor that it may be doubted whether it

will exist much longer, is not a particular one, which private
patronage, or the will of an individual, however great, can remove; but
a general cause, founded on the bent, the manners, habits, modes of a
nation, – and not of one nation alone, but of all who at present
pretend to culture.

(Knowles, *The Life and Writings of Henry Fuseli*, 1831, p.47)

Using the image of disease, Fuseli argues that the taste of the public is at
fault: 'perhaps a revolution worse to be dreaded than the disease itself must
precede the possibility of a cure' (Ibid., p.49). In the following passage, he
links the decline of great art with what he considers to be a new cultural
emphasis on the private and the domestic:

> Our age, when compared with former ages, has but little occasion for
> great works, and that is the reason why so few are produced; – the
> ambition, activity, and spirit of public life is shrunk to the minute detail
> of domestic arrangements – every thing that surrounds us tends to
> show us in private, is become snug, less, narrow, pretty, insignificant.
> We are not, perhaps, the less happy on account of all this; but from
> such selfish trifling to expect a system of Art built on grandeur, without
> a total revolution, would only be less presumptuous than insane.

(Ibid., pp.47–8)

Remember that at the time he was speaking, 1801, Britain was at war with
France – a nation that, under the leadership of Napoleon, was attempting to
claim for itself the status of cultural leader. Read the passage again. **What
causes does Fuseli cite for the decline in art he identifies? How
would you compare the words Fuseli connects with 'domestic
arrangements' with those he associates with 'public life'? What are
the explicit and implicit oppositions set up by Fuseli in the passage?**

Discussion

Modern life, Fuseli thinks, does not require 'great works', and this is
because 'private' or 'domestic' life is now valued and celebrated rather than
'public life'. Perhaps in 1801 Fuseli has identified one of the characteristic
developments within culture at this time, which saw the private and domestic spheres brought into the public domain. It is possible to see the private
sphere, what Fuseli calls domestic arrangements, as the sphere of women.
The domestic woman was being increasingly celebrated by both male and
female writers. This emphasis on the proper female sphere as that of home
and children is what is often described as the 'cult of separate spheres'.

Fuseli's adjectives for 'domestic arrangements', 'snug, less, narrow,
pretty, insignificant', are negative in comparison with the words he associates with the public sphere, 'ambition, activity, and spirit'. You may also
read them as gendered, particularly Fuseli's use of 'pretty'.

The passage works through explicit oppositions between great art and
lesser art and the public sphere and the private sphere. So if Fuseli associates
domestic arrangements and the private sphere with women there may also be
implicit opposition between male and female culture in his commentary. ■

What does seem clear is that Fuseli regrets and fears the change he perceives. Great art, he thinks, is incompatible with this new subject matter

and focus. Culture, Fuseli fears, is becoming feminized and so losing its capacity to produce great art. There is other evidence in Fuseli's writing that he associates the spread of wealth through the middle classes with the growth of the power of women to determine public taste. In his 'Aphorisms on Art', in which he refers to his time as 'an effeminate age' (Ibid., p.103), Fuseli writes:

> In an age of luxury women have taste, decide and dictate; for in an
> age of luxury woman aspires to the functions of man, and man slides
> into the offices of woman. The epoch of eunuchs was ever the epoch
> of viragoes.
>
> (Ibid., p.144)

The bourgeois culture which was seen as becoming increasingly powerful is also, he thinks, a feminized culture.

The impact of women on culture was a theme which exercised the minds of many cultural commentators. We only have to look at the portraits of mothers and children produced by Sir Joshua Reynolds, one of Fuseli's predecessors, to see what Fuseli might mean when he complains about the celebration of the private and the domestic in art. Reynolds appeared in his own Academy lectures to hold to the same values as Fuseli – valuing above all history painting based on the tradition of Michelangelo. But he excelled as a painter of portraits and many of his most striking are of children and of women. His painting of Lady Cockburn with her three sons, James, George and William, for instance, suggests a newly indulgent attitude to children (Figure 7). It hints that the baby is breast-fed, a practice which had recently become fashionable among the upper classes (who would previously have employed wet nurses).

However Lady Cockburn's husband, Sir James, would not permit a portrait of his wife to be exhibited in public. The painting was therefore exhibited at the Royal Academy in 1774 as 'Portrait of a lady with three children', and was published as a print in 1791 under the title *Cornelia*. Cornelia was a Roman mother of the Republican period who boasted that her children were her only jewels. This retitling of the painting for exhibition and for publication reveals some of the anxieties that surrounded the entrance of the domestic woman of the time into the public sphere. Lady Cockburn is celebrated in this image as a mother, indulgent towards her children and devoted to them. But her husband clearly felt that it was inappropriate to display this private identity in public. She is therefore turned into a figure from the kind of Classical culture with which upper-class men were familiar.

It could well be argued that this process of disguising private individuals when portraying them in public was common to Reynolds's portraits of men and of women. But women at the time did experience particular anxieties about their public image – anxieties not relevant to men who were seen as rightly belonging in the public eye. Some women writers used the subject of paintings of women to express these anxieties. A comparison between the exhibition of portraits in public and the publication of texts by female authors is made by a number of writers. In *Letters for Literary Ladies*, Edgeworth extrapolates from portraiture of women to discuss the issues of women publishing. But it is hard to place Edgeworth's own position because the discussion occurs in a letter from the gentleman opposed

Figure 7   Sir Joshua Reynolds, *Lady Cockburn and her three eldest sons*, 1773, oil on canvas, 141.6 x 113 cm. Reproduced by courtesy of the Trustees, The National Gallery, London.

to female education whose arguments Edgeworth clearly does not support. The gentleman *pretends* to celebrate the exhibition of 'portraits of our beauties' as a welcome freedom from Eastern misogyny (an orientalist myth of the time which is discussed further in Chapter Ten). Yet his 'thanks' to the ladies who publish private writings seem to be ironic, and in this context his praise of both exhibiting portraits and publishing merely speaks of anxieties about both public activities:

> The Turks have pictures of the hand, the foot, the features of Mahomet, but no representation of the whole face or person is allowed. The portraits of our beauties, in our exhibition-room, show a proper contempt of this insidious policy; and those learned and ingenious ladies who publish their private letters, select maxims, secret anecdotes, and family memoirs, are entitled to our thanks, for thus presenting us with full-lengths of their minds.
>
> (Edgeworth, *Letters for Literary Ladies*, 1993 edn, p.13)

Hannah More compares women with portraits in *Strictures on the Modern System of Female Education*. Here she is discussing the dangers of a man choosing his future wife at a public event such as a ball:

> If, indeed, women were mere outside, form and face only, and if *mind* made up no part of her composition, it would follow that a ball-room was quite as appropriate a place for choosing a wife, as an exhibition room for choosing a picture. But, inasmuch as women are not mere portraits, their value not being determinable by a glance of the eye, it follows that a different mode of appreciating their value, and a different place for viewing them antecedent to their being individually selected, is desirable. The two cases differ also in this, that if a man select a picture for himself from among all its exhibited competitors, and bring it to his own house, the picture being passive, he is able to *fix* it there; while the wife, picked up at a public place, and accustomed to incessant display, will not, it is probable, when brought home, stick so quietly to the spot where he fixes her; but will escape to the exhibition room again, and continue to be displayed at every subsequent exhibition, just as if she were not become private property, and had never been definitively disposed of.
>
> (More, *Works*, vol. 8, 1801, pp.178–9)

Now read the passage again looking closely at the comparison More makes between women and portraits. **To what end does More use this comparison?**

D i s c u s s i o n

More uses the comparison between women and portraits to show how different they are. She is showing a concern for women's minds as well as their appearance. But she also seems to share Sir James's sense that it is not appropriate to exhibit a wife in public. The wife 'picked up at a public place' will 'escape to the exhibition room again'. Women, both the husband and the female moralist believe, belong in private. However, More sees women and portraits as rather more alike than we might. For, just like a picture, a married woman is the property of a man. She is 'private property', 'definitively disposed of' and so, unlike a picture, unavailable for resale. ▪

The anxieties voiced by Fuseli and by More are linked but distinct. The male commentator fears the way that the public sphere is becoming moulded by female tastes and interests, celebrating the domestic world of women rather than the public world of men. The female moralist fears the effect on women of their entry into the public world of mixed society. The critic Terry Lovell writes that:

> The very segregation of women in the private sphere created the need [...] for another type of semi-public arena in which the transfer of daughters from one home to another could be negotiated. Jane Austen's world of assemblies, private balls, visiting and the London Season remains one of the most vivid fictional constructions of this carefully chaperoned and vetted intermediate sphere.
>
> (Lovell, *Consuming Fiction*, 1987, p.37)

More clearly feels that even this semi-public world threatens to undermine the separation of women in the private sphere. But it is inconclusive to try to identify a male and a female attitude to the role of women at this time. In contrast to More, the writer Mary Wollstonecraft, author of *A Vindication of the Rights of Woman,* laments the effects on women's minds of their exclusion from civil society, from public roles and duties:

> Females, in fact, denied all political privileges, and not allowed, as married women, excepting in criminal cases, a civil existence, have their attention naturally drawn from the interest of the whole community to that of the minute parts, though the private duty of any member of society must be very imperfectly performed when not connected with the general good.
>
> (Todd and Butler, *The Works of Mary Wollstonecraft,* 1989, p.256)

Confinement to the domestic sphere seems to Wollstonecraft to bring with it dangers for women's intellectual and moral development. However, she also identifies and laments certain kinds of female power and influence. She writes that:

> When [...] I call women slaves, I mean in a political and civil sense, for indirectly they obtain too much power, and are debased by their exertions to obtain illicit sway.
>
> (Ibid., p.239)

Women, then, *can* have a kind of power, though they tend to obtain it, like Mary Robinson, who in 1779 became mistress to the Prince of Wales, through sexuality. Most commentators, however, whether male or female, believe that women belong within the domestic sphere. Yet just as Lady Cockburn achieved a public identity in the print of Reynolds's portrait of her with her children, so being bound to a domestic role did not exclude women from print culture. As Gary Kelly argues:

> Commercialized print offered new opportunities to women lacking professional education, authorship did not require leaving the actual or notional confines of domestic life, and the prominence of 'domestic woman' [...] encouraged a feminization of culture on which women could claim to have some authority.
>
> (Kelly, *Women, Writing and Revolution,* 1993, p.9)

Thus we should not be surprised to see that Edgeworth, once she is allowed to publish, celebrates the figure of 'domestic woman' in her writing. Edgeworth's fictional letter from Caroline to her friend, the aristocratic Lady V, trapped within an unhappy marriage, concludes with an emphasis which is typical of this period. Lady V is enjoined to find happiness in *domestic life* as educator of her children. The kinds of power achieved by sexual attraction are seen by Edgeworth, as by Wollstonecraft, as both dangerous and ultimately self-defeating.

In her novel *Belinda*, published in 1801 (the same year as Fuseli's lecture), Edgeworth presents the ideal domestic woman. We see Lady Percival first through the eyes of the hero, Clarence Hervey:

> They found Lady Anne Percival in the midst of her children; who all turned their healthy, rosy, intelligent faces towards the door the moment that they heard their father's voice. [...] Whether her eyes were large or small, blue or hazel, he could not tell; nay, he might have been puzzled if he had been asked the colour of her hair – Whether she were handsome by the rules of art, he knew not; but he felt that she had the essential charm of beauty, the power of prepossessing the heart immediately in her favour. The effect of her manners, like that of her beauty, was rather to be felt than described. Everybody was at ease in her company, and none thought themselves called upon to admire her.
>
> (Edgeworth, *Belinda*, 1993 edn, p.89)

The chapter in which Belinda goes to stay with the Percivals is called 'Domestic Happiness'. Yet the increasing celebration in print of the domestic woman did not mean women were in fact *more* confined to a domestic role than previously. In the 1980s the media was full of images of caring fathers dandling tiny babies but that did not *necessarily* mean that men of the time were more involved in childcare than in previous decades. Even though the doctrine of separate spheres was increasingly enjoined on women in the early years of the nineteenth century, women did still have access to the public sphere, as Kelly suggests, through publication. Writing was one way in which women could be simultaneously 'domestic' and public.

The politics of sensibility

Perhaps one of the strongest influences on cultural expectations of gender in the period was the continuing influence of the eighteenth-century cult of sensibility. Sensibility, the cult of feeling, arose in the eighteenth century in response to philosophical theories that investigated the power of feeling to communicate directly between people. At its height in the 1770s, sensibility celebrated the man of feeling, endued with sympathy and pity, who felt deeply in response to the suffering of others. I introduce the idea of sensibility at this stage because it not only provides a context for some of the images of women that we see in this period, but also has strong links with Romantic writings. In focusing on feeling, sensibility takes us into an internal world of psychology. Curran argues that the link is a crucial one to understanding Romanticism when he writes that the 'poetry of sensibility is at base a literature of psychological exploration, and it is the foundation on which Romanticism was reared' (Part Two, p.288).

One of the key works of the Romantic movement is Goethe's *The Sorrows of Young Werther*, first published in 1774. This novel, which had a tremendous vogue in England in the late eighteenth and early nineteenth centuries, is a tragic love story told in the first person about the obsession that the young Werther develops for Lotte, a girl engaged to another man. The famous scene in which Werther first sets eyes on Lotte is in many ways similar to the scene you have just read in which Edgeworth first showed us her domestic ideal, Lady Percival:

> I crossed the courtyard to a well-built house and, climbing the flight of steps in front, opened the door and beheld the most charming scene I have ever set eyes on. In the hallway, six children aged between eleven and two were milling about a girl with a wonderful figure and of medium height, wearing a simple white dress with pink ribbons at the sleeves and breast. She was holding a loaf of rye bread and cutting a piece for each of the little ones about her, according to their age and appetite; she handed out the slices with great kindliness, and the children reached up their little hands long before the bread was cut, cried out their artless thanks and then either bounded away contented with their supper or, in the case of the quieter ones, walked tranquilly out to the courtyard gate to look at the strangers and the carriage in which their Lotte was to drive away.

> (Goethe, *The Sorrows of Young Werther*, 1989 edn, pp.37–8)

Lotte, like Lady Percival, is seen surrounded by children who testify to her maternal skills. But you may have noticed that unlike Edgeworth, Goethe focuses strongly on Lotte's figure, which is set off rather than concealed by her simple and modest dress. Lotte is both child and mother in this image, and seems to attract Werther all the more in this dual role.

It is characteristic of sensibility in this form to represent women in semi-maternal roles, and to value their qualities of kindliness and caring. The images of women which it celebrates are one source of the figure of the domestic woman that is so important within the culture of the Romantic period. Sensibility produces a body of literature which *seems* at least to celebrate feeling and femininity. But from the 1790s onwards, there seem to be two main strategies by which poetry, and other writing that seeks an influential place in culture, tries to dissociate itself from the feminine-marked movement of sensibility. Whereas some writers openly attack the values and conventions of sensibility, others borrow its values and conventions but attempt to mark these as masculine and as distinct from sensibility. Sensibility itself is seen increasingly as self-indulgent in its celebration of feeling.

Many of Wordsworth's poems return to the stock scenes of the literature of sensibility – such as meeting an old man on the roadside, or hearing of the distress suffered by a young woman. Yet Wordsworth's poetry also attempts to establish his treatment of such scenes as new and different from that of the female dominated literature of sensibility. As Lonsdale argues: 'The "gentle reader", whose false expectations Wordsworth mocks in a poem like "Simon Lee", was almost certainly female' (Lonsdale, *Eighteenth-Century Women Poets*, 1989, p.xli). Wordsworth's narrator rejects the expectations of the reader:

> My gentle reader, I perceive
> How patiently you've waited,
> And I'm afraid that you expect
> Some tale will be related.

(ll.69–72, Wu, *Romanticism*, 1994, p.203)

Instead of this probably female reader, Wordsworth hopes to address his poetry to a deeper and more thoughtful male reader. Lonsdale sees the Preface to the *Lyrical Ballads* as a key text in defining this newly masculine audience and voice for poetry:

> Throughout the 'Preface' of 1800, 'man', 'men', 'manly' always accompany his definitions of the poet and poetry: the poet, who will write in a 'manly' style, will use 'the real language of men' and is 'a man speaking to men'. In attacking the 'gaudy and inane phraseology' of fashionable poetry, Wordsworth (ostensibly attacking Thomas Gray) was in fact echoing the charge repeatedly levelled at women poets by reviewers and others in the 1780s and 1790s, that they were 'phrase-haberdashers' (John Williams, *Poetical Works*, 1789, ii.248–50), that they were particularly attracted by the tinsel and glare of poetic language (*Monthly Review*, New Series xiii, 1794, 77–9), that they liked tinsel ornament in poetry more than male readers (*European Magazine*, xxviii, 1795, 321–2).
>
> (Lonsdale, *Eighteenth-Century Women Poets*, 1989, pp.xl–xli)

In the literature of sensibility, the spectator is a man of feeling, who displays pity and benevolence by weeping and often gives money as charity to the victims who tell him their stories. This emotional response to suffering is seen as adequate. By the 1790s there were many who saw sensibility as an inadequate and clichéd response to the problems of the poor and the old and of women and children. In the opening stanza of 'The Human Abstract' from *The Songs of Experience*, Blake singles out this kind of response and points out the political lesson that it conceals:

> Pity would be no more
> If we did not make somebody poor;
> And mercy no more could be,
> If all were as happy as we.
> (Wu, *Romanticism*, 1994, p.74)

The value of pity, a key emotion in the literature of sensibility, is here questioned. In Blake's 1794 poem, *The Book of Urizen*, we witness the birth of the first female in a strange creation scene:

> The globe of life-blood trembled
> Branching out into roots,
> Fibrous, writhing upon the winds,
> In pangs eternity on eternity.
> At length, in tears and cries embodied,

A female form, trembling and pale,
Waves before his deathy face.
[...]
Wonder, awe, fear, astonishment,
Petrify the eternal myriads
At the first female form now separate;
They called her Pity, and fled.

(ll.315–22, 327–30, Wu, *Romanticism*, 1994, p.102)

In this negative retelling of the creation of the first woman, the 'first female form' is named as Pity, the key emotion of sensibility, and this form is viewed with horror by the 'eternal myriads'. The scene probably echoes and retells the scene in *Paradise Lost*, Book One, which tells of the creation of sin (also a woman). In Blake's version, woman is associated with sensibility and the reaction of the 'eternal myriads' is to flee. So whereas Wordsworth attempts to redefine sensibility in male terms, here Blake seems to discredit the cult of sensibility by attacking the celebration of qualities which are seen as feminine.

Stereotyped ideals of femininity from various points of view can be seen at work in political polemic of the 1790s, most dramatically through the response of the writer Edmund Burke to the early years of the French Revolution. In one of the most powerful passages of his *Reflections on the Revolution in France* (1790), Burke characterizes the Revolution as an attack on women, and the revolutionaries as unchivalrous.

> It is now sixteen or seventeen years since I saw the queen of France, then the dauphiness, at Versailles; and surely never lighted on this orb, which she hardly seemed to touch, a more delightful vision. I saw her just above the horizon, decorating and cheering the elevated sphere she just began to move in, – glittering like the morning-star, full of life, and splendor and joy. Oh! What a revolution! and what an heart must I have, to contemplate without emotion that elevation and that fall! Little did I dream when she added titles of veneration to those of enthusiastic, distant, respectful love, that she should ever be obliged to carry the sharp antidote against disgrace concealed in that bosom; little did I dream that I should have lived to see such disasters fallen upon her in a nation of gallant men, in a nation of men of honour and of cavaliers. I thought ten thousand swords must have leaped from their scabbards to avenge even a look that threatened her with insult. – But the age of chivalry is gone. – That of sophisters, oeconomists, and calculators, has succeeded; and the glory of Europe is extinguished for ever.

(Burke, *Reflections on the Revolution in France*, 1968 edn, pp.169–70)

Burke's rhetoric appears to value a certain kind of femininity and associates it with the conservative cause. His account was published in 1790, before the execution of the French king and queen, and so as events unfolded, his warning seemed to increase in significance. Contemporary readers would have recognized Burke's rhetoric as drawing on the language and values of sensibility. His appeal to his readers is through the emotions – he appeals to feeling rather than to reason. And such devices as the exclamations, 'Oh!

What a revolution! and what a heart must I have, to contemplate without emotion that elevation and that fall!', are characteristic of the literature of sensibility. Burke is portraying himself as man of feeling, responding to a woman in distress – the characteristic role of the male spectator in the literature of sensibility.

If we turn now to look at how two women wrote about the revolution, we see that women writers can adopt quite different approaches to the questions of gender and politics. Wollstonecraft and Helen Maria Williams represent two very different responses to the French Revolution. Both writers welcome the Revolution in its early stages and both are radicals. But whereas Wollstonecraft associates femininity and sensibility with the corruption of the French aristocracy whose rule has been overthrown, Williams links femininity and sensibility with the spirit of the Revolution itself. Attacking Burke, her political enemy, in *A Vindication of the Rights of Men* (1790), Wollstonecraft casts him as a ladies' man, relying on feeling not reason. Like Blake, she rejects sensibility as an ineffectual response to suffering:

> Such misery demands more than tears. I pause to recollect myself, and smother the contempt I feel rising for your rhetorical flourishes and infantine sensibility.
>
> (Todd and Butler, *The Works of Mary Wollstonecraft*, 1989, p.58)

But in a passage published in 1795, after the execution of Marie Antoinette, Williams celebrates sensibility in the figure of the radical Madame Roland, who shows sensitivity and feeling towards her fellow condemned. Here Madame Roland displays heroism and feminine charm in her appeal to the executioner:

> To be the first victim was [...] considered as a privilege and had been allowed to Madame Roland as a woman. But when she observed the dismay of her companion, she said to him, 'Allez le premier: que je vous epargne au moins la douleur de voir couler mon sang.' ['Go first: I would at least spare you the pain of seeing my blood shed.'] She then turned to the executioner and begged that this sad indulgence might be granted to her fellow sufferer. The executioner told her that he had received orders that she should perish first.
>
> 'But you cannot, I am sure', said she with a smile, 'refuse the last request of a lady.' The executioner complied with her demand.
>
> (Wu, *Romanticism*, 1994, pp.142–3)

Whereas some women writers, like Williams, take their literary identity from sensibility, others, like Wollstonecraft, see sensibility as at best an aspect of femininity which is hard for women to escape, and at worst as a means to celebrate all that is most false and decadent in the contemporary image of women. As Curran has argued, sensibility is very significant in the emergence of male Romantic poetry (see Part Two, p.291). Indeed Wordsworth's first published poem in *The European Magazine* of March 1787 was the 'Sonnet, on Seeing Miss Helen Maria Williams Weep at a Tale of Distress'. (Wordsworth had not in fact witnessed such a scene, but invents it as a suitably moving and poetic subject.) Yet, as I have already argued, the canonical male Romantic poets Blake and Wordsworth find ways to distance themselves from the 'feminine' culture of sensibility. And the historian Linda Colley has argued that in the years of the war with France (between 1793 and 1815) there are broad attempts to emphasize the masculinity of the English identity in opposition to that of the French, who are seen both as the enemy and as effeminate:

> There was a sense at this time [...] in which the British conceived of themselves as an essentially 'masculine' culture – bluff, forthright, rational, down-to-earth to the extent of being philistine – caught up in an eternal rivalry with an essentially 'effeminate' France – subtle, intellectually devious, preoccupied with high fashion, fine cuisine and etiquette [...] All of these complex prejudices [...] enabled conservatives in Britain in particular to see in the outbreak of the French Revolution a grim demonstration of the dangers that ensued when women were allowed to stray outside their proper sphere.
>
> (Colley, *Britons*, 1992, p.252)

The cult of sensibility and the promotion of domestic woman as an ideal of femininity show a concern with the place and role of women within society. It could be argued that concern about the proper role of women grows in the 1790s. Indeed I would argue that a key indicator of the changing attitudes to women can be seen in responses to the figure of Mary Wollstonecraft after her death in 1797 (of complications following childbirth). In 1798 her husband William Godwin published *Memoirs of the Author of A Vindication of the Rights of Woman*. The book told frankly of the birth of Wollstonecraft's first daughter by her lover, Gilbert Imlay, and of her two suicide attempts. The publication caused a scandal which lasted for many years and made Wollstonecraft's name and her views ones which no respectable woman could easily endorse. The scandal could well be seen as evidence of a new pressure on women towards a conventional respectability in these years. Certainly it seems that women and femininity are the subject of a new level of debate and concern in this period, and especially from the 1790s onwards.

Conduct literature

I would like to look now at the role of conduct literature in the regulation of women's reading and writing and in the production of widely disseminated images of women. One sign of anxiety about the role of women might be the rate at which books were published giving women advice on correct behaviour. William St Clair writes that:

> There was a tradition before the eighteenth century [...] But nothing which went before approached the huge flood of didactic books for ladies that started to build up in the 1780s [...] The sheer numbers of these books establish them as a cultural phenomenon unique to the revolutionary age and its aftermath.
>
> (St Clair, *The Godwins and the Shelleys*, 1989, p.505)

St Clair argues that 'a high proportion of the upper and middle classes must have owned copies of at least one advice book' (Ibid.). He traces the peaks of the conduct book phenomenon and concludes that they correlate with levels of anxiety caused by political events:

> the biggest rush comes after 1793 with the outbreak of war, the Terror in France, the treason trials, and the anti-Jacobin panic. There is a dip in the early 1800s when the short-lived Peace of Amiens (1801–1803) seemed to imply a return to normality, but numbers picked up again with the resumption of war. After Waterloo they fall rapidly back to pre-war levels.
>
> (Ibid., p.509)

It seems then that the revolutionary period gave fresh impetus to debate and concern about femininity and women's role in society. And conduct literature was a means by which views on the debate could be expressed. A central concern of conduct literature was the question of what women read. One of the most frequently republished volumes was James Fordyce's *Sermons to Young Women* (1765) in which the writer expresses strong views on the dangers to women of too much novel reading:

> We consider the general run of Novels as utterly unfit for you. Instruction they convey none. They paint scenes of pleasure and passion altogether improper for you to behold, even with the mind's eye. Their descriptions are often loose and luscious in a high degree; their representations of love between the sexes are almost universally overstrained. All is dotage, or despair; or else ranting swelled into burlesque. In short, the majority of their lovers are either mere lunatics, or mock-heroes.
>
> (Fordyce, *Sermons to Young Women,* 1796 edn, pp.149–50)

Fordyce is clear that the female intellect is limited and that 'war, commerce, politics, exercises of strength and dexterity, abstract philosophy, and all the abstruser sciences, are more properly the province of men' (Ibid.). History does have a value for women, and moral essays, such as those found in *The Spectator,* are particularly recommended:

> I need not here name the Spectator, or those who have followed him with various success in the same track; many of them ingenious, some of them masterly writers. How much are both sexes indebted to their elegant pens, for a species of instruction better fitted perhaps than most others of human device, to delight and improve at the same moment; such is its extent, its diversity, its familiarity, its ease, its playful manner, its immediate reference to scenes and circumstances with which we are every day conversant!
>
> (Ibid., p.280)

However, even if many households owned copies of Fordyce's Sermons, we can not be sure that they were read or their instructions obeyed. Jane Austen inserts a joke at his expense in *Pride and Prejudice* when the ponderous clergyman, Mr Collins, is invited to read to the Bennet sisters:

> Mr. Bennet's expectations were fully answered. His cousin was as absurd as he had hoped, and he listened to him with the keenest

enjoyment, maintaining at the same time the most resolute composure of countenance, and except in an occasional glance at Elizabeth, requiring no partner in his pleasure.

By tea-time however the dose had been enough, and Mr. Bennet was glad to take his guest into the drawing-room again, and when tea was over, glad to invite him to read aloud to the ladies. Mr. Collins readily assented, and a book was produced; but on beholding it, (for everything announced it to be from a circulating library,) he started back, and begging pardon, protested that he never read novels. – Kitty stared at him, and Lydia exclaimed. – Other books were produced, and after some deliberation he chose Fordyce's Sermons. Lydia gaped as he opened the volume, and before he had, with very monotonous solemnity, read three pages, she interrupted him with, 'Do you know, mama, that my uncle Philips talks of turning away Richard, and if he does, Colonel Forster will hire him.'

(Austen, *Pride and Prejudice*, 1990 edn, p.60)

Mr Collins's choice of Fordyce clearly marks the author out as a subject for mirth, even if it is the sillier of the Bennet sisters, Lydia and Kitty – the ones perhaps most in need of the advice of conduct literature – who are most outraged by his choice. Mr Collins 'was not a sensible man' we are told at the beginning of the next chapter, and his horror at the prospect of a novel from a circulating library is clearly presented as absurd. Yet in this brief scene we can also learn something of the circumstances in which many women read. Reading here is a public activity, not subject to individual choice. But the outrage of Lydia and Kitty makes it clear that in this household, at least, the girls' choice of novels from the circulating library usually won out over conduct literature.

It is appropriate that Mr Collins is offered, in the first place, a novel from a circulating library as this was the most important source of books for middle-class women. Whereas non-fictional writing like history, geography or essays (the kind of writing that Fordyce approves of for women) was considered worth buying, current novels, especially the expensive novels in several volumes, were not usually seen as valuable enough to buy. Gary Kelly describes how circulating libraries were commonplace by the second half of the eighteenth century. 'By 1800 humble circulating libraries could be found even in small towns and villages' (Kelly, *English Fiction of the Romantic Period*, 1989, p.4). Although the greater proportion of titles offered by these libraries was non-fiction there is evidence that most of the books borrowed were novels. There also seem to have been as many men who used circulating libraries as women. Nevertheless, it was the effects of novels and of circulating libraries on middle-class women that worried moralists, both male and female.

The rise of the magazine was probably the other greatest influence on women's reading in the period. Magazines were very widely distributed and read in the Romantic period, and a major factor in the great increase in reading and writing among the upper and middle ranks of society. From early in the eighteenth century, magazines had appealed to women readers; indeed there were a large number specifically aimed at women. They published writing on a wide range of subjects and forms, including both poetry and prose. Kelly lists the following topics as common in the miscellanies: 'history, current events, biography, moral essays, fashion, exploration, science, agricultural and industrial 'improvements', the arts – including painting, theatre, gardening, *belles lettres* – and guidance in matters of manners, fashion, taste and criticism' (Ibid., p.2). Magazines were inexpensive and probably as important, especially for provincial readers, as circulating libraries as a source of fiction and other kinds of writing. Much fiction by female authors was published in magazines in serialized form in an attempt to exploit the popularity of known authors. Some magazines encouraged readers to submit work, and towards the end of the eighteenth century some relied almost exclusively on the work of amateurs (for which they did not pay). Although this development clearly encouraged a new group of women to see themselves as authors, it has been argued that it also tended to threaten the status and earning power of professional female authors, for whom magazine work provided a significant part of their livelihood (see Turner, *Living by the Pen*, 1992). Wollstonecraft, who became an editorial assistant at *The Analytical Review* in 1787, saw herself as 'the first of a new genus', a fully professional woman journalist, and she was not always enthusiastic, perhaps not surprisingly, about the efforts of the amateur writers. But, as Todd points out, other women writers also contributed to magazines which were not specifically aimed at women in the last decades of the eighteenth century. These included the novelist and essayist Mary Hays (1760–1843) who wrote for *The Edinburgh Review* (Todd, *The Sign of Angellica*, 1989, p.220). With the rise of the famous periodicals like the *Edinburgh*, the *Quarterly*, and the *London Magazine* after 1800, the status of magazine journalism rose, writing for them became increasingly professionalized and it seems that the proportion of women writing for such magazines declined in the process.

The hierarchy of genres

Women writers frequently worked in a range of genres, producing perhaps poetry, journalism and didactic or children's literature as well as novels. The reason for this spread of work was partly financial, because few women writers could hope to maintain a middle-class lifestyle on the money they could earn from novels. But, although many entered the public arena as writers through poetry or other forms of literature, the novel probably gave the largest number of women the chance to become authors. By the end of the eighteenth century, the novel was a form that was strongly associated with women writers and at which they excelled.

This does not mean that all women writers wanted to be thought of as novelists, even if they had published novels, for the novel had a fairly low status until after 1800. Wollstonecraft who published one novel in her lifetime, and was working on another at the time of her death, is dismissive of feminine qualities that may have been considered as attributes for successful novelists. Femininity, according to Wollstonecraft, is characterized by certain mental habits, of which she singles out a female 'disregard of order' caused by a lack of education. Women, she thinks, lack the power to generalize and rely too much on 'sheer observations on real life'. The characteristic mental habits of women are ones that she ascribes, in *A Vindication of the Rights of Woman,* to their domestic and social spheres:

> Led by their dependent situation and domestic employments more into society, what they learn is rather by snatches; and as learning is with them, in general, only a secondary thing, they do not pursue any one branch with that persevering ardour necessary to give vigour to the faculties and clearness to the judgement.
>
> (Todd and Butler, *The Works of Mary Wollstonecraft,* 1989, p.92)

But 'sheer observations on real life' might be rather a good preparation for writing novels. Jane Austen, in the famous defence of the women's novel in *Northanger Abbey,* focuses on its ability to observe real life as its greatest strength as a genre. She claims that novels can reveal 'the greatest powers of the mind'.

You might like to compare Austen's account of the relative value of different kinds of literature (poetry, history, *The Spectator* and novels) with Fordyce's recommendations, which you read in the previous section:

> Although our productions have afforded more extensive and unaffected pleasure than those of any other literary corporation in the world, no species of composition has been so much decried. From pride, ignorance, or fashion, our foes are almost as many as our readers. And while the abilities of the nine-hundredth abridger of the History of England, or of the man who collects and publishes in a volume some dozen lines of Milton, Pope, and Prior, with a paper from the *Spectator,* and a chapter from Sterne, are eulogized by a thousand pens, – there seems almost a general wish of decrying the capacity and undervaluing the labour of the novelist, and of slighting the performances which have only genius, wit, and taste to recommend them. 'I am no novel reader – I seldom look into novels – Do not imagine that *I* often read novels – It is really very well for a novel.' – Such is the common cant. – 'And what are you reading, Miss – ?' 'Oh! it is only a novel!' replies the young lady; while she lays down her book with affected indifference, or momentary shame. – 'It is only Cecilia, or Camilla, or Belinda'; or, in short, only some work in which the greatest powers of the mind are displayed, in which the most thorough knowledge of human nature, the happiest delineation of its varieties, the liveliest effusions of wit and humour are conveyed to the world in the best chosen language. Now, had the same young lady been engaged with a volume of the *Spectator,* instead of such a work, how proudly would she have produced the book, and told its name; though the chances must be against her being occupied by any part of that voluminous publication, of which either the matter or manner would not disgust a young person of taste: the substance of its papers so often consisting in the statement of improbable circumstances, unnatural characters, and topics of conversation, which no longer concern any one living; and their language, too, frequently so coarse as to give no very favourable idea of the age that could endure it.
>
> (Austen, *Northanger Abbey,* 1990 edn, pp.21–2)

Look carefully at the different claims that Austen makes for the women's novel and at the case she makes against other recommended kinds of reading for women. **Which are the key words that Austen uses to try to persuade the reader of her case (look especially at how she uses 'only')?**

_D i s c u s s i o n_

Austen first of all reminds us that novels offer us 'pleasure' (a reward undervalued by the conduct writers). But she then goes on to make serious claims for women's novels (by which I mean novels both written and read by women). They are 'performances which have *only* genius, wit and taste to recommend them' (my emphasis). Now 'genius' may not be used here in the modern sense of the exceptional, inspired writer, but it is still a brave claim. The word 'taste' suggests that the reader is discerning and discriminating, like the writer. After quoting imagined women readers (picking up their apologetic 'onlys') Austen goes on to still greater claims: 'only some work in which the greatest powers of the mind are displayed, in which the most thorough knowledge of human nature, the happiest delineation of its varieties, the liveliest effusions of wit and humour are conveyed to the world in the best chosen language'. The string of superlatives establish the claim for the women's novel to stand at the top of the hierarchy of genres.

By the way, *Cecilia* and *Camilla* are novels by Burney and *Belinda* is the novel by Edgeworth I referred to earlier in this chapter. Unlike Burney in her Preface to *Evelina* (see p.93 above), Austen pays tribute to other women novelists and chooses their works as the context within which she wishes her own to be judged. In effect she outlines a female tradition for the novel in her own time. ■

Remember, Wollstonecraft lamented the fact that women tended to lack the abstract power to generalize and to order their thoughts, relying instead on observation, whereas Austen *celebrated* this power of observation as both distinctively feminine and superior to the masculine power to order. But now compare Edgeworth's account of her methods of composition. In a letter to Mrs Stark dated 1834, Edgeworth explains that she has seldom used a notebook when working on a novel:

> In short [...] the process of combination, generalization, invention, was
> carried on always in my head best. Wherever I brought in, bodily
> unaltered, as I have sometimes done, facts from real life, or sayings, or
> recorded observations of my own, I have almost always found them
> objected to by good critics as unsuited to the character, or in some
> way *de trop*. Sometimes, when the first idea of a character was taken
> from life from some original, and the characteristic facts noted down,
> or even noted only in my head, I have found it necessary entirely to
> alter these, not only from propriety, to avoid individual resemblance,
> but from the sense that the character would be only an exception to
> general feeling and experience – not a rule.
>
> (Wu, *Romanticism*, 1994, p.164)

Now consider where this places Edgeworth in the debate about women's mental powers. **Do you think her ideas are closer to Wollstonecraft's or to Austen's?**

Edgeworth seems keen to show that 'facts from real life, or sayings, or recorded observations of my own' are not the main material of her fiction. What is important is the 'process of combination, generalization, invention' which in the end provides 'general feeling and experience'. This emphasis puts her closer to Wollstonecraft as she too values generalization above observation. ∎

Both Austen and Wollstonecraft are keen to defend women as writers and readers. But whereas Wollstonecraft accepts the conventional hierarchy of kinds of knowledge and laments the failure of women to achieve the kind of education that men have, Austen celebrates a kind of mental power and a kind of writing which she sees as both distinctively feminine and as universally valuable in its understanding of 'human nature'. Both writers are well aware that there is a hierarchy of genres implicit in their time. Just as Fuseli saw history painting as being superior to the private and domestic genre of portrait painting, so Wollstonecraft values the ability to generalize over 'sheer observations on real life'. And Austen recognizes, though she does not share, the assumption that the essay, history and poetry are seen as more prestigious, more intellectually respectable forms than the novel.

One of the reasons why the novel was seen as a less important genre than the essay or poetry may have been that it was dominated by women writers and readers. In the eighteenth century, the period of the rise of the novel as a literary form, it seems likely that the majority of novels were actually written by women. As writers, women did not feel the need for a classical education (deemed necessary to writing many kinds of poetry) before embarking on a novel. And the novel's relatively low status meant that it was not too threatening a task. Moreover there was the possibility of earning money from novel writing in a society in which opportunities for female employment were all too limited. As readers, women could gain access to novels, even those which were not cheap, through the circulating libraries.

Lovell argues that this dominance of women novelists in the eighteenth century was lost as novel writing gained status in the early years of the nineteenth century:

> The preponderance of women among eighteenth-century novelists, combined with the low status of this 'literary trade', suggests that at this period of the novel's first expansion, novel-writing might have become a feminized occupation, with all the characteristics of such occupations – low pay and low status [...] But this feminization of fiction was resisted. Men were never less than a substantial minority of its producers, possibly around one third. As fiction proved popular and profitable, and as it won its literary credentials, so men moved back into a position of numerical dominance. By the 1840s the proportion of women producers of fiction had been reduced to about 20 per cent.
>
> (Lovell, *Consuming Fiction*, 1987, p.43)

Walter Scott is an example of a novelist from the early nineteenth century who was accorded a literary status far greater than that of the women novelists, such as Edgeworth, from whom he learnt and whose work he admired. By the early nineteenth century, many new novels were being taken seriously as literature, reviewed and discussed in leading periodicals.

While poetry may have enjoyed greater prestige than the novel during the early Romantic period and the novel was in some ways seen as a feminine genre, there was scope, before 1800, for women poets to be published in magazines. However, today there is no consensus on whether the Romantic period was one that saw the eclipse of women's poetry or one in which it throve. Certainly, later poets such as Keats and Byron seem to have been concerned to mark their poetry as being written by men for male readers. Critics, including Lonsdale, have written of such attempts by Keats who, rejecting the advice of his friend Richard Woodhouse, revised a key stanza in 'The Eve of St Agnes' making the action more sexually explicit. In a letter to John Taylor, Woodhouse wrote:

> though there are no improper expressions, but all is left to inference; and though, profanely speaking, the interest on the reader's imagination is greatly heightened – yet I do apprehend it will render the poem unfit for ladies, and indeed scarcely to be mentioned to them among the 'things that are'. He says he does not want ladies to read his poetry; that he writes for men …

> (Wu, *Romanticism*, 1994, p.714)

Woodhouse seems to have been aware of the importance of the female audience for poetry in terms of marketing Keats's work. But despite, or perhaps because of this, Keats was insistent on making the change which marks the poem out as not available to women. (You will be considering further this aspect of Keats's work in Chapter Six.) Similarly, whereas Byron's early poetry was a favourite with women readers (as we can tell from passages copied by women into their commonplace books – collections of favourite passages from their reading) the bawdy *Don Juan* published in 1819 was considered entirely unsuitable for women readers. Byron's many female fans were excluded by a poem with an explicitly sexual theme. The poem also reveals Byron's hostility to the gentility of a literary culture in England which was heavily influenced by feminine taste and rules of propriety.

These second generation Romantic poets seem to re-enact Wordsworth's anxieties about being subsumed within a literary culture adapted to the powerful new market provided by women readers. And even though Wordsworth is insistent that the true poet is a man speaking to men, Keats and Byron restate this using a new emphasis on sexuality to enforce the gendering of their later work as poetry for men. What may explain the anxieties of both generations of Romantic poets about female writers and readers is the fear of cultural decline that appeared also in Fuseli's Academy lectures. Thus Wordsworth and (later on) Keats and Byron were anxious to define their own literary production as something different from the mass of female-dominated literary output.

Conclusion

Critics such as Curran, who reject the views of literary worth established by the academic study of Romantic literature in this century, see the period as one dominated by women's writing in many genres. Yet those who are concerned also with the changing status of women's writing, like Lonsdale, tend to paint a bleaker picture of the fortunes of women's writing in the Romantic period. Clearly there is a considerable amount of shared culture between men and women throughout the period. It could well be argued that 'high' or 'male' Romanticism (as it is sometimes called) – the works of Wordsworth and Coleridge, Keats, Byron and Shelley – borrows significantly from female authors and 'feminine' types of literature (such as sensibility) even though it seeks to mark its own works as masculine and to sever the association with female writers and readers. Women were still writing and publishing towards the end of the Romantic period, as the prominence of the poets Felicia Hemans and Letitia Landon in the 1820s and 1830s demonstrates. Yet it may be that the kinds of writing they produce lack the adventurousness of many of the female authors of the 1780s and 1790s. The writing of Wollstonecraft, in the genres of political debate, conduct literature, journalism and novels, is hard to parallel in the years after 1800, which were characterized by an increasingly firm statement of the doctrine of the 'separation of spheres'.

Further Reading

Jones, V. (ed.) (1990) *Women in the Eighteenth Century: Constructions of Femininity*, Routledge.

Kelly, G. (1989) *English Fiction of the Romantic Period 1788–1830*, Longman.

Kelly, G. (1993) *Women, Writing and Revolution 1790–1827*, Clarendon Press.

Todd, J. (1989) *The Sign of Angellica: Women, Writing and Fiction, 1660–1800*, Virago.

Turner, C. (1992) *Living by the Pen: Women Writers in the Eighteenth Century*, Routledge.

Reading The Prelude

by Stephen Bygrave

In this discussion of Wordsworth's long poem *The Prelude*, I want to pursue some of the issues raised in Chapters Three and Four. In Chapter Three we saw the importance of the aesthetic of 'Imagination' (with a capital letter) in some of the Romantic writers' theoretical defences of their work, and in Chapter Four we looked at the situation of writers, particularly of women writers, in the 1790s. Here we turn to a monumental figure in most accounts of British Romanticism, William Wordsworth. His long poem *The Prelude* is much concerned with memory, and crucially with memories of the 1790s, the decade of revolution. Near the end of the poem Wordsworth writes that its theme has been imagination.

The Prelude is long, but so central to British Romanticism that I want to refer to much of it that you won't be asked to read. I will be asking you to consider 'Tintern Abbey', an earlier poem, first, then to look at two crucial passages from the middle and end of *The Prelude*. Finally, I want to place these passages by looking at the accounts of London and of the French Revolution which come between them. I want to see them in the context of the much longer work from which they come, because it has a story to tell. In reading *The Prelude* we will be looking for the first time at a narrative poem.

The Prelude *as narrative*

In the Introduction to this book I drew a basic distinction between lyric and narrative. Broadly, lyrics are poems written in the first person, which represent a feeling; narratives may be written in the first or third person and tell a story. Almost all stories will involve encounters with people and show their interaction. So narrative has a *social* dimension. While lyrics may be about private experience, narratives are likely to raise more public issues. We will be looking at the issues of lyric and narrative in Romantic writing in Chapter Six, but it is worth returning to the basic distinction as a way of thinking about Wordsworth's *Prelude*. The poem is lyrical in that many of its most memorable sections concentrate on the actions and feelings of an individual at a unique or typical moment. At the same time, it is a narrative in that it tells the story of Wordsworth's early life. The first two books deal with his memories from earliest childhood to the age of seventeen; the poem then recounts his experiences as a student in Cambridge, periods of living in London and elsewhere, his residence in France from 1791 to 1792, and finally how his imagination was 'impaired and restored' by these experiences.

The Prelude is autobiographical then, but it is not strictly an autobiography. It misses out many of the chief events that we would expect from a biography or autobiography – there is no mention, for example, of Wordsworth's courtship and marriage, nor of his love affair in France with Annette Vallon, which produced a child. Nor does it relate events in the order in which they occurred. The poem actually begins in the present rather than the past, and continues to place the experiences (and errors) of the past against present wisdom. In the poem Wordsworth remembers specific incidents but often suspends the story in order to meditate on their significance in the present. It is concerned with memory, then, rather than merely recounting memories.

Wordsworth worked on *The Prelude* over a period of fifty years, but never published it in his lifetime. There are three complete versions:

1   a two-part version written in England and in Germany in 1798–9;

2   a thirteen-book version completed in 1805 but not published until 1926;

3   a much-revised fourteen-book version, the result of major rewriting over some thirty years (1816–19, 1832 and 1839). This version was published by Wordsworth's literary executors after his death in 1850.

The second is the one that we will be considering here. (Unless otherwise indicated, quotations in this chapter are from Reed, *The Thirteen-Book Prelude*, 1991.) It is important to remember that the 1805 version of *The Prelude* that we will be considering was known only to Wordsworth's circle of friends. During his lifetime the long poem known to his contemporary public was *The Excursion*, published in 1814. When *The Prelude* was published after Wordsworth's death in 1850, Blake, Coleridge, Keats, Shelley and Byron were all long dead, and Queen Victoria was in the thirteenth year of her reign. Other works published in England that year were centrally Victorian texts such as Tennyson's *In Memoriam* and Dickens's *David Copperfield*.

There are two main reasons for choosing the 1805 text of the poem. The first is simply practical. The 1805 version is now the one most widely available. In an edition which reprints all three major versions, the editors suggest why, in common with most other editors, they prefer the 1805 text:

> In stylistic quality and tone [...] 1850 is very different from 1805. In successive revisions Wordsworth had smoothed out what had come to seem rough spots, clarified the syntax, elaborated the detail, and most conspicuously, had toned down, by touches of Christian piety, the poem Wordswor divine sufficiency of the human mind in its interchange with Nature.
>
> (Wordsworth, Abrams and Gill, *Wordsworth: The Prelude*, 1979,
> p.xii)

We will be looking at the 1805 version not because of its superior 'stylistic quality and tone' nor for its presumed authenticity, but for another, less subjective reason. Though it was not published until after Wordsworth's death, the 1805 version was known to his circle of friends, including Thomas De Quincey and Coleridge (whose poem 'To William Wordsworth', records his reaction on hearing Wordsworth recite from it). This chapter will suggest that *The Prelude* is a dialogue – or, at least, half of a dialogue – between friends. Coleridge applied the term 'conversation poem' to some of his own poems and that, in part, is how *The Prelude* is considered here.

When completed, the 1805 version of the poem was headed 'Poem, Title not yet fixed upon, by William Wordsworth Addressed to S.T. Coleridge'. We will turn to the importance of the poem being addressed to a named friend later. For now, we should know that it was given the title *The Prelude* by Wordsworth's widow. It is an appropriate title for a poem about how someone became a poet, and it also indicates that Wordsworth thought of it as no more than the preparation for a much longer work. Both *The Prelude* and *The Excursion* had been envisaged as portions of a great philosophical poem on man, nature and society that Coleridge had urged him to write but which was never completed. This was to have been called *The Recluse*. (Instead of this much longer poem, as someone pointed out, we have a prelude to it and an excursion from it.) *The Recluse* was to have been a massive poem in three parts. As it stands, *The Prelude* is in itself an epic poem.

Milton, as I have said (p.39 above), was the example by which Romantic writers tried to define their role; he represented political as much as poetic power to them. *Paradise Lost* is a blank verse epic about a revolution that failed. So is *The Prelude*. At the end of *Paradise Lost* Adam and Eve look back at Eden, from which they have been expelled, and face the future:

> Some natural tears they dropped, but wiped them soon;
> The world was all before them, where to choose
> Their place of rest, and providence their guide:
> They hand in hand with wandering steps and slow,
> Through Eden took their solitary way [...]
> (*Paradise Lost* XII, ll.645–9; Fowler, 1968, p.642)

Near the start of Wordsworth's *Prelude* these lines occur:

> *The earth is all before me*: with a heart
> Joyous, nor scar'd at its own liberty
> I look about; and should the *guide* I chuse
> Be nothing better than a *wandering* cloud
> I cannot miss my *way*.
> (I, ll.15–19; italics added)

The italicized phrases in these lines from the start of *The Prelude* allude directly to the end of *Paradise Lost*. As Milton supplements the Bible, so Wordsworth supplements Milton. The fallen world in which *Paradise Lost* ends already promises to be 'restored': its last two books have promised the Second Coming of Christ. Wordsworth makes his promise explicit by placing himself where Adam and Eve stood: in nature; but this is no longer punishment but 'liberty'. We will be considering further parallels as we go on.

When we describe a book or film as 'epic' we mean something that is of great length but also of great scope. An epic poem is not just long, but is concerned with great events – wars, the rise and fall of nations. With epic, we expect heroic actions and a hero to perform them. Now *The Prelude* is certainly of great length and deals with great events (the French Revolution and its aftermath), but they are not in the foreground. They form part of an autobiographical narrative. And the poem's hero doesn't perform any conventionally heroic actions. In place of battles and wars we have a psychological epic. In 1805 Wordsworth wrote in a letter that the poem would be 'not much less than 9,000 lines … an alarming length! And a thing unprecedented in Literary history that a man should talk so much about himself' (de Selincourt, *The Letters of William and Dorothy Wordsworth*, 1967, p.586).

As I have said, I am not going to ask you to read the whole of the 'alarming length' of *The Prelude*. I want to look now at an earlier and shorter work, 'Tintern Abbey', the last poem in the 1798 *Lyrical Ballads*. This will provide a way of introducing what I've called the 'themes' of *The Prelude*, imagination and memory.

'Tintern Abbey' and the 'spots of time': memory and imagination

Like *The Prelude*, 'Tintern Abbey' is a meditative poem written in blank verse and in the first person. It is a poem that leads up to *The Prelude* in a number of ways, as we shall see. Please now read 'Tintern Abbey'. There are three features of the poem that it will be helpful to bear in mind as we think about *The Prelude*.

We can consider the first by looking again at the most overtly autobiographical part of the poem, the long central passage from line 59 to about line 112. **According to Wordsworth what has been lost and what gained?**

Discussion

The memory is not just of five years ago, as in line 1, but before that. Wordsworth remembers a more direct contact with nature, a time when 'nature then […] To me was all in all' (ll.73, 76). It was an 'appetite' (l.81). The senses were more than enough; there was no need for the 'remoter charm' (l.82) of thought. But this is no longer the case.

There is consolation for this loss. There is a gain which has balanced it and is 'abundant recompense' (l.89), and that is thought. Wordsworth perceives a nature from which 'humanity' is no longer absent. It is this which he *hears* when he *looks* (ll.90–91). Nature is not now something to be passively perceived (ll.103–8), but is 'interfused' with the perceiver (l.97). There is a list of spectacular natural objects and events (sunsets, ocean, air and sky), which concludes 'And in the mind of man' (l.100). In the second half of the poem a religious vocabulary ('spirit', 'soul', 'prayer', 'faith', 'blessing', 'worshipper', 'holier') is applied to nature and its interaction with memory. This is a movement outwards towards the 'sublime' – the experience of a power in nature or religion that is greater than oneself – and it culminates in a 'moral' restoration. ■

For the second feature, we need to consider the title. The poem was published under the title 'Lines Written a Few Miles above Tintern Abbey, on Revisiting the Banks of the Wye during a Tour, 13 July 1798'. I've called the poem by the shorthand name by which it is usually known. **It would be reasonable to expect that the poem would describe or at least tell us something about that place, but does it?**

Discussion

The poem's full title locates it specifically, as do the titles of many eighteenth-century poems describing a landscape. But it locates it in time as well as space. On reading you find that actually it is not a landscape poem: descriptions of landscape come only at the beginning and at the end, and as it were 'frame' the poem. (As with 'Composed upon Westminster Bridge' and 'Anecdote for Fathers' there is a note, dictated by Wordsworth to Isabella Fenwick, which reveals that the poem was not written in front of the location given in the title.) In fact, the poem is principally concerned not with space at all but with time.

The poem ends in the same location in space and time in which it began, but it has not stayed there in between. It gives a date as well as a place of composition and begins by referring to a visit five years earlier. In 1793 Wordsworth had just returned from France, excited by what was happening there. Looking back in 1798, though, there is no overt reference to politics. The poem, as I have said, is concerned with time – with memory. ■

Thirdly, the poem concludes by turning to another person. Why is this?

Discussion

The poem is narrated in the first person, but the movement towards the sublime that we noticed above is followed immediately by a turn to another person and to a more intimate mode of address. As we'll see, there is a similar procedure in *The Prelude*. As in the Westminster Bridge sonnet, the poet had seemed alone. He prefers the repeated 'seclusion' (ll.6–7) to 'the fretful stir' (l.53) and 'the din/Of towns and cities' (ll.26–7), so the appearance of his 'dear, dear sister' Dorothy (l.122) is quite a surprise.

The poem is concerned, as we've noticed, with time. In 'Tintern Abbey' it is not the case that memory is just a matter of the past being remembered in the present; there is also a desire to store up experience, so that what happens now (which includes the experience of remembering) will be remembered in the future. All these different time scales can be bewildering for the poet (and perhaps for the reader as well). Wordsworth's sister is a reminder of continuity in all this. The turn to Dorothy is made so that she can confirm what would otherwise be a wholly private feeling of significance. It is important that she should be a 'real' person, someone with whom Wordsworth is intimate and who links him to his past. Having been through the same experiences, she too will remember what he remembers. He can be sure of her response, sure that she will understand.

I put that word 'real' in scare quotes though, because Dorothy is also a function of the poem. She is not allowed to speak, and when William looks at her he sees only himself (ll.120–21). She has a kind of mythical function. The turn to her comes with the phrase 'for thou art with me' (l.115) in which Wordsworth in the Wye valley echoes the Biblical psalmist: 'Yea, though I walk through the valley of the shadow of death I shall fear no evil, for thou art with me' (Psalm 23). If Dorothy had not been present, she (or someone else) would have had to be put there; if Dorothy had not existed it would have been necessary to invent her. ■

So, we've discussed three points arising from 'Tintern Abbey'.

1 The way imagination and memory are crucial and how these relate to nature.

2 The way the poem alludes to a specific time and place but goes on to elude that location.

3 The way the poem depends on addressing another person who can validate or guarantee the experience it records.

We will pursue all three of these points as we go on to look at *The Prelude*. But it is the first of them, the concern with imagination and memory, which is perhaps most evident in the longer poem.

We saw in 'Tintern Abbey' that space was succeeded by time – that the poem was not a description of landscape but was concerned with memory. Nature was important not as the physical features of a landscape – hills, trees, rivers, and so on – but as a 'presence' (1.95) and a 'spirit' (1.101) which produces a moral or even a religious sense. In memory natural objects become 'forms of beauty' (1.24) which can be returned to and which produce 'sensations sweet' (1.20) when they are. Both memory and nature have a moral function. Later, we will look at the way Wordsworth's response to a city (London) and to the French Revolution turns into a concern with an unchanging 'nature', and we will look at the effect of the whole poem being addressed to Coleridge.

The Prelude *and 'spots of time'*

On page 116 we considered Wordsworth's revisions to *The Prelude*. The 1799 version is in two parts, which mostly correspond to the first two books of the 1805 version. It is less discursive (or more 'lyrical') than later versions, a collection of memories of childhood incidents and activities in which nature seems to exist for the purpose of educating the child. The 1805 *Prelude* is a narrative poem rather than a collection of lyrics. The longer version doesn't only replace the lyrical with the epic but makes explicit the poet's unresolved struggles with social and political events. There is in *The Prelude* what we saw in 'Composed by the side of Grasmere Lake' in Chapter Two: a kind of resolution or consolation in 'nature'. Wordsworth has a reputation as a 'nature poet'. Despite this, there is hardly any description of nature in the sense of natural *objects* in *The Prelude* – a fact for which he apologizes near the end of the poem:

> for Nature's secondary grace,
> That outward illustration which is hers,
> Hath hitherto been barely touch'd upon.
> (XIII, ll.282–4)

If 'nature's secondary grace' is what it looks like, its primary grace is what it *does*. It is active rather than static, a power rather than an object. As such, it co-operates with the powers of the senses ('both what they half-create/And what perceive' as he has it in 'Tintern Abbey', ll.107–8). Wordsworth can see his childhood in terms drawn from nature, though nature offers an education that is not simply beneficent: 'Fair seed-time had my soul, and I grew up/Foster'd alike by beauty and by fear' (I, ll.306–7). (We saw one example of nature's awesome power in our discussion of the stolen boat episode, pp.67–8 above.)

As I suggested at the start, most of the events remembered by the poem are not obviously dramatic. Events have a private significance which the poem makes public. The early books of *The Prelude* are concerned with recreating childhood experiences through memory. Often what is recalled are physical activities – snaring woodcock, stealing a boat, skating. Others recall sights which made a powerful impression at the time but were not understood; some of these are obviously dramatic – the recovery of a drowned man (V, ll.450–81), others less so – a girl with a pitcher on her head on a windy day (XI, ll.279–316). These episodes are what Wordsworth in a famous passage calls 'spots of time'. **Please read this passage now (XI, ll.258–79).**

D i s c u s s i o n

The power of memory is evident in the words used to describe it: 'renovating', 'nourish'd' and 'repair'd'. Its power is moral. The 'spots of time' are a kind of invisible mending for the mind. 'Spots' is rather an odd metaphor. Time is a process; by definition it is mobile. But a 'spot' sounds like a place, and for Wordsworth it is something unmoving, which can be returned to. The 'spots of time' are continuing sources of moral strength. Wordsworth calls them 'the hiding-places of my power' (XI, l.335).

These lines originally appeared in the 1799 *Prelude* in a version which is much briefer, and in some ways more concise ('Such moments chiefly seem to have their date/In our first childhood'). There, spots of time retain a 'fructifying' virtue rather than the 'renovating' virtue of the 1805 version. (An interim version used the term 'vivifying'.) 'Fructifying' means making fruitful; it seems to be prospective, to be looking forward where the term 'renovating' appears retrospective, to be looking back. The passage then occurred earlier in the poem. Moved to the final book in 1805, the 'spots of time' are described long after we are familiar with them.

Again and again the poem presents us with moments at which some uncanny relationship with nature is recognized but not understood. These can be uncovered or discovered from the past to provide future sustenance: 'I would enshrine the spirit of the past/For future restoration' (XI, ll.342–3). There is an example of this in a passage from Book II: Wordsworth writes that 'the soul,/Remembering how she felt, but what she felt/Remembering not, retains an obscure sense/Of possible sublimity' (ll.334–7). The Discharged Soldier has a similar faculty: 'Remembering the importance of his theme/But feeling it no longer' (IV, ll.477–8). Perhaps then these events are like the psychoanalytic notion of childhood trauma – the poem's subtitle after all is 'the growth of a poet's mind'. ∎

In 'Tintern Abbey' we saw the way memory re-presents experience. In 'revisiting' a place where significant experiences occurred, Wordsworth revisits those experiences themselves. In revisiting them in poetry they can be understood in a way not possible at the time. In Book IV *The Prelude* there is an epic simile for memory of looking over the edge of a boat into the water and being unable to separate 'the shadow from the substance' (ll.247–78). This analogy draws on the common metaphor of 'reflecting' for thinking or remembering. Remembering is not passive but requires that the mind select from and discriminate among the images that memory presents to it. Also, as with looking into any reflecting surface, what the viewer sees is her or himself.

Keats wrote in a famous letter of 'the Wordsworthian or egotistical sublime', by which he meant the dominance not just of a style but of a personality, of a power that could not be separated from personality. As we've said, he can't have been referring to *The Prelude,* but we can see instances of what Keats noticed throughout the poem. For example, Wordsworth claims a privileged relationship with nature. He has a sense of *election,* in the religious sense of being among the chosen. The opening of the poem records Wordsworth's conviction that his 'spirit' is 'singled out, as it might seem,/For holy services' (I, ll.62–3). In Cambridge he experiences 'A feeling that I was not for that hour/Nor for that place' (III, ll.80–81), that he was 'a chosen son' (l.82). In the famous 'Was it for this ...' passage (I, ll.271–304), which began the 1799 version of the poem and alludes to the opening of Milton's *Samson Agonistes,* Wordsworth records the sense that his early life has itself been a prelude to his writing a great poem. The early books give an account of a kind of self-sufficient egotism. Nature is the teacher, the poet a star pupil.

Later this direct relationship between the self and nature, experienced in childhood and remembered as 'spots of time', is dissolved. We will be looking at how this happens. Wordsworth came to feel that a misplaced hope for political liberation had distanced him from 'nature' and from the poetic liberation he records at the beginning of the poem. Thus in one sense the whole of *The Prelude* is a poem of consolation, like 'Tintern Abbey' and 'Composed by the Side of Grasmere Lake'. In another sense it is about a crisis and a recovery, or as we'll see, a Fall followed by Redemption. But, as in 'Tintern Abbey', when the relationship with nature is recovered it is not as it was before. It is recovered by the intercession of a 'power' – a power of which the poet grows more confident as time passes and which is in interchange with a power in nature. Wordsworth doesn't claim to have been formed as a poet solely by the influence of inanimate objects but, as we'll see, in becoming a spectator of city life and of some of the events of the French Revolution he felt he had lost contact with nature.

Why did *The Prelude* need to be written at all? I suggested one answer to this question earlier by referring to the example of Milton. Wordsworth's poem has been seen as a secular version of the Christian scheme of Eden, Fall and Redemption that Milton treats in *Paradise Lost.* In *The Prelude,* memories of childhood would represent a lost Eden. *Paradise Lost is* a poem that attempts to understand the loss of Eden (the Fall) and offer consolation. In Wordsworth's poem as a whole there is a desire for a regained wholeness: 'Knowledge not purchased with the loss of power!' (V, l.449). But where and when the Fall has occurred is slower to be revealed. It comes, I think, in the account of Wordsworth's initial enthusiasm for and then disillusionment with the French Revolution in Books IX and X. But before we look at a fall, it is appropriate to look at some climbing.

The Prelude: *the mountain passages*

The passages that we are about to look at are accounts of crossing the Alps and of climbing Snowdon. They are sometimes referred to as the 'philosophical' passages in Wordsworth. But they are not philosophical in the sense that they follow a structure of logically connected argument. There may be an emotional connection to the argument, or it may follow or be part of a narrative. Both these passages recount imaginative experiences. They may even be mystical ones, and thus be difficult to talk about in rational terms. But we should not ignore the obvious. We saw how the speaker's high viewpoint in the Westminster Bridge sonnet gave us a way of talking about the poem. These passages are about mountains. Maybe their settings are metaphorical of the desire for transcendence that we identified in some of the Romantic lyrics we've looked at. Let's now consider these passages in turn.

Crossing the Alps

The first passage occurs in Book VI. Here the narrative is to do with the memory of a walking tour that the twenty-year-old Wordsworth took through France and Switzerland with his college friend Robert Jones in the summer of 1790. But, crucially, the events narrated don't end as the narrator expects and the narrative is then interrupted. Please now read the long passage from line 452 to line 572. **What feelings are recorded in the narrative?**

Discussion

A first disappointment is that Mont Blanc fails to live up to what had been expected: it is a 'soulless image' (l.454). The sight of the Vale of Chamonix to some extent compensates for this initial disappointment. It is a 'book' from which the young and old learn (ll.473–7).

The passage which follows is about two things: disappointment – and imagination. Setting out to cross the Alps by way of the Simplon Pass, the travellers are separated from their companions and eventually meet a peasant who tells them they need to retrace their steps and descend. They have missed the exhilaration of reaching the highest point and made a wasted detour uphill. The account of a walk ending with the news that the walkers have crossed the Alps without knowing it is an account of 'dejection', of 'a deep and genuine sadness' (ll.491–2). The anticipation has been out of all proportion to the event itself, which is therefore an anti-climax. The account itself is rather prosaic – until it is interrupted, that is. ■

What is this apparent 'interruption' in the narrative (ll.525–9)?

Discussion

The narrative is broken for an address to 'Imagination!'. The warrant for this interruption is in Milton's *Paradise Lost,* in hymns like those to 'light' and 'wedded love':

Hail, holy light, offspring of heaven first-born,
Or of the eternal co-elemental beam [...]

Hail wedded love, mysterious law, true source
Of human offspring, sole propriety
In paradise of all things common else [...]
(III, l.2 and IV, l.750; Fowler, 1968, pp.141 and 240)

But why is imagination recognized here? The travellers learn that they have crossed the Alps without knowing it and suddenly there is that hymn to imagination. This passage was written in 1804 about a walking tour that had taken place in 1790. Hence the 'now' in line 531. What I have called an 'interruption' might in fact be crucial. The memory of fourteen years earlier might be vital in constructing 'imagination' in the present in which the poem is written. ■

What is it that 'imagination' can do that the actual experience, as recorded in the narrative, can't do?

Discussion

The experience has been a disappointment, or occurred without even being noticed. But as in 'Tintern Abbey' loss is transformed into gain as the poet is given a revelation of the power of the mind. What imagination does is to give a sight of something greater – 'the invisible world' (l.536). This can only be 'seen' when not looked for – and when not looked *at* – 'when the light of sense/Goes out in flashes' (ll.534–5).

In the narrative a gap has been crossed, and imaginatively something similar has happened. Wordsworth celebrates the way 'that power ... came ... athwart' him (ll.527–9). Imagination is that which crosses or bridges gaps – which joins the memory of 1790 to its later writing. ■

So imagination replaces or transcends the insufficient testimony of the senses that had made Mont Blanc such a disappointment. There is a kind of process of emancipation from the brute senses. As one critic writes: 'His failure of 1790 taught him gently what now (1804) literally *blinds* him; the independence of imagination from nature' (Hartman, *Wordsworth's Poetry*, 1964, p.41). This is a difficult point, but an important one. What Hartman is suggesting, I think, is that imagination has been excessive and has led to disappointment. But this does not mean that nature is real while the imagination just produces fantasies. On the contrary, by keeping faith with imagination Wordsworth is rewarded by an experience that more than compensates. Where imagination is unexpectedly recognized in nature itself the disappointment is overcome and Wordsworth gets the sublime experience he had been hoping for.

Present experience can be overwhelmingly immediate and needs to be refracted or softened by the memory. Only later can its significance be realized: in the present in which it is remembered, and in which the poem is written. There is an important statement of this early in the poem, in Book II. 'Things' overcome the senses at the time that they occur. Afterwards they may be represented to the imagination like a strain of music which is remembered rather than heard:

in all things
I saw one life, and felt that it was joy.
One song they sang, and it was audible,
Most audible then when the fleshly ear,
O'ercome by grosser prelude of that strain,
Forgot its functions, and slept undisturb'd.

(II, ll.429–34)

Now read these lines again. What other kind of ear can there be than a 'fleshly' one?

D i s c u s s i o n

The 'fleshly ear' must be opposed to something like 'the mind's ear' (just as we speak of 'the mind's eye'). In other words, imagination is required. Imagination is superior to the brute senses. In 'Tintern Abbey' we noticed a move from landscape to memory, from space to time. In that poem there was a move not only from space to time but from the eye to the ear, from sight to hearing. It was an 'eye made quiet' that recognized 'harmony', and was eventually able to 'see into the life of things' ('Tintern Abbey', ll.48–50). Such a seeing was a way of hearing 'the still, sad music of humanity' (ll.92). Here the ear has to 'sleep' to avoid being overcome by the 'grosser prelude' of experience. Only when it does so can the mind reflect upon sensory experiences rather than being bombarded by them. ■

So, at the first sight of Mont Blanc Wordsworth and his fellow-walker 'grieved'

To have a soulless image on the eye,
Which had usurp'd upon a living thought
That never more could be.

(VI, ll.454–6)

'A living thought' is clearly preferable to 'a soulless image': it is better to 'think' than merely to 'see'. A political vocabulary is applied to nature and the workings of the mind just as a vocabulary appropriate to 'Nature' is applied to the city and to political events, as we'll see. The word 'usurp' and its derivations might be an example of this: 'usurped' also occurs in the second of the mountain passages that we shall look at.

Imagination again moves the poet from place (which is disappointing) to time (in which everything is possible). Impotence in the present is succeeded by a future of infinite possibility. The 'living thought/That never more could be' (ll.455–6) is succeeded by an intimation of 'something ever-more about to be' (l.542). Time is lost as the travellers had lost their way. Or all time is future, a 'promise' (l.534) and an 'infinitude' (l.539). Natural objects are transformed by imagination. We might compare this passage (ll.556–72) with the earlier description of the Vale of Chamonix (ll.457–68), which seems to be a much more conventional playing with elements of pastoral. Here the senses can't cope with what the scene has become – the woods are of 'immeasurable height'. Time stands still ('woods decaying, never to be decay'd,/The stationary blasts of waterfalls', ll.557–8). The rocks mutter, the crags speak, and the stream raves. But to the mind all these

125

different and contradictory phenomena appear unified. They are all seen to be like the 'workings of one mind' (l.568). Again, they are to be read: they are *characters* of the great Apocalyps' (l.570). And that mind is like the divine mind – what Wordsworth says of Nature here (l.572) is drawn directly from what Milton says of God in *Paradise Lost*: 'Him first, him last, him midst and without end' (V,l.165, Fowler, 1968, p.265). Imagination is a unifying faculty: it is the faculty which fills in gaps, which makes whole what was fragmented, which supplies what was missing, which joins what was divided.

The ascent of Snowdon

Let's now turn to the second passage. The event described here occurred in 1791, before Wordsworth went to France, but it is placed out of sequence at the beginning of the final book of the poem and is in some ways its climax. Please read it now (XIII, ll.1–119).

The passage begins quietly and rather prosaically. It is a narrative, a holiday story. We are unprepared for the suddenness of the flash of light (l.39) and the view that follows. The point is that Wordsworth is not prepared for it either. Rather than the view that had been expected, the mist produces a different scene. This is a sea of mist that empties:

Into the Sea, the real Sea, that seem'd
To dwindle and give up its majesty,
Usurp'd upon as far as sight could reach.
(ll.49–51)

Then in the 'meditation' (l.66) which follows there is another crossing: from the view reached in the narrative to the vision of the 'mighty Mind' (l.69) that it resembles.

In an essay on Shakespeare's *Coriolanus* William Hazlitt wrote that 'the language of poetry naturally falls in with the language of power'. In Wordsworth's meditation we have literally a 'language of power'. The word 'power' itself is used repeatedly. The power in nature is first heard rather than seen: in the chasm is a 'voice' (l.59). Although such an exhibition of nature's domination must be felt even by the 'grossest minds', Wordsworth's comparison is hardly egalitarian. He claims that this power is the 'express resemblance' of a faculty borne by 'higher minds' (l.90). This godlike power (l.106) is the power of imagination. **But *where* does Wordsworth claim imagination is, and *what is it?***

D i s c u s s i o n

The word 'Imagination' is used first at line 65. Imagination is located in the 'breach' that separates the two 'seas'. (Compare 'that deep romantic chasm' through which the River Alph flows in Coleridge's 'Kubla Khan'.) Imagination is located in nature and by nature. We begin to learn what it is later in the passage: 'imagination ... is but another name for absolute strength' (XIII, ll.167–8). It is once again a relationship between nature and the individual. By this point we've forgotten that Wordsworth had been accompanied on his ascent of Snowdon. As in the passage from Book VI, having sought an experience of nature as in those early memories, Wordsworth has found, it seems, only himself. Certainly, imagination, as he conceives it, is possessed by very few.

At this moment of imaginative climax there is once again an allusion to Milton. Wordsworth finds himself on the shore

> of a *huge* sea of mist,
> Which meek and silent, rested at my feet:
> A hundred hills their dusky *backs upheaved*
> All over this still Ocean [...]
>
> (XIII, ll.40–46)

The italicized phrases allude to the account of the Creation in *Paradise Lost,* when on the third day God gathers the waters:

> Immediately the mountains huge appear
> Emergent, and their broad bare backs upheave
> Into the clouds, their tops ascend the sky
>
> (VII, ll.285–7; Fowler, p.374)

Here Wordsworth shares God's viewpoint. ∎

In Book XII Wordsworth has written that 'genius' exists by an 'interchange/Of peace and excitation' (ll.8–9) supported by nature. Nature is the origin of 'that energy' by which the genius:

> seeks the truth,
> Is rouzed, aspires, grasps, struggles, wishes, craves,
> From her that happy stillness of the mind
> Which fits him to receive it, when unsought.
>
> (XII, ll.11–14)

The energy deriving from all the verbs in the second line of this quotation turns out to be potential energy found in nature's 'stillness' rather than by struggling for 'truth'. The relationship between 'nature' and the mind is reached by the senses, but the senses must not dominate. Truth is to be found only by ceasing to look for it. In a passage from Book XI the conflicting claims of 'the outward sense' and 'the mind' are again seen as a struggle (ll.170–75), this time in terms drawn from politics. The 'outward sense' is 'despotic', imposing a 'tyranny' or 'thraldom' while 'the mind' can serve 'the great ends of liberty and power'. So the ideal to be achieved is of

> A balance, an ennobling interchange
> Of action from within and from without,
> The excellence, pure spirit, and best power
> Both of the object seen, and eye that sees.
>
> (XII, ll.376–9)

This ideal is like the balance of 'Tumult and peace, the darkness and the light' claimed in the Alps passage (VI, l.567).

We can perhaps now see the scheme that the autobiographical account of *The Prelude is* meant to fulfil. The earlier 'spots of time' were

127

incidents that had impressed themselves on the mind of the young poet without his understanding them. Here the mind impresses itself on the incident. In the 'spots of time' nature was too big for the mind. In these two passages the mind exceeds what nature can offer. It is not clear whether the climactic Snowdon passage is a triumph of mind *over* nature or a triumph of mind *within* nature. The evidence from elsewhere in the poem is contradictory. The mind is 'lord and master' (XI, l.271–2) while 'From Nature doth emotion come' (XII, l.1). Despite the formula of 'ennobling interchange' (XII, ll.376), climbing Snowdon seemed to be a reassertion of the mind's dominion.

In the cases of both the 'spots of time' and the mountain passages an autobiographical account of events is followed by restoration and consolation. Both mountain passages are to do with disappointment; at least the experiences they represent are not the expected experiences. Thus they function in a way I suggested that the poem as a whole might function: as consolation. But in both cases the consolation is out of all proportion to the disappointment. Moments of anti-climax become climactic. And both culminate in a great hymn to 'Imagination'. Like many poems, these passages are concerned with events that have a private significance that we as readers come to share through their being written. They are not events that had any public significance before being written. Really they are psychological events, and events in language. But *The Prelude is* not only about the private history of an individual. In the later books, as we shall see, Wordsworth's private history unfolds against great national and international events. The twin themes of imagination and memory that we have been discussing are abstract qualities and, having looked at them in the abstract, I want to try and locate them within a material history. By *material I* mean when and where these abstract qualities were recognized and *tested. So* now we will go on to look at the books concerning London and the revolutionary period of 1791–5.

The Prelude: *London and the French Revolution*

Book VII: London

We saw that in the early books nature was a kind of teacher to the young poet, and I have said that we can see *The Prelude* as a whole as a poem of crisis and recovery: 'Nature' functions as doctor as well as teacher. I want us to turn next to the events of the crisis that the poem records.

When the poem was expanded from the shorter version, the most important additions concerned London and the French Revolution, Books VII, IX and X of the 1805 version. I'm not going to ask you to read all these books, only to discuss certain passages, but *The Prelude* is, as I've been insisting, a narrative poem, and in keeping with that I want to look at the 'mountain' passages in context, in particular at what comes between them. This should allow us to compare the way Wordsworth treats events of entirely private and solitary significance with his treatment of society and of great public events.

Book VII begins 'Five years are vanish'd', just as 'Tintern Abbey' had begun 'Five years have passed'. This time it is five years since writing the passage which opens the poem and which Wordsworth here calls its 'glad preamble'. Wordsworth now compares that opening to a storm on a mountain (ll.4–8). This book also opens with an address to Coleridge, the 'Belovèd Friend' of line 13. There is a change of season to winter as Wordsworth resumes the poem, to sing like a robin (ll.34–7). He recalls how he moved from the academic cloisters of Cambridge to 'the unfenced regions of society' (l.62), but what this book as a whole remembers is a fenced-in existence, in London. In Chapter One we looked at Wordsworth's celebration of the city in his sonnet 'Composed Upon Westminster Bridge'. I said there that this was uncharacteristic. Here in *The Prelude* the city is a kind of nightmare.

London, as he was aware, was a place to stay rather than a home (ll.76; 116–20). All the same, he had had illusions about it – indeed he saw it as a city of romance (ll.82) and exoticism (ll.227–43) that ought to transform and even cure people. However the city is a disappointment: it had held an allure for him yet such feelings are revealed as 'fond imaginations' (l.136) not borne out by 'the real scene' (l.139). It is a place where he does not understand the 'language':

> Above all, one thought
> Baffled my understanding, how men lived
> Even next-door neighbours, as we say, yet still
> Strangers, and knowing not each other's names.

(VII, ll.117–20)

London is full of signs that promise to reveal their meaning but cannot be read. House fronts are like the title pages of books (ll.176–7); advertisements are alluring but deceiving (ll.210–14); pictures 'ape/The absolute presence of reality' (ll.248–9); pantomimes and melodramas trade in cheap 'delusion' (ll.309–10). London is a series of sensory impressions that can't be made to cohere, a 'Babel din', a place of imitations – the unhappy story of a Lakeland woman, the Maid of Buttermere, is travestied on stage (VII, ll.311–64). Politics and even preaching are theatrical displays (ll.524–43, ll.543–66); there are endless 'lies to the ear, and lies to every sense' (l.574), which he thought he could 'read' (l.581) and see through, but could not. In fact Wordsworth is unable to read the city: 'The face of every one/That passes by me is a mystery' (ll.597–8). The real horror is not that this is a travesty but that it might accurately 'mimic' human life.

Wordsworth's technique in most of this book is to write a catalogue, or maybe a list – a series of confused and unsorted perceptions. All the lists come into focus on a single 'spectacle', in a brief passage about a beggar. Please now read from line 589 to line 741. **What is the context in which the encounter with the beggar occurs?**

Discussion

Before encountering the beggar Wordsworth says he was adrift, having lost 'all the ballast of familiar life' (l.604). Following this encounter comes the account of Bartholomew Fair as 'a Parliament of Monsters' (l.692). The account of the fair is another catalogue or list of the kind of which Book VII is full. ∎

How does the beggar himself strike you – and how does he strike Wordsworth?

D i s c u s s i o n

Like the rural outcasts of earlier poems, the beggar is an unworldly figure. Or maybe *other*worldly. He seems ghostly, there to teach the poet something or, like the leech-gatherer in Wordsworth's 'Resolution and Independence' to 'admonish' him. ■

What is significant about the sign the beggar uses?

D i s c u s s i o n

The beggar doesn't speak, as Wordsworth's leech-gatherer does, but has the story of his life written on a paper he wears on his chest. What is to be read there is not a lie, as so many of the sights of London are lies. But the beggar is tied to his own story; unlike some of Wordsworth's 'solitaries', the beggar does not provide the poet with a means of imaginative escape from the present situation. As in other passages we've touched on, it is not that there is too little information but too much, and it remains unsorted. ■

I've said that the account of Bartholomew Fair is another catalogue or list. The point about a catalogue or list is that it has no narrative. In a narrative, we expect things to change. In Book VII of *The Prelude* what we seem to have instead is a series of examples of false or unreadable spectacles. What Wordsworth says of the fair could have been said of many of these other examples:

> O blank confusion! and a type not false
> Of what the mighty City is itself [...]
> An indistinguishable world to men,
> The slaves unrespited of low pursuits,
> Living amid the same perpetual flow
> Of trivial objects, melted and reduced
> To one identity, by differences
> That have no law, no meaning, and no end [...]
> (VII, ll.695–6; 699–704)

(We might compare a passage on the 'gross and violent stimulants' of urban living, which occurs in the 1802 Preface to the *Lyrical Ballads*.) What allows the poet to keep his head, to maintain proportion and distinction, are the permanent forms impressed on him by 'early converse with the works of God' (l.718). He is able, he says, to differentiate the items on a list, to put them in order and have a sense of the whole from the parts:

> [...] though the picture weary out the eye,
> By nature an unmanageable sight,
> It is not wholly so to him who looks
> In steadiness, who hath among least things
> An undersense of greatest, sees the parts
> As parts, but with a feeling of the whole.
> (ll.707–12)

130

We don't actually see the evidence for such a claim in the case of the account of London. But the 'him who looks' in this manner is surely the poet himself. Wordsworth himself remains specially favoured, apart, superior, even elect. Rather than there being a change, as we expect from a narrative, the book ends by reasserting values (and ways of reading) that had been with the poet all along.

Books IX and X: France

We have seen how self-consciously Wordsworth refers to the poem he aims to emulate or to surpass, Milton's *Paradise Lost*. The crucial event of that poem is the Fall of Man, and it occurs in Book IX. So it is perhaps no surprise that Book IX of *The Prelude* also recounts a kind of Fall. It is concerned with Wordsworth in France at the time of the Revolution. In the account of his first trip to the Continent in 1790, France was unfallen, post-revolutionary, but with King and People 'espoused' to each other, the latter 'emancipated' (VI, l.394): all over Europe

> triumphant looks
> Were then the common language of all eyes:
> As if awak'd from sleep, the Nations hail'd
> Their great expectancy [...]
> (VI, ll.683–6)

Books IX and X are perhaps the most purely narrative of the whole poem, closely following the chronology of events in France from just a few months after the storming of the Bastille. They also show how that 'love of mankind' claimed to have been won in the retrospect of Book VIII is tested, and they record acutely the liberal dilemma: rather fraught sympathy turns to revulsion as those events take their course. Book IX is concerned with the period 1791 to 1792, during which Wordsworth was in Orléans, and Book X with 1793 to 1795, the period of the Terror and the war, during most of which he was following events from back in England. As he writes to Coleridge in Book X, he intended 'tracing faithfully/The workings of a youthful mind, beneath/The breath of great events' (ll.943–5). London, as we have seen, has already fallen (VII), and France seemed to promise redemption but fell (Books IX and X).

Book IX

Wordsworth had gone to France in 1791 simply in order, as he says, to improve his French (ll.36–9). This book recounts the experiences he had while there and the nature of his responses to the Revolution and subsequent events. On his way to Orléans, he stops briefly in Paris, a city with a 'hubbub' like London's. Paris is like London in that it is 'a theatre' (l.94), but the Bastille had been taken eighteen months before, and Wordsworth recognizes and sympathizes with the drama that is being played out. He is there at 'an hour/Of universal ferment' (ll.164–5). Earlier in the poem Wordsworth had recorded how

To every natural form — rock, fruit, or flower,
Even the loose stones that cover the highway —
I gave a moral life.
(III, ll.124–6)

Now in Paris, Wordsworth takes as a souvenir a stone from the ruined Bastille. He wants to regard it as a religious 'relic', yet 'I look'd for something which I could not find,/Affecting more emotion than I felt' (ll.70–71) and is more moved by a baroque religious picture. There is some unease in this. The Revolution is metaphorically organic, Wordsworth's response to it is artificial. So he says, referring to the interim between 1789 and the suspension of the king in August 1792, that he was

careless as a flower
Glass'd in a Greenhouse, or a Parlour shrub
When every bush and tree, the country through,
Is shaking to the roots
(IX, ll.88–91)

He says that, unlike the revolutionaries, he did not hate the aristocracy (ll.218–49). To him both the Lake District and Cambridge were egalitarian – Cambridge was 'a republic' (l.230) and in the Lake District he had known 'mountain liberty' (l.242) – which meant that hatred of the aristocracy was simply unknown to him. Yet the Revolution seemed *natural* (ll.252–3).

At Orléans, his friends were army officers preparing for a counter-revolutionary *putsch,* with the exception of one, Beaupuy (ll.294–438). Wordsworth has earlier described how his way of seeing the world was largely to do with his reading of poetry (ll.208–17), and Beaupuy falls in with his aspirations and literary preoccupations (ll.305–9, 445–64). The two friends share a confidence in 'the people' (ll.391–6).

Wordsworth records his sentimental reaction to the 'passing spectacles' of wartime separations and embarkations (ll.273–93), a sentimentality horribly answered by the 'domestic carnage' of the Terror that began in 1794 (X, ll.329–36), which Wordsworth only witnessed from England. There is sentiment again in the reaction to the spectacle of the 'hunger-bitten Girl' (ll.511–34), at which Beaupuy exclaims ''Tis against that/Which we are fighting' (ll.519–20).

The 'tragic tale' of Juliet and Vaudracour (IX, ll.556–936) is another sentimental story. But it is presented as a story Beaupuy has told him, and is related 'as I have heard [it]' (l.642–5). This lengthy story is a kind of coded version of Wordsworth's affair with Annette Vallon, which produced a daughter, christened Anne-Caroline Wordsworth. The episode was omitted from the 1850 version of the poem, but had been published separately in 1820. This is offered as the reason for a lack of involvement in, or of the sudden silence on, political events in France.

Book X

In Book X, Wordsworth again passes through Paris as he returns to England after the violent deposition of the king and the proclamation of a Republic in 1792. It is a month after the September massacres, in which a mob had stormed the Palace of the Tuileries. More than a thousand of the attackers and guards of the palace had died and bodies were burnt in the Place de Carrousel, a large square in front of the palace. Standing in the square on this trip Wordsworth finds it a closed book:

> looking as doth a man
> Upon a volume whose contents he knows
> Are memorable, but from him lock'd up,
> Being written in a tongue he cannot read;
> So that he questions the mute leaves with pain
> And half upbraids their silence.
>
> (ll.48–54)

And this is followed by a nightmare.

On his return to England Wordsworth witnesses the unsuccessful agitation against the slave trade (ll.203–18). Though sympathetic to those who opposed the slave trade he has no real interest in reforming it since France is, as it were, the big one. 'If France prospered' liberty would become general and other abuses too would wither away (l.223). The real turning point comes with France's declaration of war on Britain in 1793:

> No shock
> Given to my moral nature had I known
> Down to that very moment; neither lapse
> Nor turn of sentiment that might be named
> A revolution save at this one time,
> All else was progress on the self-same path
> On which with a diversity of pace
> I had been travelling; this a stride at once
> Into another region.
>
> (ll.233–41)

Wordsworth has not used the word 'revolution' for events in France; he has saved it to apply to an effect upon a particular individual's development. The declaration of war is a break which can't be assimilated to the poem's strategy of 'growth'. As Paul Hamilton points out of Books IX and X, 'Important words from the vocabulary of Wordsworth's development – "hope", "freedom", "prospect", "promise", "desire" – cluster now around public events' (Hamilton, *Wordsworth*, 1987, p.118). It was at this point that public affairs became personal ('I felt/The ravage of this most unnatural strife/In my own heart', ll.249–51). At first he 'rejoiced' (l.259) at England's defeats, and felt himself excluded at church services when thanks were given for its victories (ll.259–74).

The perversion of the Revolution's first ideals could be seen as a moral failing, a failing of individuals – 'Inly I revolved/How much the destiny of man had still/Hung upon single persons' (X, ll.136–8; here Wordsworth is using the word 'revolved' as in 'revolution'). There is hope that a single splendid individual might emerge, and that France might return to ancient law. (There's another meditation on the great man at the beginning of Book XII.) A single good person might overcome 'tyrannic power' (l.167). Looking back over 'ten shameful years ... [of] outrage and bloody power' Wordsworth laments the absence of 'one paramount mind' who might have restored the French constitution to the stability of traditional law (ll.176–88). Instead there is Robespierre.

Let's consider the passage in which Wordsworth, back home in England in 1794, hears of the death of Robespierre (ll.466–538). **What reaction does he record?**

D i s c u s s i o n

He is exultant at the fall of a man who for him represents the blood-lust that has overtaken the Revolution. (The biblical Moloch of line 468 devoured children, and in Milton's *Paradise Lost* Moloch is one of the chief rebel angels. He argues for war against God the Father.) ■

This response is put in a narrative context (where Wordsworth was and what he was doing when he heard the news). Why is this?

D i s c u s s i o n

The narrative context is an account ('which ... deserve[s]/A separate chronicle', ll.470–71) of Wordsworth's return to the Lake District village in which he was staying, a sublime skyscape above (ll.475–82) and below 'the nest of pastoral vales' (l.484) where he had grown up.

That morning he had chanced to find the grave of his former schoolmaster, an 'honor'd teacher' (l.491), who is by implication everything that Robespierre was not – he lies amongst his family, having accepted his death equably. The schoolmaster is also a kind of index of the 'promise' (l.522) Wordsworth was struggling to fulfil, and in which the Revolution marked an interruption. The scene through which he was passing now 'neither changed, nor stirr'd, nor pass'd away' (l.486) and the remains of a chapel he passes seems to him another image of continuity. (The French revolutionaries had desecrated many churches, turning some into 'Temples of Reason', others into stables or tennis courts.) It is in this mood, in which 'Without me and within ... All that I saw, or felt, or communed with/Was gentleness and peace' (ll.515–17), that he hears the news of Robespierre's death from another traveller.

So the sequence of events in the poem is: first, Wordsworth's exultation at the news of Robespierre's downfall and death; second, the walk through scenes of the poet's childhood; third, the grave of the schoolmaster, and fond memories from his pupil; fourth, the poet in harmony with a landscape of 'gentleness and peace'; fifth, the moment of hearing the news about Robespierre. The poem does relate events in France but what seems to be more important is how the poet heard of those events and what his reactions were. We are always reminded how 'the growth of a poet's mind' is the centre of the poem by the way it is not so much a narrative of events themselves as of the mind's construction of and reaction to events.' ■

The 'Hymn of triumph' (l.543) which follows continues to distinguish the ideals of the Revolution from what they had become under Robespierre: 'renovation' of the original ideals is likely, Wordsworth thinks. But as this book of the poem proceeds, it becomes more and more clear that France is set on another course. Later in Book X Napoleon can be dismissed as the latest actor in what has become a travesty, as London was a travesty (ll.930–40). Napoleon is not the ambivalently creative force he is represented as by Byron or Shelley – or even by Coleridge.

In France in the early days of the Revolution 'The soil of common life was [...]/Too hot to tread upon' (IX, ll.169–70), and in the course of these books Wordsworth comes to believe, with conservatives such as Edmund Burke, that 'the soil of common life' (a phrase which could easily come from the preface to the *Lyrical Ballads*) remains more important than attempts to make a society founded on 'reason'. Reason is an 'enchanter' (X, l.699). His experiences both of city life and the Revolution are retrospectively understood as an enchantment by 'Reason': 'My mind was both let loose,/Let loose and goaded' (X, ll.863–4). You can't build a paradise on earth: to imagine that you can is false imagination' (l.847). Wordsworth puts his faith neither in the Utopia of the French revolutionaries nor in a new heaven and earth but in a renewal of the old world:

> the very world which is the world
> Of all of us, the place on which in the end
> We find our happiness, or not at all.
>
> (X, ll.752–7)

The world looks new, or at least full of potential (ll.728–35). But this too is a deluded 'realism' – Wordsworth's actuality is confirmed by his then turning to Dorothy and to Coleridge in a passage we will look at in a moment.

I mentioned the way the poem can be seen as having a structure like the Christian scheme of Eden, Fall and Redemption. Finally it seems to have a consoling or providential structure like that of 'Tintern Abbey'. We saw in the Grasmere Lake sonnet that nature seemed, reassuringly, to be permanently available. Here, one means of restoration has remained simply in the solitary encounter with a natural world: 'I saw the Spring return when I was dead/To deeper hope' (XI, ll.25–6). At the very end, rather than assuming the public scope of the long poem, *The Prelude* returns to relate a walk in the present in which the poem has begun. This is like the ending of Milton's *Paradise Regained,* in which Christ 'home to his mother's house private returned' (Carey, *Milton: Complete Shorter Poems,* 1971, p.521), a return to the consolations of domestic life.

The third observation we made about 'Tintern Abbey' was that it turned finally to Dorothy to witness and guarantee what occurred within the poem. We have seen that Wordsworth relies on a similar strategy in the longer poem: he usually referred to the poem we know as *The Prelude* as 'the poem to Coleridge'. Could you now read lines 878–976 of Book X? **How does Wordsworth turn the narrative to the subject of Coleridge?**

In his crisis, Wordsworth had turned first towards the certainties of mathematics (ll.901–4). Meeting Coleridge lent 'a living help/To regulate my soul' (ll.90–7). Dorothy put him back in touch with himself as poet (ll.907–20), nature too revived him (ll.921–9), and both upheld him when the last prop was taken away. (There is a topical reference to the Pope's coronation of Napoleon in December 1804. Wordsworth had felt himself to be like 'a clouded, not a waning moon' (ll.91–17) but Napoleon, who had seemed like the sun, has become a pantomime effect, a 'gewgaw' or cheap plaything.)

The remainder of the book is addressed directly to Coleridge. The whole of *The Prelude* has been 'a Story destined for thy ear' (l.946). In 1804, when these lines were written, Coleridge was in Sicily on his way home from Malta. There is, then, a move out of 'time' to the 'great Society' comprised both by the living and the dead (ll.967–9) in which he and Coleridge will take their places. Coleridge will transform the sirocco, the desert wind, into an invigorating 'healthful breeze', like the breeze that opens the whole poem. ■

Like Dorothy, Coleridge was a real person, not one of the great dead poets with whom Wordsworth's poem competes. I've suggested that the poem might be seen as an act of consolation: it is written in Coleridge's absence and compensates for his loss too. A passage in the final book (XIII, ll.386–410) remembers the spring and summer of 1798 when they planned and wrote the *Lyrical Ballads* and came up with the scheme for *The Recluse*. The poem as a whole ends with another address to Coleridge, anticipating his return home and a renewed collaboration with Wordsworth. They will be 'joint-labourers' (XIII, l.439) in a great work, 'Prophets of Nature' (l.442) whose influence will outlive them: 'what we have loved/Others will love; and we may teach them how' (ll.444–5).

Of course there is a danger that such lines remain private, that, as Jon Cook writes,

> [they] become the early nineteenth-century equivalent of showing holiday snapshots, full of significant associations only if you were there. The poem becomes esoteric not because it contains arcane knowledge but because of the highly particularized nature of the associations it deals with, accessible only to that intimate circle of readers who already know the poet's life history before it is written down.
>
> (Cook, 'Paul De Man and imaginative consolation', in Wood, *The Prelude*, 1993, p.55)

As Cook goes on to say however, Coleridge is not the *only* reader of the poem but the *kind* of reader this great experimental poem demands. In another sense, then, Coleridge is not 'real' at all. In these lines his health seems to be a metaphor for the health of Europe and he is addressed in the same way that abstract entities like breezes or imagination are addressed. Coleridge is the ideal reader of a poem which, as we've seen, was read or heard only by a handful of Wordsworth's close friends. In this sense Coleridge functions in the way Dorothy functions in 'Tintern Abbey' – to guarantee the public efficacy of what might otherwise be wholly private. Coleridge stands in for us as readers, so the poem constructs him not as the historical person but as the kind of reader who will understand the poem. A poem so concerned with memories turns to private relationships in the conviction that these can stand in for political failure and that imagination can transform the past – not into poetry (*The Recluse* remained unwritten) but into a positive example for the future.

Positioning The Prelude

The Prelude is a central text of British Romanticism. But as we've seen, it was not central to Wordsworth's contemporaries, because they could not have read it. It is to our version of Romanticism that *The Prelude* is central. The reasons for this are to do with the three concerns we noticed first in 'Tintern Abbey': the use of memory to celebrate an imagination that connects the self with nature; a move from the specific to the general, or from the actual to the ideal; and the creation of an intimate audience by turning to another person. I think this last concern suggests that, despite appearances, the poem is of a provisional character. Despite its great length it is a fragment, despite all consolations the poet remains unsure of the ideal he puts in place of political ideals which failed him. Despite the common accusation that he mystifies or evades actual history, in expanding the poem after 1799 into the version we have been reading, the historical material is what he *added*.

You may feel moved by the poem as a kind of testament to crisis, but we can also see from it what the figure of Wordsworth might have meant to his contemporaries. Charges of political evasion or timeserving, of a mystification of nature and an unrealistic stress on the self outside society were laid against Wordsworth. These charges are wittily made by Byron in his own epic, as we shall see in Chapter Seven. First, since we have been reading *The Prelude* as a narrative, let's now turn to some other kinds of narrative written by Romantic poets.

Romantic verse narrative

by Graham Allen

The poets of the Romantic period were great experimenters with poetic form. If we look at the kinds of poems written during the period we see all the established forms in use – narrative, epic, ballad, ode, sonnet and others – and we also see these forms undergoing change and development. We have seen in Chapter Five how Wordsworth adapted the traditional form of the epic poem; during the Romantic period most of the established forms of poetry underwent a similar revision. Today, however, when most people think about Romantic poetry, they begin by thinking about *lyric* poetry. As we have seen, lyrical poems always involve, in some form, an 'I' and a 'you': a figure who sings or speaks and a figure to whom the words sung or spoken are directed. There are many things which can be expressed in such a form, and this structure of direct address can be said to be at the centre of the expressive theories of art and poetry we discussed in Chapter Three. Yet, as the writers themselves knew full well, there are also things which cannot be done in this form of writing. We are now going to look at a major non-lyric form, Romantic verse narrative

'Romance' in Romantic narrative

In the Introduction to this book the words 'romance' and 'Romantic' were discussed. They were said to stem from medieval and Renaissance forms like the ballad, the lay and certain epics and to involve 'exotic or far-fetched stories of knights and ladies' (p.vii above) and the adventures of a protagonist or 'hero'. These adventures and stories frequently revolved around the quest for an 'ideal'.

During the eighteenth century and throughout the Romantic period, the tradition of romance was absorbed into the newest and eventually the dominant mode of literary writing, the novel. Gothic novels such as those by Ann Radcliffe were often subtitled 'A Romance'. The Gothic novel was akin to the older tradition of romance because it relied on exotic, medieval or 'foreign' settings and presented narratives in which idealistic love was confronted by and often fell foul of dark, sinister forces. In this last respect, romance is similar to comic narratives in that the characters often go through a process of transformation, and certainly meet dangers, temptations and obstacles before the ending. In comedies the ending is invariably a happy one, of course; in romances the ending can be either 'comic' ('happy', a resolution of the major problems and misunderstandings) or, less frequently, tragic.

There is a wonderful satire on the kind of romance narrative popular in Europe from the Renaissance to the eighteenth century in Laurence Sterne's comic novel *Tristram Shandy*, written between 1759 and 1766. Despite the fact that it pokes fun at romance narratives, it can help us here.

O there is a sweet era in the life of a man, when (the brain being tender and fibrillous, and more like pap than any thing else) — a story read of two fond lovers, separated from each other by cruel parents, and by still more cruel destiny —

    Amandus — He

    Amanda — She —

each ignorant of the other's course,

    He — east

    She — west

Amandus taken captive by the Turks, and carried to the emperor of Morocco's court, where the princess of Morocco falling in love with him, keeps him twenty years in prison for the love of his Amanda —

    She — (Amanda) all the time wandering barefoot, and with dishevelled hair, o'er rocks and mountains, enquiring for Amandus — Amandus! Amandus! — making every hill and valley to echo back his name —

    Amandus! Amandus!

at every town and city, sitting down forlorn at the gate — Has Amandus! — has my Amandus entered? — till, — going round, and round, and round the world — chance unexpectedly bringing them at the same moment of the night, though by different ways, to the gate of Lyons, their native city, and each in well-known accents calling out aloud,

Is Amandus $\left.\begin{array}{l}\\\\\end{array}\right\}$ still alive?
Is my Amanda

they fly into each other's arms, and both drop down dead for joy.

(*The Life and Opinions of Tristram Shandy*, 1967 edn, p.496)

The ending of this little satirical romance is of course funny, and it is meant to pull us, its readers, down to earth by parodying other accounts of ideal love. The story captures many things about the kind of romance narrative which developed out of medieval and Renaissance romance traditions. The love between Amandus and Amanda is an idealized love. The comic similarity of their names (both Latin for 'loved') and their indestructible faithfulness to each other shows this. Their names also have a flavour of the medieval or Renaissance world rather than the eighteenth-century world in which Sterne was writing. Romances frequently take their characters into exotic, strange and unfamiliar worlds, in this piece represented by Morocco. The characters spend twenty years questing for each other and, by implication, for a return to their shared home. The way in which they find each other and their shared home (Lyons) is fantastic, implausible.

So, from this piece we can see that the kind of romance inherited by Romantic writers involves at least the following things:

1   idealized love between rather idealized characters;

2   medieval and/or exotic settings;

3   adventures and dangers faced during difficult journeys or quests for an ideal;

4   fantastic or implausible events and resolutions of problems.

In the later eighteenth century and particularly in the Romantic period, as I have said, this kind of romance narrative was used by Gothic novelists. Yet novels with more contemporary settings and subjects, novels of manners and of domestic life for example, also have strong – if different – connections to romance conventions. The novels of Jane Austen, for example, with their plots concerning love frustrated yet finally fulfilled, have significant affinities to 'romance' conventions. In the Gothic novel, the conventions of exotic locations and intensely dramatic action are sustained; in novels of domestic bourgeois life these are replaced by a world recognizable to late eighteenth- and early nineteenth-century readers. But the similarities between these distinct forms can function as a useful guide for two directions taken by romance during the period. In both cases the attachment to 'romance' can perhaps be reduced to the following two elements: (1) the quest for an ideal, usually associated with a love-plot; (2) an exploration of the relations between the sexes.

The Romantic verse narratives we are going to look at can perhaps be associated with the more Gothic kind of romance novel, in that they employ exotic and, in the case of Keats, historically distinct settings. We will be looking first at a verse narrative by Keats which employs a medieval setting.

Keats, *'La Belle Dame Sans Merci'*

'La Belle Dame Sans Merci' was written by Keats on 21 April 1819 and included by him in a draft version in a journal-letter he wrote to his brother and sister-in-law George and Georgiana Keats between 14 February and 3 May 1819. It was published in a slightly revised form in a journal called *The Indicator* in May 1820. In 1848 – after Keats's death – the poem was included in an edition of his collected works. In this edition, however, the version that was used was not *The Indicator* one but a version copied by an associate of Keats, Charles Brown. As Jerome McGann states ('Keats and the historical method in literary criticism'), it is significant that it is this 'Brown' version, checked against the first draft, that has become the established version of the poem, rather than the one Keats himself saw to publication. To read the poem properly, we need to be aware of both versions.

In a standard edition of Keats's poems, Miriam Allott writes that the poem 'is obviously connected to Keats's feelings about Fanny Brawne [his future fiancée] and is strongly influenced by memories of Spenser's fatal enchantresses in *The Faerie Queene* and by various traditional ballads expressing the destructiveness of love' (Allott, *Keats: The Complete Poems,* 1970 edn, p.500). Keats was certainly influenced by the English poet Edmund Spenser (*c*.1552–99), whose poem *The Faerie Queene* is a classic romance epic. ('The Eve of St Agnes', which we will shortly consider, was written in the same stanza form as *The Faerie Queene.*) Fanny Brawne and Keats had reached an 'understanding', just before Keats composed the poem. Because of the complexities of Keats's life, however, their relationship faced great problems. Keats met Fanny less than three years before his death. For much of that time he suffered from bad health while struggling to write some of his most important poetry. But is Allott's reading borne out by the poem's wider historical context?

Please now read both versions of the poem. The 'Brown' version is found in many anthologies and editions of Keats including Wu, *Romanticism*, 1994, pp.1051–3; *The Indicator* version is reprinted below. **As you read the poem try to identify the romance conventions it is employing. How might either version be said to alter or challenge those conventions?**

The Indicator *version of 'La Belle Dame Sans Merci'*

1
Ah, what can ail thee, wretched wight,
Alone and palely loitering;
The sedge is withered from the lake,
And no birds sing.

2
Ah, what can ail thee, wretched wight,
So haggard and so woe-begone?
The squirrel's granary is full,
And the harvest's done.

3
I see a lily on thy brow
With anguish moist and fever dew;
And on thy cheeks a fading rose
Fast withereth too.

4
I met a Lady in the meads,
Full beautiful, a fairy's child;
Her hair was long, her foot was light,
And her eyes were wild.

5
I set her on my pacing steed,
And nothing else saw all day long;
For sideways would she lean, and sing
A fairy's song.

6
I made a garland for her head,
And bracelets too, and fragrant zone;
She looked at me as she did love,
And made sweet moan.

7
She found me roots of relish sweet,
And honey wild, and manna dew;
And sure in language strange she said,
I love thee true.

8
She took me to her elfin grot,
And there she gazed and sighèd deep,
And there I shut her wild sad eyes –
So kissed to sleep.

9
And there we slumbered on the moss,
And there I dreamed – ah, woe betide –

The latest dream I ever dreamed
On the cold hill side.

10
I saw pale kings, and princes too,
Pale warriors, death-pale were they all;
Who cried – 'La belle Dame sans mercy
Hath thee in thrall!'

11
I saw their starved lips in the gloom
With horrid warning gapèd wide,
And I awoke, and found me here
On the cold hill side.

12
And this is why I sojourn here,
Alone and palely loitering
Though the sedge is withered from the lake,
And no birds sing.

(Allott, *Keats: The Complete Poems,* 1970 edn)

D i s c u s s i o n

The poem seems to be very much in the romance tradition. The language is stylized, an imitation of medieval romance. It seems much nearer to the Gothic strain of romance than that employed by female novelists such as Austen or Edgeworth or Burney. There is nothing of domestic life in it.

We are presented with a narrative in which a person (the narrator) meets a 'knight' and hears of how he has met and become 'in thrall' (enthralled, the word implies unnatural influence) to 'a lady'. This 'lady' is an idealized figure in the sense that she seems supernatural, from another world: 'Full beautiful, a fairy's child,/Her hair was long, her foot was light,/And her eyes were wild' (stanza 4). Yet this line also suggests a certain duality of nature: is the 'lady' a beautiful romance heroine (an idealization of femininity) or is she a dangerous enchantress? Are we supposed to believe that the knight really met such a lady? ■

Romance works are often set within or associated with dreams and visions and this poem certainly depends upon such a context. It is difficult to say whether the meeting with the 'lady' actually occurred, whether the knight merely dreamt or imagined it, or whether it was a vision presented to him. Whichever it was, the event clearly concerns idealistic notions of love. Before stanza 9 we have had some ambivalent description of the lady; however, as we reach the conventional stage of the story that is the lovers' embrace, the narrative itself becomes ambivalent, since the love seems to produce a dream (perhaps a dream within a dream) of a disturbing nature. Stanzas 10 and 11 recount a nightmare vision of all the previous lovers of the 'lady'. These 'pale kings, and princes', with their 'starved lips' tell the 'knight' that he has fallen into a trap: 'Who cried – "La belle Dame sans mercy/Hath thee in thrall"'. We end the poem, therefore, not with a perfect union between two idealized lovers but with a sense of alienation and despair.

We have seen that Allott compares this female figure to Spenser's 'Fatal enchantresses' and the whole poem to those romance ballads that express 'the destructiveness of love'. McGann argues by contrast with Allott that *The Indicator* poem is 'self conscious and slightly critical' in its treatment of its romance subject ('Keats and the historical method', p.41). The earlier, private version of the poem, the Brown version, had less of this 'consciousness', but was provided with an ironic commentary by Keats when he sent it to his brother and sister-in-law:

> Why four kisses — you will say — why four because I wish to restrain the headlong impetuosity of my Muse — she would have fain said 'score' without hurting the rhyme — but we must temper the Imagination as the Critics say with Judgement. I was obliged to choose an even number that both eyes might have fair play: and to speak truly I think two a piece quite sufficient — Suppose I had said seven; there would have been three and a half a piece — a very awkward affair — and well got out of on my side ...
>
> (quoted in McGann, 'Keats and the historical method', p.40)

Let's look more closely at what was entailed in the transition from private to public poetic performance. What does it mean to call the protagonist of the poem 'wretched wight' rather than 'knight-at-arms'? Definitions of 'wight' include a strong person who shows prowess in battle (a knight, therefore), and a supernatural figure. But it could also mean a 'base individual', and by the nineteenth century 'its romance meaning [...] is continually threatened by an ironic overtone' (ibid., p.34). Keats's use of the term may foreground the fact that the narrator sees the male figure as a victim and perhaps even a self-deceived one at that.

McGann also discusses the fact that the name denoting the author of the poem in *The Indicator* was not 'John Keats' but 'Caviare'. Keats apparently had in mind a line from *Hamlet* in which Hamlet describes a speech by the first player which, although it had not 'pleased [...] the million' had been like 'caviare to the general' (Act 2, scene ii). McGann argues that 'The *Hamlet* allusion shows us that Keats means to share a mildly insolent attitude towards the literary establishment with his readers in *The Indicator*, who are presumed to represent an undebased literary sensibility' (ibid., p.35). What McGann means is that Keats wrote two versions with two audiences in mind. The audience of *The Indicator*, he presumes, will be too sophisticated to expect or want what we might call undiluted romance.

The version published under Keats's supervision, then, seems to be using romance ironically, or at least ambivalently. If this is the case we have to ask ourselves: (1) why is Keats employing romance conventions ironically?; (2) what is the poem actually about? Perhaps we can use the difference between the two versions to answer these questions.

Are there any differences in the two versions in the representation of the relationship between the 'knight' and the 'lady'?

Discussion

Perhaps the most significant variant between the Brown text and *The Indicator* version comes in the first line of stanza 9. In the Brown version this line reads 'And there she lulled me asleep'. In *The Indicator* version

144

the line is: 'And there we slumbered on the moss'. Let's bear this in mind and return to the interpretation I cited earlier from Allott, where she seems to suggest an identification in the poem between Fanny Brawne and an archetypal figure of a 'fatal woman', an 'enchantress'. This reading seems to be possible in the Brown text. The 'lady', after all, 'lulls' the knight to sleep. However, in *The Indicator* version the two figures fall asleep together. In this version, then, the nightmare vision which succeeds this falling asleep cannot be attributed so easily to the 'lady'. The possibility arises that the vision of the 'pale kings, and princes' and their warning to the knight concerning the 'lady' (whom they call 'la belle dame sans merci', 'the beautiful woman without mercy') is produced by the knight's own disturbed imagination. We should note here, perhaps, that in French 'merci' can have the sense of 'no charge' as in the phrase 'don d'amoureuse merci' (a lover's gift of herself – love given as a free gift). ■

We are left with some important questions. Is the poem about a man who falls in love with a femme fatale? Or is it a poem about the delusions involved in that male invention that we nowadays call romantic (idealized) love? **What do we make, finally, of the nightmare vision presented to the knight?**

Discussion

We have already considered the possibility that Keats may be purposefully ironic about romance conventions. The feeling left at the end of the poem is surely one of a male protagonist having fallen into a kind of dream, or having had a vision of an idealized female, the effect of which is to leave him in a psychologically and physically alienated state. This process of falling in and out of a vision might well be the main point of the poem. Keats may well be employing romance to dramatize a process which is frequently represented by the Romantic poets, the experience and subsequent departure of a vision of the ideal. ■

In Keats's poem we can see the two issues we highlighted earlier working together. The poem seems to be concerned in some way with a quest for the ideal. But it represents this in terms of a love relationship. The theme of a quest for the ideal, or idealism, raises questions about the limits of human understanding and achievement and about the relationship between the material world and the spiritual world. In romance verse narratives by authors such as Keats and Shelley, however, we find an engagement with such questions in the guise of narratives concerning love relations. The question of romance or love, in other words, is often seen as an appropriate one by which to explore philosophical questions concerning the ideal, the limits of knowledge, human beings' relation to the truth and the sublime.

But are these 'philosophical' concerns the only ones which the poem dramatizes? We should perhaps add the issue of history itself. Isn't the nightmare vision the knight experiences near the end of the poem rather like a vision of history? You have already seen how important are questions of history in Romantic writing. The knight seems to quest after an ideal but what that quest seems to give him is a terrifying vision of an unspecified series of 'pale kings and princes' all of whom have fallen prey to the illusions of idealism. It may well be possible, then, to argue that Keats is using romance conventions to make a point about human history: that it is too often dictated by an idealism which inevitably leads to alienation and despair.

Keats, 'The Eve of St Agnes'

'The Eve of St Agnes' was written between 18 January and 2 February 1819 and was published in Keats's 1820 collection, *Lamia, Isabella, The Eve of St Agnes and Other Poems*. The Eve of St Agnes actually occurs during the period in which the poem was written. Once again this poem has a version which is not the one published during Keats's lifetime. Keats revised the poem in September 1819 and these revisions brought him into conflict with his publishers.

Please now read the poem with the following notes. (These focus mainly on the 'story' rather than on the manner in which that story is narrated. That is perhaps a necessary weakness in any attempt to paraphrase a literary narrative. I would urge you to consider the effects Keats produces by his elaborate and highly exotic descriptions.)

> Lines 1–9, stanza 1: Description of the wintry scene outside. Note: A 'beadsman' or 'bedesman' is a person whose job it is to pray for the souls of others. Notice the line 'Numb were the beadsman's fingers, while he told/His rosary …' (ll.5–6). A 'rosary' is a string of beads used in the Catholic religion to count a series of set prayers.
>
> Lines 10–27, stanzas 2–3. The beadsman's route from the chapel passed the crowded hall to his solitary chamber.
>
> Lines 28–45, stanzas 4–5. The beginning of the festivities. The focus moves quickly to 'one lady' (l.42). This is the 'heroine' of the poem, Madeline.
>
> Lines 46–72, stanzas 6–8. Madeline absorbed in the idea of St Agnes's Eve. The 'visions of delight' (l.47) which 'Young virgins' (l.46) are said to gain if they follow certain ritualistic actions, will reveal their future husbands.
>
> Lines 73–90, stanzas 9–10. The arrival of Porphyro 'with heart on fire/For Madeline' (ll.75–6).
>
> Lines 91–108, stanzas 11–12. Angela, the 'beldame', warns Porphyro of the danger he can expect from Madeline's family. A 'beldame' is, literally, a grandmother, but the word is often used to describe an unattractive, old, sometimes malicious woman. Notice how Porphyro calls Angela a 'gossip'. This is a traditional mock-affectionate word for an old woman.
>
> Lines 109–26, stanzas 13–14. Angela takes Porphyro to a safer place. They converse. Angela reprimands Porphyro for his recklessness in coming to the festivities. Porphyro enquires about Madeline's whereabouts. Notice how Angela describes Madeline's actions in lines 124–6.

Lines 115–117. Porphyro's words here may seem somewhat obscure. The 'holy loom', the 'secret sisterhood' described as 'weaving piously' and 'St Agnes's wool' all relate to the Feast of St Agnes, celebrated annually on 21 January at the Basilica in Rome. On this day two white, unshorn lambs are presented, the wool from which is later woven by nuns. As Angela tells Porphyro about Madeline's observance of St Agnes Eve, Porphyro hits on a plan which shocks Angela. Note: The plan is not actually made explicit here, but as we see later it involves concealing himself in Madeline's bedchamber.

Lines 145–62, stanzas 17–18. Porphyro threatens to bring attention to himself if Angela does not help him in his plan. Angela, frightened at the prospect, gives in to him.

Lines 163–80, stanzas 19–20. Angela promises to help Porphyro to hide in Madeline's bedchamber, also promising to provide him with exotic foods, 'cates and dainties' (l.173). Note: Line 171 has puzzled many critics. Miriam Allott argues that the reference is to Merlin being imprisoned in a rock by the Lady of the Lake, who had been his mistress.

Lines 181–98, stanzas 21–2. Angela conceals Porphyro in the 'closet'. She then meets Madeline, who settles Angela in a comfortable place for the night outside of the bedchamber ('a safe level matting' l.196) before returning to it alone.

Lines 199–216, stanzas 23–4. Madeline enters her bed chamber, which is described by the narrator in great detail.

Lines 217–34, stanzas 25–6. Madeline kneels and prays. As Porphyro looks on Madeline undresses and, whilst she looks towards her bed, she sees a vision of St Agnes lying within it.

Lines 235–52, stanzas 27–8. Madeline falls asleep. Porphyro, certain that she is now asleep, creeps out of the closet.

Lines 253–75, stanzas 29–31. Porphyro sets up a table upon which he lays an array of luxurious and exotic foods.

Lines 275–88, stanzas 31–2. Porphyro unsuccessfully attempts to wake Madeline. He falls into a kind of sleep or trance (l.288). Notice how Porphyro describes himself and Madeline in line 277. 'Eremites' are Christian hermits or recluses who, having separated themselves from the world, spend their lives contemplating and praising God.

Lines 289–315, stanzas 33–5. Porphyro takes Madeline's 'hollow lute' (l.289) and plays the 'ancient ditty' (l.291) 'La Belle Dame Sans Mercy' (l.292). This has the effect of waking Madeline. She is disturbed by the discrepancy between her dream or vision of Porphyro and the real Porphyro before her.

Lines 316–24, stanza 36. Porphyro, 'impassioned' (l.316) by Madeline's voice, 'melts' into 'her dream' (l.320). The focus suddenly switches to the outside world in which the moon has set and a storm is raging (ll.322–4).

Lines 325–42, stanzas 37–8. Porphyro assures Madeline that she is not in a dream. Madeline despairs at this fact and accuses Porphyro of wishing to leave her, an idea he denies.

Lines 343–69, stanzas 39–41. Porphyro points out that it is now morning and that the storm that is raging will conceal the sounds of their escape. He encourages her to escape with him to 'the southern moors' (l.351). They make their escape, passing various dangers. Notice the dramatic effect produced by the narrator's description of what they pass.

Lines 370–78, stanza 42. The time-scale shifts, allowing the narrator to summarize the world they leave behind, including the deaths of Angela and the beadsman.

Please now read through the poem again with reference to the questions below. By isolating some of the major questions that the poem poses we will be able to place our analysis of this poem within the wider context of romance conventions in Romantic verse narratives.

Question 1: Why does Keats begin the poem in the way he does?

Question 2: Do we see Madeline in a sympathetic light or does she appear foolish and superstitious?

Question 3: What does it mean to be 'deceive[d]' by 'good angels' (l.125)?

Question 4: Do we agree with Angela's negative assessment of Porphyro in stanzas 15 and 16?

Question 5: What is the purpose of the reference to Merlin in stanza 19?

Question 6: What does it mean to say that Madeline 'dreams awake' (l.232)? Does Keats allow us to distinguish between dream, vision or perception of reality in the case of Madeline?

Question 7: Given that it is not eaten, what is the significance of the exotic food in stanzas 30 and 31?

Question 8: Why should Keats have Porphyro play the 'ditty' 'La Belle Dame Sans Mercy'?

Question 9: Why is Madeline's vision or dream version of Porphyro undercut by the real Porphyro?

Question 10: What is the meaning of, 'Into her dream he melted ...' (l.320)?

Question 11: Why does Madeline call herself 'a deceived thing' (l.332), but also go on to describe herself as 'A dove forlorn and lost with sick, unpruned wing' (l.333)?

Question 12: Why does Keats end the poem in the way he does?

If we consider these questions carefully, having read the poem closely, we begin to see that most of them are illuminated by our previous discussion of romance and Keats's use of it. Like 'La Belle Dame Sans Merci', this poem seems to be subtly ironic: Keats foregrounds the literary conventions of his romance so the poem is distanced from the very conventions it seems to employ.

How does Keats make it clear that he is employing a traditional set of literary conventions?

Discussion

Questions 1, 7, 8 and 12 point to some of the devices used in the poem. Let's begin with 1 and 12. At the beginning and the end of the poem he sets up a medieval, even Gothic context for the narrative. The story of the two lovers is framed by images of cold, death and the severity of medieval Catholic religion. Indeed, the closing stanza of the poem is a superb exercise in distancing: this stanza makes readers suddenly face the fact that they have been reading a fiction, a 'romance'. Such framing allows the poem to be read naively (as pure romances) or with critical distance (with irony) by other readers.

Now let's turn to question 7. The stanzas in which Porphyro lays out the exotic foods can also be described as having a distancing effect. There is something unreal and even sickly about the descriptions of foods such as 'jellies soother than the creamy curd' (l.266). Our attention is directed to the descriptions themselves; that is to say, we respond to the literariness of the food. Marjorie Levinson has also made the point that this exotic, literary banquet seems to serve as a poetic substitute for the physical love-scene which succeeds it (*Keats's Life of Allegory,* 1988). The rich, yet strangely unnourishing food (it is all 'dessert' food – where are the protein and vitamins here?) is presented to us in a manner close to the effects of pornography. We are voyeurs here, relishing a simulacrum – the idea rather than the reality of sweet food.

Question 8 points to another device of substitution. The ballad 'La Belle Dame Sans Merci' also seems to serve as an oblique symbol for the union which follows. Keats had read a poem of that name, translated by Chaucer but known to be the work of a fourteenth-century French poet called Alain Chartier. In it a woman refuses the advances of a suitor, even when he threatens to kill himself. In the poem the woman is 'sans merci' from the male suitor's point of view. From the woman's point of view, the suitor is misguidedly idealistic and lacking in her rationality and common-sense. In other words, one of Keats's principal sources sets up a conflict between idealism and rationality or scepticism within a romance context, the (unsuccessful) courting of a 'lady' by a 'knight'. Whether we view Porphyro as an ideal romance hero, or simply as a seducer, this is an ambiguous thing for him to play at the bedside of his beloved. ■

The legend which grew up around the figure of St Agnes after the sixth century presents us with another female figure who refused the advances of suitors and was saved, on a metaphorical (or spiritual) level at least, by her extreme virtue (one might say her idealism). She was sent to a house of prostitution for refusing to marry and was finally executed, not before having shown miraculous signs of her spiritual purity. St Agnes was usually represented as a beautiful young girl with arms outstretched in prayer or with lambs in her arms or at her feet. Some versions of the legend have her being saved from violation in the brothel to which she was condemned by a storm which kept her would-be violators at home. Madeline's fate seems to ironically reverse that of St Agnes, then. Whilst St Agnes is saved by a storm, Madeline appears to be seduced during a storm. Whilst St Agnes's spiritual idealism saves her from seduction, Madeline's dreamy idealism appears to leave her open to seduction. Whatever else Keats is doing here, he seems to be playing with positive and negative senses of what we have been calling 'idealism'. A simple definition of idealism might be 'the tendency to represent things, not as they are, but as they can be imagined to be, or in their ideal forms'. Whilst the tradition of St Agnes seems to suggest that idealism is a positive virtue, Madeline's story might make us wonder whether seeing things as they are is preferable to imagining them as they might be.

Another source for the poem is Shakespeare's *Romeo and Juliet*. The theme of 'star-crossed lovers', a young man and a young woman from warring families falling in love, is taken straight from Shakespeare's play. To understand the irony of Porphyro's actions in Madeline's bedchamber we might imagine Shakespeare's hero-lover playing to the young heroine a song about a misguided male lover and his unromantic, rather severe beloved.

These two sources suggest different and even contradictory things when taken separately. However, they seem to share a common theme of idealism and its opposites: loss, frustration, violence, an environment hostile to the fulfilment of idealism or romantic desire. They also, of course, all deal with sexual relations between men and women, in which either may figure as victim of the kinds of forces we have just referred to. Is Keats using a romance context in order to stage a conflict between idealism and its various antitheses? The opening and closing parts of the poem may seem like quite conventional scene setting, but they also help to set up an opposition between Porphyro's and Madeline's 'romantic' (idealized) love for each other and the material world of suffering, decay and death which lies all around them. It seems that 'The Eve of St Agnes' is another poem that explores the human desire for the ideal within the context of a 'romance', a love relationship.

Look at questions 2, 3, 6, 9, 10 and 11. These questions relate to Madeline and our understanding of her. A traditional reading of the poem has been that it presents a beautiful and idealized picture of young romantic love. But our questions may raise doubts about Madeline in this role. They are to do with the relationship between her dreams or visions and realistic consciousness. Let's look at questions 2, 3, 6 and 9 first. **How do the allusions to visions, dreams and realistic consciousness undercut the poem's idealism?**

Discussion

In an influential essay, Jack Stillinger initiated a more sophisticated modern approach to the poem by arguing that Madeline is, as the poem states in line 70, 'Hoodwinked with fairy fancy'. In other words, as Stillinger argues, 'She is a victim of deception, to be sure, but of deception not so much by

Porphyro as by herself and the superstition she trusts in' (Stillinger, *The Hoodwinking of Madeline*, 1971, p.84). Madeline is the dupe of her own imagination. Her shock at seeing the real Porphyro before her (Question 9) is caused by the fact that she has cultivated an idealized picture of him. As our questions suggest, Madeline vacillates constantly between dream, vision and perception of the much less idealistic world around her. Her excitement and absorption in the rituals of St Agnes's Eve seem to suggest a young girl who would rather substitute her own imaginary world for the real world (including real love and real male lovers). Porphyro, the focus of that imaginative world, breaks it apart when he enters into it. ■

Do we really finish the poem, as some critics have argued, feeling that we have read a straightforward account of romantic love? Do we leave the poem feeling that Madeline's dreams and visions have been realized?

D i s c u s s i o n

The answer can hardly be an unqualified yes. Even if we are right in seeing Madeline as a young woman whose imaginary world is rudely broken apart, we still have to ask whether she was wise to cultivate such unrealistic (unworldly, 'romantic') dreams/visions in the first place. Questions 2, 3 and 11 seem to converge on this point. Is Madeline a self-deluded figure 'hoodwinked' by her own imagination? Or is she a victim?

If we decide upon the latter then we immediately face a problem with our interpretation of Porphyro. Stillinger suggests that Porphyro is a Machiavellian figure, a man who consciously goes out to seduce a young girl idealistically (romantically) in love with him. As we saw from question 4, Angela at one point seems to have this same opinion of him. Yet this is clearly only a momentary response. It would make no sense for Angela to help Porphyro, or to be frightened at the prospect of his discovery by the revellers, if she did not think him a worthy young man. If this is a romance, then Porphyro should be a 'hero', a young knight. ■

Can we get any further with the question of Porphyro's character? We need to look here at stanza 36 and thus at question 10. It is difficult to work out precisely what is going on here. Things become somewhat clearer if we look at the revisions Keats made to this and the previous stanza. The significant revisions begin from line 314 of stanza 35:

> See, while she speaks, his arms encroaching slow,
> Have zoned her, heart to heart — loud, loud the dark winds blow!
>
> For on the midnight came a tempest fell;
> More sooth, for that his quick rejoinder flows
> Into her burning ear — and still the spell
> Unbroken guards her in serene repose.
> With her wild dream he mingled, as a rose
> Marryeth its odour to a violet.
> Still, still she dreams; louder the frost-wind blows

(Wu, *Romanticism*, 1994, footnote p.1049)

By 'zoned' Keats seems to mean that Porphyro 'encircles' Madeline. Indeed, there seems to be an implication of something like 'colonization' – a gradual conquest, exploration and dividing into parts (zones are the five areas of the world distinguished by the tropics of Cancer and Capricorn, by the Arctic and Antarctic circles). However, 'zoned', in its eighteenth-century sense, also means 'wearing a zone or girdle' and hence connoted chastity.

What difference do these revisions make to this part of the poem?

Discussion

They seem to make it much clearer that Porphyro makes physical love to Madeline whilst she is in some kind of dream or trance (now described not simply as 'her dream' but as 'her wild dream'). This seems very much to back up Stillinger's point about Porphyro. Madeline here is a victim not merely of her own imagination but of the actions of her supposed ideal 'hero'. Keats's publishers clearly preferred the earlier version because it presents the physical union in a more abstract and idealized fashion. It is more 'romantic'. Keats, on the other hand, seems to have decided to undercut romance idealism with physical reality and physical desire, thus making his ironical treatment of romance more explicit. ■

Keats made these revisions to make more explicit than the original version did what happens physically between the two lovers. However, his publishers, fearing the moral impact of such explicit revisions decided to publish the original, less explicit version. As in 'La Belle Dame Sans Merci', he seems to have wished to direct his poem at an audience which would appreciate the ironical treatment of literary conventions. In an important letter, Richard Woodhouse, one of Keats's most loyal friends and supporters, discussed the arguments between Keats and his publishers over the two versions of these stanzas. The letter was written to Keats's publishers, Taylor and Hessey, and in it he gives an explanation of Keats's professed intentions:

> He says he does not want ladies to read his poetry; that he writes for men, and that if in the former poem ['The Eve of St Agnes'] there was an opening for doubt what took place, it was his fault for not writing clearly and comprehensibly; – that he should despise a man who would be such a eunuch in sentiment as to leave a maid, with that character about her, in such a situation, and should despise himself to write about it, etc., etc., – and all this sort of Keats-like rhodomontade.

> (Wu, *Romanticism*, 1994, pp.714–5)

(Incidentally, the footnote by Wu, ibid. p.1049, seems to suggest, by contrast with Woodhouse, that it is the manuscript version that is 'toned down'.) Are these reported comments by Keats surprising? We can understand them better if we remember our discussion in Chapter Three of the abuse that Keats suffered from reviewers. Reviewers did not merely abuse Keats for being lower class. They also characterized him as feminine, as a woman. Byron, as Levinson shows (*Keats's Life of Allegory,* 1988), characterized Keats as a 'Mankin' and his poetry as 'a sort of mental masturbation'.

Taking himself as a prototype of the virile, masculine poet, Byron cast Keats into an opposed role, not merely a fake but an impotent poet. Byron's sexism is blatant here, to the extent that, in these caricatures of Keats, he associates masturbation and male impotence with the feminine. To be a masturbator and/or an impotent man, the logic seems to run, is to be a fake man and to be a fake man is to be a woman. This pejorative use of the feminine is already familiar to us from the discussion of male responses to female authors in Chapter Four.

In the poems we have been dealing with so far, Keats was attempting to respond to the criticisms of his poetry. He seems to be attempting to distance himself from a 'female' literary world (supposedly dominated by the unmasculine values of sensitivity, self-absorption and emotion as opposed to the cultivated taste of the '*man*' of letters). We have already seen in this chapter how concerned Keats was to impress a specific audience. It may well be that in choosing to ironize romance conventions in a subtle way, Keats was attempting to prove that he was in fact a highly literary poet, a 'man speaking to men', to slightly misuse Wordsworth's phrase. He may have wanted to avoid being seen as a poet fit only for the unsophisticated lower classes and for female audiences supposedly concerned with the literary values of Gothic horror and excessive sensibility.

What Keats is also doing in 'The Eve of St Agnes', as in 'La Belle Dame Sans Merci', is to explore the limits of idealism. We cannot simply follow Keats's own rather hyperbolic statements, as reported by Woodhouse, and read the poem as a mock romance in which the heroine is duped by the 'hero'. Porphyro is himself a victim, as attention to question 5 demonstrates. The reference to Merlin returns us to the theme of a male figure being entrapped by an enchantress, a femme fatale. If we look at the lines which immediately follow the reference we see that Angela is concerned that Porphyro will take advantage of Madeline (see ll.179–80). **How do we sort out such a contradictory assessment of Porphyro's position? Is he victim or victimizer?**

Discussion

The poem seems to lead us to conclude that he is both. He takes advantage of Madeline, yet he himself is the victim of the idealism of romantic love. Both figures, in different ways, are victims and at the same time self-deceived. We leave the poem with an impression similar to the one created by the end of 'La Belle Dame Sans Merci'. The world in which we live is not a place in which the ideal can exist, nor can idealistic notions be sustained or sustain us. ■

In order to show that such attitudes are not unique to Keats, and to further demonstrate how Romantic poets used the conventions of romance to explore the limitations of idealism, we will end this chapter by looking briefly at Shelley's romance narrative 'Alastor'.

Shelley, 'Alastor'

'Alastor' was written between the autumn and early winter of 1815 while Percy and Mary Shelley were living at Bishopsgate near Windsor Forest. This was a relatively peaceful period in the generally turbulent early years of Percy and Mary's life together. It was a time when Shelley returned to poetry and took stock of what he wanted to do in his writing. The poem was published in *Alastor and Other Poems* early in 1816.

In 'Alastor' Shelley describes a young poet who is alienated from his home and travels east to discover the 'thrilling secrets of the birth of time' (l.128). Blinded by his visionary zeal, he spurns an Arab maiden who secretly loves and nurtures him. His restlessness eventually leads him to a valley in Kashmir, where falling asleep, he dreams of a beautiful and voluptuous 'veiled maid' who sings and plays to him. The poet dreams that he approaches the singer and they physically embrace. Awaking from his dream, he finds himself alone. The remainder of the poem narrates his quest for the beautiful maid of his vision, whom he has mistaken for a reality.

You will be returning to 'Alastor' in Chapter Ten. At this stage you do not need to read the whole poem. I would like you to read the Preface and five passages. These are:

1   Lines 1–49: an address to nature, which establishes the narrator's voice.
2   Lines 129–39, which introduce the Arab maiden.
3   Lines 140–222, which describe the appearance of the vision of the beloved and its departure.
4   Lines 469–92, which show the poet contemplating his own self.
5   Lines 672–720, which end the poem in a meditation on death, love, poetry, art and, finally, silence.

I will not supply notes for this poem, although you may wish to make your own, noting down the questions you think should figure in a full interpretation of the poem. When you have read these passages, please return to the Preface. This is an important part of the poem. **How is the Preface structured and what purpose do you think it serves?**

Discussion

It is divided into two sections (corresponding to the two paragraphs). In the first paragraph Shelley outlines the basics of the narrative. He begins by stating that 'The poem entitled "Alastor" may be considered as allegorical of one of the most interesting situations of the human mind'. Shelley's statements are sometimes rather obscure and elusive; the 'situation' he writes of here is something like the poet's quest for the ideal and his rejection of actual human sympathy.

So the poem is an allegory which depends upon the figure of the poet, the principal character of the poem. But the Preface cannot be said to simply outline the meaning of the poem. If we can come to an understanding of the Preface our reading of the poem will be more substantial. ∎

Judging from the Preface, what do you think is Shelley's attitude towards the poet?

Discussion

Shelley is clearly sympathetic towards the poet. He describes him in positive terms: 'a youth of uncorrupted feelings and adventurous genius'; 'an imagination inflamed and purified through familiarity with all that is excellent and majestic'. Yet just as clearly, he is described in terms of a problem: a problem, in fact, which leads the poet to 'an untimely grave'. ■

What is this problem?

Discussion

The answer seems to be given in the middle of the first paragraph. Shelley speaks of the poet's search for knowledge and of how it leaves him 'insatiate', that is, unfulfilled. Immediately, we recognize our theme of the quest for the ideal here. However, it is not the quest itself which seems to destroy the poet. Consider this passage: 'So long as it is possible for his desires to point towards objects thus infinite and unmeasured, he is joyous and tranquil and self-possessed. But the period arrives when these objects cease to suffice.' The problem seems to consist in a movement from contemplation of 'infinite and unmeasured' objects of thought to a search for a loved-object, 'a being whom he loves'. It is this that causes the poet's downfall. ■

The first paragraph of the Preface does not explicitly tell us why the search for a loved object should result in an 'untimely grave'. The answer is implicit in what Shelley says here, however. The poet's imagined object of love is clearly ideal. It is the culmination of all the poet's imaginative explorations. In the Preface Shelley describes the poet imagining the loved one: 'Conversant with speculations of the sublimest and most perfect natures, the vision in which he embodies his own imaginations unites all of wonderful, or wise, or beautiful, which the poet, the philosopher, or the lover could depicture' (Wu, *Romanticism*, 1994, p.835). Now let's look again at the passage in the poem in which the poet has his vision of his ideal object of love (ll.140–222). The poet's imagined object is an idealization of a perfect female 'being'. Once again we see the conventions of romance in operation here: there is a quest for truth culminating in the embodiment, in the shape of a female other, of all the quester's ideals. In the poem Shelley skilfully makes it clear that the female figure is idealized (that is, unreal, insubstantial), and he also shows how narcissistic such an ideal is. Read through the passage again (ll.140–222), looking for clues that the poet's own self is reflected back to him in the shape of the female ideal. **What is the significance of this narcissistic aspect of the poet's ideal?**

Discussion

The passage seems to rest on the fact that the poet is unable to find his imagined ideal in the world. He is unable to find it not only because the

155

ideal cannot exist in the world, but also because it is merely the reflection of his own mind, his own inner being. The poet is on a deluded quest to find himself in an externalized form. ■

This point explains the title of the poem. The title was suggested by Shelley's friend and fellow author, Thomas Love Peacock. For Peacock an 'alastor' was a demonic figure who haunts and torments a human being. Shelley's point in calling the poem 'Alastor', however, is that the 'spirit' that haunts and torments the poet is his own imagination. Look at lines 469–92. The 'alastor', in fact, is a reflection of the poet's true, alienated self rather than the idealized self-image the poet has held. Searching narcissistically for an idealized version of his own self, the poet becomes the very opposite of that idealized self-image. This is a narrative which has clear parallels with Mary Shelley's *Frankenstein*.

Shelley's characterization of the poet seems, then, to be fundamentally sympathetic, but also to point out the tragic miscalculations in his thoughts and actions. Look again at lines 129–39. **What do you think is the function of this passage?**

Discussion

The Arab maiden seems to be there to remind us that if the poet had not succumbed to an unrealizable quest for the ideal he would have been able to find love and companionship. As it is he ends in a kind of alienation which may well remind us of the ending of 'La Belle Dame Sans Merci'. (Perhaps the most intense representation of this alienation is in lines 272–95.) ■

Would you now reread the second paragraph of the Preface. The argument of this paragraph seems to be encapsulated in the passage Shelley quotes at the end: 'The good die first,/And those whose hearts are dry as summer dust,/Burn to the socket!'. This is a quotation from Wordsworth's long narrative poem, *The Excursion* (1814). One of the most important characters in this poem is called 'the Solitary'. The poem as a whole puts forward the Wordsworthian approach to nature discussed in the last chapter. Nature, Wordsworth argues, can save people from the alienation, frustration and triviality of contemporary, mainly urban life. Shelley hated the poem when he read it and this distaste seems to have encouraged him to compose 'Alastor'. (We have already seen, in Chapter One, how the second generation of male Romantic poets tended to define themselves against the work of Wordsworth.) Shelley objected particularly to Wordsworth's celebrations of a solitary relationship with nature. He believed this position to be an evasion of social and political responsibility. In a sonnet 'To Wordsworth', published in the *Alastor* volume, he argues that, having rejected his earlier commitment to 'truth and liberty', Wordsworth had become morally dead. Please read this sonnet now. **How does it help us to understand the second paragraph of the Preface?**

Discussion

This paragraph is itself concerned with solitude. It describes two kinds of solitary. The poet clearly belongs to the first kind. The second kind, we can now see, is modelled on Wordsworth. Read the sentence which begins 'But that power ... ' to confirm this.

The first kind of solitary is a 'luminary of the world' who, being 'awakened' to a 'too exquisite [...] perception' of the 'influences' of 'the Power' (that is, truth, ideal beauty, the sublime), is stricken with 'sudden darkness and extinction'. The second kind of solitary seems wholly negative in comparison. Not so much misguided as wilfully anti-social, this kind 'abjures' the 'Power' – it is rejected outright. They have no connection to other human beings and, although they live longer lives than the first kind, they 'burn to the socket', that is, like Wordsworth, they are morally dead. ∎

We have seen, then, that 'Alastor' is written out of a disagreement with Wordsworth. This insight, however, leaves us with various questions.

1   Why does Shelley in his Preface make so much of what we can call the 'Wordsworthian solitary' when that kind of figure does not actually appear in the poem itself?

2   If in the Preface Shelley opposes the poet to the 'Wordsworthian solitary', are we then to presume that the poet is in some way a representation of Shelley himself?

3   The Preface seems to leave no room for a way of life which does not in some way lead to tragedy. Does the poem continue or qualify the bleak view set out in the Preface?

We can come to some kind of answer to these questions by posing another question. Why does Shelley begin and end his poem with what seem like lyrical poems? The opening one (ll.1–49) is an invocation (call for assistance) to nature as the muse; the concluding one (ll.672–720) is a meditation on death, love, poetry, art and silence. In lyric poetry the emphasis is on the speaker's own thoughts and feelings, whilst in narrative the speaker (narrator) is not normally as important as the narrative itself. These sections are lyric in that sense. They frame the narrative rather as Walton's letters home frame the narrative of Frankenstein and the monster. They also seem to give us different perspectives to the over-idealizing one represented by the poet himself. Yet they cannot be said to present a particularly unified 'mind' or voice.

Look at lines 18–23. They seem very Wordsworthian don't they? Both in terms of the style and in terms of the idea of nature they present. Yet, if you look at the lines which follow them (ll.24–49), a very un-Wordsworthian note creeps in. Wordsworth never 'made [his] bed/In charnels and on coffins'. The section develops a sense of the inability of nature to satisfy the narrator's quest for truth. This voice seems closer to the 'poet' of the Preface than to Wordsworth.

In 'Alastor' Shelley is mixing different voices. That is to say, he is placing a Wordsworthian voice by the side of one which is nearer to his own, as it had developed up to this point. The Wordsworthian voice, it should be noted, is not that of *The Excursion*, but of the early Wordsworth whom Shelley still admired. These voices also seem to correspond to different attitudes towards nature, truth and human endeavour. The Wordsworthian voice is capable of finding truth in nature; the Shelleyan voice, if we can call it that, is more overtly idealistic and quests beyond the visible world around him. Having mixed such voices together, Shelley goes on to present a story of a poet who, as we have seen, is very similar to one aspect of Shelley himself. And yet, of course, Shelley has written all of the poem. Shelley seems to be representing dramatically various aspects of his own self: that element which is influenced by Wordsworth; the overly idealizing element; and the severely sceptical element.

'Alastor' utilizes one of the greatest strengths of Romantic verse narrative: its *dialogic* nature. In a verse narrative it is possible to juxtapose different 'voices' or points of view, to set them in a conflict or dialogue with each other. A similar dialogic aspect can be said to have generated much of the irony we discussed in relation to Keats's romances. Keats's poems, we saw, presented a kind of dialogue between different viewpoints: idealism versus rationalism; the imagined world versus the physical world. But is this dialogue in 'Alastor' merely concerned with Shelley's own multifaceted personality? Is the poem merely a dramatization of the conflicts between Shelley's idealism, scepticism and literary influences? I would say not. There will be a further exploration of the poem's relationship to a wider history in Chapter Ten. For the time being I would say that Shelley's staging of the battle between idealism and scepticism may be seen as his attempt to find an appropriate poetic, political and philosophical stance in post-Napoleonic Europe.

Finally I would like you to look again at the last section, from line 672 to line 720. **How does this section relate to the issues we have been discussing?**

Discussion

We can find all the themes we have been discussing in these lines. The figure of the wandering Jew (the 'one living man', l.677, doomed to eternal life, and wandering the earth) takes us back to the Wordsworthian solitary, the figure who, rejecting the human world, 'burns to the socket'.

The poet himself seems to represent a kind of beauty or ideal which has gone from the world forever. The narrator refuses to mourn the departure of the poet (look at lines 707 onwards). Why? The answer seems to come in the preceding lines. The world is one in which the dreams of 'dark magicians' (l.682; alchemists, who sought the key to eternal life and the means to change base metal into gold) cannot be fulfilled. Nature remains 'lovely' and yet 'Heartless things/Are done and said i' the world' (ll.690–91). ■

At the end of his poem Shelley seems to picture a world in which the quest for the ideal must succumb to something closer to political action, to attempts to alter the human world. Neither the approach of the poet nor of figures such as the Wordsworthian solitary are sufficient. Which is to say, neither an idealism centred in individual desire nor a personal scepticism about human society are appropriate positions. Another way of saying this, which seems to catch the astonishing realism of this last section, is that the old world of romance has gone. Like Keats's romances, Shelley's 'Alastor' is a romance narrative which undercuts the conventions it utilizes in order to respond to personal, social and political challenges.

I suggested earlier that if we looked at 'Alastor' we would see elements in that poem already observed in Keats's two romance narratives.

Let's sum up then. Both Keats and Shelley, we can now recognize, employ romance conventions to explore the limits of idealism. The three poems we have looked at present us with figures who are ambivalent, or to whom the reader experiences ambivalent responses. These ambivalent responses stem from the idealistic tendencies displayed by those figures. The 'knight-at-arms', Madeline, Porphyro and the poet of 'Alastor' are at once attractive figures yet the dupes of their own imaginations or their own idealism. In the three poems romantic love is employed to explore the costs of the kind of idealism associated with it. Hence, in all three poems philosophical questions concerning the limits of knowledge and the benefits of the human imagination are linked with an exploration of the relationship between the sexes. All three poems seem to be the product of a fear that blindness to reality will lead to alienation, despair and even to death. Finally, they are allusive, highly self-conscious literary productions. They are quintessentially Romantic romances, and rightfully canonical.

Reading Byron

by Stephen Bygrave

If you study Romantic writers in any British university the central figure will be Wordsworth. As we have seen, the 1805 *Prelude* was hardly read before this century, but later criticism has given that version the status of a national epic. Wordsworth has become a cultural treasure, his cottage at Grasmere a tourist attraction almost to rival Shakespeare's Stratford. However, if you were to ask anyone in continental Europe to name a British Romantic writer, the first name to occur would be that of George Noel Gordon, sixth Baron Byron. Byron was a phenomenon in his day, a bestseller even by present standards, with interest in his work magnified by a fascination with his scandalous private life. If we take Byron rather than Wordsworth as the central Romantic poet, the whole map of Romanticism looks different. Where Wordsworth stresses solitude, Byron is social, sociable and worldly. If Wordsworth is something of a 'Euro-sceptic', Byron is a committed European (he left England in 1816 to live in exile on the Continent), a figure to be compared with the German poet Goethe, who admired him. It is as such that Bertrand Russell, perhaps surprisingly, devotes a chapter to Byron in his *History of Western Philosophy*.

Like all the second generation of Romantic poets Byron partly defines himself against the figure of Wordsworth. He conducts a running argument with the idea of the great poet who has gone into retreat and into decline. In Byron's view Wordsworth had gone into retreat in the Lake District, having become High Church and High Tory, and into decline because the long poem known to his contemporaries was not *The Prelude* but *The Excursion* (published in 1814), which represented a fading of the poetic power and the political hopefulness of the 1790s. In 1818 Byron wrote that Wordsworth had been invited to aristocratic tables, 'where this poetical charlatan and political parasite picks up the crumbs with a hardened alacrity, the converted Jacobin having long subsided into the clownish sycophant of the worst prejudices of the aristocracy' (in Wu, *Romanticism*, 1994, p.771). Byron's diagnosis of the state of his country is similar to Shelley's in the poem 'England in 1819' that we considered in Chapter One (pp.7–9 above), but his point of view as an aristocratic exile allows him a perspective on the whole of Europe. After the defeat of Napoleon in 1815 the 'Holy Alliance' of Austria, Russia and Prussia had restored to their thrones most of the ruling families whom Napoleon had deposed. To many it looked like a restoration of the old order (or *ancien régime*) which had existed before the Revolution and which Napoleon had swept away.

Don Juan, the epic poem that we shall be studying, is a late and unfinished work. (By the way, 'Juan' should be pronounced to rhyme with 'new one' and 'true one'.) In the first half of this chapter I want to provide a context for *Don Juan* as a whole and to look at the Dedication to the poem; in the second half of the chapter we will look at Canto I. (I will refer to the poem by canto and stanza number and unless otherwise indicated quotations are from McGann, *Lord Byron: The Complete Poetical Works*, 1980–93.)

Byron's Dedication to *Don Juan* is ironically addressed to Robert Southey, the new poet laureate, and it attacks Wordsworth and Coleridge. You may come to think of Byron as more 'modern' than the Lake poets. But it is Byron who stresses continuity with the poets of the eighteenth century rather than the break from them advocated by Wordsworth and Coleridge. In the first canto of *Don Juan*, Byron establishes his own poetical hierarchy in a parody of the Christian ten commandments: 'Thou shalt believe in Milton, Dryden, Pope ...' (stanzas 205–6). In his pantheon, Byron puts as heirs to these poets not the 'Lakers', but the more traditional poets George Crabbe, Thomas Campbell, Samuel Rogers and Thomas Moore, his friend. Byron's modernity is to do with his scepticism about many features of Romantic writing – its claims to originality and transcendence, for example. This scepticism often takes the form of wit – there are plenty of good jokes in *Don Juan* and irreverence towards almost everything.

Byron and Wordsworth: Childe Harold's Pilgrimage

In reading *Don Juan* we may come to think that its 'digressions' are more important than the story from which they digress, and I will begin with a digression as well. I want to start with a passage from the fourth canto of an earlier work, *Childe Harold's Pilgrimage* (published in 1818), the poem that had made Byron famous. It is suffused with the influence of Wordsworth, but also represents a turning away from him. **What is there in this passage that reminds us of Wordsworth? Are there any significant differences?**

178

There is a pleasure in the pathless woods,
There is a rapture on the lonely shore,
There is society, where none intrudes,
By the deep Sea, and music in its roar:
I love not Man the less, but Nature more,
From these our interviews, in which I steal
From all I may be, or have been before,
To mingle with the Universe, and feel
What I can ne'er express, yet can not all conceal.

179

Roll on, thou deep and dark blue ocean – roll!
Ten thousand fleets sweep over thee in vain;
Man marks the earth with ruin – his control
Stops with the shore; upon the watery plain
The wrecks are all thy deed, nor doth remain
A shadow of man's ravage, save his own,
When, for a moment, like a drop of rain,
He sinks into thy depths with bubbling groan,
Without a grave, unknell'd, uncoffin'd, and unknown.

180

His steps are not upon thy paths, – thy fields
Are not a spoil for him, – thou dost arise
And shake him from thee; the vile strength he wields.
For earth's destruction thou dost all despise,
Spurning him from thy bosom to the skies,
And send'st him, shivering in thy playful spray
And howling, to his Gods, where haply lies
His petty hope in some near port or bay,
And dashest him again to earth: – there let him lay.

181

The armaments which thunderstrike the walls
Of rock-built cities, bidding nations quake,
And monarchs tremble in their capitals,
The oak leviathans, whose huge ribs make
Their clay creator the vain title take
Of lord of thee, and arbiter of war;
These are thy toys, and, as the snowy flake,
They melt into thy yeast of waves, which mar
Alike the Armada's pride, or spoils of Trafalgar.

[...]

184

And I have loved thee, Ocean! and my joy
Of youthful sports was on thy breast to be
Borne, like thy bubbles, onward: from a boy
I wantoned with thy breakers – they to me
Were a delight; and if the freshening sea
Made them a terror – 'twas a pleasing fear,
For I was as it were a child of thee,
And trusted to thy billows far and near,
And laid my hand upon thy mane – as I do here.

(*Complete Poetical Works*, vol. II, pp.184–6)

D i s c u s s i o n

There is much here that reminds us of Wordsworth: a claim for the superiority of solitude to 'society' and an assertion of man's insignificance in the
face of nature. There is also a claim for direct contact with 'nature', and, as
in Wordsworth, such contact allows an ideal merging and interchange of
the mind of the solitary poet with nature, which enables him to escape his
social role and 'mingle with the Universe' (178). In *The Prelude* Wordsworth
returns to the image of a river, but here Byron celebrates the ocean. The
sea is celebrated because of its indifference to humanity: it wrecks ships
and drowns sailors (179) and makes military hardware into its 'toys' (181).
To celebrate the sea the passage employs a long perspective like that we
saw in Shelley's 'Ozymandias'; two famous English naval victories two hundred and fifty years apart, the Spanish Armada and Trafalgar, are brought
together.

Chiefly though there is an added element here that is scarcely ever there in Wordsworth. The last of the quoted stanzas is self-dramatizing and claims a special relationship with nature, but the stroking and 'wantoning' denote a different sort of relationship. Though sexuality is not explicit – as it will be in *Don Juan* – the 'rapture' in the first of these stanzas and the breathy sensuality of the last of them are certainly not Wordsworthian. Later on, we will see that sex is not just *un*Wordsworthian; it is used to *anti*-Wordsworthian ends. ■

Byron also diverges from Wordsworth politically. It may not be obvious from these lines, but it can't be missed from the deleted note to stanza 181. Byron's use of notes is idiosyncratic. He appends them liberally to poetry, often to make specific historical connections that are not obvious in the poem itself. This note begins by explaining that a gale wrecked all the French ships taken at Trafalgar in 1805, but it concludes by talking about another famous British victory ten years later, at the Battle of Waterloo:

> For assuredly we dwell on this action, not because it was gained by Blucher or Wellington, but because it was lost by Buonaparte – a man who, with all his vices and his faults, never yet found an adversary with a tithe of his talents (as far as the expression can apply to a conqueror) or his good intentions, his clemency or his fortitude.
> Look at his successors throughout Europe, whose imitation of the worst part of his policy is only limited by their comparative impotence, and their positive imbecility.
>
> (*Complete Poetical Works*, vol. II, pp.340–41)

Despite the qualifications, this note is admiring of Napoleon and con-temptuous of the European leaders who succeeded him. Their policies are only an 'imitation of the worst part of his'. The leaders of the 'Holy Alliance' are attacked as much because of what they *are* in Byron's opinion as because of what they *do*: Napoleon's 'talents' further show up their 'imbecility' (ibid.). Earlier I spoke of Wordsworth choosing an 'aristocratic' point of view for his poem 'Composed Upon Westminster Bridge' (p.17 above) – though he is clearly not of that class. Byron consistently assumes an aristocratic viewpoint and his critique of Wordsworth depends on this class difference. As we will see, this is the position that he relies on in nar-rating *Don Juan*.

Wordsworth himself certainly regarded Byron as morally and politi-cally dangerous as well as scandalous. When the first part of *Don Juan* was published, he wanted the *Quarterly Review* to attack it not by a 'formal Critique', which would only give it even more publicity, but by directly attacking its 'damnable tendency'. Referring to critical attacks on Shelley, he writes:

> What avails it to hunt down Shelley, whom few read, and leave Byron untouched?
> I am persuaded that *Don Juan* will do more harm to the English character, than anything of our time …
>
> (quoted in Rutherford, *Byron*, 1970, pp.163–4)

There were several attacks on the poem similar to this one. *The British Critic* for example reviewed the volume containing the first two cantos of *Don Juan* as though it were a kind of self-help manual for adulterers: 'a manual of profligacy. Its tendency is not only to excite the passions, but to point out the readiest means and method of their indulgence' (Reiman, *The Romantics Reviewed: Part B*, 1972, vol. I, p.299). The sexual element in *Don Juan* is calculated to outrage not only the general conservatism (with a small 'c') of a figure such as Wordsworth but his political Conservatism as well. In fact, as I will suggest at the end of this chapter, it also affronted radicals whose zeal for reform on other issues ought to have made Byron their ally: evangelical Christians, for example, and feminists such as Hannah More.

In Chapter Two we looked at some of the political and social factors which distinguished the 'second generation' of Romantic writers from an earlier generation whose dominant figure was Wordsworth. Byron himself was born in 1788, the year before the fall of the Bastille that was the symbolic beginning of the French Revolution. In his brief career as an active radical peer he spoke against capital punishment for the frame-breaking Nottinghamshire weavers and for Catholic emancipation, but his party, the Whigs ('buff and blue') were out of power all through Byron's adult life. As he says in the poem, 'The consequence is, being of no party,/I shall offend all parties' (Canto IX, 26; *Complete Poetical Works*, vol. V, p.416). He sees formal politics as ineffectual: things recur or stay the same anyway (*Don Juan*, Canto XI, 76–83.) Byron fell from political favour in 1816 and, his marriage having also failed, he left England forever amid rumours of unnatural practices inflicted on his bride and of incest with his half-sister.

Hence Jerome McGann can summarize Byron's position as a poet in this way:

> Disheartened by his world and his own inability to alter its force or circumstance, Byron creates in his poetry a drama of the disillusioned existence. Its desperation appears in an escapist gesture of a special sort; not into the future, or into art, but into the flux of everything which is most immediate, a flight into the surfaces of poetry and life, the dance of verse, the high energy of instant sensations and feelings [...] whether of pleasure or pain.
>
> (*The Romantic Ideology*, 1983, p.127)

To be 'disillusioned' is not only to be disappointed but also to be undeceived, to see things in a newly realistic way. Byron is left with no community and no political base – but this also allows him freedom of action, or what in *Don Juan* he will call 'mobility' (Canto XVI, 96–8). 'Mobility', he writes in a note, is 'an excessive susceptibility of immediate impressions – at the same time without *losing* the past; [it] is, though sometimes apparently useful to the possessor, a most painful and unhappy attribute' (*Complete Poetical Works*, vol. V, p.769).

Reading Don Juan

Disillusion is typical of the narrative 'voice' of *Don Juan*; you don't need to read much of the poem to recognize it. The narrator is worldly and world-weary. The voice is conversational, but it is clearly not the language of conversation in 'low and rustic life' that Wordsworth says he strives for. Rather it is the voice of the urbane, cynical, worldly aristocrat:

> I perch upon an humbler promontory,
> Amidst life's infinite variety:
> With no great care for what is nicknamed glory,
> But speculating as I cast mine eye
> On what may suit or may not suit my story,
> And never straining hard to versify,
> I rattle on exactly as I'd talk
> With any body in a ride or walk.
>
> I don't know that there may be much ability.
> Shown in this sort of desultory rhyme;
> But there's a conversational facility,
> Which may round off an hour upon a time.
> Of this I'm sure at least, there's no servility
> In mine irregularity of chime,
> Which rings what's uppermost of new or hoary,
> Just as I feel the 'Improvisatore.'
>
> (*Don Juan*, Canto XV, 19–20; *Complete Poetical Works* vol. V, 1986, p.594)

An 'Improvisatore' is an Italian poet who would travel around improvising verses. This is an ideal of immediacy that Byron aims at:

> But what's this to the purpose? you will say.
> Gent. Reader, nothing; a mere speculation,
> For which my sole excuse is – 'tis my way,
> Sometimes *with* and sometimes without occasion
> I write what's uppermost, without delay;
> This narrative is not meant for narration,
> But a mere airy and fantastic basis,
> To build up common things with common places.
> [...]
>
> I have brought this world about my ears, and eke
> The other; that's to say, the Clergy – who
> Upon my head have bid their thunders break
> In pious libels by no means a few.
> And yet I can't help scribbling once a week,
> Tiring old readers, nor discovering new.
> In youth I wrote, because my mind was full,
> And now because I feel it growing dull.
>
> (*Don Juan,* Canto XIV, 7 and 10, *Complete Poetical Works*, vol. V, pp.560–61)

The pose of improvisation *is* a pose, as we can see from looking at Byron's drafts of the poem. Its conversational fluency is the product of much rewriting (see Figures 8 and 9).

Technically, *Don Juan* is a *tour de force*. It is an epic (or mock epic) written in *ottava rima*, an eight-line stanza that Byron had already used in *Beppo* (1817). Six lines rhyming alternatively are followed by a final couplet, so the rhyme scheme is *ababbcc*. The form came ultimately from the fifteenth-century Italian comic poets Luigi Pulci and Giambattista Casti, but Byron had an example nearer home in an English poem *The Monks and the Giants*, published in 1817 by 'Whistlecraft', the pen name of his friend John Hookham Frere. As we will see, the form allows Byron to play off the effect of conversation against the strict demands of the rhyme-scheme. And by using the first six lines to build something up and the final couplet to take it away, he gets many of his jokes.

Despite its epic length, like many Romantic texts *Don Juan* is a fragment. It is an unfinished poem of sixteen-and-a-half cantos written over seven years. It was begun in July 1818 and six volumes, containing Cantos I to XVI were published in Byron's lifetime. The first volume, containing Cantos I and II, was published anonymously by John Murray in 1819; and the second, containing Cantos III to V, in 1821. Murray and his own friends persuaded Byron to tone down the explicit political focus of these early cantos. The prose Preface didn't appear until 1901, and the Dedication which was to replace it was suppressed and went unpublished until 1832. The poem was reconceived between 1821 and 1822 and further volumes were published by the liberal John Hunt rather than the conservative Murray, so the later cantos could be much more explicit politically. So, for instance, a diatribe against Wellington excised from Canto III opens Canto IX.

The dedication to Robert Southey is of course ironic (Southey is later rhymed with 'mouthy'). Like Wordsworth, Southey had been at the start of his writing career a radical and a supporter of the Revolution but had become increasingly reactionary; having made peace with the Tory establishment, he was made Poet Laureate in 1813. Byron also had personal reasons for attacking Southey. As he was writing the poem he heard that Southey had been spreading a rumour that Byron and Shelley had 'formed a League of Incest' in which each had had intercourse with Shelley's wife Mary and with Claire Clairmont. (Byron rejected this allegation in a letter to John Cam Hobhouse of 11 November 1818.)

The hero of the Dedication is Milton (10), its real villain is Robert Stewart, Viscount Castlereagh. As Foreign Secretary from 1812 to 1822 Castlereagh pursued a policy of alliance with reactionary states. He represented Britain at the Congress of Vienna in 1815, and at the later Congress of the European Alliance at Aix-la-Chapelle in 1818. The Dedication also refers to the fact that Castlereagh, who was Irish, had put down the Irish rebellion of 1798 as Lord Lieutenant of Ireland and pushed through the Union of 1800. Byron was contemptuous even of Castlereagh's suicide in 1822: 'So Castlereagh has cut his throat; — The worst/Of this is, — that his own was not the first' (*Complete Poetical Works*, vol. VI, p.578).

The Dedication has four main parts:

1 an attack on Southey and the other 'Lake poets' (1–9)

2 an invocation to Milton (10–11)

3 the attack on Castlereagh (12–14)

4 a statement of Byron's position and a final 'dedication' to Southey (15–17).

I would like you now to read the Dedication, thinking about the following questions on each of these four parts.

(1) What are the 'Lakers' attacked for?

Discussion

Considering the personal animus Byron held against Southey, the attack on the Lake poets is surprisingly good-humoured. Southey is 'representative of all the race' (l.2) of those who, having been radicals in their youth, have undergone a 'conversion' (l.42), and are now enjoying favour under the Regency. This enables them to publish long and incomprehensible works in prose and verse (Byron singles out Wordsworth's *Excursion*, 1814, by name). They are attacked for their egotism and 'narrowness' (5), but still allowed credit for their poetry. ■

Figure 8   George Gordon Noel Byron, *Don Juan,* autograph unsigned manuscript first draft of Cantos I–V; Canto I, stanza 158. The Pierpont Morgan Library, New York. MA 56–57. Photo: David A. Loggie.

1 She ceased & turned upon her pillow;—pale

2 ~~But beautiful she lay—her eyes shed tears~~
        ~~lays~~
        ~~lies~~
        ~~lays,~~   ~~lies~~
                  ~~the starting tears~~
                  ~~and drop the tears~~

3 ~~Reluctant past her bright eyes rolled—as a veil~~

4 ~~Like Summer rains through Sunshine~~
  ~~As~~   ~~drop~~
             ~~flow fastly~~

3 ~~From her bright eyes reluctant rolled the veil~~
                ~~flows as a veil~~
                ~~leaps~~

4 ~~Of her dishevelled tresses dark appears~~
        ~~dark dishevelled tresses~~

5 ~~Wooing her cheek—the dar   black curls strive but fail~~
  ~~Contrasting with her cheek—& bosom~~
                  ~~they~~
          ~~her   & strive but fail~~ [3]

2 She lay, her dark eyes flashing through their tears,

3 ~~As~~ Like Skies that rain and lighten; as a veil

4 Waved and ~~oerflowing~~ her wan cheek appears
          oershading

5 Her ~~hair~~ streaming hair—the black curls strive but fail

6 To hide the glossy shoulder which ~~still~~ uprears

7 ~~It's symmetry with~~
  ~~In shining~~
  ~~It's whiteness through them all—with lips~~
  It's snow through all—~~she lay with soft lips~~
           ~~her   lips   sweet lips lay apart~~
                ~~ripe lips lie apart~~
  her soft lips lie apart,

8 And louder than her breathing beats her heart.

[3] The next four lines were written crosswise in the right-hand margin, after he had finished the couplet.

Figure 9 Transcription of George Gordon Noel Byron, *Don Juan* autograph unsigned manuscript first's draft of Cantos I–V; Canto I, stanza 158. Reprinted from *Byron's Don Juan*: vol. 1, *The Making of a Masterpiece*, 2nd edition, edited by Truman Guy Steffan. Copyright © 1957, 1971, renewed 1985. By permission of the University of Texas Press, Austin.

(2) We have seen the importance of Milton to all the Romantic writers. Why is he invoked here?

Discussion

Unlike the Lake poets, as Byron sees it, Milton never betrayed his political principles. Milton is here seen primarily as a political example (or even as a prophet) rather than as a poet. Byron is not nostalgic as Wordsworth is. He doesn't invoke Milton to show how the present is worse than a mighty past, and can't be altered. Byron is angry at what he sees to be present oppression: Milton is invoked to attack Castlereagh. ■

(3) Is the attack on Castlereagh similar to that made on the Lake poets?

Discussion

The contemporary poets of the opening may be vain, self-serving and reactionary but in the end these offences are as nothing against the politician's power to have people killed. Stanza 14 refers to the post-Napoleonic carve-up of Europe. But it is interesting to note the position from which Byron's anger and disdain issue. Having been called, in effect, a murderer, Castlereagh is then attacked for his mediocrity, and for being a bad speaker. He is not just a 'tool' [of] tyranny' but a *vulgar* tool (l.93). Byron moves from politics to discourse in stanza 13 – indeed he sees politics *as* discourse: the last of Castlereagh's failings is a failing in *style*. This is not denunciation so much as a put-down in class terms. Byron is a liberal, a radical, even in some ways a revolutionary, but he is no democrat. ■

(4) What is 'Byron's own position'?

Discussion

Literally, he is in Italy – a country that had been placed under Austrian domination since 1815. Of course stanza 16 is ironic, the Dedication is not a bit of 'honest, simple verse' (l.130). The stanza ends with a couplet which, like Shelley's 'England in 1819', lists political symptoms – this time of all Europe ('slaves, allies, kings, armies') – before revealing its hand: as laureate it will be Southey's function to celebrate these in (bad) verse. Byron is also explicit about his own politics: buff and blue (l.132) were the colours of the Whigs. In an era when 'apostasy's so fashionable' (l.134) Byron implicitly associates himself with a commitment to unfashionable literary and political principles. ■

The Dedication functions as a very good introduction to the poem. It is rude (indeed libellous), lays out its own ideological principles and accustoms us to the witty and cynical voice of the narrator. However, it gives us no hint of what the events of the poem are to be.

There is another element in the Dedication that I haven't so far mentioned: sex again. Lack of sexuality features as a moral condemnation: Castlereagh is called an 'intellectual eunuch' and a 'dry bob' (Dedication, ll.88 and 24) – Regency slang for *coitus interruptus*. There is a similar condemnation of Wordsworth in terms of sexual lack by Shelley in *Peter Bell the Third* in 1819:

> ... from the first 'twas Peter's drift
> To be a kind of moral eunuch,
> He touched the hem of Nature's shift,
> Felt faint – and never dared uplift
> The closest, all-concealing tunic.
>
> (XI, ll.167–71; Webb, *P.B. Shelley: Poems and Prose*, 1996, p.170)

Telling the story of *Don Juan* should reveal how central is sex and sexuality.

Don Juan: *plot, timescale and plan*

The figure of Don Juan originated in a seventeenth-century Spanish play by Tirso da Molina. Don Juan became a familiar figure through, for example, Molière and Mozart (*Don Juan,* 1665; *Don Giovanni,* 1787; first English performance 1817). In both of these cases, however, the story begins with the hero fully formed and in mid-career. Byron begins with Juan's upbringing and education – though his character doesn't 'develop' as the hero of a novel does. Throughout the poem is a running joke based on the mythical status of the hero as a seducer: Don Juan should be a libertine and a kind of devil who is eventually punished by being sent to hell. Byron's Don Juan is always *being* seduced – he is passive, acted upon rather than acting. His Juan is not cynical and diabolical either – though the narrator is.

As we will see, the first canto is largely concerned with the sixteen-year-old Juan's adulterous affair with Donna Julia. After his mother Donna Inez sends Juan away from Cadiz, Canto II involves him in a shipwreck and he is cast adrift on an open boat where the other survivors resort to cannibalism. He is washed ashore on a Greek island and is discovered by Haidée, daughter of the pirate ruler, Lambro. Juan and Haidée go on to enjoy an idyllic love affair. Their idyll is shattered by her father's return (Cantos III and IV). Haidée dies and Juan is shipped off to be sold in the slave market at Constantinople. In Canto V Juan, now a possession of the Ottoman Sultan, is introduced to the Sultan's favourite wife, Sultana Gulbeyaz who for ease of access installs him in her husband's harem disguised as a woman (Canto VI). Juan escapes and flees towards the border. The shipwreck episode in Canto II had been carefully derived from various documentary sources, but Canto VII is the first to deal with specific historical events – the Russo-Turkish war and the siege of the Turkish city of Ismail by Russian forces, begun 30 November 1790, in which Juan fights as a mercenary. After the city falls and is sacked Juan is sent with dispatches to St Petersburg. Canto IX finds him at the court of Catherine the Great, where Juan becomes her 'man-mistress'. Catherine sends him as an ambassador to England. Byron himself had left England once and for all in 1816 and 'The English Cantos' (X–XVII) are partly a memoir. (Byron had burned his own memoirs on the advice of his friend Hobhouse in 1809. He had visited Seville with Hobhouse around the same time. Another set of memoirs, begun at the same time as the poem, was burned after his death.) Juan experiences a London social 'season', is seduced by a duchess at a country house party and when the poem breaks off, in its seventeenth canto, is becoming involved with his hostess, Lady Adeline.

Byron at first claimed the poem 'had no plan' but McGann has shown how in a letter to Murray in February 1821 Byron saw the plot developing. Juan, sixteen at the start, was to die on the guillotine in 1793. Thus the period the poem deals with is 1787–93. Juan's career was to be played out against the early phase of the Revolution. The period covered by the narrative, however, was intended to be concurrent with the poem's 'improvisatory' writing. A parallel was to be drawn with the Europe of 1818–24. A third period with which the poem deals is that of Byron's career during what he called his 'years of fame' (1812–15), in the Napoleonic wars. This device enables Byron to use the past to condemn the present – so Milton is invoked to condemn the poet Southey and the politician Castlereagh – but largely Byron stresses the *similarity* of the post-war world to the world of the *ancien régime* it had supposedly supplanted.

Many anthologies print only extracts from the earlier cantos of *Don Juan*. These extracts tend to leave us with the story of Don Juan himself, cutting away the apparent 'digressions'. In Laurence Sterne's eighteenth-century novel *Tristram Shandy*, a novel which has affinities with Byron's poem, the narrator argues that his digressions are central:

> Digressions incontestably are the sunshine; — they are the life, the soul of reading; — take them out of this book for instance, — you might as well take the book along with them; — cold eternal winter would reign in every page of it; restore them to the writer; he steps forth like a bridegroom, — bids All hail; brings in variety and forbids the appetite to fail.
>
> (*Tristram Shandy*, 1967 edn, p.95)

The centrality of the digressions suggests why, as Byron insisted in a letter to his publisher after publication of the first two cantos, the poem could have no 'plan'. Like *Tristram Shandy* the poem never had a detailed plan; rather it is episodic. *Don Juan* was composed and published serially, like a novel, allowing Byron to incorporate the reactions of his readers to earlier episodes as he wrote.

Hero and narrator

The first words of the poem proper are 'I want a hero'. 'Want' here means both to lack and to desire and, as may be obvious to you by now, the true hero of *Don Juan* is not Juan but the narrator of the poem, a figure who shares many characteristics with Byron himself. Scattered through the poem is an autobiographical narrative (which we will return to later), and throughout it there is a self-conscious representation of the poet as hero, 'The grand Napoleon of the realms of rhyme' as he refers to himself (Canto XI, 55).

Byron was, after Napoleon, the most famous man in the world in the early years of the nineteenth century. He is famous now and was in his lifetime partly because the poet is confused with the poems, the Romantic heroes are confused with their producer. This is a confusion that Byron exploits. His image of youthful, risqué glamour has led one writer in recent years to compare him with James Dean and another to cite Elvis Presley (Carter, *Expletives Deleted*, 1992, p.169; Paglia, *Sexual Personae*, 1991, pp.347–64). The mock title the 'Napoleon of the realms of rhyme' refers particularly to his earlier career, the 'years of fame' following the enormous success of *Childe Harold* I, II (1812) and III (1816). (The final canto, part of which we have considered, was published in 1818.) In *Don Juan*, however, the narrator stresses both his world weariness and his age.

During the 'years of fame' the 'Byronic hero' was developed in verse romances and dramas: *The Giaour, The Bride of Abydos, The Corsair* (a poem considered in Chapter Ten, which sold 10,000 copies on its first day of publication in 1814), and *Lara*. The Byronic hero of these works is a moody outlaw nursing some secret guilt, a rebel in a non-political guise. Through him, Byron succeeds in translating a complex politics into a more abstract defence of 'Liberty'. (Byron was, after all, an active peer in a country where Napoleon was the enemy.) Once in exile, Byron had contacts with the *Carbonari,* a faction fighting for the independence of Italy from the Austrians, and he died in the struggle for Greek independence from the Turks. Despite his gestures towards 'Liberty', Byron is quite as capable of cynicism about such matters as he is about everything else. This is a complete poem written in 1820:

Stanzas

When a man hath no freedom to fight for at home
Let him combat for that of his neighbours;
Let him think of the glories of Greece and of Rome,
And get knocked on his head for his labours.

To do good to mankind is the chivalrous plan,
And is always as nobly requited;
Then battle for freedom wherever you can,
And, if not shot or hang'd, you'll get knighted.

(*Complete Poetical Works*, vol. IV, 1986, p.290)

The poem is deeply ironic – at the expense of those politicians who might indeed have been knighted for their efforts in foreign policy, but also at Byron's own expense. At home, 'freedom' is a lost cause; but at the time this poem was written, uprisings in Spain and Naples led Byron to believe that Italy would rise against Austria. And he was to die 'combating' for the freedom of Greece from Turkey, leaving *Don Juan* unfinished.

I hope to have provided some useful contexts for reading Byron and to have suggested some of the connections between sexuality, politics and humour which run through *Don Juan*. In the rest of this chapter we will be looking at Canto I of the poem, which is a self-sufficient narrative.

Canto I

To give you a sense of all the issues in this canto, I'm going to ask you to read passages from it at some length. Let's split it in half. We need to separate 'story' from 'plot'. Story is *what* happens, plot is *how* it happens. In this case we can separate the story (what happens to Juan) from the plot (how it happens, and what the narrator says about it – and about a host of other matters) fairly easily. Story and plot comment on each other. We will read through the poem first of all, looking both at *what* happens and at *how* it happens. Then I want to go back and look at the two principal female figures and at Byron's treatment of 'pleasure' and sexuality. Would you now read right through Canto I as far as the end of stanza 117? **Make brief notes on what happens.**

Discussion

My notes are as follows. There is a mock epic opening (1–7) – that is, an opening which is modelled on those of conventional epic poetry but which is clearly satirical. 'My way is to begin with the beginning' (l.50), the narrator claims, but this is not what he does. Stanzas 8–36 are to do with Juan's parents and their relationship, leading eventually to the death of his father. As in the Dedication, references tend to be to the contemporary world in which Byron writes: thus Donna Inez is a bluestocking (16). And they tend to call attention to the narrator: he reflects generally on marital relationships (21) and educated women (22) from a position outside of marital relationships (23), though he knows the family and seems in the past to have played a part in their story (24).

Stanza 25 shows Juan as a child; 37 shows him as an heir (to not much); his education follows (39; 44). Juan goes from the age of six to sixteen between stanzas 50 and 54. The next twelve stanzas (55–66) are concerned with Donna Julia. (The narrator retails gossip that her husband, Don Alfonso, and Donna Inez had been lovers.)

Stanzas 69–85 present Juan and Julia, at first from her perspective – she is aware of him at first as a 'pretty child' (69) – then from his perspective (86–97). Stanzas 97–102 narrate Donna Inez's complaisance. Stanzas 102–17 narrate what happens on 6 June, Juan's first 'fall' as it is referred to later (127). ∎

I hope you are finding the poem funny. There is nothing more deadly than trying to explain jokes, but **could we say how they work and what kind of humour it is?**

Discussion

Even from here we can see many instances of the way the final couplet of the *ottava rima* delivers a punchline. Consider for example, 'But – Oh! ye lords of ladies intellectual,/Inform us truly, have they not hen-peck'd you all?' (22), or 'What men call gallantry, and gods adultery/Is much more common where the climate's sultry' (63), or the description of Donna Julia in stanza 61, or Julia's 'fall' to Juan (117).

Much of the humour is ironic. Irony exploits a gap between what is said and what we as readers infer. I think that the gap, or ironic distance, between, for example, what Juan thinks and what we are likely to think is maintained by two things:

1   our awareness of the narrator's personality. He seems at first to be a meddling middle-aged bachelor friend of Juan's family, but we are chiefly aware of him as a sophisticated roué (80) who is writing a poem, the problems of composing which we are brought into. For example he calls attention to his ingeniously laboured rhymes and the fact that he can't remember which commandment is 'thou shalt not commit adultery' (98).

2   our awareness of the contemporary world in which the narrator writes (for example, the jokes at the expense of Wordsworth and Coleridge as the lovesick Juan wanders about, in stanzas 90–91). ■

Perhaps we can now read on to the end of the first canto (118–222), again making notes on what happens.

D i s c u s s i o n

The second half of Canto I begins with the narrator expatiating on 'Pleasure' – he says he is incorrigible (119). He takes us forward six months, to November, but the long digression continuing the theme of 'Pleasure' goes up to stanza 134. Stanzas 134–87 present a scene from a farce. Don Alfonso bursts in on Julia and her maid Antonia with friends, servants and his attorney 'To prove himself the thing he most abhorred' (line 1112) – that is to catch Julia in adultery and prove himself a cuckold. We have had a hint that Juan is there and of where he is hidden, but it is not until they have all gone that Juan appears (166). He now hides in the closet. Alfonso returns, finds Juan's shoes (180–1) and sets up a commotion. Alfonso goes for his sword and meets Juan in the doorway as the latter attempts to flee. They fight, and Juan's only clothing falls off as he makes his escape. Subsequently Juan is sent on a Grand Tour, Julia to a nunnery.

Her letter (192–7) is a kind of coda. (We will look at this letter in some detail in a moment.) There is then another coda, by the narrator, which returns us to another world, one governed by commercial considerations (199; 209–11). He claims that the story is true – we may infer that by this he means realistic. This ending is elegiac, but there is another joke at the expense of Southey. ■

Julia and Donna Inez

We have seen only one brief example of Byron in wholly serious mode – in the extract from *Childe Harold's Pilgrimage* with which I began. Almost everything in *Don Juan* seems to have been fair game for a joke. **Now re-read Julia's letter (stanzas 192–7). Is this an exception? Do we take it wholly seriously?**

D i s c u s s i o n

I think we do. This is the first time any of the characters in the poem are allowed to speak for themselves at any length. By this I mean that Julia speaks rather than being spoken for, and that she speaks without interruption from the narrator's commentary upon writing which otherwise goes on throughout. If we were to come across this passage as a poem in its own right there would be no problem about how to read it. This is sentimental in the eighteenth-century sense of that word. It is an outpouring of feeling, and has a validity as such. There is pathos in Julia's acceptance that her affair with Juan is at an end although her love isn't. This is the last we hear from her. The narrator later speaks of his own heart being 'a thing apart' (215), apparently confirming Julia's claim that 'man's love is of his life a thing apart' (194). ■

We have been reading Julia's letter as though it were a free-standing lyric. However, its function within the context of the poem may be different. It is striking partly because it seems to be independent of the experienced, cynical and masculine view of sexuality within which it is embedded. There are other examples of this happening in the poem – the death of Haidée in Canto IV – but they are rare enough to stand out where they do occur. A hostile essay by Francis Jeffrey in the *Edinburgh Review* of February 1822 took this passage as one example of Byron's amorality, because 'a shameless and abandoned woman' writes in 'the very spirit of warm, devoted, pure and unalterable love' (Reiman, *The Romantics Reviewed: Part B*, 1972, vol.II, p.937). Jeffrey's sideswipe at Byron is based on a hostility to his politics as well as the moral content of his fictions, but it does raise the issue of *why* this passage alone in Canto I and exceptionally in the whole poem, should have escaped irony. Even if we take its context to be only the rest of this first canto, Julia might be seen as a victim of hypocrisy – her sin was not to have committed adultery but to have been found out.

Or Julia herself might be hypocritical too: 'love is taught hypocrisy from youth' (72), and her letter might be seen as yet another attempt at deceiving herself about her love for Juan and Juan's for her. But if so, the narrator is unusually reticent on this point.

The passage is also a good example of how subsequent events may cause us to revise our first reading. In the next canto of the poem Juan is cast adrift on an open boat and begins to re-read Julia's letter, when lovesickness is succeeded, grossly, by seasickness (II, 18–23). After some days without food Juan's shipwrecked companions eat his dog and then resolve on cannibalism. They decide to draw lots for which of their number should be eaten. The only paper that can be found is Julia's letter, so it is torn up (II, 74). This undignified fate for the letter could be seen as destroying its poignancy, or alternatively as intensifying its pathos.

There is another possible way of reading Julia's letter, and one that is perhaps less flattering to Byron. Let's consider the submission that Julia is made to express. Having lost everything and been in effect imprisoned because of the affair, Julia has 'nothing to reproach, nor to request' (193), and has 'no further claim' on Juan (192). She is still fixated on him: 'all is o'er/For me on earth' (196) – at twenty-three! – except a love for Juan that makes her 'To all, except your image, madly blind' (195). She acknowledges that he will have other lovers. His freedom of movement contrasts with her incarceration. He will range over 'all European climes' (194). Julia is made to generalize this contrast as a gender difference: 'woman's whole existence' is to stay at home, and be in love. Her own future 'imprisonment' is unfortunate but convenient. She will continue to love Juan, but without conditions. Her love will be unrequited; its object can further his sexual education. Julia's letter is sealed *Elle vous suit partout* (she or it follows you everywhere), which was the motto on Byron's own seal. Is this undemanding constancy a fantasy on Byron's part? Is it evidence, in other words, that he is a libertarian in terms of sexual behaviour only when it is *male* sexual behaviour? It could be seen, at least, as marking a limit on his demands for sexual licence. And yet the apparent absence of irony might also suggest some nostalgia on the part of the author for Julia's directness of feeling, some ambivalence about his own cynical pose, which within the limits of this pose he can only place in the mouth of a woman.

It seems to me that these interpretations are all possible ways of reading Julia's letter, although we may not be able to decide between them. If we remember the Dedication, we will know that Byron's jokes are not *only* cynical, that it is not the case that he has no agenda. He does believe that some actions are ethical, others not. The problem comes with trying to determine his position. He attacks Wordsworth as sexless, po-faced and reactionary; but that does not mean that everything about Byron and his work must therefore be 'radical'.

I have tried to sketch a general problem of how we are to understand gender relations in *Don Juan* by focusing on a single important passage, and I want to pursue this problem more generally by turning first to the other principal female figure in this first canto of *Don Juan*, Donna Inez, Juan's mother.

Donna Inez is satirized as a 'new woman', a 'lady intellectual' who reads the didactic novels of the 'bluestocking' Hannah More (I, 16) and who eventually sets up, like More, a Sunday School (II, 10). (Byron excised from the proof a couplet about her treatment of the boys: 'Their manners mending, and their morals curing,/She taught them to suppress their vice and urine', *Complete Poetical Works*, vol. IV, 1986, p.92.) When we last hear of her she has remarried and writes to Juan in Moscow, where he is the 'man-mistress' of Catherine the Great, praising 'the Empress's *maternal* love' (X, 32). **What role does Donna Inez play in Canto I?**

Discussion

Donna Inez and Don José 'ne'er agreed except in doting on' their son (25), and on hypocritically maintaining the show of their marriage. 'Wishing each other, not divorced, but dead', they nevertheless 'lived respectably as man and wife' (26). She gets 'professional' help to control her husband (27–8, 32–3). At his death he leaves two mistresses, though not much else; the narrator pruriently reports gossip that Donna Inez and Alfonso had also been lovers (66). So her puritanism is seen as hypocritical. As we have seen, it is hinted that she once erred herself but now her passion is kept under wraps. She supervises the strict education of her son – an education which omits sex (39–50). Forbidding Juan the family missal because of its crude pictures, she keeps it for herself. The narrator hints that Donna Inez may have had 'motives' for overlooking the affair between her son and her friend; and he professes ignorance too of how Don Alfonso's suspicions could have been raised (139). She wants only to avoid scandal (190–1). The narrative therefore punishes her by making her own actions lead to the disaster they were aimed at avoiding. ■

Some of Byron's friends thought they recognized Donna Inez as a satirical portrait of Byron's wife: Lady Byron too had 'tried to prove her loving lord was *mad*' (27). In other ways she is like his own mother, who had certainly supervised his education. Donna Inez is characterized chiefly as a hypocrite, and hypocrisy or 'cant' is the traditional target of the satirist. Byron wrote to Lady Blessington:

> I am so changeable, being everything by turns and nothing long — I am such a strange mélange of good and evil, that it would be difficult to describe me [...] There are but two sentiments to which I am constant — a strong love of liberty, and a detestation of cant.
>
> (Countess Blessington, *Conversations of Lord Byron*, 1969 edn, p.221)

For Byron 'cant' is everywhere in the modern world, exemplified by the Toryism of Castlereagh, by the portentousness, obscurity and religiosity of the 'Lake School', by evangelicalism and by a stress on utility rather than pleasure. So he seems to be defending an Enlightenment tradition (rational and sceptical of authority) against an emergent Victorianism, as in his blasphemous parody of the commandments, with which we began. Blasphemy and sexuality are conjoined: Byron sees religion, economics and sexual repression as a cluster which needs to be attacked. Hence the scandal of the poem. For reasons we have discussed, in the first canto of the poem this is primarily sexual scandal. As Byron writes in a letter to his friend Douglas Kinnaird:

> As to 'Don Juan' — confess — confess — you dog — and be candid — that it is the sublime of *that there* sort of writing — it may be bawdy — but is it not good English? it may be profligate — but is it not *life*, is it not *the thing*? Could any man have written it — who has not lived in the world? and tooled in a post-chaise? in a hackney coach? in a Gondola? against a wall? in a court carriage? in a vis a vis? — on a table? and under it? I have written about a hundred stanzas of a third Canto — but it is damned modest — the outcry has frightened me. — had such projects for the Don — but the *Cant* is so much stronger than *Cunt* now a days, — that the benefit of experience in a man who had well weighed the worth of both monosyllables — must be lost to despairing posterity.
>
> (Marchand, *Byron's Letters and Journals*, 1975, vol. 6, p.232)

In the letter Byron strikes a pose much like that of the poem's narrator – he is a 'man of the world', both sexually experienced and sexually voracious. Feminine desire (and homoerotic desire) is represented elsewhere in the poem, but the view of gender in its first canto is close to that in this letter. 'Life' is defined in sexual terms: men so define themselves and women are so defined. Sex is a motive force, as much for those who seek to contol it as for lovers. In the final lines of this quotation, the outcry against *Don Juan* is seen as a strong but hypocritical alliance against pleasure.

Pleasure

As we have noticed in Canto I of the poem there is a long digression on 'Pleasure' (119–34). I have already suggested that the digressions may be more important than the narrative from which they digress, so it is worth paying some attention to this passage. It may be self-defeating to try to discuss 'pleasure' – like explaining a joke – but it is clearly an important theme in the poem, in stanzas 153 and 217 for example.

Could you now re-read stanzas 118–33? **(1) What does Byron mean by 'Pleasure'? (2) What is the purpose of the apparent digression-within-the-digression of stanzas 128–32? (3) Why might society seek to control 'Pleasure'?**

D i s c u s s i o n

1   By 'Pleasure' Byron evidently means sexual pleasure above all else. Love and leisure are synonymous for the narrator. The narrator's resolve to reform 'next winter' (119) is like the apocryphal prayer of St Augustine – who was referred to in stanza 47: 'O Lord make me chaste – but not yet'. It presents the narrator as lovably incorrigible. He is not jaded: he doesn't want new pleasures, like Xerxes – more of the old will do (118). Liberty is always up against constraint: freedom is always freedom *from* some strict demand or other. This is apparent even in the virtuosity of the form in which the speaking voice is set against the demands of the rhyme scheme (120).

Stanzas 122–27 make up a list of possible objects of desire, some with sentimental appeal and some which appeal to other kinds of desire (for revenge, drink, money, and so on). It is not that rainbows, birdsong and so on *aren't* pleasurable, but that less sentimentally appealing activities like arguing with a 'tiresome friend' are *also* pleasurable. There is then a kind of realistic impulse – all these things occupy the same world. Of all of them, first love is the sweetest. It is a Fall and afterwards nothing can be the same (127). Afterwards, you always know something you didn't know before.

2   If this sounds sentimental, stanzas 129–32 discuss in cynical terms some of the uses to which new knowledge was being put. Stanza 127 has compared love to Prometheus 'filching' fire from heaven, for which he was punished by Zeus. In Mary Shelley's novel, the scientist Frankenstein was 'The Modern Prometheus'. In these stanzas Byron considers what gifts the scientist of his own day, the modern Prometheus, had brought humankind.

He is sceptical that 'progress' is inevitable: for every medical advance that saves lives there is a Waterloo to end them. 'The great' (pox) (l.1040) is syphilis (these references were removed from early editions of the poem), which was said to have come from America. The mention of America leads into an ironic allusion to the theories of the political economist Thomas Malthus, who had argued (in terms we would now call 'Darwinian') that famine and disease acted as 'natural' correctives to 'thin' (l.1044) a population that had outgrown the resources to support it. Byron suggests that it is curious to believe that a 'civilization' that could act on such a belief (by letting the Irish starve for example) should think itself superior to one in which sexually-transmitted disease originated. Is *our* 'pseudo-syphilis' – Europe's social disease – really to be preferred to *their* physical disease? As with innovations in poetry, scientific innovations may not represent progress at all. And evangelical religion may have patented new ways of saving souls (132), but not of saving lives or improving them.

3   The narrator concludes (133) that pleasure has no 'end', in the two senses of that word. That is, it exists for its own sake, having no goal but itself; and the desire for it is also infinite. As this stanza also suggests, it is therefore seen as a 'sin' that must be controlled. And, as Byron was well aware, there is a third, gross meaning of 'end'. ■

At the level of plot, what follows this digression is the farce scene which leads to the lovers being discovered and ultimately punished. As with Julia's letter (and within the development of individual stanzas) it might be that a 'serious' treatment of an issue is comically undermined. In this instance, though, the discovery of Julia's adultery with Juan seems rather to reinforce the point that people are naturally inclined towards pleasure and should be free to pursue it: at any rate, where the opportunity exists for sexual adventure it will be taken.

I have said that Juan does not take the lead in any of his amours. Julia is said to have 'consented' to adultery (117), but she is not represented as succumbing to pressure from Juan. Rather, both lovers succumb to an impulse that is irresistible – even the climate bears some responsibility (63). So, on the one hand, erotic love is simply something people can't resist, and therefore they could not be free. On the other hand, it could be seen in public terms. At the least it does no harm – it is trifling in comparison with the political activities of the European courts and stately homes where it takes place; at most it might subvert the hypocritical constraints of institutions like the church and the family.

Byron seems to be both a libertine *and* a libertarian. It may be that his Romantic individualism simply cannot be applied to anyone but himself. On the other hand, he may be offering an alternative to another kind of radicalism – to the contemporary feminism we considered in Chapter Four, for example (see Caroline Franklin, 'Juan's sea changes', 1993). A conservative feminism with connections to evangelical Christianity and an appeal to images of idealized motherhood was not likely to engage him.

The first canto of *Don Juan* is not politically explicit in the way that the Dedication is, and it does not deal directly with contemporary politics in the way that the later cantos do. But the poem's pursuit of 'Pleasure' is not an idle pursuit and has political implications of its own. It sees sex not only as an animal instinct or as a distraction from more important affairs, but as a pursuit that is central to life in society. A belief in this kind of liberty did not only have consequences for the erotic life of Spanish aristocrats, it also presented Byron's readers with a scandal and a challenge. The problem is that neither liberty nor cant is absolute: they mean different things to different people. Similarly, love and sexuality are different matters for men and women. It may be that Byron, this time like Wordsworth, mistook his personality for evident truth about the world.

Conclusion

Byron's voice may, then, seduce us into overlooking alternative voices, including those of women. But first I want to return to where this chapter began, to the comparison with Wordsworth. In Chapter One I suggested that British Romantic writing might be described as a set of voices arguing over a similar agenda. By now we can see that Byron may fulfill more closely than Wordsworth the prescriptions of the Preface to *Lyrical Ballads*. It is Byron rather than Wordsworth who seems to be a 'man speaking to men' in their 'real language', a language in which there is no 'essential difference [from] the language of prose'. This is to suggest that Wordswoth and Byron may share an agenda.

Each can also seem to redraw the world in the shape of his own personality. If Wordsworth and Byron would agree that the language of poetry ought to be 'the real language of men', and agree on accepting the gendered implications of that definition, they would still interpret the interests of those 'men' differently. As we have seen, there is in Byron's work an explicit sexuality which is not there in Wordsworth. However, it is a male sexuality, or a fantasy about female sexuality, which reveals the limitations to Byron's insistence on a general 'Liberty'.

Further reading

Christensen, J. (1993) *Lord Byron's Strength: Romantic Writing and Commercial Society*, John Hopkins University Press.

Sales, R. (1983) 'Lord Byron's Speaking Part' in *English Literature in History 1780–1820: Pastoral and Politics*, Longman, pp.204–231.

Thorslev, P.L. (1962) *The Byronic Hero: Types and Prototypes*, University of Minnesota Press.

Women poets 1780–1830

by Amanda Gilroy

Introduction: gender and poetry

In Richard Polwhele's 'The Unsex'd Females: A Poem' (1798), the speaker ridicules a number of women writers and invites the (implicitly male) reader to:

> Survey with me, what ne'er our fathers saw,
> A female band despising NATURE'S law,
> As 'proud defiance' flashes from their arms,
> And vengeance smothers all their softer charms.
>
> (Quoted in Jones, ed., *Women in the Eighteenth Century*, 1990, p.186, lines 11–14)

In thinking about the relation between gender and writing in the Romantic period, we should note that Polwhele claims an inherited masculine perspective, locating his contemporary readers in the context of their fathers' experience. According to Polwhele, women's writing is an affront to God-given, 'natural' gender roles. In this masculine way of seeing, women are objects of the male gaze; they are defined by their appearance and behaviour. It follows that if women engage in certain types of writing, this will involve the loss of the 'softer charms' that are bound up with these ideals of femininity.

By the beginning of the nineteenth century, women writers such as Anna Barbauld, Anna Seward, Charlotte Smith and Mary Robinson had entered the literary scene. They were influential poets in their time with their work going through many editions, but they have subsequently been erased from literary history or pushed to its margins. Women writers were very popular, and women readers gained a new (economic) visibility through the rise of fashionable magazines (such as *La Belle Assemblée* and *British Ladies' Magazine*), which contained an eclectic mix of fashion and literary content with adverts, engraved portraits, embroidery patterns and gossip columns (see Adburgham, *Women in Print*, 1972). The shift from a system of aristocratic patronage to the modern system of writers, publishers and booksellers operating within a consumer market (discussed by Stephen Bygrave in Chapter Two) gave women increased opportunities to publish their work, which included political pamphlets and travel-writing, as well as novels and poetry.

Male poets were increasingly forced to respond to women writers such as Joanna Baillie (1762–1851), a Scottish poet and successful dramatist, who published a seventy-two page polemic arguing for naturalness in poetic language two years before Wordsworth wrote his 'Preface' to the second edition of *Lyrical Ballads* (1800), in which he makes the same plea. Baillie and other women poets preceded Wordsworth in bringing the vigour of common life and language to their poems. Thus, his 'Preface' endorses a cultural revolution that was already taking place. But Wordsworth also tries to reclaim the genre of poetry for men in the face of competition from women writers. His famous dictum that a poet is 'a man speaking to men' has been read in some studies as encapsulating the democratic emphasis of Romanticism. Significantly, Wordsworth's phrase makes his figure of the poet self-consciously masculine. Even metre, according to Wordsworth, should be 'manly'.

Indeed, many of the characteristic preoccupations of Romantic poetry were part of a defensive response to women's writing. In an increasingly open marketplace, male poets constructed an ideology of 'self-possession': they frequently represented their male figures, and by implication them-selves, as solitary and self-sufficient. They used images of conquest (moun-tain climbing, for example) that constituted them as masters of, rather than mastered by, the domestic affections that were thought to dominate women's poems (see Ross, *The Contours of Masculine Desire*, 1989, especially chapter 1).

In contrast, Romantic poems placed women as muses, who functioned simultaneously as inspiration and as entities onto which men projected aspects of themselves: for example, Blake writes of woman as the prophet's 'emanation', that is, an entity existing only as something that flows out from the male source. Dorothy Wordsworth's role in *The Prelude* was to foster William's 'intercourse' with his poetic self. In this masculine tradition, women were located as passive, quasi-natural objects, like Wordsworth's Lucy in 'A Slumber did my Spirit Seal', who is absorbed into 'earth's diurnal course' and against whom Wordsworth's speaker can assert his difference as an active speaking subject.

Any study of women's poetry during this period must take into con-sideration the constraints on its production and reception. As mentioned in Chapter Two, by the late eighteenth century there were models, the 'bluestockings', for women writers to emulate. However, the bluestocking circle was largely confined to upper-class women who, though they had greater access than most women to the classical education regarded as a prerequisite for writing poetry, did not have to make a living from their writing. Prose was a more accessible genre for women writers than poetry. The novel was a more flexible, less prestigious form, which had been asso-ciated from its beginnings with women writers and readers.

And yet women increasingly wrote poetry, not just as a civilized lei-sure activity, but as a professional endeavour. Especially in the later part of the period many of the most popular poets, such as Letitia Elizabeth Landon (L.E.L.), published their poems in annuals and ornamental gift-books, which were directed towards a largely female readership. L.E.L. edited and wrote most of *Heath's Book of Beauty* in 1833, and contributed to countless other giftbooks such as *The Keepsake* and *Forget Me Not*. These books were lavishly produced and highly ornamental; to give and to own them signified the possession of sensibility and of bourgeois affluence. They promoted, particularly through their illustrations, an ideology of feminine beauty, providing models for women to emulate and confirming that the ideal woman was the object, not the subject, of the gaze. (George Eliot recognizes the class and gender significance of the giftbooks in *Middlemarch*, where Ned Plymdale gives Rosamond Vincy the latest

Keepsake. Eliot writes with some irony that 'Mr Ned was satisfied that he had [given] the very best thing in art and literature as a medium for "paying addresses" – the very thing to please a nice girl' (*Middlemarch*, 1994 edn, p.269). Rosamond is the epitome of conventional femininity, and is, unsurprisingly, a reader of L.E.L.)

One drawback of contributing to giftbooks and annuals was that it frequently entailed writing to order, producing poems to go with engraved illustrations and keeping to strict deadlines. It also meant working within a circumscribed domain of acceptable literary femininity, writing from the heart about the heart's concerns, with betrayed love being a favourite theme. Did these limitations have an effect on the quality of the writing? Certainly they made it easier for male reviewers to trivialize women's writing.

So how could women write poetry *and* display what Polwhele called 'their softer charms'? How could they go public, and still preserve their association with the private sphere? The following discussion will examine how women poets negotiated a space for themselves within contemporary discourses of gender and authorship. We will place our readings in the context of the development of models of femininity in the period, and of how these affected both the production and reception of women's poems. One way of recovering the 'historical particularity' of literary works is to look at contemporary reviews: we will consider the way that discourses of gender, aesthetics and morality are bound together in the reviews.

Sonnets and sensibility

The first poem I want you to read is Charlotte Smith's 'Sonnet XXXII. To Melancholy. Written on the Banks of the Arun, October 1785'. Charlotte Smith's life (1749–1806) provided plenty of reasons for sadness. In 1783 she, and her several young children, joined her dissolute husband in a debtor's prison (he was convicted of embezzlement). The first edition of her *Elegiac Sonnets* was published in 1784 at her own expense, though she hoped to make money to ease the family's dire financial straits. Subsequently she struggled to raise nine children, but even after separating from her husband in 1787, she could not block his legal access to the income produced by her successful publications.

You have already encountered some Romantic sonnets, and we will return to the significance of the sonnet form. **But firstly, as you read the poem, look out for words that describe the landscape that the poet sees, but which also seem to indicate mood, the 'melancholy' of the poem's title.** (Note on line 10: Thomas Otway, 1652–85, was a Restoration dramatist for whom the most important tragic emotion was pity. In the eighteenth century he came to be seen as the supreme pathetic tragedian, and a forerunner of the cult of sensibility.)

D i s c u s s i o n

The poem's subtitle 'To Melancholy' seems more important than the speci-ficity of place and time suggested by the second subtitle, but the setting Smith evokes is important to the mood of the poem. The poet calls up a

Gothic landscape of shadows and strange sounds. The visual details conspire to frustrate clear vision: the emphasis is on an in-between, border-land state – it is dusk ('autumn spreads her evening veil'), there are 'mists' and a 'phantom', that is, a ghostly figure, hardly visible, whose very presence suggests absence (the absent living figure which the phantom once was). The qualifying adjectives in the octave, especially 'grey', 'dim', 'shadowy' and 'pale', add to this effect. There are similar effects in terms of sound, for the landscape is suffused with 'hollow sighs'. Again, think about the function of the adjective: these sighs have no meaning other than as signs of emptiness. Notice, too, the alliteration in the phrases 'strange sounds' and 'mournful melodies', which produce an echo effect, the verbal equivalent of shadows. The alliteration enacts an aural haunting. ■

The wood is 'half-leafless'. Smith displays a good eye for nature in many of her poems, but here the detail is symbolic as well as literal: the negative suffix contributes to the emptying out of any positive features in the landscape, while 'half' suggests a place that is neither quite one thing nor the other.

The phantom 'seems to fleet before the poet's eyes': the verb 'fleet' emphasizes that this vision is momentary, while 'seems' throws the status of the vision into doubt. We start to question whether this is an objective or subjective sight. The language is emotionally charged.

Now read the poem again. Think about whether the speaker is project-ing her feelings onto the scene (I say 'she' here on the assumption that there is some connection between the speaker and the woman poet). **Another way of putting this is to ask: *why* is the speaker melancholy?**

D i s c u s s i o n

We are not given any specific reason for the speaker's pensive sadness; what we can say is that nature reciprocates the speaker's feelings. Smith uses the eighteenth-century device of personification: 'autumn spreads her ... veil', the wood 'sighs', the wind is 'saddened', so that nature becomes a mirror for the speaker both reflecting and fostering her melancholy.

The melancholic focus may have had a personal source, but the speaker's melancholy is also a literary pose. Smith's haunted landscape and sad speaker derive partly from the 'graveyard' poetry of mid-eighteenth century writers such as Thomas Gray (1716–71). His best-known poem, 'Elegy Written in a Country Churchyard' (1751) helped to establish the figure of the poet as one of melancholic, vulnerable sensitivity. Misery and death were typical themes, and graveyards favoured places for the production of poems. ■

Smith's speaker, then, displays the fashionable quality of sensibility. As we have seen, sensibility privileged supposedly 'feminine' qualities such as morality and feeling – what Edmund Burke called the 'softer virtues' (Burke, *A Philosophical Enquiry*, 1987 edn, p.110). Among women writers of the period, Hannah More, Ann Yearsley and Mary Robinson, were all drawn to the discourse of sensibility. There were different nuances even in the heyday of sensibility: in the same decade that Smith was adopting the literary pose of melancholy, Hannah More celebrated the social sensibility that is the 'sweet precursor of the gen'rous deed' ('Sensibility', line 249, extract quoted in Wu, *Romanticism*, 1994, p.26). She asserted that feelings of pain and pity must lead to action, not merely to words. The notion of sensibility provided what was considered to be an acceptable 'voice' for women poets, but it was still a voice that remained outside the domain of rationality. Mary Wollstonecraft argued in her *A Vindication of the Rights of Woman* (1792) that women should think as well as feel if they were to break out of their ideological corsets.

Now read the poem again. *Who* is the speaker?

D i s c u s s i o n

The speaker is a proponent of sensibility and, significantly, she is a poet (line 6). In the sestet she envisages a meeting with Thomas Otway, whose 'sighs' echo those of line 3, but with the difference that they are 'deep' rather than 'hollow'. We have moved then from a misty landscape to a pensive poet, and from hollowness to depth. Something positive – indeed, the poem itself – has been generated out of apparently negative experiences. ■

The final address to Melancholy and the speaker's reference to her 'visionary mind' suggests a figure of the poet as a prophet. **Do you recognize Smith's poetry as 'prophetic'? Does she make any grand claims for her visions, or for her language?**

D i s c u s s i o n

We get no sense here of Shelley's later model of the poet as an 'unacknowledged legislator'. Nor is Smith's language forward looking. It is not the plain speaking that William Wordsworth advocated in order to revolutionize poetry. Smith used the kind of eighteenth-century diction that Wordsworth argued against in his 'Preface' to *Lyrical Ballads*. If she was 'prophetic', Smith was a prophet of the pensive (female) heart; she was one of the first women poets of the period to demarcate this domain as peculiarly feminine. ■

Smith's volume *Elegiac Sonnets* demonstrated her virtuosity with the sonnet form. The volume went into a fifth edition in 1789; by 1851 eleven editions had been published. Twelve poems, of which seven are sonnets, were included in Alexander Dyce's *Specimens of British Poetesses* (1827). This was the first anthology to redress the exclusion of women's work from poetry collections, and Smith was accorded more space than any other poet in the volume. As well as being a role model for women writers, Smith was read appreciatively by the likes of Wordsworth, Coleridge, Bowles, Scott and Keats. Her sonnets are evidence that she was working at the forefront of a revival of a poetic form that is closely associated with Romanticism. Her work, then, could be used to undermine Wordsworth's claim that a poet was a man speaking to men.

Separate spheres

We have noted the phenomenon of sensibility, and its importance for women poets. In terms of finding contexts for our reading of female poetry, we should be prepared to look outside mainstream political events. Women did write explicitly about politics – Ann Yearsley, Anna Barbauld and Hannah More all wrote poems arguing for the abolition of slavery; Felicia Hemans wrote about Greece, the Pilgrim Fathers and emigration – but more often their focus was on domestic politics. A range of factors influenced this general rule.

The women poets we will study, in particular Felicia Hemans and L.E.L., were subject to the constraints of an increasing prescriptiveness about acceptable behaviour and roles for women. They wrote during what may be seen as a transitional period: if, chronologically, their work is 'Romantic', they display many of the concerns of the Victorian 'poetess', that figure who has entered our literary mythology as the spokeswoman of sentimental morality and religious responsibility. In 1861, Jane Williams summed up the literary and social persona of the Victorian 'poetess' in her praise of the 'sublimely blended purity and piety' of the work of Felicia Hemans (quoted in Leighton, *Victorian Women Poets*, 1992, p.27). The notion of separate but complementary spheres for men and women limited women's poetic horizons. Legal and economic structures restricted the options available to women and supported a hierarchical gender system in which women were seen as secondary to men.

Conduct books (advice manuals for women offering instruction on social and domestic behaviour) were one element of a public discourse on middle-class female behaviour in the eighteenth century. They were a powerful means of defining emergent middle-class identity (see Jones, *Women in the Eighteenth Century*, 1990) and focused on women's role in the private and domestic sphere. In this section we will consider the style and content of these discourses. Thus, in his conduct book John Bennett instructed young ladies in behaviour that he derived from Milton's *Paradise Lost*:

> *His* Eve reveres her husband. She listens to his conversation, in order to be instructed. In *him*, she feels herself *annihilated* and absorbed. She always shows that deference and consciousness of *inferiority*, which, for the sake of *order*, the all-wise Author of nature *manifestly* intended.
>
> (*Letters to a Young Lady*, 1795, vol.II, p.90)

In fact, Milton's Eve displays a subversiveness that is totally absent from this account; this Eve is no more than a passive cipher who confirms the superior status of masculinity. The woman is 'annihilated and absorbed', just as the legal existence of a woman was 'incorporated' into that of her husband.

Why should this shift towards a more rigid oppositional, or binary, model of sexual difference have taken place in the late eighteenth and early nineteenth centuries? One way of understanding it is to connect it with the dislocation of social roles experienced in a period of revolutions, industrialization, urbanization and the growth of dissenting religions. These events shattered the supposed stability of the eighteenth century, and inspired a type of revolution in the manners and morals of the British people. If we look at these events specifically from the perspective of gender, we can trace the development of a new kind of domestic space, a realm of tranquil domesticity, untainted by public problems – woman's realm. Women poets necessarily engaged with these ideological shifts, with responses ranging from complicity to opposition.

A more direct constraint on women poets was the image of the 'poetess' cultivated by influential reviewers. It is important that we define the characteristics of the 'poetess' in order to assess the ways in which the poets we are studying submit to or subvert this paradigm. I have chosen to present a fairly lengthy, edited extract from George Gilfillan's essay on Felicia Hemans in *Tait's Edinburgh Magazine*, June 1847. This article was written very late in terms of the period that is traditionally called Romantic, and it sums up many of the concerns that had preoccupied reviewers for the preceding three decades. Note that the figure of the 'Blue, in papers and morning wrapper' is a reference to the learned, literary ladies called the 'Bluestockings'; 'papers' alludes to the pieces of paper used in the process of curling women's hair (locks of hair were wound up in paper and then secured). The author also makes a mock-heroic allusion to Milton (Mulciber is thrown out of heaven down to hell: 'from morn / To noon he fell, from noon to dewy eve', *Paradise Lost*, I, lines 742–43). **Read the extract carefully and then summarize its main points.**

> We have selected Mrs. Hemans as our first specimen of Female Authors, not because we consider her the best, but because we consider her by far the most feminine writer of the age. All the woman in her shines. You could not (unknowing of the author) open a page of her writings without feeling this is written by a lady. Her inspiration always pauses at the feminine point. It never 'oversteps the modesty of nature', nor the dignity and decorum of womanhood [...] We are reluctantly compelled [...] to deny her, in its highest sense, the name of poet [...] She is less a maker than a *musician* [...] Her works are a versified *journal* of a quiet, ideal, and beautiful life – the life at once of a woman and a poetess, with just enough, and no more, of romance to cast around it a mellow autumnal colouring [...] Mrs. Heman's poems are strictly effusions. And not a little of their charm springs from their unstudied and extempore character. This, too, is in fine keeping with the sex of the writer. You are saved the ludicrous image of a double-dyed Blue, in papers and morning wrapper, sweating at some stupendous treatise or tragedy from morn to noon, and from noon to dewy eve – you see a graceful and gifted woman, passing from the cares of her family, and the enjoyments of society, to inscribe on her tablets some fine thought or feeling, which had throughout the day existed as a still sunshine upon her countenance, or perhaps as a quiet unshed tear in her eye. In this case, the transition is so natural and graceful, from the duties or delights of the day to the employments of the desk, that there is as little pedantry in writing a poem as in writing a letter [...] Mrs. Hemans is distinguished above all others by her intense womanliness. And as her own character is so true to her sex, so her sympathies with her sex are very peculiar and profound. Of [...] the proper sphere and mission of woman [...] she has a true and thorough appreciation; and her 'Records of Woman,' and her 'Songs of the Affections,' are just audible beatings of the deep female heart [...] females may be called the natural guardians of morality and faith. These shall always be safe in the depths of the female intellect, and of the female heart – an intellect, the essence of which is worship – a

heart, the element of which is love [...] After all, the nature of this poetess is more interesting than her genius, or than its finest productions. If not, in a transcendent sense, a poet, her life was a poem.

(Gilfillan, 'Female authors', 1847, pp.360–2)

D i s c u s s i o n

Your list of the main points might look something like this:

1   The reviewer highlights the importance of the propriety of women's poetry and the limits of feminine inspiration.

2   This requirement disqualifies Hemans from the title of 'poet'.

3   Her poems are described as a 'versified journal', and writing them is like writing a letter. In other words, her poems are described in terms of less valued genres, ones that traditionally record women's private experience.

4   These poems are 'effusions' and the 'audible beatings of the deep female heart'. Female poetry is a type of emotional spillage, a physiological effect not an intellectual endeavour.

5   There is a 'natural' continuity between the woman poet's life and work: the 'poetess' is simply an extension of the woman, with all the same characteristics. This is confirmed by the content of her verse which is 'the proper sphere ... of woman'.

6   Women are presented as the caretakers of morality, the good house-wives of literature.

7   If female poetry is merely an extension of their lives, then according to Gilfillan's audacious mirror-logic, the woman's life (and by implication the woman herself) is a poem. Hemans is an object (a poem) not a subject (a poet). ∎

Describe the point of view of the writer of the extract.

D i s c u s s i o n

Summing up the point of view of the reviewer, we might say that he is an admiring observer of the perfect poetess. He sees her through rose-coloured spectacles as a sentimentally romantic figure wandering around with a tear in her eye. Her poeticizing is unobtrusive and 'unstudied': Gilfillan defuses any threat that women's writing might pose to patriarchal society. Gilfillan's complacency is only disturbed by his vision of the blue-stocking, whom he belittles by the mock-heroic allusion to Milton (while a reader who remembers that Mulciber is falling might also think about feminine falls from sexual virtue). The bluestocking is improperly dressed, in the nineteenth-century equivalent of dressing-gown and curlers, and unfemininely 'sweating' over her work. Here we get an insight into the voyeurism that is just beneath the surface of the overtly sentimental view of women. Moreover, the faultline in his reasoning is exposed. The blue-stocking's attitude is paradoxically 'natural' – she does not know she is being watched. Hemans, on the other hand, and 'poetesses' like her, write their spontaneous effusions within the frame of a gaze that *expects* signs of their essential womanliness. The ideology of femininity encourages them to be consciously unselfconscious. ■

These attitudes had serious implications for women writing poetry in the first half of the nineteenth century. In order to establish an audience, women poets had to live up to the ideal of the 'poetess'. In the rhetoric of the reviews, socio-moral values were translated into literary criticism, so that Mrs Hemans was selected for assessment not because she was the best female author but because she was 'the most feminine writer of the age'. Women poets were expected to write from and about a separate sphere of home, beauty and virtue. Their poetry, which was improvised rather than inspired, was simply an extension of their domestic roles.

One dark consequence of this elision between life and text was that a single slip from virtue could damage a poet's reputation irrevocably. In the stern words of a *Blackwood's* reviewer, 'no Englishwoman ever wrote verses worthy of being twice read, who had deviated from virtue' (vol.XLI, 1837, March, p.408).

Writing from the heart

In this section we will look at three poems by women poets, all of which have as their subject another woman poet. We will focus on three main topics: the growth in the number of poems about the realm of domestic affections, poems designed to have a direct emotional effect on the reader; the importance of virtue for women writers (in this context we will consider the elision of life and text made in so many reviews of female poetry); and the nature of the relation between women writers.

The three poems are: Felicia Hemans, 'The Grave of a Poetess'; L.E.L., 'Stanzas on the Death of Mrs Hemans'; Elizabeth Barrett Browning, 'L.E.L.'s Last Question'. (It is worth looking, too, at Barrett Browning's other poem on Landon, 'Stanzas Addressed to Miss Landon'. All four poems may be found in Wu, *Romanticism*, 1994.) Read all the poems now to get some sense of the continuities, and differences, between them.

Felicia Hemans and Mary Tighe

Now read 'The Grave of a Poetess' more carefully. The poem is Felicia Hemans's tribute to Mary Tighe, the author of *Psyche with Other Poems* (first published in 1805). The poem was published in Hemans's *Records of Woman* in 1828. **Describe what Hemans thinks are the most important characteristics of Tighe's writing.** In thinking about this question, you might find it helpful to focus particularly on the last two stanzas of the poem.

> Thou hast left sorrow in thy song,
>   A voice not loud, but deep!
> The glorious bowers of earth among,
>   How often didst thou weep!

Where couldst thou fix on mortal ground
   Thy tender thoughts and high?
Now peace the woman's heart hath found,
   And joy the poet's eye.

(lines 45–52)

D i s c u s s i o n

According to Hemans, Tighe's 'song', that is, her poetry, is characterized by 'sorrow' and her life by weeping ('How often didst thou weep!'). Her poetic voice conforms to the demands of feminine discourse in that it is 'not loud, but deep'. 'Deep' here refers not to her tone of voice – we tend to think of a deep voice as masculine – but means something more like 'deeply felt'. Her thoughts are described as 'tender' and elevated ('high'); they cannot find a home in everyday life. ■

What is the significance of the connection that is made between Tighe as a woman and as a poet? Once again, you might find it helpful to focus particularly on the last two stanzas of the poem.

D i s c u s s i o n

Twice Hemans links gender and poetry explicitly (lines 14–16, 51–2); in the latter example – 'Now peace the woman's heart hath found, / And joy the poet's eye' – the parallel syntax binds the woman and the poet, and the pun on 'eye' ('I') enforces a parallel between the poet's identity and the female heart. This is a conjunction that recurs again and again: the organ that seems to generate women's poetry, in the view of the poets themselves and their reviewers, is the heart. ■

Mary Tighe is enshrined in this poem as a paradigm of suffering femininity. Contemporary readers would also have known of her delicate constitution and premature death, so that her tender poetic voice was seen as biologically grounded in her frail body. **How does Hemans respond to the death of this icon of femininity? Think about her response in formal terms.**

D i s c u s s i o n

She asserts that she is 'mournful' (lines 13 and 17), but rather than heightened emotion, what is most noticeable about the poem is its metrical and formal regularity – each quatrain has alternate lines of eight and six syllables with regular iambic stress. Hemans cannot show what Wordsworth calls 'the spontaneous overflow of powerful feelings' ('Preface' to *Lyrical Ballads*) for to display such power is to risk being unladylike. ■

The 'propriety' or correct conduct that Hannah More saw as the crucial ingredient in the making of a lady ('propriety' is a keyword in her influential *Strictures on the Modern System of Female Education*, 1799) also had *formal* consequences, as is made clear in these lines from Anna Barbauld's poem 'On a Lady's Writing':

Her even lines her steady temper show,
Neat as her dress, and polished as her brow;
[...]
And the same graces o'er her pen preside,
That form her manners and her footsteps guide.
(Barbauld, *The Poems*, 1994 edn, p.70, lines 1–2, 5–6)

Baubauld posits a direct connection between the poet and her poem: in this paradigm, metrical neatness, a regular rhyme scheme and polished language mirror feminine fashion and confirm female good manners. As we have seen, reviewers during the Romantic period increasingly emphasized the connection between a woman's life and her text as a way of enforcing contemporary ideologies of femininity.

How does Hemans relate herself to the other poet?

D i s c u s s i o n

Hemans's 'mourning' is also an act of identification: 'And mournful grew my heart for thee' (line 13) she writes, identifying with 'the woman's heart' of her precursor poet.

Women poets acknowledge the intertextuality that is so often hidden or unacknowledged by male Romantic poets (other than their agonistic relation to Milton). The politics of sisterhood rather than rivalry inform Hemans's elegy on Tighe, as they inform the volume as a whole which is dedicated to another woman writer, Joanna Baillie (see Ross, *The Contours of Masculine Desire*, 1989, pp.302–3). ■

L.E.L. and Felicia Hemans

The sense of a supportive network of women writers is confirmed by the next poem that we will consider, L.E.L.'s 'Stanzas on the Death of Mrs Hemans' (first published in *New Monthly Magazine* in 1835). L.E.L.'s reaction to Hemans's death (and her poetry) is overtly emotional: 'But the quick tears are in my eyes, / And I can write no more' (lines 111–12). This might be seen as another example of the affectional poetics that is a defining characteristic of women's writing during this period. The poem reflects self-consciously on the nature and role of the poet. This preoccupation has been regarded as typical of Romantic writing, but for L.E.L., as for other women poets, the question of poetic identity is bound up with the question of gender identity, and you should bear this in mind as you now read the poem.

Let us consider the key term in L.E.L.'s characterization of her fellow poet. According to L.E.L., her fellow poet is an 'angel', but L.E.L.'s use of a masculine pronoun in line 40 is not an act of linguistic cross-dressing, but a way of suggesting an androgynous asexuality. The description of woman as 'angel' emphasizes women's purity and suggests that they have innate religious inclinations. In her poem 'The Rights of Woman', Anna Barbauld alluded to 'That angel pureness which admits no stain' (line 6): this is the *essence* of woman. (Barbauld was praising precisely the 'angel pureness' that Mary Wollstonecraft saw as a limited and limiting virtue in

A Vindication of the Rights of Woman). But here Hemans is not an angel who floats above daily life, but one 'who sings of earth' and 'Whose cares are at his feet' (lines 39–40). L.E.L. suggests that Hemans is a domestic angel, whose poetry deals with everyday 'cares'. The impulse of her poetry is not transcendent, but is those 'common thoughts and things' that make up the daily round of a woman's life, what Hemans called 'woman's weary lot' ('Indian Woman's Death Song', line 36). L.E.L. addresses Hemans as 'weary one' (line 105), and writes, 'They say that thou wert faint and worn / With suffering and with care' (lines 101–2). She seems to be a prototype for that ideal Victorian figure, the wife and mother described by Coventry Patmore in his influential verse-novel of the same name, as 'the angel in the house'. This second generation of women poets, and in particular, Felicia Hemans and L.E.L., provided the connection between eighteenth-century sentimentalism and Victorian sentimentality.

We noted earlier the elision of life and text made by reviewers of women's poetry. **Is there any evidence in this poem that the female poets accepted this notion?**

Discussion

You will probably have noticed that many of the same words are used to describe both Hemans's life and her poetry. There is a parallel between the 'song' that is made from 'common thoughts and things' (line 29) and the life that beautifies 'common scenes' (line 16). The adjective 'sweet' is repeated several times, again as a way of asserting the continuity between life and text: Hemans's life is 'So pure, so sweet' (line 13); her song is 'subdued and sweet' (line 38), and it bears the soul (of poet and reader) 'on a sweet and swelling tide' (line 31). L.E.L. uses the traditional metaphor of poems as flowers (see the opening lines), and deploys this figure to conflate poet and poem: 'The red rose wastes itself in sighs / Whose sweetness others breathe!' (lines 83–4; again note that the defining characteristic here is 'sweetness'). ■

Wordsworth also wrote about Hemans, deploying the same terms as L.E.L.: 'Mourn rather for that holy Spirit, / Sweet as the spring, as ocean deep' ('Extempore Effusion, Upon Reading in the Newcastle Journal the Notice of the Death of the Poet, James Hogg', 1835). She is 'holy' and 'sweet', more like an angel than a woman or a poet. The use of the same epithets confirms the notion that L.E.L. repeats the conventional patriarchal view of women in her tribute to Hemans. Hemans's poems mirror her life, and this means that the character of the poet can be seen in intimate terms, as 'an old familiar friend' (line 96). Significantly, in her poem 'On Wordsworth's Cottage, near Grasmere Lake', though she acknowledges that Wordsworth's poetry has made the hours 'sweet' (line 31), L.E.L. inscribes the distance between them in conventional poetic terms: 'Great poet, if I dare to throw / My homage at thy feet' (lines 28–9). But we may deduce from her exaggerated humility her consciousness of her different position.

Sentimentally, then, L.E.L. asserts the transparency of life and art, stating explicitly of Hemans that her 'songs and image blend' (line 94). In an article on Hemans published in the same issue of the *New Monthly*

Magazine, L.E.L. wrote that 'nothing is so strongly impressed on composition as the character of the writer' (p.425). The abiding image of Hemans is of a domestic icon, whose moral life gave value to her poems. It is important to know that this 'image' was assiduously cultivated by Hemans herself. She had married Captain Alfred Hemans at the age of eighteen in 1812; he departed for Rome in 1818, apparently for health reasons, and never returned. Hemans was thus in the curious – and potentially scandalous – position of supporting herself, her mother and her five sons through her writing, in the absence of her husband, an absence that was decorously glossed over by early commentators. She adopted the role of the dutiful, suffering wife, and extolled in her poems the virtue of domestic affections (continuing the trend established by her second volume of poetry, *The Domestic Affections, and Other Poems*, published in 1812).

L.E.L. ascribed to Hemans 'a music of thine own'. Does she give us a clear idea of what this music sounds like? What images are used to convey the particular quality of Hemans's poetic creativity?

D i s c u s s i o n

As we have already noted, Hemans's poetry is 'subdued' and 'sorrowful', just what might be expected from a 'poetess'. In this poem female creativity is figured in terms of music, perfume and pulsations, breath and breezes. Hemans was acutely receptive to outside influences (the 'fine chords' of her soul were 'highly strung' (lines 58, 60); her poetry was as natural as breathing, a type of exhalation that her readers registered as a pervasive perfume. ■

This imagery takes us back to the idea of contemporary critics that women's poetry lacked conscious artistry (though working against this is the comparison between the poet and the sculptor, lines 25–8). Reviews of Hemans emphasized precisely her unconscious skill. Remember Gilfillan's comment: 'Mrs Hemans's poems are strictly effusions. And not a little of their charm springs from their unstudied and extempore character'. In their emphasis on the spontaneous, bodily expression of emotion, Gilfillan and L.E.L. recapitulated the rhetorical figures characteristic of the cult of sensibility. The result was a focus on the woman's body rather than on her text.

There is another view present in this poem, one that does not accord so well with domestic ideology. How, for example, can Hemans reconcile public fame and private duties? (Look especially at lines 49–56 and 69–76.)

D i s c u s s i o n

L.E.L. isolates fame as an explicit problem. She writes of the 'fated doom' of 'the priestess of the shrine' (lines 51–2); again, this is religious vocabulary, an interpretation supported by the word 'hymn'. But more importantly, the 'priestess' is a less accessible figure than the domestic angel. According to L.E.L., the 'gift of song' is 'dearly purchased': the crowd of admirers are 'dazzle[d]' by the poet's 'meteor wreath', an image that suggests the poet as a sort of shooting star, spatially separated from others. Ultimately, Hemans's 'triumph' is a 'sacrifice', she 'tremble[s] at fame' and 'loathe[s] its bitter prize'. This is strong stuff. L.E.L.'s message is that the currency of poetic genius is isolation rather than connection, fame at the expense of family. ■

We know that in her own life Felicia Hemans combined family and fame. Her matronly public persona conformed to the image of ideal womanhood and 'trembled at fame', even as she published successfully. L.E.L. cultivated quite another image. She was more like an actress than an angel. We have noted that the poet is separate from and above the admiring crowd – she is the object of their gaze. There are several implications of this position: (a) as the object of the public gaze, the woman is pushed to the margins of conventional morality which would place women in the private sphere of home and hearth; (b) on the other hand she may conform to another paradigm of femininity: the beautiful woman who is the object of the patriarchal gaze; (c) as a performer, she displays her artistic authority.

Corinne

There is a significant literary context for Hemans's life and work. In many ways, as Angela Leighton argues, Madame de Staël's novel, *Corinne: or Italy*, created the myth of the woman poet and thus offered a possible model to several generations of women writers (*Victorian Women Poets*, 1992). *Corinne* was published in France in 1807, and there were many English translations (the ode translations in the 1833 version were by L.E.L.). The story concerns a spirited, Anglo-Italian heroine who progresses through Italy performing and improvising (singing, dancing and reciting verses) for adoring crowds, which include her English lover, Lord Nelvil. Corinne is beautiful and talented, but her life is tragic for she loses her lover to the angelic, English heroine, Lucile. Corinne dies after a final, inspired performance.

Felicia Hemans commented on de Staël's novel that 'some passages seem to give me back my own thoughts and feelings, my whole inner being, with a mirror, more true than ever friend could hold up' (quoted in Leighton, *Victorian Women Poets*, 1992, p.30). Hemans wrote a poem called 'Corinne at the Capitol' (dealing with a famous scene in the novel when Corinne is crowned in Rome). In this poem, Hemans celebrates the power and beauty of the heroine and the rapturous reception she is given, but concludes that 'happier far' than this laurelled figure is 'She that makes the humblest hearth / Lovely but to one on earth!' (this is the triumphant concluding couplet of the poem). Hemans, then, rejects the glamour of public admiration for the virtues of home. Corinne's success takes place in what is perceived to be the freer culture of southern Europe. Perhaps this type of thing is just not possible in England. The paradox is that her choice of private and domestic respectability is made in a public statement. As Angela Leighton points out, Hemans 'asserts a woman's voice in poetry which, far from being closed in private introspection, is rousingly theatrical and catching' (ibid., p.13).

If we turn to L.E.L. we find that she, too, was drawn to the Corinne story. Throughout her work the glamorous figure of Corinne is a favoured persona, most explicitly in her second volume of poetry, *The Improvisatrice* (1824), which is a series of fatal love stories, narrated by an Italian woman poet, clearly a literary descendent of Corinne. The volume was a huge success, going through six editions in its first year. But L.E.L. did not just treat the Corinne myth poetically; she put it into practice. An unmarried (until towards the end of her life), self-supporting woman writer, she lived in the public gaze. Her life and career were marred by scandalous accusations of sexual liaisons with several men.

If Hemans purports to shrink from the male gaze and ostensibly rejects fame, why might L.E.L. invite it? We cannot answer this question on the basis of her elegy to Hemans, but we may find clues in the images of the 'poetess' promoted by reviewers. L.E.L. could not subscribe to the domestic ideal espoused by Hemans, but she could subscribe to the alternative ideal of female beauty. Edmund Burke saw the characteristic effects of the beautiful as 'that sinking, that melting, that languor' which inspired 'melancholy' (Burke, *A Philosophical Enquiry*, 1987 edn, p.123). As modern critics point out, Landon promoted herself and her poetry as an embodiment of Burke's female beauty (Mellor, *Romanticism and Gender*, 1993). Burke's categories of the 'Sublime' and the 'Beautiful' operated as a hierarchical opposition. The sublime was associated with vast objects, ruggedness, and the experience of terror, while beautiful things were small, smooth and curvy. This opposition could be mapped in gender terms as masculine/feminine.

It would be a mistake, however, to see L.E.L. as passively submissive to contemporary gender ideology. She was a clever businesswoman who marketed this image for her own ends. The use of initials, for example, encouraged speculation about her and generated interest in her work (see Leighton, *Victorian Women Poets*, 1992, pp.46–7). Felicia Hemans and L.E.L. negotiated in different ways the demands of the cult of the 'poetess'. Their poems cannot be read simply as submissions to the ideology of femininity, for they are also capitalizing on those ideals.

Elizabeth Barrett Browning and L.E.L.

As you may be aware, our next poet, Elizabeth Barrett Browning, is usually regarded as a Victorian poet. But we will look at an early poem by Barrett Browning, one of two poems on L.E.L. Please read 'L.E.L.'s Last Question'. The poem responds to one of two poems that L.E.L. wrote on her way to Africa in 1838 with her new husband, Captain Maclean. Two months after her arrival there she died from prussic acid poisoning (probably suicide or an accident, but possibly murder). L.E.L.'s last two poems had been published in the *New Monthly Magazine* in January 1839; in one of these, 'Night at Sea', she addresses her 'absent friends', asking 'Do you think of me, as I think of you?' This is the refrain picked up by Barrett Browning in 'L.E.L.'s Last Question', which was published later that month in *The Athenaeum*. She expresses sympathy towards the other poet, but she also turns away from her.

What are Barrett Browning's main objections to L.E.L.?

Discussion

At the end of the fourth stanza, Barrett Browning points out that L.E.L asks. 'Think ye of me, friends, as I of you?' and not 'Do you praise me, oh my land?' (lines 27–8). The implication is that L.E.L. asked the wrong question, that her desire for personal remembrance pales in the context of national

197

recognition. Barrett Browning's larger perspective recurs in the questions asked in the penultimate stanza:

> Do you think of me as I think of you?
> Oh friends, oh kindred, oh dear brotherhood
> Of the whole world, what are we that we should
> For covenants of long affection sue?
>
> (lines 50–3)

The shift from 'friends' to 'kindred' to 'brotherhood of the whole world' deflates the importance of the personal. In the final stanza, L.E.L.'s demand seems presumptuous when placed against Christ's love and sacrifice. As well as criticizing the self-centredness of L.E.L.'s question (it is 'Not much, and yet too much', line 55), Barrett Browning dissociates herself from the 'one tune of love' that marks L.E.L.'s poetry. ■

L.E.L.'s own pronouncements locate love as the essence of womanhood. In the Preface to her volume of poetry, *The Venetian Bracelet* (1829), L.E.L. asserts that love is 'her source of song':

> I can only say, that for a woman, whose influence and whose sphere *must* be in the affections, what subject can be more fitting than one which it is her peculiar province to refine, spiritualise, and exalt? I have always sought to paint it self-denying, devoted, and making an almost religion of its truth ...
>
> (Quoted in Mellor, *Romanticism and Gender*, 1993, p.114)

Barrett Browning brings L.E.L.'s poetry down from these exalted heights. In her view, L.E.L. is not the disciple of a religion. Her poetry is 'some elfin disturbance' (line 19) in a child's dream. In accordance with the dominant notions of female spontaneity and sensibility, L.E.L.'s poems 'poured' out from her heart (line 29), full of romantic visions of 'knightly gestes and courtly pageantries' (line 22). The result is divorced from life.

Perhaps the most pointed criticism comes in the second stanza, in the following lines:

> And little in this world the loving do
> But sit (among the rocks?) and listen for
> The echo of their own love evermore;
> Do you think of me as I think of you?
>
> (lines 11–14)

Like Narcissus falling in love with his own image in the pool, poetry such as L.E.L.'s is in love with the subject of love and with its own language. It all sounds the same – 'one tune of love' that recurs again and again like an 'echo'.

L.E.L.'s refrain from 'Night at Sea', echoed and deflated in Barrett Browning's poem, is itself an echo of some lines from Felicia Hemans's 'A Parting Song': 'When will ye think of me, my friends? / When will ye think of me?' Such poetry, then, refers only to itself; it just echoes other texts rather than engaging with contemporary reality. These echoes are alluring, but threaten to drown out an individual voice, a threat that is pointed through the allusion to the sirens, who sit on rocks, singing and luring sailors to their deaths.

In her poetry, Barrett Browning tries to break free from the constraints of 'feminine' verse, challenging the easy emotionalism of heart-focused poetry, and the 'smooth' (line 30) versification of her predecessors. The response of the reviewers confirms that women's poetry was always seen in terms of sexuality: Gilfillan, who voted Mrs Hemans 'the most feminine writer of the day', called Mrs Browning 'the most masculine of our female writers'.

In criticizing L.E.L.'s 'one tune of love', Barrett Browning is an early voice in a new trend. John Lockhart takes up this issue in his comments on Caroline Norton's work (some of whose poems are included in Wu, *Romanticism*, 1994) in his essay 'Modern English Poetesses', published in the *Quarterly Review* in September 1840. After praising 'that intense personal passion' which makes her 'the Byron of our modern poetesses' (p.376), Lockhart advises Mrs Norton

> to break through the narrow circle of personal and domestic feelings,
> and adventure herself upon a theme of greater variety and less morbid
> interest. There is a great difference between writing always *from* the
> heart and always *about* the heart, even the heart of a beautiful woman
> of genius.
>
> (p.382)

The implication is that to write 'from the heart' produces a poetic text that is heart-felt but outward-looking, while to write 'about the heart' implies a text that is self-fixated and inward-looking. Norton's poetry, according to Lockhart, lacks 'progress to any spiritual end, and ... retrospect to any moral source'. Lockhart annotates the shift in taste from the theatrical sensibility of Charlotte Smith, where pathos was an end in itself, to the Victorian demand for socially responsible pathos. There is no room for empty emotion once the poetess, safely ensconced in the home, becomes the spokeswoman of the nation's duties and virtues.

So far we have looked at poems which seem to suggest the existence of a female writing tradition that is somewhat at odds with mainstream Romanticism. The very term 'poetess', which comes into widespread usage in the 1820s, is revealing, emphasizing the difference between male and female poetry. But alongside the poetry of the heart that develops out of the discourse of sensibility, we should note that there were female poets such as Anna Barbauld who criticized an 'unearthly' Romanticism divorced from the contingent 'things of life' (in her poem 'To Mr Coleridge').

You might like to look back at this point to a poem you thought about in Chapter One, Mary Robinson's 'London's Summer Morning'. Note how her use of a listing rhetoric celebrates and particularizes the human life of the city (see especially lines 9–14). This is not Wordsworthian 'emotion recollected in tranquillity' (see his 'Preface' to *Lyrical Ballads*) nor a transcending of the life of things; rather, it demonstrates a loving attention to the ordinary. No hierarchies of significance are set up, and sight is allowed to be itself without having to generate insight into the poet's self.

Women and nature

All the poets we have looked at wrote for publication; though the currency of their verse was private feelings, their poems circulated in the public market-place, with all the ideological constraints that this entailed. In many ways Dorothy Wordsworth conforms to the paradigm of the selfless 'angel in the house', ministering to her brother's domestic needs and facilitating his poetic production. Her journals were fodder for his imagination; some of William's most famous poems depend on Dorothy's words and images. Critics have recognized the 'poetry' of her prose – Virginia Woolf credited her with 'the gift of the poet' – but less attention has been paid to her actual poetry (for a detailed account, see Levin, *Dorothy Wordsworth and Romanticism*, 1987).

Please read 'Floating Island at Hawkshead', a poem that was published in Dorothy's lifetime, but anonymously within William's poems of 1842. This poem has been read by feminist critics as a type of manifesto of an alternative model of subjectivity to that provided by male Romantic poets, and one we must take account of in our mapping of Romanticism. **What do you notice about the way nature is represented in the first stanza?**

Discussion

The first stanza of the poem could be summed up by the word 'harmonious'. At this stage no specific speaker is identified and what we have are the neutral tones of commonplace quasi-religious thoughts. Each noun in the list of the second line receives more or less equal stress, suggesting the balance of nature, while the connectives in the third line bring the apparent polarities of 'Sunshine and storm' and 'whirlwind and breeze' into agreement. The subtitle of the poem is 'An Incident in the Schemes of Nature'; the word 'schemes' points to a deliberate pattern. ∎

What is the relationship between the speaker and the natural scene in the second and third stanzas?

Discussion

In the second stanza we shift from the general to the particular, and from neutrality to emotion. The poet's 'I' is invoked for the first time when the floating island comes into being, which suggests that the speaker's subjectivity may in some way be identified with the existence and fate of the island. ∎

The undermining of 'a slip of earth', its severance from the security of the shore, and subjection to the exigencies of the wind, is analogous to the marginalization and subjection of women in male-dominated society, as well as the more personal displacements of Dorothy Wordsworth's own life (she did not live with her brother until adulthood, and then assumed second place when he married Mary Hutchinson).

Yet within a circumscribed existence the island is the location of constant activity and the generation of life – it is a 'peopled *world*' supporting birds, berries, flowers and insects. The poet uses the deictic 'there' three times, holding our imaginative gaze to this fluid space, reiterating its present-ness. (You might find it useful to refer back to the discussion of deictics in Chapter Two, pages 51–2 above). Dorothy Wordsworth represents external nature as interior domestic space, for this world is 'a tiny room'. In other poems, such as 'A Cottage in Grasmere Vale' and 'A Sketch', she emphasizes the security of homes situated in nurturing landscapes (the cottage, or 'little nest' sheltered by trees in 'A Sketch'). In this poem, the island's survival is tenuous in the context of nature's arbitrary powers. The fragile place – the island, or, metaphorically, the speaker's identity – which is created out of displacement, the severing of a piece of earth, is ultimately dispersed.

Read the final two stanzas again. What is the speaker's perspective on the disappearance of the island (look especially at the change of pronoun), and what does her response to this loss tell us about the 'self' of this poem?

Discussion

Significantly, this is not a solitary experience. In the penultimate stanza the poet invokes the reader ('you') to witness the absence of the island. Though the tone remains tentative ('*Perchance* ... your eyes *may* turn' [my italics]), we as readers take up the task of giving the island a place in the world again; the very act of noticing its absence constitutes a memorial to the lost island. The shift in pronouns through the poem from 'I' to 'all' and 'you' posits a network of relations, locating the individual within a community. The island has 'passed away' – this verb suggests something more than mere disappearance, for the phrase is traditionally used as a euphemism for death, a connotation supported by the word 'Buried' at the beginning of the final stanza. Yet working against the sense of annihilation is the poet's writing about the continuance of 'lost fragments' which though unseen 'remain / To fertilize some other ground'. Vision is 'undermined' (line 6), but the island and the viewing self may be integrated into the larger schemes of nature. We might say that there is a 'buried' narrative here, which tells of a self that is other than the monolithic, transcendent self characteristic of some male Romantic writers. This female self does not seem to have an essence, a core identity, but is subject to change and is constituted through a series of relations. ∎

So this self does not fit easily into notions of Romantic self-consciousness derived from male poets of the period. As Anne Mellor observes, the poem represents 'a self that *does not name itself as a self*' (*Romanticism and Gender*, 1993, p.156). We can analyse the implications of this issue in more detail by looking at Dorothy Wordsworth's self-estimation of her writing, and the intertextual dialogue between her poem and her brother's work.

Dorothy Wordsworth did not claim the title of 'poet' for herself. She felt overshadowed by her brother's achievements, calling her own work merely 'verses' or 'rhymes'. In a late poem called 'Irregular Verses', she explains that she '*reverenced* the Poet's skill', and though she '*might have* nursed' a desire 'To imitate the tender Lays / Of them who sang in Nature's praise', 'bashfulness' and 'shame' prevent her (my italics). She is not inter-ested in claiming a special place in Nature's schemes or in asserting the authority of her poetic 'I' as the privileged reader of Nature. Her poetry certainly differs from the notion of the 'egotistical sublime' which Keats finds characteristic of William Wordsworth. If we take this as the model of poetic production, Dorothy Wordsworth's poem can seem a record of self-effacement, the absence of an 'I' at the end of the poem marking the loss of self. But she may well be revising William's poetics of confrontation and transcendence.

There is a specific intertextual context that may help us here. In the Thirteen-Book *Prelude* William Wordsworth denounces his own self during his Cambridge days by analogy with a floating island: 'Rotted as by a charm, my life became / A floating island, an amphibious thing, / Unsound, of spongy texture' (Book III, lines 339–41). The island's 'amphibious' nature transgresses the boundaries of singular identity. This imaginary 'floating island' is presented explicitly as an image for the poet's own identity, which would seem to have no centre and no security. Such a fractured self cannot imaginatively appropriate and transcend the external world. This negative experience is, however, valorized by Dorothy Wordsworth in her vision of a fluid self, which is dispersed in nature.

Conclusions

Women poets of the Romantic period developed 'a music of [their] own'. This is not to suggest that men's and women's Romantic poetry function as a binary opposition. Indeed, the emphasis throughout Romantic writings on the validity of private experience unintentionally legitimates female poetry, for women preside over the private sphere. But there is what Virginia Woolf called 'a difference of emphasis'. The dominant note is writing from/about the heart. Some women poets, however, deal with Romantic themes, such as nature, though the perceiving self differs from that constructed by male Romantic poets. Other women writers dignify the domestic and the quotidian as the subject matter of poetry. They perceive themselves as part of a sisterly endeavour.

The rediscovery of the women poets can affect our sense not only of 'what was Romanticism?' but 'when was Romanticism?'. As Stuart Curran points out, 'early' poets such as Anna Barbauld, Hannah More and Charlotte Smith are 'the missing link' in the history of poetry in the later eighteenth century, while a 'second generation of women poets ... published far into the Victorian period' (Part Two, p.282).

Much of the writing we have been looking at was hugely popular in its own time. Since then, though, it has tended to be erased from literary history, or seen as minor. Until recently, for example, you were unlikely to have studied the women poets on a university literature course. I have suggested that there are reasons why these works have been excluded from the canon – that is, excluded from those lists of texts that are highly prized. Their exclusion testifies to the politics of taste by which canons are constructed. The female prophets of affection were downgraded as subsequent generations of critics upheld the male Romantic poets' own myths of originality and transcendence.

Further reading

Ashfield, A. (ed.) (1995) *Romantic Women Poets, 1770–1838: An Anthology*, Manchester University Press.

Breen, J. (ed.) (1994 edn) *Women Romantic Poets 1785–1832: An Anthology*, Dent.

Davidoff, L. and Hall, C. (1987) *Family Fortunes: Men and Women of the English Middle Class 1780–1850*, Routledge.

Stephenson, G. (1995) *Letitia Landon: the Woman Behind L.E.L.*, Manchester University Press.

Chapter Nine

Romantic allegory

by Graham Allen

In this chapter we will be concentrating on two poems: S.T. Coleridge's *The Rime of the Ancyent Marinere* and William Blake's *Visions of the Daughters of Albion*. The chapter is divided into three main parts: first, through analysis of a passage from the 'Ancient Mariner', we will look at the nature of allegory as a mode of writing and reading; secondly, we will examine the manner in which the canonical Romantic poets responded to the tradition of allegorical writing and reading; thirdly, we will consider the poems by Coleridge and Blake as allegory.

When Coleridge first published his poem in *Lyrical Ballads* (1798) it was entitled *The Rime of the Ancyent Marinere*, and this is how the poem is referred to throughout this chapter. However, Coleridge went on to revise the text very considerably, including modernizing the spelling and introducing a large number of interpretive marginal glosses. This revised version was published in *Sibylline Leaves* (1817), under the title *The Rime of the Ancient Mariner*, and was reprinted, with minor changes, in Coleridge's *Poetical Works* (1828). The complete texts of both versions are included in Beer, *Poems of S.T. Coleridge*, 1993, and unless otherwise indicated quotations in this chapter are from this edition.

Allegory as a mode of writing and reading

Allegory is a mode of writing which has its origins in Greek literary forms and in the religious tradition of the Old and New Testament. In the late eighteenth century allegory was a well-established literary form and of particular significance for the Romantic poets were the allegorical works of John Milton. The Greek root of our word 'allegory' means 'saying one thing while meaning another'. From this definition we can see that allegory presupposes that language can communicate meanings in subtle, indirect ways. When a text appears to contain multiple meanings, when it contains figures, images or symbols which appear to point to meanings other than those which are most obvious and immediate, when, indeed, a text seems to possess what we might call 'depth', and inspires its readers with a sense that if they were to look 'beyond' or 'below' the most obvious meanings, other layers of meaning would emerge, then we can be reasonably sure that the text was written as an allegory.

The complexity of meaning in allegory and the questions that may be raised about whether a work does have intended allegorical meaning make it a specially difficult form for the reader. The reader has to make a judgement about whether an allegorical mode of interpretation is appropriate for a particular text. This is why I have called it a mode of reading as well as a mode of writing.

Before we go on to analyse the place of allegory in Romantic poetry, I want to establish a general understanding of what allegory is. Allegorical texts typically have layers of meaning and I want to begin by looking at a passage with this characteristic. The passage I have in mind comes from part III of Coleridge's *The Rime of the Ancyent Marinere*. Considering this passage as an example of allegorical writing and specifying the particular qualities it possesses will help us towards an understanding of what is involved in allegory. Before we look at the passage in detail, please read the whole of the 1798 version of the *The Rime of the Ancyent Marinere*. In parts I and II, after the initial meeting between the ancient mariner and the wedding guest, we have been told of the mariner's shooting of the albatross, of the various interpretations made concerning this action, of the ship's breaking through into the 'silent sea', and of the dropping of the breeze. This last event, of course, leaves the mariner's ship stranded. The final stanza of part II shows the mariner, now alienated from his fellow crew members, wearing the dead albatross round his neck.

At the beginning of part III a ship is sighted on the horizon, at first no bigger than the mariner's 'fist'. It is with the nearing of this other ship that the passage I want to examine begins. Please read it again.

> The western wave was all aflame,
>   The day was well nigh done!
> Almost upon the western wave   165
>   Rested the broad bright Sun;
> When that strange shape drove suddenly
>   Betwixt us and the Sun.
>
> And strait the sun was fleck'd with bars
>   (Heaven's mother send us grace)   170
> As if thro' a dungeon grate he peer'd
>   With broad and burning face.
>
> Alas! (thought I, and my heart beat loud)
>   How fast she neres and neres!
> Are those *her* Sails that glance in the Sun   175
>   Like restless gossameres?
>
> Are these *her* naked ribs, which fleck'd
>   The sun that did behind them peer?
> And are these two all, all the crew,
>   That woman and her fleshless Pheere?   180
>
> *His* bones were black with many a crack,
>   All-black and bare, I ween;
> Jet-black and bare, save where with rust
> Of mouldy damps and charnel crust
>   They're patch'd with purple and green.   185
>
> *Her* lips are red, *her* looks are free,
>   *Her* locks are yellow as gold:
> Her skin is as white as leprosy,
> And she is far liker Death than he;
>   Her flesh makes the still air cold.   190

(pp.224, 226)

What aspects of the above passage do you find most striking?

There is an emphasis on imagery drawing on the elements of nature.

We start with a sunset which is dramatically disrupted by the other ship's appearance. In the second stanza the outline of the other ship 'flecks' the sun with 'bars', from behind which the sun is said to 'peer'. This creates a juxtaposition of a phenomenon usually associated with grand and dramatic beauty – sunset – with images of imprisonment. It is out of this symbolic sunset that the other ship approaches.

At this point we need to remember that the ancient mariner's ship has been stranded, due to the lack of breeze for its sails. The other ship, however, seems to move without the assistance of any wind. This immediately marks it out for us as a supernatural entity. This is the context in which the mariner asks his questions in the third and fourth stanzas. As readers we are given a clue here that we are moving from a natural into a supernatural context; a context, in other words, of highly charged significance, which suggests deeper levels of meaning (one of the characteristics of allegory that I have identified).

The next two stanzas deal with the two figures on the supernatural ship. **What features are most striking about this pair of figures?**

Discussion

The figures are clearly supernatural. Indeed, they are figures taken from mythology and religious literature. One of them is Death. Coleridge follows mythological tradition by making Death a male figure. Indeed, the description in the fifth stanza seems reminiscent of the traditional representation of Death as the 'grim reaper', a skeletal figure with blackened and cracked bones. The other figure is female and is more difficult to relate to any recognizable figure from mythology. In the 1817 version of the poem Coleridge calls her 'the Night-mare LIFE-IN-DEATH'. In the version we are looking at the line reads 'And she is far liker Death than he'. She is, then, a figure who more closely resembles death than Death himself. Whatever tradition Coleridge was plundering for his representation of the female figure, it seems appropriate to place her in the company of other literary *femmes fatales*, seductive female figures who lure men to their ruin. We have already seen an example of this kind of figure in Keats's 'La Belle Dame Sans Merci' in Chapter Six. ■

The two figures, then, represent two aspects of death: literal, material death and a kind of 'death-in-life'. In the next stanza they are shown playing a game of 'dice', another traditional image which associates death with chance and/or fate. The female figure wins, as she herself announces, and this victory appears to set up the events of the rest of part III, which I would like you now to re-read. **What do we make of this victory of the female 'Life-in-Death' figure over Death himself? and what relation does this 'victory' have to the rest of this part of the poem?**

Discussion

The events in the remainder of part III are relatively easy to list: first, the supernatural ship departs; secondly, we recognize that the moon has risen (with the departure of the supernatural ship, we have begun to move back to a natural context); thirdly, each of the crewmen curses the mariner before dropping down dead. What the female 'Life-in-Death' figure wins, it would appear, is the ancient mariner himself. Death appears to have been awarded a consolation prize consisting of the rest of the crewmen. There is a strong sense that what happens to the ancient mariner has a direct effect on the fate of his fellow crewmen. Why this should be the case, however, is not directly stated. ■

So far we have merely detailed the basic features of this passage. We have looked at the imagery, the symbolism and the apparent significance of the events of the passage. The feeling remains, however, after such an analysis, that we have not exhausted the passage's meaning. There are implicit connections – causal relations – in the passage which cannot be interpreted by a conventional attention to imagery, symbolism and the events of the passage (that is, the plot). This is where an understanding of allegory becomes extremely useful. **What else do you think remains left unsaid by our analysis? Are there levels of meaning that we have not as yet described?**

Discussion

On one level, as we read the passage, we attend to what we might call the basic or literal story: a ship arrives with two supernatural figures on board and all the ancient mariner's fellow crewmen die. On another level, we connect all this with the theme, already established in the poem, of the ancient mariner's relationship to the world outside him. The mariner's killing of the albatross seemed evidence of a destructive response to nature. It is an action that also left him alienated from his fellow crewmen. The passage that we have just looked at can be said to develop allegorically the theme of human destructiveness and the alienation that follows as a consequence from it. The passage, allegorically, dramatizes the ancient mariner's alienated state; he is left alone, possessed by a 'death-in-life', a severe mode of alienation, and is, inadvertently, the cause of the death of his companions. We read the imagery and symbolism and events of the passage as an indirect dramatization of this theme of destruction and alienation. This theme concerns the individual actions and thus the morality of the mariner, but we cannot help but also view it as concerning human beings in general. Beyond this there is a recurring impression of a spiritual tussle between good and evil; the forces of evil having achieved dominance at this point. ■

This reading establishes at least four different yet interrelated levels of meaning: the level of the story in its literal sense (what actually happens in the passage); an ethical level, concerned with the mariner's actions and motives; a level at which the actions and motives of the mariner seem to reflect upon human beings in general; a religious or spiritual level concerning an ultimate conflict between the forces of good and evil.

These four levels, in fact, correspond relatively closely to the four levels of allegory which were established by medieval and Renaissance writers and which were inherited by subsequent generations up to the Romantic period. The history of the development of this scheme is complex, and each level has been called by more than one name. (If you want to study the emergence of the modern view of allegory more fully you should consult John MacQueen, *Allegory* (1970) and Isabel Rivers, *Classical and Christian Ideas in English Renaissance Poetry* (1979; Chapters Ten and Twelve). For a more sophisticated discussion of allegory see Angus Fletcher, *Allegory* (1964).) In the following account of the fourfold allegorical scheme I have used the most straightforward name available for each level.

The four levels of allegory

1 Literal level   (Story)

2 Ethical level   (Moral meaning)

3 Historical level   (Social–political meaning)

4 Apocalyptic level   (Spiritual meaning)

Let's consider these levels in turn, starting with the literal level. Allegory developed in an attempt to discover the 'truth' presumed to reside within ancient myths. Myth can be defined in many different ways, but in all myths there is a strong narrative element. They are, on a simple level, the stories which underpin and thus define any specific culture. There is a strong link between allegory and myth. One might say that allegory is the interpretation of myth, or the re-telling of myth, for historically specific purposes. By this I mean that the central myths of a culture are re-told or adapted to suit particular circumstances. The myth of Prometheus provides a good example in terms of the Romantic period. In the myth Prometheus stole fire from the gods and gave it to humanity and his punishment for this was to be chained to a rock by Jupiter and tortured daily. In the Romantic period, Prometheus is often referred to as the archetypal revolutionary, resisting heroically the power of a despotic monarch, namely Jupiter. We will be looking briefly at Shelley's *Prometheus Unbound* later in this chapter. Many other writers of the period use the association between Prometheus and revolution in their work, including Mary Shelley, Blake, Byron and Keats. This particular re-telling of the myth, however, could only occur in a period, such as the late eighteenth and early nineteenth centuries, in which social revolution itself was a serious possibility. So we can say that the Romantic reading of the myth of Prometheus is suited to contemporary social and political circumstances.

In many forms of narrative literature we find that a distinction can be maintained between *story* and *plot*. By *story* I mean the events of any narrative as they are supposed to actually occur. By *plot* I mean the manner in which these events are arranged in a specific narrative. For example, as we saw in Chapter Five, the *story* of Wordsworth's *The Prelude*, if presented in its strict chronological sequence, would provide us with a very different narrative to the one actually presented in that poem. The act of casting a particular story into a specific plot is called 'emplotment'. For example, there may be only one story concerning the battle of Waterloo, yet each time the story is re-told it is told differently: each time it is 'emplotted' according to the interests and beliefs of the person doing the telling. When we read a text allegorically, we concentrate less on the emplotment of the story than on the hidden levels of meaning built into the story or myth. However, the fact that in allegory plot is less important than story does not mean that all allegories have uncomplicated narratives. Many allegories employ complex modes of emplotment. However, the ultimate purpose of a traditional allegory is not to display the author's skill at embellishing a story, but rather to lead the reader into the hidden layers of meaning 'below' or 'behind' the story.

With these considerations it is possible to produce a more sophisticated version of our initial map of allegory.

1 Surface

Plot (manner of presentation of the *story*)

2 Depth

(a) Literal level (story/myth)
(b) Ethical level
(c) Historical level
(d) Apocalyptic level

From this we can now understand the literal level (the story itself) not as the surface plot (the word order on the page), but as the first level of depth. However, in each specific allegorical work the story is subjected to a specific mode of emplotment. The ethical or moral level concerns our understanding of such a story in terms of the moral or ethical themes it tacitly conveys. This level is traditionally seen as pertaining to the morality of each individual human being, in distinction to the next level, the historical level, which concerns the manner in which the story sheds light upon and relates to the social and political events of the day.

In our analysis of the passage from *The Rime of the Ancyent Marinere* we did not deal with anything we might call history. There did not seem to be a level of meaning which possessed social or political significance. What we suggested, instead, was that the mariner's individual actions and motives seemed to reflect something about human beings in general. What was happening was a characteristic feature of reading texts from earlier periods. The historical contexts of Coleridge's poem are not immediately apparent to modern readers. It might well be that the aspects of the mariner's character, situation, and actions which we initially thought to have a general, universal significance, are actually relevant to historically specific social and political issues. Fears about the increase in technology, about a growing utilitarian attitude towards human society, about a perceived decrease in religious faith, about an encroaching process of urbanization, all of them features of the time within which Coleridge was writing, might in fact be the direct points of reference for this level of Coleridge's allegory. We must, however, be careful when reading the poem on this level. *The Rime of the Ancyent Marinere* is a poem that could be said to evade any specific references to a historical level of meaning. It is a poem which seems to highlight the other levels of allegory and to underplay the historical level. Despite the possibility of placing the poem in such general historical contexts, it may be better to argue that Coleridge purposefully avoids direct historical references and to ask why he does so. One answer to that question may be that the historical level, when dominant within an allegorical work, ties that work to specific times, places, events, and, potentially, specific meanings. Coleridge's poem, as we will see later, appears to resist such clarity and openness to definite interpretation. We will come back to the issue of the historical meanings of Romantic allegory later in this chapter.

The final, apocalyptic level, takes us into the area in which the ultimate shape and significance of human history is considered.

It is perhaps worth noting that it is not necessary for an allegorical piece of work to employ all four levels at the same time. We have just considered, in fact, the possibility that an allegory might underplay or even evade one of the levels entirely. Each time we read an allegory we need to determine precisely what levels are in play and what relation exists between them. When we look at the allegorical scheme in this way, we begin to see why it is often said that there are few 'pure' allegories. Such a work, if it were to lead the reader directly to its specific hidden meanings, would need to eradicate the influence of emplotment. The more important is the plot, the harder it is for the reader to look 'beyond' it to the concealed meanings behind the story.

Using the scheme I have outlined, reconsider the allegorical meaning of the passage from *The Rime of the Ancyent Marinere*.

Discussion

We have already covered the literal level of the passage comprehensively. We now recognize that there is a distinction to be made between the ethical and the historical levels of the passage's meaning. On the former level, the passage develops the poem's treatment of an individual's response to the world around him, to nature in the largest sense of that word. It also develops the theme of alienation, which the poem seems to suggest dominates those individuals who take a destructive or unimaginative approach to nature. We have just discussed possibilities for the historical level. At this level, the mariner comes to represent some aspect or aspects of the society Coleridge lived and wrote within. The passage also seems to make clear that all these issues, ethical and social, are underpinned by a spiritual conflict foregrounded by the two supernatural figures: Death and 'Life-in-Death'. ■

Reading texts in terms of the four levels of allegory raises important questions. For example, how do we decide whether a text was written as an allegory? The answer must be that there is no hard-and-fast rule. However, what is important is to recognize the implications involved in treating or not treating individual texts as allegories. Questions concerning the implications of allegorical writing and reading form an important part of Romantic poetic theory and we shall turn to these in the next section.

Romantic writings and allegory

In considering the role of allegory in Romantic writings it is best to begin with the criticisms that Romantic writers levelled against it. Wordsworth and Coleridge seem to agree that allegorical writing is far too restrictive and manipulative to constitute great art. When Wordsworth, in the 1802 Preface to *Lyrical Ballads*, rejects poetry in which is found 'personifications of abstract ideas' he is directly rejecting allegorical modes of poetry. Allegory, in its 'purer' forms, attempts to direct the reader to various meanings 'behind' or 'within' the literal story. This is necessary because if the meanings that readers find in an allegorical work are too numerous, and the significant ones cannot be identified, the allegory will have failed in its purpose. Allegory was therefore regarded as a mode of literature which attempted to manipulate its readers by restricting the possibilities of meaning within the story it presented.

If we restrict ourselves to the canonical poets of the period, it becomes reasonable to speak of a Romantic critique of allegory. We can see such a critique if we look at Coleridge's distinction between allegory and symbol. In a lay sermon published as *The Statesman's Manual* (1816) Coleridge argues that 'Allegory is but a translation of abstract notions into a picture-language which is itself nothing but an abstraction from objects of the senses'. Coleridge contrasts such a practice with the use of the artistic symbol, which 'always partakes of the Reality which it renders intelligible; and while it enunciates the whole, abides itself as a living part in that Unity, of which it is the representative' (White, *Collected Works of S.T. Coleridge*, 1972, vol.6, p.30).

What Coleridge disliked about allegory was that it made poetry, and art generally, into a secondary process. That is to say, allegorical works are meant to help their readers recognize the great truths which they fictionally or mythically represent. Indeed, the process assumed to be at the heart of traditional allegory can usefully be understood in terms of *re*-presentation, a presenting of something which existed prior to the existence of the allegorical work itself. However, for Coleridge, true poetry does not merely represent eternal verities, it is itself essentially creative.

Coleridge's criticism of allegory is strikingly similar to remarks made by William Blake in his *A Vision of the Last Judgement*. Blake distinguishes between the creative 'Imagination' and the mechanical operations of the mind thought to be at the centre of allegory. Blake states that 'Vision or Imagination is a Representation of what Eternally Exists. Really and Unchangeably. Fable or Allegory is Form'd by the daughters of memory' (Erdman, *The Complete Poetry and Prose of William Blake*, 1982, p.554).

Both Coleridge and Blake seem to define allegory in opposition to the creative 'Imagination'. The 'Imagination' does not merely represent, but is part of the things, the 'eternal things', it represents. Allegory, in contrast, seems to be a rather static, uncreative repetition of things, no way bound up in their essential nature. Why did the Romantics find it necessary to criticize the allegorical mode of writing and reading?

If writers such as Blake and Coleridge believed in the creative nature of the poetic imagination, and in an enlargement of the role of the poet in the production of truth and beauty, then allegory necessarily suffered as a consequence. It may well be, in fact, that allegory, in its more traditional forms, requires the kind of simple belief in an eternal world to which the canonical Romantic poets could no longer subscribe. Or it may be that allegory suggested an outmoded, passive role for the poet; poets simply reporting back to the reader the eternal truths which they have been privileged to be shown.

Perhaps this Romantic reaction against allegory stems from the characterization of the 'figure of the poet' as a kind of god or part of the eternal. When Blake states that 'All deities reside in the human breast' and when Shelley declares that 'Poets are the unacknowledged legislators of the world', they are claiming a role for poets far beyond the kind of reporter role which allegory appears to sanction; they are, in fact, claiming that poets are themselves embodiments of the 'Truth' or the 'Eternal'. Keats encapsulated this Romantic rejection of traditional allegory when he wrote the following: 'A Man's life of any worth is a continual Allegory – and very few eyes can see the Mystery of his life...Shakespeare led a life of Allegory: his works are the comments on it' (Letter to George and Georgiana Keats, 14 February to 3 May 1819; in Forman, *The Letters of John Keats*, 1931, vol.II, p.327). Given that allegory seemed to be out of favour amongst some of the leading theorists of Romantic poetry, why did Romantic poets continue to write allegories or to use allegorical techniques? We will not be able to fully answer this question until we have looked at other examples of Romantic allegory. However, over the next few pages I want to begin to answer this question by considering a passage from Shelley's *Prometheus Unbound* (1820).

In the allegorical works read by the Romantics – Edmund Spenser's *The Faerie Queene,* John Milton's *Paradise Lost,* John Bunyan's *The Pilgrim's Progress,* or, from a European source, Dante's *Divine Comedy* – the fourth level of the allegorical scheme stabilizes the play of meanings inevitably created by the layered nature of allegorical writing. I mean by this that in these works the 'myth' being employed – all of these authors work within dominantly Christian cultures – does not merely supply the literal story of the work, it is also seen as the ultimate truth to which the author would, by means of the work in question, lead the reader. Allegory, traditionally conceived, is the interpretation or re-telling of 'myth' for historically specific purposes. By writing his allegory of the fall of Satan, of Adam and Eve, and of Christ's final victory over Satan, Milton hoped, as he put it, 'To justify the ways of God to men'. In Milton's *Paradise Lost,* the ethical and the historical levels of the allegory are made subservient to the literal and the apocalyptic levels.

It is significant that many of the great Romantic allegorical poems mix Classical or original narratives with those available in the Old and New Testaments. Keats's allegorical works *Hyperion* and *The Fall of Hyperion* employ the Classical myth of the overthrow of the Titans by the younger Olympian gods. Shelley, likewise, used Classical myth as his narrative base in *Prometheus Unbound.* In the first act of this drama we see Prometheus bound to a rock, a punishment inflicted on him by Jupiter for befriending humankind. In Classical myth Prometheus was depicted as the friend of humans, and was thus a symbol of the revolutionary spirit for many Romantic writers.

Please read the passage below. It represents a central moment in the opening act of *Prometheus Unbound.* Prometheus in this act gradually learns to transcend the power exercised over him by Jupiter, the epitome of the tyrant-king. The act establishes a major theme of the poem: that the true revolution should take us beyond the logic of power, the logic of master and slave, rather than just reversing these roles and thus perpetuating social power relations. Before he can achieve liberation, however, Prometheus must recall (that is, remember, repeat, but also revoke, take back) the curse he had formerly directed towards Jupiter. Shelley uses the dramatic device of having the Phantasm (an apparition) remind Prometheus of what he had formerly said to Jupiter.

Phantasm.

<blockquote>

Fiend, I defy thee! with a calm, fixed mind,
  All that thou canst inflict I bid thee do;
Foul Tyrant both of Gods and Human-kind,
  One only being shalt thou not subdue.   265
Rain then thy plagues upon me here,
Ghastly disease, and frenzying fear;
And let alternate frost and fire
Eat into me, and be thine ire
Lightning, and cutting hail, and legioned forms   270
Of furies, driving by upon the wounding storms.

Ay, do thy worst. Thou art omnipotent.
  O'er all things but thyself I gave thee power,
And my own will. Be thy swift mischiefs sent
  To blast mankind, from yon ethereal tower.   275
Let thy malignant spirit move
In darkness over those I love:
On me and mine I imprecate
The utmost torture of thy hate;
And thus devote to sleepless agony,   280
This undeclining head while thou must reign on high

But thou, who art the God and Lord: O, thou
  Who fillest with thy soul this world of woe,
To whom all things of Earth and Heaven do bow
  In fear and worship: all-prevailing foe!   285
I curse thee! let a sufferer's curse
Clasp thee, his torturer, like remorse;
Till thine Infinity shall be
A robe of envenomed agony;
And thine Omnipotence a crown of pain;   290
To cling like burning gold round thy dissolving brain.

Heap on thy soul, by virtue of this Curse,
  Ill deeds, then be thou damned, beholding good;
Both infinite as is the universe,
  And thou, and thy self-torturing solitude.   295
An awful image of calm power
Though now thou sittest, let the hour
Come, when thou must appear to be
That which thou art internally;
And after many a false and fruitless crime   300
Scorn track thy lagging fall through boundless space and time.

</blockquote>

Prometheus. Were these my words, O Parent?

The Earth.   They were thine.

Prometheus. It doth repent me: words are quick and vain;
  Grief for awhile is blind, and so was mine.
  I wish no living thing to suffer pain.   305

(Hutchinson, *Shelley: Poetical Works*, 1970, pp.213–14)

Shelley's use of the myth of Prometheus is not the same as Milton's or Bunyan's use of Christian myth. In his Preface to the poem he makes it quite clear that he is prepared to alter radically the basic narrative of the Classical myth. Shelley uses the myth as a basis for generating other meanings than those that may have been central to it originally.

Read the passage again and try to use the allegorical scheme we have been discussing to interpret its various meanings. **How is the power-relationship between Prometheus and Jupiter represented? What is the significance of the original 'curse' and its 'recalling'? What relation do the different levels of allegorical meaning have to each other?**

D i s c u s s i o n

Let's begin by looking at the poem on the 'literal story' level. The passage presents an intensely poetic expression of the defiance of a figure in the position of a slave towards a figure in the position of master. The master/slave opposition is, in fact, expressed here through religious imagery: the master figure is designated as 'God and Lord', as possessing 'omnipotence', but also as 'Foul Tyrant both of Gods and Human-kind'. This religious imagery, however, seems to reinforce the basic subject-matter of the speech, which is clearly about power. The 'tyrant'/'God' figure, namely Jupiter, is represented as the most powerful entity in the universe. Yet, if we read the passage more closely, we begin to realize that Jupiter's power is not so much absolute as temporarily leased to him from those whom, like Prometheus, he tyrannizes. ■

The second stanza contains the lines, once spoken by Prometheus to Jupiter: 'Thou art omnipotent./ O'er all things but thyself I gave thee power,/ And my own will'. With a careful reading of the passage, we see that what at first sight seems to be a straightforward expression of the power relations between oppressed and oppressor, is in fact based on an opposed relation of power: the master has his power only because the current slave, Prometheus, has given it to him.

Once we have recognized this important point we read the utterance of the curse in the third stanza in an altered light. Prometheus's outburst ('I curse thee! let a sufferer's curse/Clasp thee, his torturer, like remorse') which seems, initially, a natural expression of defiance from an oppressed subject, actually increases Jupiter's power. Prometheus's words in the final stanza of the speech, 'let the hour/Come, when thou must appear to be/That which thou art internally', apply also to himself.

The 'hour' referred to has, of course, now come. In hearing his own curse to Jupiter repeated back to him, Prometheus is confronted with his own role in the establishment of the power structure which presently exists. The scene, in fact, represents the moment of insight, when Prometheus comes to understand the oppressive system of power he has himself suffered under. The insight is that this system was partly the result of his own actions, his own 'will', and thus need not continue; it can be 'will[ed]' out of existence. The final line of the whole passage, 'I wish no living thing to suffer pain', begins to take Prometheus beyond the logic of power itself, since it implies that he is no longer willing to construct Jupiter as a hated 'tyrant'/'God'.

With this last statement we begin to be able to develop an allegorical reading of the passage. On an ethical level it appears that what is being dramatized is the idea that individuals within society are complicit in the logic and structure of power. If individuals cease to construct those that oppress them as inevitable, absolute rulers, then they will transcend the power-structures they find themselves imprisoned within. Prometheus here, as was the case with the ancient mariner, is a figure who allegorically personifies a characteristic shared by all members of society. Again, as in our discussion of *The Rime of the Ancyent Marinere*, once we recognize this aspect of the ethical level of the allegory, we can move on to the historical level.

As we noted in earlier chapters, the Romantic period was one domi-nated by the idea, and indeed the reality, of revolution. On a historical level, the passage we have been discussing represents an allegorical treat-ment of social and political revolution. Shelley's idea of revolution seems to be one in which a bloodless act of transcendence, occurring on both an individual and a collective level, destroys the material system of power. As we read the passage, we, as individual readers, experience the 'insight' achieved by Prometheus himself. By that shared attainment of a vision of social relations transcending the logic of power, Shelley seems to hope that his allegory will lead us from an individual (ethical) moment of vision to a collective (historical) moment of vision. The revolution, in this sense, begins as we begin to interpret the meaning of Shelley's allegorical text.

What view of revolution do we come away with after having studied this passage?

Discussion

Shelley's passage clearly emphasizes the ethical and the historical elements of allegory. The passage presents us with an allegorical treatment of a spe-cific social and political issue, the nature of revolution. Yet in using the myth of Prometheus, and in treating the subject of revolution in terms of individual 'insight' or vision, it also universalizes this issue. Shelley's alle-gory of revolution is historically specific and yet also idealized. This ideali-zation seems to take us from a historical perspective to a perspective associated with the apocalyptic level of allegory. ∎

What prompted our examination of this passage from *Prometheus Unbound* was the question why, given the many critiques of it that exist in Romantic writing, allegory remained such an important form during the Romantic period. The passage, and our discussion of it, give us some answers to this question: first, on the level of style, and, secondly, on the level of historical context. I want to look at these in turn.

The issue of style is tied up with the issue of poetic influence. In Chapter Two we saw how Milton was a powerful influence on the work of many Romantic poets. Milton's poetry is one of the greatest examples of allegorical writing in the British literary tradition. The Romantics' use of Milton's poetry, despite what they might have thought about allegory on a theoretical level, inevitably added an allegorical element to their work. The frequent use of and reference to Biblical models, which to an extent complements the use of Milton, is clearly another source of the allegorical approach in Romanticism.

Another important explanation for the importance of allegorical form in Romantic poetry can be found in our analysis of the structure of allegorical writing and interpretation. In a time of political conflict, when it becomes difficult or dangerous to express directly one's own political and social beliefs, then allegory can become an indirect way for writers to communicate their beliefs. The writer of an allegory can express political beliefs covertly by foregrounding the literal, and even the ethical and the apocalyptic levels, apparently at the expense of the historical level. Or specific political beliefs can be expressed in the guise of universal ideals. We need to remember that writing in the Romantic period was a particularly dangerous occupation in Britain. It is likely that the development of allegorical modes of writing in the Romantic period constituted a form of response to this environment of censorship and cultural repression. (There is good reason to believe also that one of the principal motivations for the concentration on individual poetic consciousness and individual acts of poetic utterance during the Romantic period was another kind of response to the dangerous political environments within which the Romantic poets lived and wrote.)

The political environment means that it is particularly important to analyse the manner in which Romantic allegorical works treat the concept of history, both in terms of the specific history within which the authors were living and writing, and in terms of the total shape of history (the spiritual view of history associated with the apocalyptic level) which allegorical works have traditionally explored.

Blake's Visions of the Daughters of Albion

As we have begun to see, it is often useful, when dealing with an allegorical work, to begin with the narrative element, the literal level of the *story* and its particular mode of emplotment. Please now read Blake's *Visions of the Daughters of Albion* (1793), but before you do so read the following paraphrase of the poem, which includes notes on some of Blake's obscure or invented names.

> Oothoon, a virgin associated with America, plucks a flower in a vale belonging to a figure called Leutha. Oothoon journeys towards Albion (Blake's term for England) but is raped by a fierce, violent figure named Bromion (literally 'thunderer' or 'roarer'). Oothoon's beloved, a male figure called Theotormon ('tormented by God') cannot now accept Oothoon, whom he sees as having been defiled by Bromion. The rest of the poem involves a series of set speeches in which Oothoon declares her spiritual purity and Bromion and Theotormon reiterate their static mental positions.

Notice how my paraphrase of the story collapses at the end. Most of the poem is not so much a narrative as a conflict between three figures representing three different states of mind. Why does Blake write in this way?

Figure 10   William Blake, Frontispiece or final plate, from *Visions of the Daughters of Albion*, 1793, relief-etchings with watercolour additions, 17 x 12 cm. Copyright British Museum.

Isn't he contradicting himself by using allegory, a form we have already seen him criticizing (p.212 above)?

Despite his distinction between Allegory/Fable and Vision/Imagination, Blake could not escape from allegory. His poetic work as a whole can be said

Figure 11   William Blake, 'Where the cold miser...', from *Visions of the Daughters of Albion*, Plate 8, 1793, relief-etchings with watercolour additions, 17 x 12 cm. Copyright British Museum

to develop, in an accumulative fashion, a network of allegorically significant characters and events which, in their totality, represent his overall poetic system. This system is an extended allegory. In *Visions*, for example, we are introduced, for the first time in Blake's work, to the character of Urizen (his name, apart from sounding like 'your reason', also echoes the word 'horizon'), who reappears in the *Book of Urizen* of 1794. Urizen is Blake's version of the orthodox image of a sky-god, Jehovah, the Jewish and Christian god, an oppressive monarch, like Shelley's Jupiter, who institutes a universal law under which all individuality is stifled. Urizen is the god whose law of repression Theotormon has internalized and against whom Oothoon directs a defence of her own spiritual purity and physical freedom in Plate 8 of *Visions of the Daughters of Albion* (see Figure 11).

Blake's purpose in his poem, however, is not to present a fully developed allegorical system; it is, rather, to present the reader with a spiritually and psychologically challenging vision. We might say that Blake needed to develop his own allegorical system in order to create his poems; he writes in his long, prophetic book *Jerusalem*: 'I must Create a System or be enslav'd by another Mans'. Each of Blake's complex allegorical works is meant to create an imaginative view of the world (a system) that might rival and even replace the dominant views of human society sponsored by church and state (the orthodox and official 'systems'). Each of Blake's poems, however, is the presentation of a visionary moment, or series of moments, emanating from that overall, allegorical system. Blake's poems are meant to be experienced, rather than simply interpreted. As we saw in Chapter One, Blake combined poetry and design in his prophetic works. He did so in order to create a unique mode of visionary expression, and in some ways this defies simple interpretation. An analysis of Blake's work, such as the one we are attempting here, can take us some way towards an interpretation, but a complete engagement with his work would involve a simultaneous response to both text and design.

Would you now look at the two plates from *Visions* reproduced in Figures 10 and 11? In all but one of the existing versions of Blake's book, the first plate (Figure 10) serves as a frontispiece; in the other version it serves as a tailpiece along with Plate 8 (Figure 11). This second plate is, in all but one of the variant productions of the book, the last design. These designs are, then, the first and the last thing we see in the book. In the single variant, they are two halves of the last thing we see. Figure 10 shows Oothoon and Bromion tied back-to-back; Theotormon tortures himself with his jealous, inner imaginings concerning the two figures before him. Figure 11 shows us a liberated Oothoon, moving towards Albion, some of whose daughters look toward her.

Blake placed an epigraph on the title page of his poem which reads 'The eye sees more than the heart knows'. When we consider that these two plates form the margins of this particular text this epigrammatic statement begins to appear extremely significant. **How is the idea of 'seeing' and 'knowing', or 'vision', represented in these two plates?**

Discussion

In Figure 10 Bromion is the only character who looks beyond himself and the frame of the design. Oothoon seems to be studying her own reflection; Theotormon refuses to look beyond his own internally created nightmare visions. We cannot tell what Bromion sees. Whatever it is, it seems, from the expression on his face, to have terrified him. Blake's placing of the two plates at either end of the text might suggest, however, that what Bromion sees is the vision of the liberated Oothoon returning, like an avenging fury, as depicted in Figure 11. ■

If we take this view of the two plates, then they would appear to suggest that the poem's central significance lies in a conflict between two opposed visions of Oothoon herself. Blake, in his epigraph and in his text, is arguing that it is possible for the 'Imaginative' faculty to transcend the habitual logic of conventional morality (the logic of the 'heart'). Blake's poem and its accompanying designs present us with a dramatic situation, a triangle of love, rape, jealousy and sexual awakening, in which the female participant is viewed from two distinct perspectives. From a conventional, Christian perspective, Oothoon's rape ties her morally to her violator, Bromion. However, from what Blake would call the 'Imaginative' perspective, the perspective of true 'Vision', Oothoon has merely passed from 'Innocence' through 'Experience' out to the threshold of true spiritual and physical liberation, to the state of 'Imagination'.

Our discussion of the poem so far seems to relate solely to the ethical level of allegory. I want now to turn to the historical level of the poem's allegory. Blake's *Visions* was published in 1793, one year after the publication of Mary Wollstonecraft's pioneering feminist work, *A Vindication of the Rights of Woman*. Blake had met Wollstonecraft along with other leading radicals of the day at the home of the London publisher Joseph Johnson. Wollstonecraft's book draws analogies between the condition of women in English society and the condition of slaves in the still existent slave trade. Wollstonecraft argues that to deny women the opportunities of education and an active role in society is to transform them into domestic slaves. What connects women and slaves, for Wollstonecraft, is that they are both seen and treated as commodities. **Are there any signs in Blake's poem of the influence of the kinds of feminist arguments made by Wollstonecraft?**

Discussion

Both male characters in the poem represent the ideology which supports the slave trade and the domestic enslavement of women. Bromion's speech (ll.107–118) is certainly repressive. Theotormon's inability to accept Oothoon's spiritual purity after her violation shows that his view of the world is dominated by the same ideology that justifies Bromion's logic of violent oppression. The dialogue between the two male characters ends with Bromion reaffirming the law (or logic) of Urizenic oppression, best captured in the line 'And is there not one law for both the lion and the ox?' (l.116); a line which echoes one from Blake's *The Marriage of Heaven and Hell:* 'One law for the lion and ox is oppression'. ■

We see further connections with Wollstonecraft's feminist arguments if we look at Oothoon's relation to the figure of Leutha. Oothoon falls from innocence into experience, a fall allegorized in miniature in 'The Argument'. But more than this, it is a fall into a patriarchal ideology which views female sexuality as sinful. Oothoon's plucking of 'Leutha's flower' is, on one level, simply the awakening of her own sexual desire for Theotormon. However, Leutha, in Blake's system, represents a kind of female sexuality which disguises its true nature behind a demure, polite and passive mask, just the kind of socially expected mode of female repression and sublimation that Wollstonecraft had attacked.

What Blake's poem, like most of his poetry, attempts to do is to connect social repression with individual repression. I mean by this that Blake believes that the manner in which the state manages to keep people in a slave-like position is to encourage them to believe that their own desires are sinful and in need of policing. Social repression, for Blake, works in and through psychological repression. This method of forcing people into a mode of self-policing was, in Blake's own time, achieved largely through the doctrines of the Established Church. You can see a simpler expression of this idea in the two 'Chimney Sweeper' poems in *Songs of Innocence and Experience*.

We can relate these comments directly to Blake's allegorical technique. Blake's poem *Visions of the Daughters of Albion*, and his work in general, strives to show the inter-relatedness of the ethical (individual), the historical (social, political), and the apocalyptic (spiritual) dimensions of human existence. Only when individuals achieve spiritual vision, Blake argues, will individual liberation and social revolution occur. Having said this, we are faced with a question of some importance to our interpretation of the poem. **Does Oothoon's movement from physical oppression to spiritual vision, or what Blake called 'Imagination', actually liberate her?**

D i s c u s s i o n

Blake's *Visions* is a poem about the way in which society keeps women in a slave-like position by encouraging them to accept an ethos of sublimation and repression. Oothoon, spiritually and psychologically, moves beyond this ideology; but for her imaginative, liberated vision to be fully realized, society itself must become equally enlightened and liberated. The drama of Blake's poem centres on the struggle of one individual towards spiritual vision or the state of 'Imagination'. However, the poem is so constructed as to make it clear that only when the other, male figures around that individual also achieve such a state will the female figure be liberated. The poem, after all, ends not with a successful revolution, but, each morning, with the defiant wailing of Oothoon, while her counterpart, Theotormon, sits 'Upon the margined ocean, conversing with shadows dire' (1.217). As in Shelley's *Prometheus Unbound*, Blake's allegory makes a direct link between individual and social liberation. ∎

In the same year that he printed *Visions* Blake printed another poem entitled *America: A Prophecy*. In this poem Blake argues that the American Revolution, two decades earlier, prefigured the beginning of a new, liberated world order, a new age which the French Revolution had begun to realize. Blake's *Visions*, then, connects with an interpretation of contemporary history in which the present age is seen as the beginnings of a phase of history in which personal liberation will lead to social liberation. Oothoon is an allegorical realization of this view of history. In other words, the view of history which *Visions* implicitly promotes is still very closely tied to an allegorical tradition in which the ethical (individual), the historical (social), and the apocalyptic (spiritual or total history) are ultimately connected. Let's now return to Coleridge's poem and try to analyse in more depth its allegorical dimension.

Coleridge's *The Rime of the Ancyent Marinere*

Despite its generally chronological sequencing of events, Coleridge's poem is an allegory in which the relation between story and plot is complicated. The poem presents what can be called a framed narrative: the story is told by the mariner to the wedding guest; another narrative voice presents us with that scene of story-telling, the framing. An 'Argument' is attached to the front of the poem. In 1817, in the last of a series of revisions to his poem, Coleridge added a detailed marginal gloss to his poem, thus adding one more 'voice' through which the story is mediated. As Jerome McGann has pointed out, these various levels of narration do not necessarily help to clarify the nature of the story being told. In many ways they serve to distance the original events, turning them into a legend or even a myth. The mariner seems to hypnotize the wedding guest into hearing his story. He states that, on arriving back after his adventures, it 'left [him] free' to tell his story to the hermit. However, he goes on in the 1817 version (which is slightly different to the 1798 version):

> Since then, at an uncertain hour,
> That agony returns,
> And till my ghastly tale is told,
> This heart within me burns.
>
> I pass, like night, from land to land;
> I have strange power of speech;
> The moment that his face I see,
> I know the man that must hear me:
> To him my tale I teach.
>
> (VII, ll.582–90; p.253)

We leave the poem, therefore, wondering whether the mariner has really purged himself of his sin by confessing his story, or whether he remains in the grip of a demonic possession. The poem's last lines concern the wedding guest: 'A sadder and a wiser man/He rose the morrow morn'. However, we cannot help but wonder whether the wedding guest has himself now become contaminated with the strange need to re-tell the original story. All of these issues serve to create a poem which questions the meaning of the story it presents: is it a story about a passage, to put it in Blake's terms, from 'Innocence' through 'Experience' to the state of 'Imagination'? is it a story of supernatural possession? or is it merely a legendary tale with no serious allegorical significance?

In his *Biographia Literaria* Coleridge explained that his contributions to the jointly authored *Lyrical Ballads* were supposed to be tales of the supernatural, whilst Wordsworth's contributions were supposed to be concerned with the 'things of every day'. Coleridge states that in his tales the readers were to be encouraged to suspend their 'disbelief'. There is a suggestion here that Coleridge viewed his main contribution to the collection, *The Ancyent Marinere*, as a fantastic rather than an essentially moralistic poem. In a remark recorded on 31 May 1830, Coleridge stated that he thought the poem had too great a 'moral' and that it should have been less didactic and more imaginative (Abrams, *The Norton Anthology of English Literature*, 1993, vol.2, p.346).

Coleridge modelled his poem on the ballad, an older style of poetry which often told a moral tale and which was becoming increasingly popular in the late eighteenth century. From the statement above, it seems that Coleridge thought in retrospect that he had put something into his poem which could be taken as its 'moral'. Perhaps it was this imitation of the ballad that led Coleridge to write his poem in this way. This explanation seems somewhat inadequate, however, since the more one reads the poem, the more one gains the impression that Coleridge is purposefully playing with his reader, setting up possible meanings which are never fully established. If the poem has a 'moral', it is not an easy thing to locate and describe.

Can our understanding of allegorical techniques help us to sort out the problem of the poem's 'moral' (or 'meaning')? When studying the allegorical nature of a text it is often worth focusing on what seem to be the crucial events in the narrative. Allegorical meaning often clusters around significant events. **(1) What are the key allegorical events in this poem? (2) What connections can be made between these key events?**

Discussion

1   The three most important events in the poem seem to be the mariner's shooting of the albatross, his encounter with the phantom ship, and his instinctive blessing of the water-snakes.

2   One thing which strikes most readers of the poem is the apparent lack of motivation for the main events, particularly the mariner's shooting of the albatross at the end of part I. However, what can be said is that there seems, from simple chronological sequence, to be a connection between this event and the ship's breakthrough into the uncharted waters of the Pacific Ocean (II, ll.99–102). The environment they enter once in these waters is hostile and even vengeful, an aspect of their new environment which seems somehow connected to the next important event, the arrival of the supernatural ship.

The mariner now appears to be the only living thing left, until he mentions the water snakes (IV, l.265) which he spontaneously blesses (IV, ll.276–80), an action which relieves him of the burden of the dead albatross. This moment seems a turning point in the story, the mariner's movement towards home apparently commencing the moment he can bless the world around him. ∎

It does seem possible to locate an allegorical meaning in this series of events. In Coleridge's 'Dejection: An Ode' he writes of a state of mind which can be described as a 'life-in-death' (see stanzas 2 and 3). This unimaginative state, as the poem shows, stems from an inability to interact with the natural world outside the poet. It seems possible to see the series of events in *The Rime of the Ancyent Marinere* as an allegorical presentation of a pattern central in the work of both Coleridge and Wordsworth. This pattern involves an initial recognition of an alienation from nature which is finally transcended through the emergence of an imaginative understanding of the 'marriage' between the human mind and the natural world outside that mind. Coleridge, in his poem 'The Eolian Harp', writes of the 'one intellectual Breeze,/At once the Soul of each, and God of all', a unity between mind and nature which can only be experienced in an imaginative state, a state in which the individual consciousness learns to see beyond itself.

If this is the allegorical meaning behind these central events in the poem, then we can say that the allegory has an ethical and an apocalyptic dimension. The marriage between mind and nature takes place in each individual consciousness, yet it also symbolizes the final destination of history, the establishment of a 'new heaven' and a 'new earth' prophesied in the last book of the Bible. Although this interpretation gets us some way, it does not deal with the final effect of the poem. We cannot leave the poem feeling confident that we have understood precisely what Coleridge intended. This reading also does not deal with any allegorical meaning at the historical level.

If this is a poem about a movement from a state of isolation and/or alienation to an imaginative integration with the natural world, why does the mariner seem such an uncanny figure at the poem's close? why is the hermit so unsettled by the mariner? why does the conclusion present a figure who is driven by a supernatural force, rather than a figure who, after various trials and adventures, returns happily back to his homeland?

Perhaps one possible answer to these questions arises when we return to Coleridge's distinction between symbol and allegory. If you remember, Coleridge considers allegory to be too didactic. He argues that it is inferior to symbol, since it does not involve the author (or by implication the reader) in imaginative activity in establishing what the work represents (see p.212 above). It might be the case that the historical level of the *Ancyent Marinere* resides in the very fact that the poem refuses any single, simple interpretation. If Coleridge's purpose is to help foster the imagination of his readers, and thus to effect some form of social change, then it might be that he chose to do so by creating a text which, because it denies any simple interpretation, challenges the reader to participate in the production of its meaning.

This principle, that the reader is an active participant in the production of meaning, is, in one sense, an anti-allegorical one, if we accept the traditional idea of allegory as the communication of abstract concepts via disguised means, 'saying one thing whilst meaning another'. Yet, having seen a desire in Blake, Shelley and Coleridge to include their readers in the realization of the vision (and thus the meaning) represented in their texts, we seem to be moving nearer to a definition of a specifically Romantic mode of allegorical writing. This would be a mode of allegory not at all opposed to but consistent with what Coleridge calls 'Symbol' and Blake 'Imagination'. This kind of Romantic allegory, it would seem, foregrounds the relation between writing and reading; it highlights the participation of the reader in the production of meaning.

Further reading

Fletcher, A. (1964) *Allegory: The Theory of A Symbolic Mode*, Cornell University Press.

Colonialism and the exotic

by Nigel Leask

We have by now built up a picture of Romanticism as 'composed of a set of different and competing voices' arguing over a particular social and political agenda (see p.23 above). One point of contact between quite disparate literary works has been their response to common historical events: for example, in the years between 1789 and 1815, the French Revolution and the Napoleonic Wars contributed to an atmosphere of ferment in which fundamental notions about politics, social class, gender and religion were thrown into question in a veritable 'war of ideas'. And yet a problem arises in the undeniable fact that much literature of the Romantic period is concerned with escape from day-to-day reality, with images and narratives remarkable for their historical or geographical exoticism. We have seen examples of exotic settings in *The Prelude* and in *Don Juan* (Chapters Five and Seven). The apparent escapism of these exotic images seems at odds with the social and political concerns we have observed in so much Romantic literature.

Romantic writers adopted their exotic images from various sources including medieval and Gothic culture and its survival in contemporary folk culture, and the world of ancient Greece or medieval and Renaissance Italy. They also looked to the Orient, which usually meant the Islamic world familiar to European readers of the translation of *The Arabian Nights* or the India of Hindu antiquity and Mogul domination. It is on this fascination with the Orient, evident throughout the Romantic period, that discussion in this chapter is focused. Through the works of the poets and writers S.T. Coleridge, P.B. Shelley, Lord Byron and Thomas De Quincey I aim to show how the apparently conflicting claims of oriental escapism versus the here-and-now of social and political concerns may be reconciled.

Coleridge and the Orient

These conflicting claims are well illustrated in a comment made by Coleridge in 1797. Although still closely embroiled in the political turmoil of the revolutionary decade, the poet none the less wrote to his friend, the radical orator John Thelwall:

> I should much wish, like the Indian Vishna, [Vishnu] to float about along an infinite ocean cradled in the flower of the Lotos, and wake once in a million years for a few minutes – just to know that I was going to sleep for a million years more.
>
> (Griggs, *Collected Letters of S.T. Coleridge*, 1956, p.350)

In this letter Coleridge, who is making a rather private allusion to his recent experiments with opium, identifies with the Hindu deity Vishnu in a state of eternal reverie prior to his creation of the world. But only two years previously, in his poem 'Reflections on Having Left a Place of Retirement',

Coleridge had written of his resolve to abandon his rural cottage at Clevedon for a life of political and religious activism:

> I therefore go, and join head, heart and hand,
> Active and firm, to fight the bloodless fight
> Of Science, Freedom, and the Truth in Christ.
>
> (ll.60–2, Beer, *Poems of S.T. Coleridge*, 1993 edn, p.97)

There appears to be a contradiction between these two statements, one extolling Hindu mysticism, the other Christian political radicalism. Can they really emanate from the same writer? Look at the first statement and what it says about the Orient in terms of a cultural stereotype – that is a fixed, immutable image of a people and its customs. Then focus on the second in terms of what it says about western culture. **Can these contradictory statements be explained in terms of Coleridge's sense of identification? Which culture do you think we learn most about from these statements?**

Discussion

In the first statement Coleridge is personally identifying with a cultural stereotype which associates the Orient with narcotic reverie, myth and mystical contemplation. According to the stereotype, the oriental subjects have no power over their will, and live in an exotic, timeless never-never land closer to the realm of mythology than history. We might say that the oriental is represented as the 'other' of the westerner, who in contrast lives in a 'progressive' and purposeful historical present motivated by moral choice and action. Orientalist stereotypes work by setting up a dichotomy between familiar and exotic cultures. These are defined according to abstract essences ('timelessness', 'myth', 'mysticism' versus 'history', 'rationalism', 'moral purposefulness') rather than by human dialogue and the concrete experience of cultural difference.

There is evidence here of a tension between cultural description and personal vocation. Coleridge's identification (as poet and opium-user) with the 'Orient' is in marked contrast with his 'western' resolutions in the 1795 poem. The contrast is in many ways emblematic of the poet's life-long struggle between an active and a contemplative life. Apparently objective descriptions of a different culture can here be seen to be tied up with a whole set of psychological and moral values internal to western culture. Thus orientalist stereotypes tell us more about western culture than they do about oriental culture. ∎

'Kubla Khan'

A comparable interest in drug-induced reverie is the starting-point for Coleridge's poem 'Kubla Khan', which has been seen as the greatest orientalist poem in the English language. Although the poem was not actually published until 1816, Coleridge tells us in the 1816 Preface that it was written in the summer of 1797 in an Exmoor farmhouse. Elsewhere he mentions that his poem (he calls it a 'fragment'), 'with a good deal more, not recoverable [was] composed, in a sort of Reverie brought on by two grains of opium, taken to check a dysentery' (Beer, *Poems of S.T. Coleridge*, 1993 edn, p.206).

The poem's Preface describes how at the time of falling into his opium-induced reverie Coleridge had been reading Marco Polo's account of the Mongol emperor Cublai Can's (Kubla Khan) 'palace and stately garden' at 'Xamdu' (Xanadu) in a collection of seventeenth-century travel accounts entitled *Purchas his Pilgrimage*.

Read both the poem and the Preface now and consider the source of Coleridge's poetic inspiration. Is there a link between his reverie and the dream of Vishnu and the Lotos?

Discussion

Both Coleridge's reverie and the dream of Vishnu and the Lotos find their imaginative vision in a version of the Orient. But is the poem really about the Orient at all, or is it just an attractive setting for a poem about human creativity? We may want to read 'Kubla Khan' and other orientalist poems as fables of the Romantic self, but we cannot ignore the exotic settings. They are not merely backdrops to the psychological or creative development of the poems' protagonists. ∎

Compare Coleridge's literary influence (Samuel Purchas) with Wordsworth's thoughts about the negative influence of books in 'The Tables Turned' from *Lyrical Ballads*:

> Books! 'tis a dull and endless strife;
> Come hear the woodland linnet –
> How sweet his music! On my life,
> There's more of wisdom in it.
>
> And hark, how blithe the throstle sings!
> And he is no mean preacher;
> Come forth into the light of things,
> Let nature be your teacher
>
> (ll.9–16, Wu, *Romanticism*, 1994, pp.235–6)

The case of Coleridge reveals a danger in over-generalizing about an immediate experience of *nature* as the source of Romantic inspiration. Coleridge was by no means exceptional in building his poem upon a traveller's account of an exotic Orient in this way; the oriental poems of Robert Southey, Lord Byron and Thomas Moore also often drew upon travel books or scholarly studies of eastern customs to capture an authentic setting, often footnoting their sources to underline their accuracy.

Let us turn to the Preface of 'Kubla Khan' which tells how, after dreaming that he had composed two to three hundred lines of poetry based upon Purchas's book, Coleridge woke from his reverie. He had just written down the fifty-four lines of the extant poem when he was interrupted by 'a person on business from Porlock'. Returning to his pen, Coleridge discovered to his chagrin that he had forgotten the remainder of what would have been a considerable epic poem in its full form. He tells the reader that he has nevertheless decided to publish the fragment he had dredged up from his reverie as a 'psychological curiosity' rather than for its 'poetic merits'.

Whether or not we believe Coleridge's account of the poem's composition – written, we should remember, nearly twenty years after the event – there is no doubt that he did regard it as something of a 'psychological curiosity' in so far as it represented the pleasures and inspiration of opium-induced reverie. The fact that Coleridge intended to present his readers with an account of the 'pleasures' and the 'pains' of opium (to anticipate the section titles of De Quincey's *Confessions of an English Opium Eater*, which we will consider shortly) is evident in the Preface's concluding remark: 'As a contrast to this vision, I have annexed a fragment of a very different character, describing with equal fidelity the dream of pain and disease' (Beer, *Poems of S.T. Coleridge*, 1993 edn, p.205).

'Kubla Khan' is clearly designed to represent the pleasures of opium reverie. In contrast, the fragment to which Coleridge refers here is 'The Pains of Sleep' (1803) in which he described the hellish dreams which torment the opium addict, powerless to break the circle of dependence. The euphoric oriental paradise described in 'Kubla Khan' has become an oriental hell in which the poet discovers himself impotent to redress terrible wrongs inflicted upon him:

> A lurid light, a trampling throng,
> Sense of intolerable wrong,
> And whom I scorned, those only strong!
>
> (ll.18–20, ibid., p.381)

Evident here is an ambivalence in the Romantic representation of the Orient as an exotic vision. Instead of opening the gates of paradise, and turning the poet into Vishnu floating on a Lotos leaf, the oriental reverie could be a terrifying experience in which his western identity and will-power were overwhelmed by uncanny and alien forces. We will see that such Romantic attitudes to the Orient are not simply reactions to the pleasures and pains of opium but also have broader cultural, political and economic ramifications closely linked to European imperial expansion in 'the East'.

'Kubla Khan' is written in the rhapsodic visionary style associated by orientalist scholars like Sir William Jones with the poetry of oriental nations. In his 'Essay on the Poetry of the Eastern Nations' of 1772, Jones had argued that whereas European culture was marked by reason, oriental culture exemplified imagination in a superior degree (a clear example of the orientalist dichotomy mentioned above). Just as contemporary European poets were looking to folk ballads and supposedly 'ancient' European epics in order to regenerate an over-refined and over-intellectualized modern literature, Jones believed that by the study of Asiatic literature: 'we would be furnished with a new set of images and similitudes' (Jones, *Works*, 1799, pp.547–8). Like Wordsworth's condemnation of 'poetic diction' (by which he meant the tired repertoire of neo-Classical poetry) in his Preface to *Lyrical Ballads*, Jones complained that we have 'subsisted too long on the perpetual repetition of the same images, and incessant allusions to the same fables'. Jones's essays and translations of Sanskrit, Persian and Arabic literature were indeed instrumental in creating a literary taste for things oriental, exemplified here by Coleridge's 'Kubla Khan'.

Although Coleridge claimed that his poem was a fragment without design, it is in fact a highly organized work of imagination. It is divided into two sections: the first describing Kubla's pleasure dome and the mighty fountain which rises in the midst of his paradisical garden, giving birth to the sacred river (ll.1–30); and the second, the inspired poet's vision of the Abyssinian maid singing of Mount Abora (ll.37–54). The movement between these two geographically disparate settings (Asian Tartary and African Abyssinia) is facilitated by a linking stanza: 'The shadow of the dome of pleasure/Floated midway on the waves' (ll.31–2) which combines the polarities of sun and ice, fountain and cave. There is no particular reason why Coleridge should have picked upon Kubla's Tartary or the maid's Abyssinia for his setting, although both places had been proposed by biblical scholars as original sites of earthly paradise. What is significant here is their interchangeability for the Romantic poet as exotic, oriental locales, rather than their actual geographical location in quite different continents. The dream-like 'Kubla Khan' is in this respect quite distinct from the many travel accounts of exotic countries published in the period, which, in contrast to the fabulous Renaissance travelogue of Samuel Purchas, stress the geographical accuracy and 'firsthand' quality of their narratives.

'Kubla Khan' as orientalist poem

Perhaps more ink has been spilt by critics upon the literary sources and meaning of 'Kubla Khan' than upon any other Romantic poem, so I will limit myself here to developing a sense of its significance as an orientalist work. Coleridge's reading of Purchas, combined with two grains of opium, had prompted an exotic reverie in powerful contrast to the prosaic world of Porlock, where he was staying at the time of composing the poem. Following in the tradition of eighteenth-century orientalist narratives like the popular *Arabian Nights* and William Beckford's novel of 1785 entitled *Vathek*, the Orient of 'Kubla Khan' is represented as a place of almost magical beauty and power, but also of tyranny, eroticism and danger. It would be a mistake to attribute this to Coleridge's private fantasy for, like the image of Vishnu floating on a lotos, these qualities were also widely held contemporary stereotypes about the Orient. Kubla himself is the type of the oriental tyrant in search of god-like power over his dominions. He 'decreed' the pleasure-dome and 'girdled round' fertile ground for his private garden. The main protagonist of Beckford's novel, the Caliph Vathek, seeks divine power from a mysterious Indian wizard and is punished at the novel's conclusion by eternal damnation in the subterranean hell of Eblis. In similar fashion, Kubla Khan's power is threatened by the eruption of the fountain in the 'deep romantic chasm' breaking his ordered dominion into 'huge fragments' like 'chaffy grain beneath the thresher's flail' (ll.21–2).

Lines 12–30 are often cited as an embodiment of the uncontrollable libidinal energy associated with much Romantic art, clearly evident in the sexual imagery of 'And from this chasm, with ceaseless turmoil seething,/As if this earth in fast thick pants were breathing'. The more the Khan seeks to exert control over his territory for his own pleasure, the more the revolutionary force of natural energy thwarts his designs. The only thing he can hear from the revolutionary 'tumult' of the 'sacred river' thrown up by the fountain is the downfall of his dynasty: 'Ancestral voices prophesying war!'

I want to look now at Shelley's famous sonnet 'Ozymandias' which has already been discussed in Chapter Two (see p.52 above). **Reread the sonnet and compare the fate of Coleridge's Khan with Shelley's oriental tyrant. How does each poet present the role of the artist in their work?**

Discussion

Like Ozymandias (the Greek name for the Egyptian pharaoh Rameses II), the Khan's empire will soon exist only in ruins, which will remain amid shifting desert sands to mock his stern 'decrees'. Now compare the fate of Shelley's tyrant with the work of the sculptor who has captured his 'sneer of cold command' for all time and thus 'mocked' the pharaoh's claim to omnipotence. Shelley presents the work of the artist as transcending the fall of empires, surviving long after political tyranny has been overthrown by the inexorable passage of time. Coleridge expresses a similar idea about the artist in 'Kubla Khan'. In contrast to the Khan's negative interpretation of the fountain, Coleridge's 'poet' figure discovers a harmonious 'mingled measure' in the sacred river roaring through the caverns, blending images of light and shadow, heat and cold, in a manner which is characteristic of Coleridge's descriptions elsewhere of the workings of imagination. ■

The music of the sacred river leads the poet in the final lines of 'Kubla Khan' to remember his vision of the Abyssinian maid with her dulcimer singing of the Miltonic earthly paradise of Mount Abora:

> Could I revive within me
> Her symphony and song,
> To such a deep delight 'twould win me,
> That with music loud and long,
> I would build that dome in air,
> That sunny dome! those caves of ice!
>
> (ll.41–7, Beer, *Poems of S.T. Coleridge*, 1993 edn, p.207)

The poet's ideal order (note that it is expressed in the conditional voice) is a form of reverie strongly contrasted with Kubla's tyrannical 'girdling' of his dominion. At the same time his inspiration is drugged and rather uncanny. The oriental vision which redeems him from the prosaic world of Porlock also has the effect of separating him from the sympathies of ordinary people, fearful of his mad, inspired figure:

> [...] all should cry, Beware! Beware!
> His flashing eyes, his floating hair!
> Weave a circle round him thrice,
> And close your eyes with holy dread,
> For he on honey-dew hath fed,
> And drunk the milk of Paradise.
>
> (ll.49–54, ibid.)

The oriental renaissance

Our reading of 'Kubla Khan' may now help to provide us with an answer to the problem with which we began – what is the historical meaning of the powerful Romantic leaning to the exotic? How does the poem's employment of stereotypes link it to the Romantic discourse of the Orient? Coleridge's poem supports the argument of the French writer Raymond Schwab, who ventured in 1950 to dub the European Romantic movement the 'oriental renaissance'. An extract from Schwab's book, *The Oriental Renaissance*, appears in Part Two (p.294). Please read this now and consider why Schwab chose the term 'renaissance'. **Can you see a connection between the phenomenon we are studying here and the Italian Renaissance, the cultural 'rebirth' of the fourteenth and fifteenth centuries?**

D i s c u s s i o n

In the title of his book Schwab was not referring to a renaissance occurring in oriental cultures themselves, but rather to a wave of European scholarly and artistic interest in the languages and cultures of Eastern nations from about 1760 onwards. Europeans suddenly realized that their classical and religious heritage was not unique, and that they were themselves descended from more ancient oriental cultures. ■

Schwab described the Romantic movement as in part motivated by the orientalist scholarship of Anquetil-Duperron, Sir William Jones and Friedrich Schlegel (in France, Britain and Germany respectively) into the ancient and modern languages, literatures, and religions, of Persia, India, Egypt and Arabia. Think about the relationship between this cultural renaissance and Jones's desire to import the imagery and style of oriental poetry into Europe to replace the rather tired neo-Classicism that Wordsworth also criticized (see p.230 above). This definition of Romanticism as an encounter between European and non-European cultures is one that we have not yet considered in our approach to the subject. Taking our departure from traditional views of Romanticism as a quintessentially European phenomenon, we must now try to think of it as something more global.

What exactly was the nature of Europe's encounter with other cultures in the late eighteenth and early nineteenth centuries? Jones once again offers an important piece of evidence in trying to build up the picture. In the course of his studies of the classical Indian language Sanskrit, Jones 'discovered' that Sanskrit, Greek, Latin and the Germanic languages of Europe shared a common ancestor, which he traced to an ancient Persian language now lost. If this were true of languages, could it not also be argued that the peoples of Europe and Asia shared a common oriental ancestry? The suggestion worked like yeast upon the minds of European poets, historians and philosophers, extending the historical and geographical borders of Europe beyond the Mediterranean basin in which Greece and Rome were situated into the heart of a mysterious and ancient Orient, now regarded as the origin of mankind. Accordingly, the self-image of Europe experienced a profound change as attention was drawn to the oriental origins of Greek and Roman civilization and even of the Christian religion itself. The world was older and wider than Classical or Renaissance scholars had ever imagined.

Shelley, 'Alastor, or the Spirit of Solitude'

The new mood of geographical and historical expansion is well illustrated in Shelley's poem 'Alastor, or the Spirit of Solitude' (1815). Shelley's young 'poet', you will remember from Chapter Six, alienated from hearth and home, travels east to discover the 'thrilling secrets of the birth of time' (1.128). Blinded by his visionary zeal, the young traveller spurns an Arab maiden. His restlessness eventually leads him to a valley in Kashmir which, like Tartary or Abyssinia, was another suggested location for the original earthly paradise. Falling asleep, he dreams of a beautiful and voluptuous 'veiled maid' who sings and plays upon a lute songs of liberty and virtue. The poet dreams that he approaches the singer, who is evoked in extremely erotic language, and the couple make love. Awaking from his dream, he finds himself alone on the cold hillside. The remainder of the poem narrates his quest for the beautiful maid of his vision, whom he has mistaken for a reality.

Now read the poem and compare it to Coleridge's 'Kubla Khan'. **Can you see a resemblance in the way each poem represents the relationship between East and West?**

D i s c u s s i o n

Note the eroticism of both descriptions. In these orientalist narratives both Coleridge and Shelley represent the relationship between East and West as gendered; that is to say, as a European man falling in love with, or being seduced by, a fascinating oriental woman, who leaves her lover disappointed and broken-hearted. ■

Shelley based the central episode in 'Alastor' on a popular novel of 1811 by Lady Sydney Morgan entitled *The Missionary*, which took a stand against the contemporary movement to allow British missionaries to convert the natives of the Indian subcontinent to Christianity. The novel's climax described Hilarion, a Portuguese missionary, falling in love with a beautiful Hindu priestess called Luxima – a latinized form of the Hindu goddess Lakshmi. He failed to convert her, and in the end was himself converted to a form of Luxima's own religion of love after her heroic death saving his life. We know how much Shelley admired *The Missionary* from his comment in a letter of 1811: 'Luxima the Indian is an Angel. What a pity we cannot incorporate these creatures of Fancy: the very thought of them thrills the soul' (Jones, *Collected Letters of P.B. Shelley*, 1964, p.107). Although Shelley's maiden in 'Alastor' sings about the European revolutionary themes of liberty and virtue instead of Luxima's Hindu hymns, she is clearly inspired by Lady Morgan's mysterious priestess.

Shelley's comment about Luxima may help us judge the poet's intention in 'Alastor's' desire to recover his dream-companion. Is Shelley condemning his protagonist's hopeless quest in 'Alastor', or does the poem contain an autobiographical element which describes Shelley's own fascination with the Orient? It is worth noting here that in 1821 Shelley applied to his friend Thomas Love Peacock, a senior administrator in the East India Company, for a diplomatic post in India. Peacock turned down his request on the grounds of the poet's fragile health. **Consider Shelley's attitude to the dreamer and the dream. If the dreamer represents a western male, and the veiled maid an oriental woman, what can we learn about Shelley's attitude to the East?**

D i s c u s s i o n

We can now see that 'Alastor' reveals Shelley's profound ambivalence toward the visionary imagination figured here – as in Coleridge's 'Kubla Khan' – as a beautiful eastern woman. On the one hand, the desire in the poet stimulated by the woman helps him to transcend a cold and unfeeling world where there is no space for his idealism. On the other hand, pledging his life to the quest for the lost woman leads to a further alienation from society, and in the case of 'Alastor', to a premature death on the stony Caucasian mountains. ■

Orientalism and imperialism

Perhaps we can see in Shelley's ambivalence the lineaments of a general European ambivalence concerning the Orient, and the 'exotic' worlds being opened up by British imperialism in these years. The Palestinian critic Edward Said pointed out in an important book entitled *Orientalism* (1978), that it is precisely the question of imperialism that lies at the bottom of the Romantic fascination with the Orient. Our tendency to think of British imperialism as getting under way in the Victorian period makes us forget that the outcome of the Napoleonic Wars of 1793 to 1815 left Britain with governing power of 200 million people, about 26 per cent of the total world population in 1820. The fact that a very large proportion of these were Asian (the others being mainly African, Afro-Caribbean, Polynesian, Australian Aboriginal and Native American, as well as 'other' European peoples including Irish, Greeks, Spaniards and Sicilians) reflects the largely eastward drive of British expansion during the Napoleonic wars. Said criticized Schwab and others for having failed to consider the factor of imperialism in writing about the encounter between European and Asiatic cultures. He argued that the 'oriental renaissance' and its intellectual offspring, far from purely representing a form of intellectual curiosity on the part of European scholars and artists, was the cultural ramification of European imperialism: 'a Western style for dominating, restructuring, and having authority over the Orient' (Said, *Orientalism*, 1978, p.3).

Said argued that European cultural stereotypes were based upon traditional prejudices about the East rather than sensitivity towards, or dialogue with, members of the cultures themselves. Europeans were often blind to the specificity of different Asian nations, lumping together Egyptian, Arabic, Indian and Chinese into one confused 'imaginary geography'. Think about Coleridge's easy move from Tartary to Abyssinia in 'Kubla Khan'. Moreover, these orientalist representations traditionally tended to view Asian societies as static and corrupt, ruled over since time immemorial by tyrannical khans, pashas or maharajahs. Asian men were depicted as passionate, cruel and unreliable, lording it over their indolent, sensuous womenfolk, whom they jealously locked up in their harems. Only the civilizing mission of European colonialism could help liberate these luckless oriental peoples from their tyrannical rulers. As we saw above, this was often described in terms of gender: the salvation by Europeans of Asiatic women from their traditional bondage, described by the Indian critic Gayatri Spivak as 'White men saving brown women from brown men' (Spivak, 'Can the subaltern speak?', 1988, p.296). Said and others have pointed out how this helped to legitimize the European colonial enterprise of extracting as much loot as possible from other people's lands, to which they had no real claim apart from conquest, usually facilitated by superior military technology. It is interesting to note that the word 'loot' is of Hindi origin which reminds us of when and how it was first used.

To go back to the problem posed at the beginning of this chapter, we can see now that the Romantic exotic represented far more than simply an escapist flight from history. For in the empire-building years 1790 to 1830 historical reality was itself exotic for many British – and European – peoples. If we look at British writers alone, it is instructive to note that Wordsworth, Coleridge, Shelley, De Quincey, Robert Southey, Thomas Moore, Walter Scott, Thomas Love Peacock and Charles Lamb all had personal or professional stakes in Britain's Indian empire. Perhaps, then, we can not expect to find any real resistance to imperialism among Romantic writers, even those on the left of the political spectrum, as we might among twentieth-century writers. Exposure of abuses in British colonies – such as the famous impeachment of the Governor-General of British India, Warren Hastings, in the years between 1788 and 1794, on the grounds that he had governed British India in a rapacious and unscrupulous fashion – led to criticism of the manner of rule, but almost never to the principle of imperialism itself. After all, we are talking about a period preceding the rise of nationalist independence movements in Britain's colonies. This is not to say that British Romantic writers were all gung-ho empire-builders, and as we have seen, they often contemplated the Orient with a certain ambivalence, with fear as well as fascination. We should therefore be on the lookout for anxieties rather than principled opposition to empire in the literature of the period.

Byron, The Corsair

One writer who more often poured scorn on Britain's imperial aspirations than most was Lord Byron. Yet in this light it is ironic that Byron's tremendous poetical success was partly based upon his ability to capitalize upon the popular taste for things oriental. Indeed, probably the most popular orientalist poem of the Romantic period was *The Corsair* (1814) by Byron. This sold 10,000 copies on the day it was published, and in the months following went through seven editions and 25,000 copies. The market appeal of orientalist poetry was slightly embarrassing to the aristocratic Byron, who prided himself on being 'above' writing for commercial gain. I think this is evident in the flippancy of the following lines from his Venetian poem 'Beppo':

> How quickly would I print (the world delighting)
> A Grecian, Syrian, or Assyrian tale;
> And sell you, mix'd with western sentimentalism,
> Some samples of the finest Orientalism!
>
> (Page, *Lord Byron Poetical Works*, 1970, p.629)

What was the recipe of Byron's commercial success? An extract from *The Corsair* with contextualizing notes appears in Part Two of this book (p.303). (All page references to *The Corsair* are to Part Two.) Please read the extract now. Look particularly at the description of Conrad, the aristocratic leader of a band of pirates who live by terrorizing the coastal waters of Turkish-dominated Greece:

> Sun-burnt his cheek, his forehead high and pale
> The sable curls in wild profusion veil;
> And oft perforce his rising lip reveals
> The haughtier thought it curbs, but scarce conceals.
> [...]
> There was a laughing Devil in his sneer,
> That raised emotions both of rage and fear;
> And where his frown of hatred darkly fell,
> Hope withered fled – and Mercy sighed farewell!
>
> (ll.203–6, 223–6, pp.303–4)

Byron portrays Conrad as a disappointed idealist ('a man of loneliness and mystery' (l.173, p.303), a kind of fallen angel who has turned into a free-booting pirate, pledged to wreak havoc with Turkish shipping and resist the stern power of the local Turkish Pasha. Conrad and his corsairs are Europeans and nominally Christians with Spanish names like Pedro, Juan, Anselmo and Gonsalvo. There is a tacit expectation that the European reader will identify with them in their struggle against the Turkish foe, much as a 1950s cinema audience would be expected to identify with the 'cowboys' and not the 'Indians' in a 'western' movie. Indeed, Conrad exhibits the mixture of reckless courage and chivalric sentimentality of a 'western tough-guy', the main difference being his aristocratic outlook on the world. His only virtue lies in his faithful love for his Greek wife Medora, who represents a conventional romance heroine. His fidelity epitomizes his chivalric regard for women in general, although it is a virtue that will cost him dear. Chivalry and a sense of gentlemanly fair play clearly represent for Byron the superiority of European over oriental values, although here as in his other oriental tales he is concerned more with the failure of these values than their triumph.

When Conrad is called out upon an urgent and dangerous mission to infiltrate the Pasha's court and strike a pre-emptive blow against the Turkish forces which are mustering to capture the corsair band, Medora's sorrowful reaction is described in the following terms:

> O'er every feature of that still, pale face,
> Had sorrow fixed what time can ne'er erase:

The tender blue of that large loving eye
Grew frozen with its gaze on vacancy,
Till – Oh, how far! – it caught a glimpse of him,
And then it flowed, and phrenzied seemed to swim,
Through those long dark, and glistening lashes dewed
With drops of sadness oft to be renewed.

(ll.491–98, pp.305–6)

Medora is descended from the heroines of sensibility in the novels of the late eighteenth century – particularly the virtuous heroines of Gothic novels such as Anne Radcliffe's *Mysteries of Udolpho* and *The Italian* – who were often characterized by passivity, sensitivity and fidelity. **How does this representation of the virtuous European woman differ from that of the oriental women in 'Kubla Khan' and 'Alastor'?**

Discussion

Pallor, vulnerability and inwardness seem to be the signs of Medora's passive dedication to Conrad, matching his own chivalric, protective attitude to women, his 'one virtue' set against 'a thousand crimes' (l.696, p.317). One cannot imagine Medora like Coleridge's oriental 'woman wailing for her demon lover' in 'Kubla Khan'! ■

Let us now turn to the passage describing the Pasha Seyd's court, which Conrad will shortly infiltrate disguised as a dervish, or Islamic holy man. It is worth noting here the fascination with disguise in orientalist narratives. Byron even had himself painted by Thomas Phillips in full Albanian costume, a striking image of Romantic Orientalism which you can see in Figure 12.

High in his hall reclines the turbaned Seyd;
Around – the bearded chiefs he came to lead.
Removed the banquet, and the last pilaff –
Forbidden draughts, 'tis said, he dared to quaff,
Though to the rest the sober berry's juice,
The slaves bear round for rigid Moslem's use;
The long Chibouque's dissolving cloud supply,
While dance the Almahs to wild minstrelsy.

(ll.28–36, p.306)

Consider some of the ways in which this passage is 'orientalist' in Said's sense; how it reinforces cultural stereotypes based on traditional prejudices. Think about the meaning of the 'forbidden draughts' and the fact that the Pasha breaks Islamic law to quaff them. Compare this to the 'sober berries' brought round for the 'rigid Moslem's use'. And note Byron's use of the Turkish words 'Chibouque' (water pipe) and 'Almah' (dancing girl). **What is the literary effect achieved by these realistic details of Seyd's exotic court?**

Discussion

Encapsulated here we find the orientalist stereotype of the eastern tyrant, surrounded by his henchmen, described with careful attention to exotic

Figure 12   Thomas Phillips, *George Gordon Noel Byron*, 1813, oil on canvas, 76.5 x 63.9 cm. Reproduced by courtesy of the National Portrait Gallery, London.

detail. (Byron prided himself that his travels in the Near East had acquainted him firsthand with Turkish customs.) There is also an implication of Islamic hypocrisy – at any rate a hostile representation of Islam. Byron insinuates that Seyd flouts the Islamic ban on alcohol ('forbidden draughts') while his followers are constrained to drink nothing but coffee ('sober berries'). Completing the picture are the 'Almahs', suggesting the 'wild' sexual licence of

Seyd's court, and the 'Chibouque' which suggests languor and narcosis. These details give an authoritative, firsthand quality to Byron's verse, the authority of a poet who has travelled in the Orient. ■

At a pre-arranged signal, Conrad, reinforced by his corsairs, throws off his oriental disguise and reveals himself fully armoured ready to fight with Seyd and his guards. All is going well when Conrad, in a characteristic act of chivalry, interrupts his men and urges them to save the Pasha's concubines from the blazing harem: 'Oh! burst the Haram – wrong not on your lives/One female form – remember – *we* have wives' (ll.202–3, p.306). This delay proves fatal to the corsairs, who are rapidly overwhelmed by the Turks, and their leader seized and thrown into prison. There Conrad faces death by impalement (a typical example of 'oriental cruelty'). However, Conrad's act of chivalry has won him an admirer in an unexpected quarter. Gulnare, Seyd's mistress and the 'Haram queen', having been rescued by Conrad has fallen in love with him. Visiting the captured corsair in his dungeon, she warns him that he faces death and offers to help him escape from the Pasha's grasp. But Conrad's gentlemanly code of honour prompts him to turn down the offer and accept his fate: 'Not much could Conrad of his sentence blame,/His foe, if vanquished, had but shared the same' (ll.370–1, p.308). To accept Gulnare's offer would be to break the gentlemanly code of conduct upon which Conrad prides himself. It would also, more problematically, be to put himself (a married man faithful to his patient Medora) into the hands of a lower-class woman, a prostitute and a Turk.

In the event, Gulnare makes up Conrad's mind for him. Burning with resentment against her tyrannical lover Seyd, she takes the law into her own hands and brutally assassinates him while he sleeps in bed. Despite his vaunted fidelity to Medora, Conrad has almost imperceptibly been seduced by Gulnare's heady charms; at one point Byron likens her to Cleopatra casting her erotic spell over Mark Antony (see l.550, p.311). Here is Conrad's horrified reaction upon realizing what Gulnare has done, noting a bloodspot upon her cheek:

> That spot of blood, that light but guilty streak,
> Had banished all the beauty from her cheek!
> Blood he had viewed – could view unmoved – but then
> It flowed in combat, or was shed by men!
> (ll.426–29, p.316)

Like Lady Macbeth, Gulnare has broken the rules of allowable feminine behaviour and has become 'unsexed'. Remember that in refusing to kill Pasha Seyd, Conrad says:

> To smite the smiter with the scimitar;
> Such is my weapon – not the secret knife –
> Who spares a woman's seeks not slumber's life.
> (ll.363–5, p.315)

What does this tell us about Conrad's chivalric, 'European' code of honour in contrast to Gulnare's oriental conduct?

Discussion

Although Conrad's code of honour is a paradigm of aristocratic virtue, it is hopelessly ineffectual in practical situations. He is willing to allow himself to be killed brutally by Seyd simply because he has lost the game (as a result of his chivalry in saving the concubines). Conrad may dislike Seyd's tyranny, but he is incapable of doing anything to overthrow it. Gulnare throws all codes of honour to the winds (indeed, as a concubine and a Turk, what can she gain by upholding aristocratic honour?) but in so doing effectively puts an end to Seyd's tyranny and rescues Conrad. Hers is thus a genuinely revolutionary action, although it jeopardizes everything that Conrad's 'European' code of honour stands for. ■

In the light of this narrative consider how Byron deploys the cultural opposition East/West for his dramatic and psychological purpose in 'The Corsair'. **How does Conrad regard the newly empowered Gulnare? Why do you think that his contemporary British readership found it so fascinating?**

Discussion

Conrad is horrified by Gulnare's assassination of Seyd, but is powerless to resist. A strange inversion of gender and class takes place as Gulnare exchanges her passive 'womanly' qualities for those of a revolutionary male, and Conrad adopts a passive stance, allowing himself to be led (and even kissed) by the dominant Gulnare. For a contemporary readership, Gulnare represents an exorbitant and horrifying character, creating a frisson akin to that of the best Gothic villains. 'Civilized' values of political behaviour and sexual role-playing are thrown into question by this episode, which contributed to Byron's 'demonic' reputation in contemporary England. ■

The real pathos of Byron's poem, however, lies in the fate of Medora, and this may have appealed in particular to Byron's female readers, versed in the tragic fate of the abandoned heroine which was typical of the novels of sensibility. Gulnare leads the zombie-like Conrad to his rendezvous with one of his ships and the couple are carried away to freedom. While returning to the corsair's island, Gulnare declares her love for Conrad and, despite his declared revulsion from the 'unsexed' Turk, he succumbs briefly to the seductive charms of the woman who has liberated him. Although Byron declares that 'even Medora might forgive the kiss/That asked from form so fair no more than this,/The first, the last that Frailty stole from Faith' (ll.549–51, p.317), it assumes great symbolic importance in the poem's conclusion. Arriving home, Conrad discovers to his consternation that his wife lies dead in her tower, ostensibly broken-hearted by his reported capture and imminent execution by the Turks. (She has died unaware of Conrad's liberation.)

If we read the final sections of *The Corsair* carefully, however, it seems more likely that she has been – at least symbolically – killed off by Conrad's 'betrayal' of her love. Gulnare's kiss has killed her, and in a sense she has been replaced by the seductive, unscrupulous oriental woman. In the poem's conclusion we are told that Conrad, broken-hearted at his wife's death, vanishes in a boat: 'His death yet dubious' (l.694, p.317). Of Gulnare we hear no more, as if Byron was unsure as to how he should finish his tale of chivalry defeated and love betrayed. Perhaps this is evidence that, as a character, Gulnare has got 'out of control' and that Byron is uncertain how to resolve the narrative once all allowable codes of conduct have been broken. Conrad's enemy Seyd lies dead, brutally assassinated in bed by his former lover rather than slain in battle by his enemy. Conrad's gentlemanly standards (symbolized by Medora) have been doubly compromised, once by Gulnare's oriental treachery in the manner in which she secured his freedom, and again by her kiss, which represents her usurpation of the place of his 'European' wife.

If the military and sexual tactics of Conrad and his band represent the 'official' ideology of European imperialists, 'white men saving brown women from brown men', the outcome of Byron's poem represents its collapse and betrayal. Gulnare's rescue of Conrad from prison and his subsequent seduction is something more along the lines of 'brown woman saving white man from brown men – only to seduce them away from their own white women'. This is an inversion of the normal imperialist programme, which has the effect of sundering the hero from the values of his own civilization. As Medora's tragic death makes clear, Conrad has 'turned Turk' and betrayed the values of his own culture. The danger and anxiety implicit in the oriental subject-matter of Coleridge's 'Kubla Khan' and Shelley's 'Alastor' become much more explicit in Byron's poem. The really disquieting suggestion made by the poem, however, is that the European male on the colonial frontier is far from being secure in the knowledge of his moral and cultural superiority. The colonizer (and I think we can read Conrad in this light without forcing the issue) is deeply vulnerable and risks the fate of 'turning Turk', of being absorbed into the oriental world which he has sought to subordinate to his own standards of civilization. In conclusion we might say that although *The Corsair* contains many elements that fit Said's account of 'orientalist' representation, it can hardly be said to assert the triumph of the West with any confidence. It is a paradigmatic case of imperial anxiety.

Thomas De Quincey and the Confessions of an English Opium Eater

Romantic anxieties of empire reach their zenith in the baroque prose writings of Thomas De Quincey, and particularly in the 1821 *Confessions of an English Opium Eater*. 'Not the opium-eater, but the opium, is the true hero of the tale: and the legitimate centre on which the interest revolves', the author declares with an assertiveness which seems to question the book's very status as a 'confession' (De Quincey, *Confessions of an English Opium Eater*, 1971 edn, p.114). Although on one level De Quincey's book can be read as a Romantic inquiry into the world of dreams and imagination, its fascination with 'the dark idol' of opium places it within the category of Romantic orientalist literature. After all, opium was one of the staple commodities of British trade in the Far East as well as the source of bizarre Romantic dreams and visions. Opium produced in British India was sold to

China in increasingly vast quantities throughout the nineteenth century in return for China tea, particularly after the opium wars of the 1840s and 1850s had forcibly opened Chinese markets to 'official' British drug-dealers. Along with the slave trade, abolished in 1807, this was one of the least salubrious chapters in the history of European colonialism.

Perhaps partly for this reason there is something profoundly disquieting about the *Confessions*. On the one hand, De Quincey advocated aggressive imperial expansion in the East, and later gave his hearty support to the opium trade with China. On the other hand, like the drug-besotted orientals victimized by this trade in human misery who filled his dreams, De Quincey himself appears to dwell in a shadowy land of dependence and paranoia. Even the book's title – the *English* opium eater – lays emphasis on the *un*-English nature of opium eating, more commonly associated with Turks, Chinese or other 'orientals'. Like most Europeans, De Quincey actually consumed the drug in the liquid form of laudanum, tincture of Turkish opium dissolved in alcohol. (It was a potent mix, and widely taken by rich and poor alike in England as the only really effective pain-killer, cheaper than many forms of alcohol.) De Quincey's title thus plays on the oriental associations of 'opium-eating', thereby portraying himself as an 'orientalized' Englishman.

Even in our own day, discussion of drugs is closely enmeshed with questions of race and culture, and there is still a tendency to 'orientalize' the drug culture. Can you think of examples in contemporary literature or cinema? (William Burroughs's novel *The Naked Lunch* and Francis Ford Coppola's film *Apocalypse Now* spring to mind.) Despite his loss of stable identity, De Quincey was not interested in moralizing about drug abuse. 'An inhuman moralist' he wrote 'I can no more endure in my nervous state than opium that has not been boiled' (ibid., p.88). For this reason the *Confessions* spends more time and energy proclaiming the pleasures rather than the pains of opium. You might like to refer to Coleridge's poem 'The Pains of Sleep' for an unambiguously negative account of opium addiction. Unlike De Quincey, Coleridge kept his life long addiction to the drug a guilty secret. He imprecated mercy on De Quincey for publishing the *Confessions*, 'if his book has been the occasion of seducing others into this withering vice through wantonness' (Gillman, *Life of S.T. Coleridge*, 1838, p.250).

Despite the personal misery which it brought him, De Quincey regarded opium as a commonly available and inexpensive substitute for the pleasures of imagination described by poets like Wordsworth and Keats. 'Happiness might now be bought for a penny, and carried in the waistcoat pocket: portable ecstasies might be had corked up in a pint bottle: and peace of mind could be sent down in gallons by the mail coach' (De Quincey, *Confessions of an English Opium Eater*, 1971 edn, p.72). Even in the 'pains of opium' section of the *Confessions* which purports to describe De Quincey's terrible bondage to the drug, he spends most of the time dwelling upon his 'romantic agony' – the powerful and terrifying dreams resulting from his medical condition as a dependent. His representation of the massively aggrandized landscapes and incidents of these dreams exemplifies De Quincey's notion (developed in an essay of 1823 entitled 'Letters to a young man whose education has been neglected') of a sublime 'literature of power', counterbalancing the triviality and materialism of everyday urban life in the West. **Can you see the connection between this 'literature of power' and the excitement and allure of empire building in distant lands which formed an important theme in early nineteenth-century British imperialist culture?**

Discussion

Romantic exoticism might have been an important ingredient in the construction of nineteenth-century imperial culture. The most insignificant European self could find itself aggrandized in the colonial situation, at times obeyed and humoured like a species of minor deity. The 'construction of civilization' in non-European cultures appealed to the idealism of many Europeans, seemingly blind to the ethical problems underlying imperialism. Above all, life on the imperial frontier seemed to be replete with an excitement and stimulus wholly lacking in bourgeois urban life. It is thus an easy step from De Quincey's 'literature of power' to the sublime inflation of the collective European self under the sign of imperialism. ∎

The Grasmere Malay

In De Quincey's writings of the 1820s, we can already see the dark shadow of cultural and racial bigotry which looms large over the later nineteenth-century literature of empire, but which was still only implicit in the poems of Coleridge, Shelley and Byron. Let us examine an exemplary scene of cultural encounter in which De Quincey discovers the Orient in the heart of the English countryside. I refer to an incident in the 'pains of opium' section of the *Confessions* which describes the appearance of a turbaned Malay at the door of De Quincey's cottage in Grasmere – in point of fact Wordsworth's Dove Cottage, which he had rented from the poet. Please read this section now. Note particularly the unambiguously racist terms that De Quincey employs in his comparison of the Malay with the young English girl:

> ... a more striking picture there could not be imagined, than the beautiful English face of the girl, and its exquisite fairness, together with her erect and independent attitude, contrasted with the sallow and bilious skin of the Malay, enamelled or veneered with mahogany, by marine air, his small fierce restless eyes, thin lips, slavish gestures and adorations. Half-hidden by the ferocious-looking Malay was a little child from a neighbouring cottage who had crept in after him and was now in the act of reverting its head, and gazing upwards at the turban and the fiery eyes beneath it, whilst with one hand he caught at the dress of the young woman for protection.
>
> (Wu, *Romanticism*, 1994, pp.677–8)

In the light of our previous discussion of cultural stereotyping, compare the description above with Byron's description of Medora and Gulnare. **How are the Malay's cultural attitudes represented in his physical appearance? What values are associated with skin colour in this racist passage?**

Clearly skin colour equals culture here, without any regard for the Malay's human qualities (De Quincey feels able to characterize the Malay without any knowledge of these qualities, given that the two men have no language in common). Don't miss the sexual paranoia underpinning the passage; De Quincey feels called upon to protect the English woman and child from the menace of this oriental 'tiger-cat'. De Quincey was not alone in fearing Malays more than other 'oriental' peoples: the Revd Sydney Smith described Malays as 'the most vindictive and ferocious of living beings. They set no value on their own existence, in the prosecution of their odious passions' (quoted in Leask, *British Romantic Writers and the East*, 1992, p.210). ■

Although De Quincey's writing is often haunted by a fear of drug-besotted impotence when called upon to defend innocent English women and children from varieties of oriental savagery, in this case he does manage to contain the situation. Addressing the Malay in classical Greek (the nearest thing to an oriental language which he can muster), De Quincey induces him – who clearly cannot understand a word of his address – 'to worship me in a most devout manner'. De Quincey has 'saved [his] reputation' and persuaded the pacified Malay to rest on the floor for an hour before continuing on his journey – but only just. His parting gift to the Malay displays greater resolution. 'To him, as an orientalist, I concluded that opium must be familiar'. As a result he gives the visitor a lump of opium big enough to poison 'three dragoons and their horses'. To De Quincey's consternation the Malay bolts it all down in one, and then departs on his way. De Quincey never discovers his body, so he surmises that the 'coarser' oriental nervous system is resistant to such huge overdoses. Despite feigning compassion as the motivation for this lethal 'gift', it is probable that De Quincey employs the drug to overpower the Malay, just as the British East India Company sought to overpower the Far East by flooding it with cheap opium (exchanged for China tea and other sought-after commodities) manufactured in the Company's opium factories at Patna in India. The anecdote of the 'Grasmere Malay' is thus an emblem proleptic of the British opium trade upon which British imperial power in the Orient was consolidated, particularly after the opium wars had forced open the immense Chinese markets.

In a sense, however, it is the Malay who has the last word, at least in De Quincey's troubled dreams narrated in the final section of the *Confessions*: 'this Malay [...] fastened afterwards upon my dreams, and brought other Malays with him worse than himself, that ran amuck at me, and led me into a world of troubles' (Wu, *Romanticism*, 1994, p.678). De Quincey describes in a passage of superb baroque prose the oriental nightmares which afflict him in the wake of the Malay incident. This passage is perhaps the finest manifestation of imperial bad conscience in English Romantic literature, as well as the most consummate example of Romantic Orientalism:

> I was stared at, hooted at, grinned at, chattered at, by monkeys, by
> paroquets, by cockatoos. I ran into pagodas and was fixed for
> centuries at the summit, or in secret rooms. I was the idol, I was the
> priest, I was worshipped, I was sacrificed. I fled from the wrath of
> Brama through all the forests of Asia. Vishnu hated me. Seeva laid wait

for me. I came suddenly upon Isis and Osiris. I had done a deed, they
said, which the ibis and the crocodile trembled at. I was buried for a
thousand years in stone coffins, with mummies and sphinxes, in
narrow chambers at the heart of eternal pyramids. I was kissed with
cancerous kisses by crocodiles, and laid confounded with all
unutterable slimy things amongst reeds and Nilotic mud.

(Ibid., p.681)

What De Quincey fears more than anything, following on from the fears
of Coleridge and Byron, is absorption in the nightmare world of the
Orient: 'Southern Asia, in general, is the seat of awful images and associations' (Ibid., p.680). In his dream De Quincey has lost the self-possession
and command which he exhibited in his encounter with the Malay. Like
the drug-user who loses his will and is 'possessed' by his drug, De
Quincey fears that the European subject will be 'possessed' by the Orient
which it has set out to dominate. In this passage the English opium eater
has become the Malay, and discovers that he has tried to poison his own
double.

How does this passage compare with Coleridge's 'Kubla Khan'? **Compare De Quincey's representation of the Hindu god Vishnu with that
in Coleridge's letter of 1797 to John Thelwall (see p.227 above)**.

D i s c u s s i o n

Once again the European has taken on the persona of an oriental deity
(what De Quincey's French admirer and translator Charles Baudelaire called
'le homme-dieu'). Remember the charmed circle woven around the
inspired poet of 'Kubla Khan'? Imperial and technological domination of
Asiatic and African states did seem to afford European colonizers a 'godlike'
power over their millions of subjects. Yet the god here is sacrificed as well
as worshipped. On the evidence of this and similar passages we have
looked at, European colonizers, with their tidy sense of rationality and
history, seem deeply threatened by the enormous spatial and temporal
vistas opened up by the East. Coleridge's dream of the million years' sleep
of Vishnu, and the 'forests ancient as the hills' in 'Kubla Khan' revolve upon
the ancientness of the Orient. As De Quincey puts it: 'The mere antiquity of
Asiatic things, of their institutions, histories, modes of faith, etc., is so
impressive, that to me the vast age of the race and name overpowers the
sense of youth in the individual. A young Chinese seems to me an antedi-
luvian man renewed' (Wu, *Romanticism*, 1994, p.680). ■

The youthful vigour of Europe when set against the antiquity of the Orient
easily loses its sense of superiority and of rational purpose; like the *English*
opium eater it becomes fixated and addicted to the Orient which it had set
out to dominate. The price the inspired writer pays for god-like powers is
to lose his command and be sacrificed: 'I was worshipped, I was sacrificed
[...] I had done a deed [...] which the ibis and crocodile trembled at' (ibid.,
p.681). Moreover, the 'cancerous kiss' of the crocodile refers us back to
Conrad's fatal kiss of Gulnare in *The Corsair*, the kiss that destroyed
Medora, personification of the frail chivalry of western civilization. The
West labours under the anxiety that it will be destroyed by its unquench-

246

able and lawless desire for the 'oriental other'. Moreover, like the opium addict, it will be impotent to resist this fatal attraction.

Conclusion

We began by thinking about the contradiction between Romanticism as a literature of social and political engagement and as a flight from reality to an exotic Orient. We observed certain constant traits in Romantic writing about the Orient, which we related to cultural stereotypes concerning oriental tyranny, indolence and eroticism. This helped to explain the recurrence of common themes and images in a variety of orientalist works. The Romantic poet figures in Coleridge's 'Kubla Khan' and in Shelley's 'Alastor' both appeared to be fixated by a desire for the Orient, in both poems personified by a beautiful visionary maiden.

We could have followed a well-trodden path in interpreting these visionary females as symbols of Romantic imagination, objects always desired, never attained. Resisting the temptation to read them merely as metaphysical or psychological projections, however, we referred them back instead to their historical and cultural context in what Schwab called 'the oriental renaissance'. We saw how scholarly investigation into oriental cultures from the mid-eighteenth century had added a new historical and geographical dimension to Europe's sense of its own cultural origin in the classical world of the Mediterranean basin. Scholars like Jones posited the common cultural heritage of the Hindu, Persian, Graeco-Latin and European traditions. The Romantic reaction against eighteenth-century neo-Classicism manifested an obsession with mapping these earlier and more distant origins, as it were 'orientalizing' the European Classical tradition.

At the same time we noted that this new sense of the past coincided with a massive increase in European/Asiatic cultural encounters. Following Said, it was suggested that the 'oriental renaissance' was more than simply a humanistic 'discovery' of Europe's oriental heritage; it was also a symptom of the rise of European imperialism. The transition in the course of the eighteenth century from small-scale European trading stations situated on the margins of Asian states to full-scale colonies, entailing the political control of large non-European populations, necessitated the study of indigenous languages and cultures. Europeans liked to see themselves as the vigorous 'youthful' descendants of ancient oriental cultures, returning to their ancestral roots to introduce historical progress and new forms of civilization. Although many colonizers genuinely believed that they were bringing the benefits of European manners, social relations and technology to colonized people, their notion of a 'civilizing mission' was a mask for social and economic exploitation.

With reference to *The Corsair* by Byron, we discussed both the sheer popularity of orientalist literature in early nineteenth-century Britain and the anxieties about imperialism which begin to emerge in that literature. Colonization was often symbolized in terms of gender, and as an unsuccessful or unrealized romance between a European male and an oriental female. In *The Corsair*, we noted how the conventional European romance heroine was upstaged and 'killed off' by a a beautiful but lawless Turkish harlot. Gulnare's triumph over Medora led to the 'orientalization' of the European male hero Conrad, in an exemplary narrative of imperial anxiety.

By deploying the notion of anxiety we began to question Said's account of the triumphalism of orientalist discourse, whereby the West marches assertively and triumphantly upon a down-trodden and passive Orient. Orientalist discourse was far more fissured, insecure, anxious than Said's account allows for. Imperial anxiety was followed through in the writings of De Quincey's *Confessions of an English Opium Eater*, where we found an increasingly paranoiac representation of cultural and racial difference. The ruling metaphor of sexual desire which marked the poetry of Coleridge, Shelley and Byron has now been translated into a metaphor of drug addiction, with its darker overtones of madness and dependence. Imperialism seems to be a deadly attraction for Europe which might lead on the one hand to economic power and cultural aggrandizement, on the other to loss of self and cultural degeneration. We found this perfectly embodied in the Malay incident in *Confessions*, both in the autobiographical anecdote in which De Quincey 'sees off' his oriental visitor, and the dream in which he is visited by a terrifying, hallucinogenic vision of oriental revenge and European degeneration.

A literary-critical understanding of the global and imperialist dimensions of Romanticism has been very long in coming. This is partly because of an enduring tendency to think of Romantic literature as essentially concerned with the 'private' relationship between the mind and nature, or of the reflexive relationship of the mind with itself. It is also because of the way in which British history was rewritten in the era of decolonization that followed the Second World War as a national and European, rather than a global, concern. When Romantic critics 'rediscovered' history in the 1980s, it was to the French Revolution and to the rise of British national culture in the crucible of the Napoleonic wars that it turned. But Romanticism was the product of the colonial 'margins' as well as the European 'centre'. English writing in this period was strongly marked by a burgeoning global imperialism which, as I pointed out above (p.235), could by 1820 count 26 per cent of the world's population as British subjects.

The task of post-colonial criticism is to show an awareness of this imperial history in reflecting upon the history and composition of English literary culture. On account of that history (marked, lest we should be beguiled by the rhetoric of 'commonwealth', by the inequality of its power-relations), Britain today has a tremendous cultural and ethnic heterogeneity. To make sense of this present and all its rich opportunities, criticism must be aware of the inequalities and anxieties of a shared imperial history in constructing our literary canon.

Further Reading

Bayly, C.A. (1989) *Imperial Meridian: The British Empire and the World 1780–1830*, Longman.

Leask, N. (1992) *British Romantic Writers and the East: Anxieties of Empire*, Cambridge University Press.

Majeed, J. (1992) *James Mill's 'History of British India' and Orientalism*, Clarendon Press.

Said, E. (1978) *Orientalism*, Penguin.

Suleri, S. (1992) *The Rhetoric of British India*, Chicago University Press.

Reading Kleist and Hoffmann

by Richard Allen

This chapter discusses two stories by German writers from the early years of the nineteenth century – 'The Betrothal on Santo Domingo' by Heinrich von Kleist (1777–1811) and 'The Sandman' by Ernst Theodore Amadeus Hoffmann (1776–1822). Although the texts date from the same period as much of the poetry dealt with in previous chapters, studying German prose is a departure from what has gone before and some explanation is in order. This chapter allows you to take a step towards reading texts that are generally described as Romantic from outside British literature. Working through the stories by Kleist and Hoffmann will give you a glimpse first of a wider Romantic movement spreading across Europe, and second of Romantic writing in prose rather than poetry. It is important, however, to understand the limitations of this chapter. It cannot offer a summary of writing in German literature of the period on the scale of the account of writing in English given in the book so far. And it cannot do more than introduce you to the close reading of a single text by each author. (In the case of Kleist, though his stories are perhaps his most widely known works now, it can be argued that his major works were plays. And Hoffmann was as much an authority on music and a composer as a writer of stories.) The chapter cannot 'sum up' German Romanticism, although in each case I try to relate your reading to what I see as major Romantic issues: Romantic 'irony' in the case of Kleist, the 'uncanny' in the case of Hoffmann. But I hope this chapter can provide further ground on which to test the idea set out in Chapter One that 'Romantic writings share a broadly similar historical context and our reading gains from knowledge of this context' (see p.7 above).

The Betrothal on Santo Domingo

Please read 'The Betrothal on Santo Domingo' now. (All references to 'The Betrothal on Santo Domingo' are to Taylor, *Six German Romantic Tales*, 1985.) As you read, bear in mind the idea in Chapters One and Two of 'reading in history', and that the story was first published in 1810–11.

Can we transfer the idea that it is important to 'read in history' from English Romantic poetry to this German story?

Discussion

From the very first sentence the story seems to demand an awareness of history. We learn that it is set at 'the time when the natives were murdering the white men' and there is reference to a historical figure, General Dessalines. Hoango is placed within this historical situation and, although our interest soon becomes focused on the plight of Gustav, the historical dimension is never far from the centre of the narrative. Moreover if we are not able to supply this kind of context we are not able to assess fully the threat to the Strömli family. At the end of the story after a brief reference to

251

the siege of Port-au-Prince the story is specifically located at some point in 1807. And note that the story was first published in a collection in 1810–11. There are thus three levels to reading this story in history: Herr Strömli looks back from 1807 to the events in the story, Kleist looks back from 1810–11 to the events of 1807, and the reader looks back from 'now' to 1810–11 and 1807. ■

A little research now shows how much meaning was contained in the opening sentence for early readers of the story. And that research carries us straight from the text to the French Revolution just as with our reading of much English Romantic poetry. 'The natives were murdering the white men' refers to events in the French colony on the island of Hispaniola (now Haiti) and to the aftermath of a revolution which had begun in 1789. While undoubtedly stimulated by events in France, the horrors of slavery in the sugar plantations meant that the slaves hardly needed external prompting to revolt against their masters. Over the following ten years black people waged their struggle for freedom, but their war was deeply complicated by events and involvements from outside. The French at times offered models of revolution and freedom but at other times exercised only savage repression. The British offered themselves as a different kind of virtuous model by their official adoption of the anti-slavery cause; they were also at war with the French and had extensive sugar interests of their own. Meanwhile, the United States of America was keen to establish a sphere of influence in the Caribbean. The presence of these outside influences meant that the rebellion in French Hispaniola was of wide interest in Europe. The attention of radicals was also stimulated by the life and actions of the black revolutionary leader, Toussaint L'Ouverture. In referring to General Dessalines, Kleist's story not only calls up this history but silently evokes Toussaint, who had been Dessalines's superior in the struggle. The force of Toussaint's inspiration and vision can be gained from the final paragraph of an open letter he wrote to the French citizen government in 1797:

> Do [you] think that men who have been able to enjoy the blessing of liberty will calmly see it snatched away? They supported their chains only so long as they did not know any condition of life more happy than that of slavery. But today when they have left it, if they had a thousand livres they would sacrifice them all rather than be forced into slavery again.
>
> (Quoted in James, *Black Jacobins*, 1980, p.196)

Toussaint's reputation in Europe can be seen in a poem Wordsworth wrote in 1802. In that year came news that Toussaint had fallen foul of Napoleon (who threatened to reintroduce slavery) and had been captured and imprisoned in France.

> There's not a breathing of the common wind
> That will forget thee; thou hast great allies;
> Thy friends are exaltations, agonies,
> And love, and man's unconquerable mind.
>
> ('To Toussaint L'Ouverture', ll.11–14, Wu, *Romanticism*, 1994, p.275)

In his pioneering book, *Black Jacobins*, C.L.R. James writes of Toussaint:

> Despite Toussaint's despotism, his ruthlessness, his impenetrability, his unsleeping suspicion of all around him, his skill in large-scale diplomacy and petty intrigue, to the end of his life he remained a man of simple and kindly feelings, his humanity never drowned by the rivers of blood which flowed so plentifully and so long. His 'no reprisals' sprang from a genuine horror of useless bloodshed [...] He was incapable of meanness, pettiness or vindictiveness of any kind.
>
> (James, *Black Jacobins*, 1980, p.254)

Toussaint died in 1803 but his desire for an independent Haiti was achieved by Dessalines in 1804. This brings us to the events directly represented in 'The Betrothal on Santo Domingo', for soon after, as James writes in words as stark as those used by Kleist, 'early in the new year, 1805, the whites in Haiti were massacred by the order of Dessalines. All histories are full of this' (ibid., p.370). What James tells us that Kleist does not, however, is that the massacre ordered by Dessalines needs to be seen in the context of a similar policy pursued by the French, a policy that, particularly from 1802 to 1804, led to 'the massacre of as many blacks as possible. The drowning of over a thousand in Le Cap harbour at one stroke was no act of panic – it was deliberately done. This started the race war' (ibid., p.371).

What can we say about the way Kleist represents this history in 'The Betrothal on Santo Domingo'? We might begin, cautiously, by noting that there are dangers in comparing a story written early in the nineteenth century with a historical account written more than a century and a half later. It is likely that James had access to historical sources not available to Kleist, such as private diaries and administrative documents. That said, events in Haiti were regularly reported at the time. The press in France reported events in their colony, and insofar as Toussaint was associated with the revolutionaries in France his fame also spread. There is also evidence that Kleist had a particular interest in French affairs. He lived in Paris for a while and was a fervent admirer of Napoleon. Despite coming from a noble family with a strong German military tradition, in October 1803 Kleist tried to enlist in the army his hero was gathering to invade Britain. He was refused. Later his allegiances change. Once back in Germany he joined the nationalist cause. In 1807 in Berlin, then under French control, he was arrested by the Napoleonic government as a spy. He was held in the same prison in the Jura in which Toussaint had died four years before. All this suggests that Kleist was in as good a position as anyone to be informed about Toussaint's life and ideas and the situation in Hispaniola.

Let us now consider in more detail what we learn from Kleist's story about Haiti before independence and about relations between the races at that time. Look particularly at the opening of the story and at the character of Gustav von der Ried. **Does Kleist provide evidence of the slave basis of the French colony? Where does the character of Gustav von der Ried stand in relation to the French slave-owning class?**

There are clear signs of the slave basis of the French colony, first in the details of Hoango being freed but less explicitly in the fact that both Babekan and her daughter Toni are of mixed race – by implication the result of the sexual exploitation of black women by white men. General evidence of this sexual exploitation is further implied in the details of Toni's birth. Babekan has been on a trip to Paris 'with the wife of Monsieur Villeneuve' and has had a child by a Monsieur Bertrand. However, the emphasis on the surface of the story is on the wickedness of the black revolutionaries. No recognition is given to the systematic cruelties of slavery except in the passing reference to Babekan 'having been cruelly punished as a child' (p.72). Balancing this is the account of a slave woman infecting her former master with yellow fever (p.81) – a detail akin to those Kleist may have read of in contemporary accounts (Dyer, *The Stories of Kleist*, 1977, p.33).

Let us now look at the way Gustav von der Ried is introduced. Every step is taken to dissociate him from the French slave-owning class. He is not French but Swiss with a German name; Switzerland was the birth place of Rousseau, the novelist and advocate of individual rights and freedom. Like Rousseau's heroes Gustav has an open, trusting disposition. He is a reluctant participant in the army, not a career mercenary but a man travelling with no less than seven members of his family: 'my old uncle, his wife and five children' (p.75). The paragraph beginning 'He knew in the depth of his heart' ending with Gustav's assertion that 'the angels [...] would take the part of those who were in the wrong and act in their own way to preserve both human and divine order' (p.81) seems to embody all this. It presents a man who is essentially an individual, governed by his instincts rather than by nationalism. And it presents an image of life in which problems are solved not by political action but by some other-worldly power. ∎

The story of Gustav and Toni rapidly builds to a climax with the sentence 'We need not relate what then happened' (p.85). No doubt the prevailing demands of literary decorum lead to Kleist's self-censorship here, but the reader is in no doubt about what lies behind the moment. There is the erotic fascination that Toni's young body exerts for Gustav and the effect of her quiet assent to his claim that she is 'waiting for a white man on whom to bestow her favours' (p.83). To these Kleist adds Gustav's story of his relationship with Marianne Congreve. On reflection the reader sees that what is presented as an entirely spontaneous act of sex between Gustav and Toni is built on deceit and ambiguity. The erotic fascination Toni exerts begins as a trick. Gustav is attracted by her physical appearance, which is half-caste and sallow, even as we are reminded that he finds this kind of appearance 'repellent' (p.82). Even more striking is the way he almost unconsciously sees a resemblance between Toni and Marianne Congreve who had, in effect, died of love for him.

This complexity continues. The remainder of the story is dominated on the surface by the tension between an instinctive love and events driven by historical necessity, but both elements are qualified. Love may be deceit. Historical necessity may only be the working out of the ambitions of evil men like Hoango. The story also operates on more than one level. At one level we are drawn close to the experience and feelings of Gustav and Toni, on another level we can see the full picture and the implications of the actions of each of the characters in a way they cannot. The phrase 'Romantic irony' can be used to describe this complexity. In literature the word irony can have different shades of meaning. In Shakespeare's *Julius Caesar*, Antony declares 'Brutus is an honourable man' (Act 3, scene 2); the phrase is directly ironic since his audience understands he means exactly the opposite. In Chapter Six it is suggested that Keats may be using romance conventions in an ironic way. In this case one might say irony amounts to a sort of detachment, Keats plays with the conventions so that the result is different to what one might expect from a simple or sincere use of them. There are links between this kind of irony and Romantic irony but in this chapter I want to downplay these links. I want to keep 'Romantic irony' as a separate label to refer to something that was consciously developed in German philosophical and literary writing and spread to become one of the most common features of late Romantic works in Europe.

The most fundamental development of the idea is credited to Friedrich Schlegel (1772–1829) during the 1790s. The philosophical basis of Romantic irony lies in the attempt to hold together two quite opposed ideas which Anne Mellor describes as first the pessimistic 'denial of any absolute order in natural or human events', and second the optimistic sense of an 'overflowing and exhaustless vital energy' in the world (Mellor, *English Romantic Irony*, 1980, p.7). Schlegel's ideas were produced in response to the philosophy of Kant and we can connect them to the work of Kleist who, in March 1801, also experienced what critics have called a 'Kant crisis'. Before then:

> Kleist had worked out for himself a rigid and rigorous 'Lebensplan' [life plan], the goal of which was knowledge and happiness, to be achieved through the pursuit of virtue and the dedicated application of reason and will-power. Now a study of Kant revealed to him that absolute knowledge was unattainable by the conscious application of reason and that the knowledge obtained by such means was at best relative and transitory, conditioned by standpoint and subjectivity. At one stroke Kleist saw his ideals and ambitions in ruins and the purpose of his existence shattered [...] But paradoxically the ruin of his extravagant hopes in conscious rational endeavour confirmed the emergence of the poet in him. It [...] liberated his mind [...] and made possible the varied treatment of the problem of knowledge, truth and appearance that occurs with increased subtlety in all his works.
>
> (Dyer, *The Stories of Kleist*, 1977, pp.7–8)

If we now look at the following summary of what is involved we may see how Schlegel's idea of Romantic irony can be applied to 'The Betrothal on Santo Domingo'.

> For the early generation of pure romantics 'irony' could capture simultaneously a situation's opening toward the infinite and its limitations, the ideal and the real [...] Where the [irony] [...] that seems to prevail in much of seventeenth and eighteenth century writing tried to cut pretensions and yearnings down to size by occupying a safe

middle ground, romantic irony tended to spread out in all directions, to relativise [all the elements] [...] As understood by Schlegel and [...] Kleist, romantic irony was a statement on the complexity of the world.

(Nemoianu, *The Taming of Romanticism*, 1984, p.165)

How might these ideas be used to describe the characters of Gustav and of Toni? If this kind of irony does exist in the story, who is in a position to appreciate it at the point when Gustav and Toni fall into each other's arms?

Discussion

Gustav's situation seems to contain the simultaneous 'capture' of an 'opening toward the infinite and its limitation' (ibid.). In Toni he seems to have found not only a true love and erotic passion but implicitly to have brought about the impossible, namely to achieve a union with the dead Marianne Congreve. The 'limitations' of the situation are obvious in that first he is caught within Hoango and Babekan's snare and second Toni is not Marianne. Applying the idea to Toni is a little more difficult at this point but there is a suggestion that she has also discovered a love which transcends her everyday world just as she becomes more enmeshed in that reality. This is to see the characters as parallel. Perhaps they can also be seen as complementary with Gustav at this point most associated with 'vital energy' and Toni with 'the denial of any absolute order in [...] human events' (Mellor, *English Romantic Irony*, 1980, p.7).

At the mid point of the story neither Gustav nor Toni seems to be allowed full recognition of the irony of their respective situations. The reader is perhaps the only person fully aware of the situation and thus fully aware of the various ironies. ∎

When readers have a full sense of the meaning and implication of events it can have the effect of placing them at a point of detachment, like someone looking down from a hilltop on events below or a historian looking back on events in the past. Kleist is often regarded as adopting this position; some critics use the word 'Classical' to describe this detached stance. The beginning and the end of 'The Betrothal on Santo Domingo' do place the reader in such a position of detachment and early in the story this is achieved with the use of a historical perspective. In the last sentence a moment of contemplation which could be termed Classical is invited. There is reference to the monument Herr Strömli erects to the memory of Gustav and Toni and the story itself can be seen as another kind of monument to their love. The reader is encouraged to feel like a visitor to the memorial, silently contemplating past events. But surely we are also drawn closely into the development of the relationship between Toni and Gustav, for example in the eroticism of their union and the shock of their deaths. The use of both proximity to and distance from events seems to lead the reader to feel the truth of the Romantic ironic view of life. As we read we have simultaneously a sense of possibility, of things opening out, and a sense of awful limitations. We experience something of the feeling Kleist may have had when he contemplated simultaneously the possibilities offered by

Toussaint and the consequent savagery of all sides in the Haitian struggles. It is again worth going back to Schlegel: Mellor argues that for him 'irony can free the imagination to discover or create ever new relationships, to participate in the fertile chaos of life'. Schlegel himself wrote:

> man's most precious possession, his inner happiness, depends in the last analysis, as anybody can easily verify, on some [...] point of strength that must be left in the dark, but that nonetheless shores up and supports the whole burden and would crumble the moment one subjected it to rational analysis.
>
> (Quoted in Mellor, *English Romantic Irony*, 1980, p.10)

Do these words of Schlegel have a relevance to the ending of 'The Betrothal on Santo Domingo'?

D i s c u s s i o n

It seems to me that they go pretty far to describing Gustav's final situation. His 'inner happiness', surely, depends on his love for Toni; we see this developing in instinctive irrational terms so that it is very much a 'point of strength' that exists 'in the dark'. Towards the end Gustav tries to live the relationship in different and more rational terms. He thinks through Toni's action in tying him to the bed and can only understand it as treachery. The result is fatal to them both. With the collapse of his 'point of strength' the whole fabric of his life crumbles and death is the only result. The moment of freedom becomes ironically the moment of death. ■

Schlegel's words may have further resonance if we consider the way the reader is drawn into the emotion of the actual moments of Toni and Gustav's death. For readers wondering how to sustain an 'inner happiness' and make sense of the world, the story can become the 'point of strength'. But it remains a 'point of strength that must be left in the dark'; in the end it must be something that depends hardly at all on rational explanation. Kleist's story leads the reader to share in a moment when love, the supreme value beyond all others, only finally triumphs and achieves its full significance by coming together with death. We are drawn into a supremely complex moment, ironic because the opening out and the limitations completely coincide, but also transcendent because at that moment the limitations of life are entirely overcome. It is a moment that recurs in Romantic works of the period we are discussing and in later works influenced by similar ideas.

War, restoration and the middle class in Europe

Before moving on to discuss 'The Sandman' I want to emphasize the culture and political situation in Europe in the period from which Kleist and Hoffmann's stories emerged. The political and economic stresses and changes in Europe in the period following 1790 are a recurrent theme in this book and are again important here. The conquests of Napoleon and the expansion of the French Empire in continental Europe were a crucial element in the process of change, particularly after 1800. But their impact varied in different parts of Europe. In some areas – particularly in Mainz and close to France on the left bank of the Rhine – French radical ideas spread quickly and made a big impact. In other parts, the established rulers collaborated with Napoleon and radical ideas gained less hold. Similarly nationalism was felt in different ways across Europe. In some parts it flourished among those who welcomed Napoleon's sweeping away of old, often feudal, structures. Elsewhere it grew up later as part of the opposition to the dominance of France and imperial rule.

The swings in Kleist's own allegiances to which I referred earlier (see p.253 above) provide a graphic illustration of how revolutionary politics and war proved inescapable forces for many. It is hardly surprising that we find literary works marked by these forces. E.T.A. Hoffmann also travelled through Europe and was caught up in the turmoil. In 1806 he lost his job in the Prussian Civil Service, which was disbanded after Napoleon conquered the country. Hoffmann then abandoned his official career in favour of music. This took him to Bamberg in Bavaria, a state also under French control, where the French influence helped to bring about some changes and redistribution of power. He then went to Leipzig and Dresden in Saxony, again under French control, but where the French shored up the old structure (not least because the ruler of Saxony was prepared to contribute large numbers of men to the French imperial army).

After the defeat of Napoleon and the signing of the peace treaty at the Congress of Vienna in 1815 there was what can be described as a restoration. This saw the return of overthrown monarchies and methods of government that the Napoleonic empire had brushed aside. Paradoxically, however, in Germany restoration consolidated change, so that what had in 1790 been 314 independent territories became just 34 individual states. Moreover, in Germany as elsewhere, the Napoleonic upheavals were only a contributing factor to social and economic changes which had begun in earnest in the eighteenth century. These changes were characterized by a growth in the power of the middle class, by industrialization, and by a shift of the population from farming and the countryside to factory work and the city. As the Revolution in France progressed radicalism became increasingly the property of the middle class, which also prospered beneath imperial trappings of the Napoleonic period. In exporting radicalism France also exported the dominance of the middle class. Equally the nationalism which followed the sweeping away of old structures was often dominated by the middle class.

Although the Kleist text speaks directly about the situation of the revolution in Haiti it can also stand as a parable of revolution and ideals in Europe. The figures descended from the ideals of revolution like Hoango (and Napoleon) are viewed with intense suspicion while those like Gustav, who can be seen as embodying individualism – predominantly a middle-class quality – are treated with considerable sympathy. Gustav's tragic fate in the story is perhaps a sign of how difficult it was to feel confidence in middle-class and individual values. Kleist's own suicide in 1811 can be seen as reinforcing this point although the exact reasons behind the act are obscure. Perhaps Kleist was driven by the failure of his own dreams for himself, both personal and political (see Dyer, *The Stories of Kleist*, 1977, for a useful account of Kleist's life).

Connections between historical events and personal life can also be made in the case of Hoffmann in the years before 'The Sandman' was first published in 1816–17. In 1813, for example, he was in Dresden and then Leipzig, both of which had seen major battles in the previous year – at Dresden Napoleon had been victorious but the Battle of Nations at Leipzig is generally accepted as a milestone in the process of his eventual defeat. In this period of his life, indeed, Hoffmann has been described as 'dodging Napoleon's retreating armies and the Russian armies passing them' (passage quoted in Barron, 'Prison or pleasure dome', 1987, p.55). Can we add to this kind of detailed biographical evidence? The author of the discussion of Hoffmann in a recent history of German literature has no doubt that this is possible:

> Hopes that the premises of freedom and equality would be transformed into political reality had been doubly dashed [...] by the path from the French Revolution back to monarchy [...] and by the increasingly glaring social contradictions ensuing from socio-economic development towards middle-class capitalism. The prevailing reaction to this tide of restoration and increasing social contradictions was one of alienation. The mood of awakening of the Early Romantic period now gave way to a sombre, sarcastic and fragmented view of current conditions. A classic example of this new phase in the Romantic movement is the work of E T A Hoffmann.
>
> (Beutin, *A History of German Literature*, 1993, pp.240–1)

Elsewhere, writing of Hoffmann's novel *Kater Murr* (*Tom-Cat Murr;* 1820–2) the same author writes that it 'brings to light the failure of the Romantic creative artist in the face of the conflict between ideals and real life' (ibid., p.213). The key ideas I want to pick up from Beutin here are 'alienation' and the idea of the artist leading a double life in 'the face of the conflict between ideals and real life', and in the next section we shall consider if and how these ideas can be applied to the specific case of 'The Sandman'. (All references to 'The Sandman' are to Cohen, *Tales from Hoffmann*, 1951.)

The Sandman

Please read or reread the story now. As you read, particularly the opening pair of letters, ask yourself if either: (1) 'alienation'; or (2) a double life; or (3) a 'conflict between ideals and real life' are relevant terms.

D i s c u s s i o n

1   'Alienation' does seem to be a relevant term for this story. The opening sentences show Nathaniel saying in effect, 'I am sorry I have not written but I have been feeling alienated from you and from everyday life through no fault of yours'. Clara's response is to urge him to 'recognise this strange enemy' and get back to normal. By implication she urges him not to follow the example of his father, who like many 'experimentalists' was 'alienated from his family'. A second point that you might have picked up is that in the story told by Nathaniel in his letter he is shown as alienated from his father's work. First he is shut

out by his father, then as he watches from a hiding place what he sees is entirely alien to him.

2   The idea of a double life also seems relevant. The most obvious example of someone living in this way, perhaps, is Nathaniel's father. With his family he is the perfect image of a loving father while with Coppelius 'his mild features' become 'a repulsive, diabolical countenance' (p.115). In a slightly different sense the opening of the story hangs on whether the barometer seller – Guiseppi Coppola – has a double life as Coppelius.

3   The idea of a 'conflict between ideals and real life' is perhaps more difficult to work with. Nathaniel perceives a gap opening between a life with the 'fair, angelic' Clara and the 'cruel threatening fate' (p.109) that hangs over him. Equally there is a conflict between the ideal home life described in the third paragraph beginning 'Excepting at dinner-time' (p.110) and his father's work. But to square these with the idea of a 'conflict between ideals and real life' we have to define 'real life' in strange terms, and see the images of Clara and family bliss as ideals rather than real life. ∎

Alienation is an important term in another sense. Hoffmann has Nathaniel describe his father's work as if it was a kind of sorcery but, as in the case of Mary Shelley's novel *Frankenstein* (1818), what he describes is a kind of scientific experiment – an early form of research into the possibility of creating a robot device which will replicate human actions. The way Hoffmann presents this work, however, prevents us seeing that science in the form of these experiments can be a progressive force acting in harmony with humankind. Instead it is dark and mysterious, something entirely alien. The reader, like Nathaniel, is effectively alienated from invention and innovation, which are equated with death and the breaking of taboos. In a similar way, one might argue that in the figure of Coppelius Hoffmann presents an entirely alienated image of the lawyer – a central figure in the modern world because of his work in drawing up contracts and safeguarding inheritance. It would be difficult to imagine a more threatening or malevolent image of the law than Coppelius presents. The detail of his spoiling the children's food, for example, suggests directly that the law does not safeguard but contaminates what it touches. Looking forward, it is significant that the lawyer who should safeguard inheritances is instrumental in introducing the automaton, an alien and sterile creature.

Before leaving these two letters it is worth dwelling for a moment on the sentence towards the end of Clara's letter – 'Lothaire's last words I do not quite comprehend' (p.120). The effect of this sentence is perhaps two-fold. First and most immediately it creates Clara's character as that of a woman prepared to be guided by her brother, willing to accept whatever he tells her. But secondly it may prompt readers to turn back to the words in question and ask if they understand them. The words 'we ourselves kindle the spirit, which we in our strange delusion believe to be speaking to us. It is the phantom of our own selves' (p.120) are thus thrown into relief and we carry them forward into the tale. They then lend an additional resonance to Nathaniel's words in his next letter: 'I cannot get rid of the impression which the accursed face of Coppelius makes upon me' (pp.121–2). If we follow Lothaire's words we must understand Coppelius as some kind of phantom projected from Nathaniel's own self.

So far in this discussion I have not referred to the story of the Sandman itself. To our minds the grotesque threat offered by the Sandman tale at a child's bedtime seems self-defeating, and at best likely to produce nightmares. But early nineteenth-century culture was less subject to scruples about cruelty. It is a common feature of the stories collected by the Brothers Grimm and published in 1812, though this quality has been much softened in translations and revisions. That Hoffmann makes a tale told to children central to the beginning of his story may seem incidental or part of its horror but it can also be used to make a connection between the story and the culture from which it emerges. The Grimm brothers' stories were only partly intended for children. Their larger role was to play a part in the reconstruction of German culture, bringing back to life a much older culture which lay behind the modern world. This was obviously part of a nationalist agenda and, because Germany was politically so fragmented, culture was a particularly important part of that agenda. In the face of a plethora of different contemporary examples of Germanness, the Grimms offered an image of an ancient unified culture. They also offered an image of the way that culture could be transmitted from one generation to the next in the scenes of story telling around the family hearth. The same desire to evoke a German nation that transcended modern fragmentation can be found in Johann Gottlieb Fichte's *Addresses to the German Nation* (1807–8). Fichte evoked the idea of 'spirituality' which in this context might be quite close to the idea of another world created in the Grimms' stories. He wrote:

> whoever believes in spirituality and in the freedom of this spirituality,
> and who wills the eternal development of this spirituality by freedom,
> wherever he may have been born and whatever language he speaks, is
> of our blood; he is one of us, and will come over to our side.
>
> (Quoted in Gildea, *Barricades and Borders*, 1987, p.55)

'The Sandman' can be seen as at the same time joining in this kind of message and parodying it by turning this 'spirituality' into something irrational, fascinating and deeply disturbing. Nathaniel is made to express the desire that also grips the reader: 'if I, I myself, could penetrate the mystery and behold the wondrous Sandman – that was a wish which grew upon me with the years' (p.111). The mysterious conversion of the Sandman into Coppelius only continues and deepens the fascination. The power of these moments in the story, indeed, led one reader, Sigmund Freud, to feel that the 'main theme' of the story was not Nathaniel's pursuit of Olympia but:

> on the contrary, something different, something which gives it its
> name, and which is always re-introduced at critical moments: it is the
> theme of the 'Sandman' who tears out children's eyes.
>
> (Freud, *An Infantile Neurosis and Other Works*, 1955 edn, p.227)

Freud made 'The Sandman' the centre of an essay 'The "uncanny"' which he wrote in 1919. Hoffmann, he writes, is the 'writer who has succeeded in producing uncanny effects better than anyone else' (ibid.).

You will find an extract from Freud's essay in Part Two of this book on page 318. Please begin reading it now and stop at the end of the paragraph which begins 'We know from psycho-analytic experience' (p.320). Freud's discussion of the story up to this paragraph is reasonably straightforward. His summary shows him taking a genuine pleasure in the story. After the summary there are three paragraphs of commentary. **What is Freud's main point in each of these paragraphs?**

Discussion

In the first paragraph beginning 'This short summary' his main point is that it is plain from the devices used that Hoffmann's purpose is not to make us detached observers; rather he 'intends to make us [...] look through the demon optician's spectacles' as perhaps 'the author in his very own person once peered through such an instrument' (Part Two, p.320).

In the next paragraph he elaborates this point. We should not take what I called earlier a Classical stance, 'we are not supposed to be looking [at] a madman's imagination, behind which we, with the superiority of our rational minds, are able to detect the sober truth'. What is most important is 'the impression of uncanniness'.

Then in the third of these paragraphs Freud goes on to discuss the details of the sprinkling of sand in the eyes and the tearing out of the eyes in terms drawn from his 'psycho-analytic experience' – 'a study of dreams, phantasies and myths has taught us that anxiety about one's eyes, the fear of going blind, is often enough a substitute for the dread of being castrated' (ibid.). To focus for a moment on the story Nathaniel tells of his childhood, Freud is suggesting that it is perfectly normal for Nathaniel to be so affected by the story of the Sandman. It is a sign that he is experiencing the kind of anxiety about his developing masculinity that Freud thinks all boys feel. That Nathaniel remembers this incident so vigorously when he is older suggests to Freud that he still carries the same anxiety with him. In retrospect we can also understand from the opening of his first letter and the beginning of the story the direction this anxiety has taken. We learn he has isolated himself from his family, his friends and particularly from Clara. But what weighs most on Nathaniel's mind is that while 'the dear form of my lovely Clara passes before me in my dreams [...] A horrible thing has crossed my path' (p.109). Lothaire's words that I focused on earlier, which make these strange presences 'the phantom of our own selves' (p.120) may strike you as relevant here. ■

Please continue reading to the end of the extract now. The paragraph after those we have just considered, beginning 'Moreover, I would not recommend' (Part Two, p.321) and its associated footnote are at once the most concise expression of Freud's view of the story and the most difficult. What he is aiming to do is to retell the story of Nathaniel as if it were one of his medical cases, and the language changes accordingly. He also allows himself to imagine he is speaking to colleagues who are familiar with his ideas. That said, I think it is worth spending some time puzzling through the footnote. To my mind it makes the following key points:

1   All the older figures in the story are representations of a father-figure and the threat which provokes Nathaniel's anxiety stems from these

father-figures. Only his 'real' father is even partly good and the fact that the explosion that causes his real father's death leaves 'his face burned, blackened and hideously distorted' (p.116) perhaps shows him suffering the same fate as Nathaniel himself.

2   There is a strong parallel between the relationship of Nathaniel's father and Coppelius with Nathaniel on the one hand, and that of Coppola-Spalanzani and Olympia on the other. This makes Olympia into a kind of double for Nathaniel. Seeing this relationship makes Freud able to make sense of the detail – which he accurately describes as 'frightening' – of Coppelius screwing off the hands and feet of the child Nathaniel (p.232) and of Olympia's ideal femaleness being that of an automaton. The first detail is another image of the anxiety and fear of castration and the threat here comes from a kind of father-figure; the second is an image of the complete subservience to the father-figure which loss of masculinity and manhood would entail.

3   Nathaniel's abandonment of his love for Clara and his pursuit of Olympia is to be understood as an abandonment of 'the real, external object of his love' consequent on an inability to pass from his childish relationship with his father to a successful adult relationship with him.

4   The events of the story reflect back onto Hoffmann himself and represent the fact that 'the writer's relationship with his father was always a sensitive subject with him'.

I hope you will find Freud's reading of 'The Sandman' interesting even if you do not want to follow it entirely yourself. The last sentence of the footnote (Part Two, p.325) indicates that Freud wants to relate the text to Hoffmann's own life. The link here is between story and author; Freud scrutinizes Hoffmann as he might one of his patients. I would like to suggest, however, that there are ways in which we *can* think of Freud's reading of 'The Sandman' within the 'reading in history' method used in this chapter and in the book as a whole. Following this track in a simple sense we might perhaps ask why Freud took up this apparently fantastic story. The tearing out of eyes, screwing off of legs, and its general violence is a rendition of the horrors of battle that were all too familiar to the German people around 1815. And it may have held just the same meaning and fascination for Freud and other readers around 1919 after another period of war and carnage. But if we see Freud's choice of the story as rooted in history, how do we understand his psychoanalytic interpretation of it. Freud's reading, it might be argued, makes the story meaningful because through it we can understand how the 'uncanny' can bring out something strange and hidden in individuals and relationships. What is hidden is a representation of the father–son relationship and, more particularly, the plight of a young adolescent boy struggling towards manhood. To a Freudian reader it is just those parts of the story which resist rational explanation which provide a direct conduit to its truth and to feelings that lie hidden in our everyday lives. (Perhaps my use of that rather general 'our' here will make you pause for thought. Surely here, if anywhere, is a story that needs to be considered with a gendered perspective, a story of fathers and sons which a man will read differently from a woman.)

These two ways of thinking about the story may seem mutually incompatible. To the psychoanalytically oriented the idea that it is simply a war-time story fails to take deeper meanings into account, while to the reader sceptical of the Freudian scheme, Freud reads far too much into the story. **Is it possible to find a reading which acknowledges both approaches?**

Discussion

For many who follow Freud the scheme which is revealed in the story is a universal one; the story is important precisely because it reveals a structure which operates within the family regardless of historical period. But others prefer to see Freud's work as much more tied to his own historical period. From this point of view Freud's interest in 'The Sandman' can be explained as in part due to the fact that Hoffmann was writing in a period which was beginning to witness historical trends (the rise of nationalism, a Germanic culture and a modern German state) which had a parallel in Freud's life-time. Perhaps also Hoffmann's middle-class point of view was not dissimilar to Freud's own. Within our 'reading in history' approach we can see the 'uncanny' in the story as revealing a central element in developing middle-class culture. That is tension between father and son within the enclosed world of the middle-class family. Hoffmann sees the father as a dominating presence, linked with threats to the son, even when the son, in this case Nathaniel, idealizes his father. It is Nathaniel's father, remember, who treats Coppelius 'as though he were a superior being' (p.114) and Coppelius who embodies Nathaniel's worst fears. The story insists on the threat to the child which comes from this dominating presence and the almost insuperable problem the son has in achieving adulthood and father-hood for himself. ∎

I have been stressing the need to see 'The Sandman' within the context of German culture, but insofar as the rise of the middle class was a phenom-enon which can be recognized across Europe, it is not surprising that one can cite analogous representations of the father–son relationship in other cultures. One example which comes to mind, not least because it might also be said to have 'uncanny' elements, is the relationship between Mag-witch and Pip in Charles Dickens's *Great Expectations*. In Magwitch we have a father who is benevolent, providing his son with money, but also monstrous. Early in Dickens's novel Magwitch threatens to 'have your heart and liver out' (1994 edn, p.4) and evokes a second and more threatening young man hiding within. The analogy with Coppelius screwing off Nathaniel's hands and the simultaneous presence of Nathaniel's father and Coppelius is striking. And just as 'The Sandman' describes the failure of Nathaniel to begin the process to becoming a father-figure himself, so at the end of *Great Expectations* Pip is left pretty much alone, especially in the earlier discarded ending which shows him cut off from a relationship with Estella and Biddy.

In following Freud's analysis we have rather put to one side the story of Nathaniel and Olympia which is central to the later part of the story. In this final part of my discussion of 'The Sandman' I want to suggest that this can lead us to much the same kind of reading of the story as we have been exploring, confirming the value and significance of reading this story in its history. To focus this discussion please look at the paragraph beginning

'Nathaniel had totally forgotten' (p.138). **What does the first part – up to 'free choice in the matter' – tell us about the relationship of Nathaniel and Olympia?**

Discussion

Olympia is perfect in Nathaniel's view; she completely absorbs his attention, pushing aside family and friends. But the relationship is based not on good sense or equal companionship but on one-sided feelings symbolized by the 'extravagant sonnets, stanzas and canzoni' Nathaniel reads to Olympia 'for hours on end'. Nathaniel views the relationship as a 'wonderful harmony' but the reader sees that it consists of blind enthusiasm on his part and an absolute and almost unresponsive stillness on hers. Olympia's stillness makes it particularly ironic when Spalanzani gives 'his daughter a free choice' in deciding whether to marry Nathaniel, for there is no evidence she can act for herself at all. ■

Every detail of the description of Olympia in this paragraph seems designed to create a sense of strangeness to match that already accumulated around Coppola and Spalanzani. But not far beneath the surface there is a commentary on the love between an individual man and an individual woman that supposedly underpinned middle-class marriages, and, through those marriages, the whole fabric of work and society. Nathaniel and Olympia represent a parody of these values. Nathaniel's love blinds him to everything except his adored Olympia. Olympia has no personality; her only role is to provide the apparently loving gaze that Nathaniel needs to prove his own value to himself. But Nathaniel's sense of self-worth is not that of an adult involved in meaningful activity, rather he is like a child playing with a toy, and before we understand Olympia to be an automaton we understand that she is exactly like a doll. Again a comparison with Dickens is appropriate, for the situation is similar to that he portrays in *David Copperfield* between David and his doll-wife Dora. Dickens allows us to feel the lack of fulfilment David comes gradually to feel as well as the impracticality of the relationship. Hoffmann's ending is altogether more violent and far more catastrophic for the hero. The subject of Hoffmann's story was one which continued to be significant across Europe generally throughout the nineteenth century. We can compare Nathaniel and Olympia with Torvald Helmer and his wife Nora in Ibsen's play *A Doll's House,* first produced in Norway in 1879. Here the audience sees the story from the woman's point of view and the woman is allowed to present an analysis of the situation. She explains to her husband:

> When I was at home with Papa he told me his opinion about everything, and so I had the same opinions; and if I differed from him I concealed the fact, because he would not have liked it. He called me his doll child, and he played with me just as I used to play with my dolls. And when I came to live with you [...] I was simply transferred from Papa's hands to yours. You arranged everything according to your own taste [...] When I look back on it it seems to me as if I have [...] existed merely to perform tricks for you.
>
> (Ibsen, *A Doll's House*, 1992 edn, p.66)

It is very much a case of the 'doll' answering back – in contrast with the image Hoffmann presents of Olympia, who is eventually literally torn apart by the two men who both claim to own her (see p.140).

It is also interesting that Ibsen allows Nora to suggest that her husband can only be different 'if your doll is taken away from you' (1992 edn, p.70). This is what happens at the end of the play, but describing Torvald's future life lies beyond the scope of Ibsen's text. In 'The Sandman' Hoffmann, in contrast, allows us to see what happens when Nathaniel's doll is taken from him (and in fact broken). At first normality seems to return – 'Nathaniel awakened [and] every trace of [...] madness had vanished' (pp.142–3). But this respite is temporary. He still carries Coppola-Coppelius's telescope, which he is described as reaching for 'mechanically' (p.143) and is trapped within that way of seeing. Deprived of his doll and part mechanical himself, his impulse is to try to turn Clara into a new kind of doll, thus drawing on the 'fathers' generation' model represented in the story by his own father and Spalanzani and the demon Coppola/Coppelius. Just as Olympia was shown, as it were, hanging upon Nathaniel's every word, Nathaniel makes Clara hang literally from his grip, entirely dependent on him.

Again we have a story that pivots on a moment of love which is inextricably linked with death. Nathaniel's relationship with Clara will not cohere. At one moment they are an image of domesticated bliss – 'The two lovers stood arm-in-arm on the highest gallery of the tower, and looked down upon the misty forests, behind which the blue mountains rose like a gigantic city' (p.143). At the next Nathaniel 'shrieked out in a piercing tone, "Spin round, wooden doll! – spin round!"' (p.144). At the risk of over-simplifying the story we might see these extreme moments as images of the fragmentation that Hoffmann, like Kleist, saw around him in Europe: a fragmentation made up of competing elements – revolutionary, reactionary, political, social, supernatural and uncanny, domestic – all with a potential to provide *the truth*. So we are not looking at things falling apart, but at forces with the potential to unify all competing against and destroying each other. The unity that love might create between Nathaniel and Clara as man and wife is blown apart by the force of different relationships. Nathaniel is united with Coppelius – they are a kind of uncanny father and son; Clara is united with Lothaire, sister and brother together again.

Conclusion

I suggested that in 'The Betrothal on Santo Domingo' Kleist sets out the death-in-love and love-in-death moment of Gustav and Toni as a moment of 'inner happiness' and a 'point of strength': a memorial to inspire those who remain. Hoffmann's story can be seen as offering similar possibilities. The final paragraph offers something akin to the memorial put up by Herr Strömli at the end of Kleist's story. But these moments are highly ambiguous. On the one hand I want to accept that these last moments, typical of many in Romantic works, provide meaning and a sense of unity after all that has happened. But I also see the woodcut-like image of Clara's 'quiet domestic happiness [...] in a remote spot' (pp.144–5) as perhaps hardly more effective than Herr Strömli's memorial stone.

Both 'The Betrothal on Santo Domingo' and 'The Sandman' excite through the force with which they assert Romantic dreams of unity – between Gustav and Toni, Nathaniel and Clara, Nathaniel and Olympia. But both also excite through the power of the images which conjure up the ironic vision of the contemporary world – a vision which leaves Toni dead; Clara bereft of Nathaniel; Olympia, eyes torn out, dragged away by Coppelius; and both Gustav and Nathaniel literally smashed to pieces.

Further reading

Dyer, D. (1977) *The Stories of Kleist: A Critical Study*, Duckworth.

Mellor, A. (1980) *English Romantic Irony*, Harvard University Press.

Nemoianu, V. (1984) *The Taming of Romanticism: European Literature and the Age of Biedermeier*, Harvard University Press.

Conclusion

Stephen Bygrave

To conclude our study of Romantic writings let's look again at two issues that have recurred in our discussions:

1 defining Romanticism;
2 reading in history.

This will be a chance to pull strands together and to identify some questions which remain open in discussion of Romantic writings.

Defining Romanticism

Is it possible to identify tendencies (the word you will remember I used at the beginning of the book, p.6 above) which are common to Romantic texts? I hope that at the least you will now understand that this question might be answered in two ways: on the one hand 'Romantic' might describe a particular *kind* of writing, on the other it might describe some of the writing from a particular *period*. You will have found both of these descriptions in this book and each has its implications. To focus our discussion, I want to look again at René Wellek's discussion of the 'concept of Romanticism' which was referred to in the Introduction. (A longer extract from Wellek is included in Part Two, pp.326–35.) Wellek's writing is difficult because of the range of terms and names which he uses, but he keeps coming back to a series of phrases which occur in a key sentence in the first paragraph (quoted in the Introduction, pp.vii–viii above).

The phrases are 'imagination for the view of poetry, nature for the view of the world, and symbol and myth for poetic style' (p.326). (By 'symbol and myth' Wellek means by and large what has been described in this book as allegory.) They are criteria – which Wellek links to the history of Western philosophy – for defining a work as Romantic, so that theoretically if we encounter a new work we can identify whether or not it is Romantic by measuring it against these criteria. However, this is neither what Wellek does, nor what he claims to do, in the extract; rather he looks in turn at the poets and identifies these qualities in their work. You might wonder which is the chicken and which the egg here – is he checking the writers against a definition, or is he assuming that these are Romantic writers and deducing the criteria from their work? Something of this process can be seen in the references to Wordsworth on pages 327 and 332. In the first reference the fit between the poet and the idea of imagination is very close, but in the second Wellek seems to say both that Wordsworth *is* a 'romantic poet' *and* that he hardly matches one of the three criteria because he is 'farthest removed from symbolism and mythology'.

Wellek's analysis is useful because the elements he identifies – imagination, nature, symbolism and myth – are commonly identified as key elements in Romantic writing. **Do the kinds of approaches taken in this book suggest some 'limitations' in Wellek's way of thinking?**

Discussion

I think there are three main limitations.

1   The first concerns the question of coherence. As we have seen, when you look at Romantic writing (even if we restrict ourselves to texts by the six poets he considers), the claim that their conceptions of imagination, nature and symbol and myth are 'the same' needs at the least to be seriously qualified. Wellek does qualify his case – at different points Blake (p.328) and Byron (p.331) are both allowed to stand somewhat apart – but he does not go as far as questioning the selection of his six poets as *the* Romantic group.

2   This leads us to the second limitation, which is suggested by Amanda Gilroy in her conclusion to Chapter Eight. Wellek's definition of the tendencies of Romantic poetry leads him to exclude any writers beyond those in the orthodox canon from whom he has derived his definition. Hence the systematic omission of women writers from the canon.

3   In general, Wellek does not see Romantic writing as a kind of dialogue with the historical circumstances in which it is produced (although he does argue that Blake, for example, tries to give 'a vision of politics and morals' (p.331)). Indeed, towards the end he seems explicitly to dispute the value of such an approach, writing that an emphasis on the politics of Romantic writing will be an overemphasis: 'On the whole, political criteria seem grossly overrated for judging a man's basic view of the world and artistic allegiance' (p.334). But having noticed this stress in his work you might also have realized that Wellek does see the writers he discusses in a kind of history – at one point he refers to the 'ancestry' of Romantic ideas. The point is, however, that this is to place writers not within the political and social history of their time, but within a history of abstract thought (what in academic terms is known as the History of Ideas). ■

Let's pursue these points a little further. The first concerns coherence. Wellek centres his opening discussion on Wordsworth's notion of the imagination and says emphatically that Byron 'does *not* share' this conception (p.331). Wellek's position here is quite orthodox. Most studies of Romantic writing have taken Wordsworth to represent the mainstream and Byron a tributary. We suggested how Byron and Wordsworth might be contrasted in Chapter Seven. The two certainly detested each other, but could it be argued that the ideal of the poet and of poetry advanced by the younger Wordsworth is more truly fulfilled by Byron than by Wordsworth himself? It is surely *Don Juan* rather than *The Prelude* which could be described as 'a natural delineation of human passions, human characters, and human incidents' and as having been written in the 'language of conversation' ('Advertisement to *Lyrical Ballads*, 1798'; Wu, *Romanticism*, 1994, p.166); it is surely Byron rather than Wordsworth who seems to be a member of a recognizable social community.

Let's turn now to the second limitation we have identified, the issue of the canon and its inevitable exclusions. This issue was raised in the Introduction, but we can now see more clearly what is involved. To suggest that Byron, or Blake, rather than Wordsworth should be the central figure in British Romantic writing would only be to rearrange the conventional canon. As we have seen, the canon tends to exclude some male writers (such as John Clare) and may exclude women writers completely. Although in this book we have devoted most space to texts from that conventional canon we have tried to be less exclusive. I hope that in this way we have suggested the limitations of a tight definition of Romanticism.

As we have seen, for example in Chapters Eight and Ten, the conventional canon depends on certain assumptions about gender and race. Celebrating the ideals of Romantic texts without questioning these assumptions may be to say that art which has value is beyond politics and history. The case I made in Chapter One is that this is never true for texts, and that it isn't true for us as readers either. I suggested there that we always read with particular purposes in mind.

This leads us into the final point, that the 'political' or 'historical' kind of approach adopted through the book contrasts with Wellek's abstract and ideal approach. For example, in writing about the Romantic writers' interest in nature, their turning from the neo-Classicism of the eighteenth century, and their use of symbol and myth, Wellek draws attention to a visionary or prophetic strain present in one way or another in Romantic writing. For example, he quotes with approval the view that Keats possesses the capacity to build 'afresh', to body 'forth anew a reconstructed universe' (p.328); later he sees Shelley as striving toward but never achieving absorption 'into some nirvana' (p.333). Other critics thinking in this vein have gone on to see Romantic writings taking on some of the functions of religion: attributes that had been ascribed to God were now ascribed to 'Nature'. I would like to suggest that we can recast this idealist emphasis if we think back to the seventeenth-century poet John Milton, whose example was of such importance to many Romantic writers (see Chapters Two, Five and Nine for discussion of Milton and the Romantic writers). Milton's epics may appear to be religious, but it can be helpful to think of them as using religious terms to mount a political argument. Perhaps we should learn to read the idealistic and visionary language we find in Romantic poetry in a similar way, as political discourse.

This depends on the questions we ask about texts and on the sorts of context in which we put them. In Chapter Ten, for example, Nigel Leask was concerned with Romantic Orientalism (and even perhaps saw Romanticism *as* Orientalism). This interest in the uses Western writing has made of 'the Orient' has followed a recent reassessment by scholars of the legacy of European colonialism in the Romantic period, and its impact on the culture of Britain as much as on that of overseas countries. Similarly, an interest in the women writers of this period really began only after feminism had made a political impact in the 1970s. Much of the work of women writers could until recently only be read in a research library; it is the influence of feminism that has led to many of these works being republished and becoming available to a wider audience. In both these instances literary texts are seen as part of a political world rather than separate from it. All this is to say that there is an argument not only about what the canon of Romantic writings should be, but also about how they should be read. In other words, the questions which seem important for us to put even to familiar texts are influenced by the history we inhabit. We *read* in history just as texts are *written* in history.

The Wellek extract shows how the question of which writers are chosen interacts with questions about what constitute the Romantic tendencies. This book has stressed the importance of the historical context in which texts were written, and this is no less important in thinking about how those texts may be described in the present. I want to call this a question of 'ideology'; it is the subject of the next section.

Romantic writings and ideology

We can see what ideology means in relation to Romantic writing by returning to our discussion of 'The Chimney Sweeper' from Blake's *Songs of Innocence* in Chapter One (pp.30–33 above). The speaker of that poem talks himself (and attempts to talk a fellow sweep) into accepting conditions that ought to be unacceptable. That poem, you will remember, contained a vision of the resurrection. The speaker argued that their conditions must be accepted because only temporary – temporary in this context meaning lifelong. Though no-one in authority was there to force the speaker to mount such an argument, it was clearly in the interest of those with power and wealth that those like the sweeps should accept their lot. The poem therefore exemplifies the concept of ideology in three ways: (1) that a set of beliefs such as religion (the idea of resurrection) can be seen as an ideology; (2) that such a set of beliefs may not serve the best interests of the believer (the sweeps); (3) that a writer such as Blake, in try-ing to make sense of his experience of the world may produce work which has its own ideological interests. Let's explore such issues further.

Interestingly, the word ideology is itself a product of the Romantic period: it seems to have been first used in Napoleonic France – Napoleon's 'ideologues' were responsible for what we would now call propaganda, or perhaps public relations. (The history of this word and concept is concisely described in Raymond Williams's book *Keywords*, 1976.) To draw a discussion of Romanticism and ideology together we might begin by taking a cue from this early use of the term by asking just how Romantic writings could be seen as working like 'propaganda' or 'public relations'. Such a question in fact presupposes another, for propaganda is always designed to work in someone's interest, and to someone's benefit. **How might the Romantic writings you have studied in this book be said to be in someone's interest?**

D i s c u s s i o n

The simplest way of responding would be to go back to earlier comments about the political connotations of some of the poems we have looked at – we might say that at various times the poetry of Blake, Wordsworth, Shelley, Byron and so on was in the radicals' interest. Shelley's 'England in 1819' (see p.7 above) is an obvious example, although it was written when the poet was living far away from England and not published until twenty years later. If we ask who might have read Blake's or Shelley's poems, we can perhaps open the question further. Blake's lavishly illustrated books were too expensive for most people to buy. Shelley's later radical poems were not published in his lifetime because booksellers feared government persecution and imprisonment. So, when we ask 'In whose "interest" is a poem working?', we need to know more about its context. In Chapter One I suggested a set of questions in relation to context (Who wrote a text? When was it written? Who was it written for? How did they read it?, and so on). The answer to some of these questions may involve individuals but more often than not we will be talking about *class* interests. But we will also need to remember that some interests may cut across classes, for example race and gender. As Susan Matthews argues in Chapter Four, it may have been in the interest of male Romantic writers to differentiate their writings from those of the popular female writers of the day and mark them as 'masculine', and by doing so to preserve their male authority. When we understand in whose interest something works, we can also often know whose interest it is against – another vital element in ideology. ■

Put simply, it is in each person's 'interest' to have a view of the world which enables them to 'make sense' of the situation and circumstances in which they find themselves. This notion of ideology is particularly associated with the thinking of the French philosopher Louis Althusser (1918–90). This ideological process of 'making sense' of our worlds is especially relevant to cultural works; to paraphrase Althusser, it is how we imagine our relation to our real conditions of existence. (For a fuller exposition, see Althusser, 'Ideology and ideological state apparatuses'.) My use of the word 'imagine' here recalls the importance attributed to that term in Wellek's account of the Romantic movement. There imagination tended to signify something visionary; here it is something different.

Many of the passages we looked at in Chapter Five celebrate the power of the 'Imagination' to heal and restore, to supply the faith which had earlier been lost after the disappointments of the French Revolution. The close of 'Composed by the Side of Grasmere Lake' is a good example of the imaginary making sense of real conditions. (This poem, and the ending in particular, is discussed in Chapter Two, pp.49–55 above.) The poem imagines a mysterious voice able to bring 'tranquillity' to 'earth's groaning field'. Imagining a 'Great Pan' who can resolve a problem is one way of being able to make sense of a difficult world. But such a resolution can sometimes just be temporary; it is more in our interest, perhaps, to make sense of two competing aspects of life if we can bind them together. This is done not by the Great Pan but by the poetry as it holds together 'Ravage' and 'tranquillity' in the last line.

To some, religion is part of an ideological process because it enables us to make sense of our situation in the world. Christianity, for example, might make sense of suffering by seeing it ultimately as part of God's purpose. This idea can be quite directly transferred to discussion of Romantic writing and ideology. In Chapter Ten, for example, Nigel Leask discusses Coleridge's 'Of the fragment of *Kubla Khan*'. Coleridge describes how his poem appeared spontaneously through an act of inspiration. In other words, he claims for it an authority from beyond everyday life; such a claim is akin to the supernatural appeal made by religion.

All these are instances of what we might call ideological effects in texts we have looked at. However, we might want to ask whether we can identify a broader ideology or set of interests at work. Can we say that there are tendencies and preoccupations present in these texts which have a unified ideological effect; that, in other words, Romanticism amounts to an ideology?

One way of beginning to answer this question might be to register that when Romantic writers did claim that art and politics were separable it was often to assert that the former was superior to the latter. (This issue is discussed in Chapter Two, which deals with the figure of the poet, and in Chapter Three.) Alongside this, we may put a specific comment by Graham Allen – 'Blake's poems are meant to be experienced, rather than simply interpreted' (Chapter Nine, p.220 above); in other words poetry is not to be seen as referential, not part of a language of reason. It is very difficult to argue with a poem. The language of a Romantic poem may be so powerful as to inhibit your own thinking. It leaves you – in other words – absorbed in the poet's imagining of his or her relation to the real world. So perhaps part of Romantic ideology is that in celebrating powers such as vision or the imagination, it suspends rational questioning.

I want here simply to suggest two further possible unifying factors (as suggestions for further thought rather than as some kind of definitive answers). We have often been dealing with texts which are explicitly about ideal entities (love, beauty, art, nature, and so on) and all the authors of this book have argued that they can be located within particular histories – indeed that they need to be so located. We began this book with two lyric poems, one by Wordsworth and one by Clare. Might Richard Allen's comments on Kleist and Hoffmann in Chapter Eleven – and in particular his discussion of their preoccupation with irony, alienation and double lives – enable us to circle right back to those two texts with which we began? If we think of Clare's 'I Am' with its wavering sense of self, couldn't we now see this as the effect of alienation? Both there and in Wordsworth's 'She dwelt among th' untrodden ways' an ideal is located in the past and in childhood. Couldn't we now see the workings of Romantic irony in the 'difference' between the ideal and the actual in Wordsworth's poem?

We mentioned above the power of Romantic writing, but a different emphasis is possible. One characteristic of nearly all the texts we have explored, not just the theories we considered in Chapter Three, is a self-conscious commentary on the act and meaning of writing. Doesn't this self-consciousness in the texts prompt a self-consciousness in our own reading? In Chapter Nine it is suggested that the Romantic notion of allegorical reading 'highlights the participation of the reader in the production of meaning' (p.226 above). Might we go a stage further and emphasize that we ourselves have the power to interpret Romantic writings in our own terms rather than theirs? Texts make sense of the world and we make sense of texts, but our interests may be different from theirs.

Reading in history: a postscript

Throughout this book you will have found poems which are as familiar as any in the English language, part perhaps of your own reading experience. We have tried to show that these poems benefit from being read in history and in the course of this have, we hope, made some of the history of the period familiar to you. The emphasis on reading in history should not lead us to ignore the fact that for many readers some Romantic texts can seem very immediate. They can give us the sense that they deal with our own feelings and our own world in something like our own language. But perhaps their very immediacy makes it difficult for us to stand back from the claims and assumptions made within them. In the first chapter I suggested that paying close attention to the language of texts is indispensable. But this did not give us the whole picture. Knowing more about the contexts in which texts were written may have given us a different way of reading them. Our reading of Blake's 'The Chimney Sweeper' in Chapter One did not mention ideology but discussed irony. Irony is, like allegory, a mode in which we infer something other than what is said or written. The speaker of Blake's poem is possessed by a certain ideology, but that is not the ideology *of the poem*. The speaker can justify the system within which he is placed; the poem, however, attacks it.

So I want to end by saying that we should never forget that in a sense works of the past can never be really familiar; the contexts in which they were written were very different from those in which we read them now. The changing perspectives that have come with feminist criticism and with analysis that tries to unpick the effects of colonialism in British culture again help us; to live and read in the period of Romantic writings was different from living and reading now. But it may be that the particular tendencies which have been retrospectively described as Romantic represent an ideology which continues to affect the way that our culture views for example the role of the artist. To ignore this possibility, it has been argued, leaves you still inside the Romantic ideology, failing to notice that we have (or we *ought* to have) outgrown the cultural claims and assumptions that were bequeathed to us by Romantic writing.

In a book published in 1983, with the title *The Romantic Ideology*, Jerome McGann explores this issue. He writes:

> The works of Romantic art, like the works of any historical moment [...] transcend their age and speak to alien cultures because they are so completely true to themselves, because they are time and place specific, because they are – from our point of view – *different*.
>
> (McGann, *The Romantic Ideology*, 1983, p.2)

You may have registered a paradox here – Romantic works are said both to 'transcend their age' *and* be 'time and place specific', to 'speak to alien cultures' *and* to be 'completely true to themselves'. In our own age, Romantic works survive not because they represent some kind of universal truth – to think this is to surrender to their power – but because they are specific to their time and therefore *different*. This book has recommended that we read them in history, asking what interest they serve, what history they make and remake. In learning how writings of the past are different, we can learn about ourselves. In understanding how they are written in history we can understand how we read in history. If this seems to create distance, even loss, then it is a loss for which there is, as Wordsworth writes in 'Tintern Abbey', abundant recompense.

Part Two

Romantic poetry: The I altered

by Stuart Curran

From: Curran, S. (1988) 'Romantic poetry: The I altered', in A.K. Mellor (ed.) *Romanticism and Feminism*, Indiana University Press, pp.185–203, 205–7.

Let us suppose they all died young: not just Keats at twenty-five, Shelley at twenty-nine, and Byron at thirty-six, but Coleridge in 1802, Wordsworth in 1807, and Southey on the day in 1813 he became poet laureate. Let us suppose too of the other candidates for fame in verse that Blake was mad, that Campbell and Hunt were journalists, Moore a songster, Rogers a bonvivant, Scott a novelist, and the rest vicars of the church. Let us then suppose a retrospect on British Romanticism just after the death of Byron in the inimitable tones of *Blackwood's*, celebrating this 'Age of Genius, only second to that of Elizabeth' and attempting to identify its particular source, 'the strong influence in operating the change that has taken place in our poetic literature.' It might run along these lines:

> We [are] delighted with the opportunity afforded us of offering our tribute of admiration to one, who, in point of genius, is inferior to no individual on the rolls of modern celebrity – whose labours have given a tone and character to the poetic literature of our nation – whose works were the manuals of our earliest years, and were carried by us, in our school-boy days, to shady nooks, and unfrequented paths, and our most favourite solitudes – whose touching portraitures of the workings of the human soul awakened in us an enthusiasm, to the full as ardent as that which is only inspired in our present youth by the effeminizing sensuality of Moore, or the gloomy and bewildering fascinations of Lord Byron – whose deep and affecting morals, illustrated by the moving examples of her scenes, touched the heart and mind, and improved the understanding by the delightful means of an excited imagination – and whose pages we have never returned to, in our days of more matured judgment, without reviving the fading tints of admiration, and justifying our early estimate of her high intellectual superiority.[1]

Without the pointed pronouns, a modern reader would surely anticipate from this description a contemporary estimate of the greatness of Wordsworth. But, instead, the subject is Joanna Baillie, who, two years before Wordsworth's celebrated preface, had published her own seventy-two-page argument for naturalness of language and situation across all the literary genres. Today, if she appears in modern literary histories, Joanna Baillie is fortunate to be able to duck into a footnote, usually derogatory. And yet, aside from the authority of its preface, her three-volume *Series of Plays: in which it is attempted to delineate the stronger passions of the mind* (1798–1812) was hailed in comparison to Shakespeare and, of all contemporary influences, exerted the most direct practical and theoretical force on serious drama written in the Romantic period. That with the exception of Shelley's *Cenci* we do not read this corpus and almost none of it is revived in the theater is apt testimony to the caprices of history with fame. The caprices of historians with history are quite another matter. Manifest distortions of the record have accrued, and these are the subject of this essay.

If we revert a generation from *Blackwood's* assessment of the contemporary scene, we might focus our perspective at a point midway between Baillie's and Wordsworth's prefaces, which is to say, before Baillie's impact on her culture had taken place. This is how Mary Robinson, a major literary voice of the 1790s, characterized its landscape:

> The best novels that have been written, since those of Smollet, Richardson, and Fielding, have been produced by women: and their pages have not only been embellished with the interesting events of domestic life, portrayed with all the refinement of sentiment, but with forcible and eloquent, political, theological, and philosophical reasoning. To the genius and labours of some enlightened British women posterity will also be indebted for the purest and best translations from the French and German languages. I need not mention Mrs. Dobson, Mrs. Inchbald, Miss Plumptree, &c. &c. Of the more profound researches in the dead languages, we have many female classicks of the first celebrity: Mrs. Carter, Mrs. Thomas, (late Miss Parkhurst;), Mrs. Francis, the Hon. Mrs. Damer, &c. &c.
>
> Of the Drama, the wreath of fame has crowned the brows of Mrs. Cowley, Mrs. Inchbald, Miss Lee, Miss Hannah More, and others of less celebrity. Of Biography, Mrs. Dobson, Mrs Thickness, Mrs. Piozzi, Mrs. Montagu, Miss Helen Williams, have given specimens highly honourable to their talents. Poetry has unquestionably risen high in British literature from the productions of female pens; for many English women have produced such original and beautiful compositions, that the first critics and scholars of the age have wondered, while they applauded.[2]

Robinson's landscape is then further delineated with a list of thirty-nine exemplary women scholars, artists, and writers, many of whom the modern reader could not have identified before the publication of Janet Todd's *Dictionary*. These thirty-nine articles of faith, as it were, were universally known among the literate of the 1790s and, indeed, could be multiplied several times over. Although our concern is with poetry, the breadth of the list should remind us from the start that by the 1790s in Great Britain there were many more women than men novelists and that the theater was actually dominated by women, all the more so as Joanna Baillie's fame and influence spread. In the arena of poetry, which in the modern world we have privileged as no other in this age, the place of women was likewise, at least for a time, predominant, and it is here that the distortions of our received history are most glaring. Its chronology has been written wholly, and arbitrarily, along a masculine gender line.

That such distortions started early can be perceived in the midst of *Blackwood's* extolling of Joanna Baillie. For the reviewer, identified as William Harness, implicitly sets Baillie within a nationalistic Scottish milieu dominated before her entrance by James Beattie, whereas clearly the major poetic voice in England in the ten years between 1785 and 1795 was that of William Cowper. But the curious centering of Beattie, who staked his exaggerated claims on one unfinished poem, should alert us to how difficult it is for the customary history to center any poet writing in Britain in the last third of the eighteenth century. After the death of the mercurial and self-destructive Charles Churchill in 1764, there occurs (according to the standard account) a remarkable trough in English poetry, which cannot be filled in by two honored poems each from Oliver Goldsmith and Samuel Johnson, nor by the inventions of the brilliant Chatterton, an adolescent suicide, nor by those two antithetical voices of the Scottish Enlightenment, alike inventors of a spurious past, Macpherson and Beattie. And yet there was a rush to fill that trough by an entire school of poets – women poets – who came to maturity in the 1770s out of the intellectual energy of the bluestocking circle of Elizabeth Carter and Elizabeth Montagu. They were well aware of one another, sometimes conceiving themselves as rivals of one another, and found an audience that followed their careers and bought their books. That they constituted a coterie, however far-flung from its London origins, is absolutely true, with all the disadvantages we might associate with it, but with energy, determination, and staying power to enforce a transformation in the history of British letters. Aside from intellectual encouragement, it is important to note, this coterie in its broadest manifestation furnished the economic base on which women writers depended for material support. Thus, while Goldsmith was writing his two poems and Beattie his one, a succession of women poets came to prominence: Anna Barbauld with five editions of her poems between 1773 and 1777; Hannah More with six sizable volumes of verse between 1773 and 1786; Anna Seward, the Swan of Lichfield, whose *Monody on the Death of Major Andre* of 1781 went through successive editions and was followed in 1784 by her influential amalgamation of genres, *Louisa, a Poetical Novel*, making her a literary force to be reckoned with until her death a quarter-century later; Charlotte Smith, whose *Elegiac Sonnets* of 1784 went through ten expanding editions in fifteen years; Helen Maria Williams, who capitalized on the fame of her first two books of poetry by publishing a collected *Poems, in Two Volumes* in 1786, when she was yet twenty-four; and Mary Robinson, whose first poetic volume was published in 1775, and who the year before her death in 1800 could survey a literary landscape and see it dominated by women intellectuals.

These six poets, however ignored today or misconceived in their own time, along with Cowper impel the history of poetry in the last quarter of Britain's eighteenth century. They are, as it were, the missing link, all the more missing since, deluged with reprints as the literary academy is today, only Seward's works have shared in that effort; indeed, only two of these six, Anna Barbauld and Hannah More, found their way into Victorian editions. As literary figures, these women poets are by no means isolated; there are dozens of other women of lesser ambition or simply less prominence who emulated them and thereby swelled their ranks into a literary phenomenon without parallel in earlier history. The six had their veritable differences in temperament and ideology – Anna Seward disparaged the propriety of Charlotte Smith's sonnets, for instance, and it is unlikely that Hannah More would have acknowledged the acquaintance of Mary Robinson, though a former student at the Misses More's Bristol academy, once she became celebrated as 'Perdita,' Mistress of the Prince of Wales – but even so, they could not help being linked in the public mind. They, and their emulators, are the unacknowledged subtext to Mary Woolstonecraft's *Vindication of the Rights of Woman* (1792), their achieved and independent excellence intimating a radical reordering of existing social institutions.

The dates of the six poets are instructive, for only one of them – Mary Robinson – died relatively young; Anna Barbauld lived until 1825, Helen Maria Williams until 1827, and Hannah More until 1833. And they were followed by a second generation of women poets who likewise confound our normative assumptions about the chronology of Romanticism. These are the dates of a handful of the most prominent: Joanna Baillie (1762–1851); Mary Betham (1776–1852); Margaret Hodson (1778–1852) – truly of a second generation, she dedicated her historical epic, *Margaret of Anjou*, in 1816 to her mother Margaret Holford, whose *Gresford Vale* was published in 1798; Mary Russell Mitford (1787–1855); Amelia Opie (1769–1853); Sydney Owenson, afterward Lady Morgan (1783–1859); Caroline Bowles Southey (1786–1854); Jane West (1758–1852). These are not only long-lived women, but for the most part they published far into the Victorian period and it would appear more productively and influentially than any male Romantic contemporary, with the exception of Leigh Hunt. Here, too, were it to be pursued, is a second missing link, only less important than the first because the terms were by this point so firmly set and the energy was so self-fulfilling. Still, in the writings of the two most famous women poets of this generation, Felicia Hemans and Letitia Landon, who died respectively in 1835 and 1838, we can discern what is otherwise almost strikingly absent in the male Romantic universe, an actual transition into the characteristic preoccupations of Victorian verse. Since, moreover, Hemans and Landon were the first women to earn a sizable income from writing only poetry, being accorded recognition in the public mind as professional poets, their success, whatever value we place on it today, testifies to a major transformation in the world of British letters. In fifty years women had come from the margins of that world to an assured, professional place at its center.

Hemans and Landon, to be sure, paid a price for their celebrity, at once fulfilling and defining a literary niche that, however important historically, may explain, if not exactly justify, their later neglect. For the bourgeois public of the 1820s and 1830s their names were synonymous with the notion of a poetess, celebrating hearth and home, God and country in mellifluous verse that relished the sentimental and seldom teased anyone into thought. There are other and darker strains in their voluminous production – a focus on exile and failure, a celebration of female genius frustrated, a haunting omnipresence of death – that seem to subvert the role they claimed and invite a sophisticated reconsideration of their work against the complex background of the transition between Romantic and Victorian poetic modes. But such an analysis must itself depend on our understanding of their principal inheritance, which is not that of the British Romanticism that died young but rather of a half-century of women writers who determinedly invaded a male fiefdom and reconceived its polity. On the surface the interests of these poets seem little different from the dominant poetic genres and modes of thought we associate with their time. They wrote satires as well as sonnets, tragedies along with *vers de société;* a few even wrote epics. But to look with attention and historical discrimination is to realize that some of the genres we associate most closely with British Romanticism, notably the revival of the sonnet and the creation of the metrical tale, were themselves strongly impelled by women poets; that some of the distinctive preoccupations of women poets eventually color the landscape we think of as Romantic; and that others are so decidedly different as to suggest a terra incognita beneath our very feet.

I

We are so accustomed to referring to English Romantic poetry as a poetry of vision that we have numbed ourselves to the paradox that what the word signifies is exactly the opposite of what we mean by it. We mean that it is visionary, borne on what Keats called 'the viewless wings of poesy' and obsessed, like Keats's major odes, with imaginative projection as an end in itself. The actual vision might be said to be the province – until late in the careers of Byron and Shelley, even the exclusive province – of women poets, whose fine eyes are occupied continually in discriminating minute objects or assembling a world out of its disjointed particulars. The titles of three of Anna Barbauld's poems, written over a span of forty-five years, are indicative: 'Verses Written in an Alcove,' 'An Inventory of the Furniture in Dr Priestley's Study,' 'The First Fire, October 1st, 1815.' If a woman's place is in the home, or in the schoolroom as in Anna Barbauld's case, or in the garden, then the particulars of those confined quarters are made the impetus for verse. Thus a characteristic subgenre of women's poetry in this period is verse concerned with flowers, and not generally of the Wordsworthian species. Merely to distinguish texture, or scent, or a bouquet of colors may seem a sufficient end in itself, enforcing a discipline of particularity and discrimination that is a test of powers. One senses exactly such a purpose behind Mary Russell Mitford's debut with a collection of her adolescent *Poems* in 1810, which is virtually a sampler of floral embroidery, the apprentice work of a literary seamstress. Yet, this category of seemingly occasional verse, from whose practice men are all but excluded, has the capacity to encode values, not just of culture but also of perspective, as in a different medium Georgia O'Keeffe's magnifications have proved to our century. The world of Charlotte Smith's 'Flora' is fantastic, even surreal; and it is small wonder that so many poems for the nursery or children in this period, verses like Mrs. Montolieu's *The Enchanted Plants* (1800) or Alice LeFanu's *The Flowers; or the Sylphid Queen* (1809), invest the garden with imaginative propensities. It is not, however, merely a 'rosy sanctuary,' like that of Keats in his 'Ode to Psyche,' built as a retreat 'In some untrodden region of [his] mind,' which in general parlance might be considered the quintessential garden of English Romanticism; rather, it exists for its own sake, for its capacity to refine the vision of the actual. Its significance is quotidian.

Quotidian values, although present and celebrated in the verse of the Enlightenment and Victorian periods, have been largely submerged from our comprehension of Romanticism, with its continual urge for visionary flight, for an investment in symbols. Even the fragmentary, as in 'Kubla Khan,' has served to implicate planes of reality beyond the power of words to image. Yet obviously the fragmentary can have more mundane and perhaps less self-congratulatory functions: to suggest a decentered mind or a society compounded of incongruities, for instance, or, for opposing ends, to document the sheer energy of life or its resolute thingness. Such are the ends one discerns from the experiments of Mary Robinson in poetic montage, which at once recall earlier satiric catalogs like Swift's 'Description of a City Shower' and assimilate new and startling cultural elements to the mix. Although we can discriminate particular elements and even recurring patterns, the poems resist reduction to thematic uses. They artfully refuse to reconcile their discords, whether of class, occupation, or mores. The opening of the eleven–stanza 'January 1795' may be taken as an instance:

> Pavement slipp'ry, people sneezing,
> Lords in ermine, beggars freezing;
> Titled gluttons dainties carving,
> Genius in a garret starving.
>
> Lofty mansions, warm and spacious;
> Courtiers cringing and voracious;
> Misers scarce the wretched heeding;
> Gallant soldiers fighting, bleeding.
>
> Wives who laugh at passive spouses;
> Theatres and meeting-houses;
> Balls, where simp'ring misses languish;
> Hospitals, and groans of anguish.

We are barely conscious here that the backdrop to these clashing juxtapositions is the war with France, so carefully does Robinson go out of her way to separate her references. Not until the final two stanzas does she return to the arena of bleeding soldiers and anguished groans:

> Gallant souls with empty purses;
> Gen'rals only fit for nurses;
> School-boys, smit with martial spirit,
> Taking place of vet'ran merit.
>
> Honest men who can't get places,
> Knaves who shew unblushing faces;
> Ruin hasten'd, peace retarded;
> Candour spurn'd, and art rewarded.[3]

Peace would be 'retarded' for another two decades, with enormous cultural consequences, while these incongruities played out their attrition on a world stage to the point of exhaustion. But that is deliberately not the theater of Robinson's poem; rather, it is merely one aspect of the universal pursuit of mundane and amoral self-aggrandizement.

What had already become the longest war of modern history is also the backdrop to Robinson's even more remarkable 'Winkfield Plain; or, a Description of a Camp in the Year 1800,' an evocation of sheer energy continually reverting to its sexual base.[4]

> Tents, *marquees*, and baggage-waggons;
> Suttling-houses, beer in flagons;
> Drums and trumpets, singing, firing;
> Girls seducing, beaux admiring;
> Country lasses gay and smiling,
> City lads their hearts beguiling;

Dusty roads, and horses frisky,
Many an *Eton boy* in whisky;
Tax'd carts full of farmers' daughters;
Brutes condemn'd, and man who slaughters!
Public-houses, booths, and castles,
Belles of fashion, serving vassals;
Lordly gen'rals fiercely staring,
Weary soldiers, sighing, swearing!
Petit-maitres always dressing,
In the glass themselves caressing;
Perfum'd, painted, patch'd, and blooming
Ladies – manly airs assuming!
Dowagers of fifty, simp'ring,
Misses for their lovers whimp'ring;
Husbands drill'd to household tameness
Dames heart sick of wedded sameness.
Princes setting girls a-madding,
Wives for ever fond of gadding;
Princesses with lovely faces,
Beauteous children of the Graces!
Britain's pride and virtue's treasure,
Fair and gracious beyond measure!
Aids-de-camps and youthful pages,
Prudes and vestals of all ages!
Old coquets and matrons surly,
Sounds of distant hurly-burly!
Mingled voices, uncouth singing,
Carts full laden, forage bringing;
Sociables and horses weary,
Houses warm, and dresses airy;
Loads of fatten'd poultry; pleasure
Serv'd (to nobles) without measure;
Doxies, who the waggons follow;
Beer, for thirsty hinds to swallow;
Washerwomen, fruit-girls cheerful,
Ancient ladies – *chaste* and *fearful*!
Tradesmen leaving shops, and seeming
More of *war* than profit dreaming;
Martial sounds and braying asses,
Noise, that ev'ry noise surpasses!
All confusion, din, and riot,
Nothing clean – and nothing quiet.

'Winkfield Plain' is a tour-de-force in more ways than one, for no man could have written this poem so conscious of the place of women within the economy of war and no woman in English society but an inhabitant of the demi-monde like Robinson, would have dared to. As realistic genre-painting it is years ahead of its time: its vision of the actual is penetrating. It may be true that little of Mary Robinson's copious oeuvre falls into the genre of realistic montage; but a quick comparison with the major realist among the male poets of the 1790s, Robert Southey, would suggest what literary victories are implicit in her refusal to categorize by class or politics or morality. The quotidian is absolute.

Morality is, on the other hand, the true subject of the brilliant *Essays in Rhyme on Morals and Manners* that Jane Taylor published in 1806. But the moral vantage point is only attained through the accumulation of minute detail, each piece precisely calibrated to ground morality in quotidian life. Taylor, who is the only woman poet in England during the Romantic period to have been honored with a twentieth-century selection, immediately reminds us, with her fine irony, of Jane Austen; but there are obvious differences in perspective. A devout Methodist, she is the analyst of its bourgeois underpinnings, and, like many Dissenting women, she is not to be dismayed by squalor. Above all, she understands what it is to work [...]

Taylor's capacity to reveal the inner life as a thing is, it could be asserted, unrivalled in English literature before Dickens; and she possesses what for the ends of comedy he often sacrificed, a quiet compassion for its costs. That we feel for those who cannot is the impetus for the moral bond Taylor would establish with her reader. Taylor's moralizing is deeply embedded in the Dissenting aesthetic that we have wished away from the Romantic period, but that is nonetheless present as a crucial link between Enlightenment moral satire and Victorian concerns with social- and self-improvement. To ignore it is in effect to marginalize both the burgeoning role of women as social teachers in early nineteenth-century culture and the literary interests of the increasingly educated lower classes.

If the quotidian has its view, it also has its sound. The timbre that can be discerned in these poems by Robinson and Taylor is that of the vernacular, what we are accustomed to call, following Wordsworth, 'the real language of men.' It was even more so, with fine irony, the language of women – not to say also, of Dissenting culture and of the lower classes. Not only is a vernacular not confined to men, but it is at least arguable that women poets, with their relative freedom from establishment conventions and their investment in the quotidian, are those who explored most deliberately the extent to which its language could be incorporated in poetry. If it could describe, if it could moralize, it could also incite. Perhaps the bridge that spans the long distance from the pastoral drama and tragedy with which Hannah More began her career to the evangelical agitation for which she is now known is simply a woman's voice and a woman's professional experience. From the theater she had learned how to know her audience and how to command its attention, as is exemplified in this stanza from a piece called 'The Bad Bargain':

> But the great gift, the mighty bribe,
> Which Satan pours amid the tribe,
> Which millions seize with eager haste,
> And all desire at least to taste,
> Is – plodding reader! what d'ye think?
> Alas! – 'tis money – money – chink![5]

The importance of More for the future directions of British fiction has recently been admirably charted by Mitzi Myers.[6] But the ease of such verse, its dramatic involvement of the reader, and the introduction of everyday slang had equal consequences for poetry, the poetry of the leveling Romanticism first enunciated by Joanna Baillie.

II

If women tended to see differently from men, it was axiomatic in the eighteenth century that they felt differently too. A singular phenomenon, suddenly appearing in mid-century and not only coinciding with the rise of women poets but also its very hallmark, was the cult of sensibility, which, despite Rousseau's impact on this culture, was largely a female creation. It was unquestionably a central concern in writing by women, whether in the ubiquitous romances or in poetry. The relative fame accorded Henry Mackenzie's novella of 1771, *The Man of Feeling*, should not blind us to the crucial fact foregrounded in his title: that men, too, can feel. The obvious literary struggle on the part of women authors was to convince those men that women, too, can *think*; but precisely because of the powerful shibboleth against the learned woman, an ideological control of remarkable intensity, sensibility was all the more to be cultivated, even celebrated. Hannah More's tribute to the bluestockings of 1782 entitled 'Sensibility: An Epistle to the Honourable Mrs. Boscawen' centers its world of learned exchange within an ambience of refined fellow-feeling, suggesting that this is the natural atmosphere in which intellectual development is fostered and shaped. What had been widely considered the defect of a female mind is there shrewdly reclaimed as its distinguishing virtue.

In the culture of sensibility it was relatively easy for women to assert their superiority by the very act of writing. A decade before More's celebration of a collective endeavour, Anna Barbauld had illustrated the process in 'The Mouse's Petition, Found in the TRAP where he had been confin'd all Night [by Dr. Priestley],' a poem whose considerable charm masks a studied self-reflexiveness.[7]

> O HEAR a pensive prisoner's prayer,
> For liberty that sighs;
> And never let thine heart be shut
> Against the wretch's cries!
>
> For here forlorn and sad I sit,
> Within the wiry grate;
> And tremble at the approaching morn,
> Which brings impending fate.
>
> If e'er thy breast with freedom glowed,
> And spurned a tyrant's chain,
> Let not thy strong oppressive force
> A free-born mouse detain!
>
> O do not stain with guiltless blood
> Thy hospitable hearth!
> Nor triumph that thy wiles betrayed
> A prize so little worth.
>
> The scattered gleanings of a feast
> My frugal meals supply;
> But if thine unrelenting heart
> That slender boon deny, –
>
> The cheerful light, the vital air,
> Are blessings widely given;

Let Nature's commoners enjoy
The common gifts of Heaven.

The well-taught philosophic mind
To all compassion gives;
Casts round the world an equal eye,
and feels for all that lives.

If mind, – as ancient sages taught, –
A never dying flame,
Still shifts through matter's varying forms,
In every form the same;

Beware, lest in the worm you crush,
A brother's soul you find;
And tremble lest thy luckless hand
Dislodge a kindred mind.

Or, if this transient gleam of day
Be *all* of life we share,
Let pity plead within thy breast
That little *all* to spare.

So may thy hospitable board
With health and peace be crowned
And every charm of heartfelt ease
Beneath thy roof be found.

So when destruction lurks unseen,
Which men, like mice, may share
May some kind angel clear thy path
And break the hidden snare.

Like all fables, 'The Mouse's Petition' has its interior shades of meaning. Even if addressed with youthful affection to an admired family associate, the poem is a direct assertion of the claims of feminine sensibility against male rationality. Making a virtue out of the necessities of feminine existence, its winning style enacts the claim of its underlying metaphor, a release from prison. And in this 'The Mouse's Petition' is of a piece with the collection in which Barbauld first published it in 1773, an act of liberation through, not from, femininity. In the clarity and delicacy of its style, it challenges the male universe exemplified by Priestley's scientific experiments. If it is not itself weighty, it embodies as it reflects the tensile strength of a cultural movement gathering momentum.

The poetry of sensibility is at base a literature of psychological exploration, and it is the foundation on which Romanticism was reared. From within the bluestocking circle itself arose a lively debate between the claims of sensibility and those of stoicism, the latter being centered in Elizabeth Carter's 1758 translation of Epictetus and Mrs. Greville's 'Ode to Indifference.' The debate broadened in the poetry of the later eighteenth century into an entire subgenre written by women, who represented the contrary currents either within the same poem (as in Helen Maria Williams) or in companion pieces in which 'To Sensibility' would be countered with the title 'To Apathy' (as in Mary Robinson) or 'To Indifference' (as in Hannah Cowley and Ann Yearsley). The existence of such a feminized

'L'Allegro' and 'Il Penseroso' is much more than simply a curiosity. It is the mark of the formation of an independent and shared woman's poetic, and the paradox of its analytical exposition of fine feeling should suggest as well its suitability as a locus for an encoded treatment of the female condition. Ann Yearsley, known as the Milkwoman of Clifton, near Bristol, and a protégé of Elizabeth Montagu and Hannah More, is a case in point. She is not, by and large, a poet of lasting claims, being an example of the proletarian genius that the late Enlightenment, with its humanitarian principles, promoted. But precisely because of those credentials her rendering of the complex reveals the values that underlie these conventions, what they encode. The poem she chooses to introduce her *Poems on Various Subjects* of 1787, the expanded fourth edition of the *Poems on Several Occasions* published a few years earlier, is 'Addressed to Sensibility.' It ends with this passage:

> ... ye who boast
> Of bliss *I* n'er must reach, ye, who can fix
> A rule for sentiment, if rules there are,
> (For much I doubt, my friends, if rule e'er held
> Capacious sentiment) ye sure can point
> My mind to joys that never touch'd the heart.
> What is this joy? Where does its essence rest?
> Ah! self-confounding sophists, will ye dare
> Pronounce *that* joy which never touch'd the heart?
> Does Education give the transport keen,
> Or swell your vaunted grief? No, Nature feels
> Most poignant, undefended; hails with me
> The Pow'rs of Sensibility untaught.[8]

Crude as this blank verse is, it embodies a defense of the right of women, with no capacity for education beyond that offered by boarding school or indulgent parents, to literary status, and, beyond that, a claim for an underlying affinity with maternal nature and through it to those elements that are essentially, fundamentally human. In other words, once again to recall Wordsworth's phrase, and here with an exact propriety, it is women who truly do speak 'the real language of men.'

Yet even as such an analytical mode as verses to one's own sensibility may implicate serious social concerns, its primary impulse was introspective, and the far-reaching consequence was to create the first sustained literary exercise in women's self-reflexiveness. And in turn, that mode slowly permeated the whole of English Romanticism. Likewise, we can trace into the mainstream of Romanticism the dialectical counterpoint between emotional extremes that is the subject and substance of the poems on female sensibility. Yet also the very extremity of this self-reflexive dialectic continually verges on a feminine version of Romantic irony. In the orchestrated emotional abandon of Mary Robinson's sonnet sequence, *Sappho and Phaon*, lies a fictionalized embrace of psychological self-destruction that is virtually a *Liebestod*. [...]

Charlotte Smith made a virtual career out of self-pity. She rises from it in her novels, but it is the obsession of her poetry and, to judge by her letters, of her life. But, in sober fact, she had ample justification. In 1783 she joined her wastrel husband, to whom she had been forcibly married in mid-adolescence, in debtors' prison, surrounded with a veritable brood of their children. In effect, from that point on they were her sole responsibility, and her recourse was to write – and write. The first edition of her *Elegiac Sonnets* in 1784 brought her sudden fame and opportunity, but for her the profession of letters was not an indulgence in feminine liberation nor in middle-class mobility; it was an absolute necessity. By 1787 she had separated from Benjamin Smith with responsibility for nine children but no legal freedom. Instead, her husband could comfortably pursue his ways with the insurance of a new and more secure source of income to relieve his chronically dire straits, that guaranteed by his wife's publishing contracts. There was no escaping him, nor was there any legal means, though Smith pursued them all, of independently attaching money left from his father to set up trusts for her children. So it went until her last year, when during her own decline, in a cruel irony, she received news of her husband's death.

Although Smith is virtually an archetype of the female condition of the late eighteenth century, and in her wide influence a promulgator of its values, her situation in the abstract is replicated by the history of Mary Robinson. Left fatherless in adolescence, she was married off by an Austenesque mother to a man who spent on women what he did not lose in gambling or in the assumption of loans at exorbitant rates of interest, a style of living that also lodged her, with their infant daughter, in debtors' prison. Her way out by economic necessity was through the stage, where she became a star before she was twenty. Attracting the attention of the young Prince of Wales, she resisted but at last stepped into the demi monde of his promises, which within a year dissolved in scandal. Left to herself, unable to return to the stage, Robinson contracted rheumatic fever at the age of twenty-three and was thereafter invalided for the rest of her life. A small annuity was finally procured from the prince, and she found a rather more stable, if not always steady, lover, with whom she traversed European spas in a futile search for a cure. There at least she could exist in society, from which she was almost rigidly excluded in England. But with the declaration of war in 1792 she was forced to return to London, where for the next eight years she wrote for a living. Hers was an unsatisfying, lonely existence, especially after she was again jilted in 1796, and it is reflected constantly in her poetry. If one adds her voice to Charlotte Smith's, the result is something beyond merely somber tones. It is veritably existential.

The constant theme of Charlotte Smith's *Elegiac Sonnets* is of rootless exile. Permanence is situated in the external phenomena of nature; even the most impermanent objects – the moon, storm clouds, the ocean, a shipwrecked denizen of a desert island – have an integrity that recoils on the speaker's sense of emptiness. The grotesque forty-fourth sonnet, 'Written in the Churchyard at Middleton in Sussex,' is astonishing in its trope, the interior life being first compared with a seaside cemetery washed away by a tidal wave – 'their bones whiten in the frequent wave ... With shells and sea-weed mingled' – and then contrasted; for the living woman cannot attain the entropic nonmeaning of dissolution she desires: 'I am doom'd – by life's long storm opprest, / To gaze with envy on their gloomy rest.'[9] But if extreme, the sonnet is of a piece with the collection that surrounds it, the whole portraying a disembodied sensibility at the mercy of an alien universe and without discernible exit from its condition. The entire sonnet revival of the Romantic period was impelled into existence by this vision, and, even where (as with Wordsworth) the tonalities are reversed, the underlying dynamic of an isolated sensibility informs all the sonnets written in Smith's wake.

Her most finished poem, beyond the collection of *Elegiac Sonnets*, is *The Emigrants* of 1793. Its dedication to William Cowper is forthright in acknowledging his desultory meditation of *The Task* as her model. But his is ultimately a poem of ringing optimism – at least it aspires to that end – whereas the underlying metaphorical strategy of *The Emigrants* is to connect Charlotte Smith as center of perception to the exiles from France's Terror, wandering the Kent shore cut off by but a dozen miles from their homeland, which is as present and as inexplicable to them as the suddenness of their reduction from opulence to penury. Their compounded loss of language, country, and means threatens their very sense of cultural and personal identity, and as the poem increasingly focuses on them as emblems of alienated humanity, the greater becomes their correspondence to the solitary figure observing them. In an uncanny way Charlotte Smith creates her own identity in the poem by absorbing their emptiness. In the process the details of her own vicissitudes are inflated to mythic status, and the intrusion of her legal frustrations as an embryonic version of the nightmare Dickens was to depict in Chancery seems justified by the abuses of state power from which these exiles have fled. [...]

Smith gambles daringly in *The Emigrants*, and perhaps she does not wholly succeed, for the stakes are too large for the table on which she plays. But by the end of the poem we have before us a wholly recast model. Cowper is willing to allow the world to flow through his centering consciousness, but he is characteristically self-effacing rather than absorbent. In 'The Emigrants,' most fully of Charlotte Smith's poems, one understands the deep impulse behind Wordsworth's generous praise of her in 1833 as 'a lady to whom English verse is under greater obligations than are likely to be either acknowledged or remembered.' In his tribute he singled out her 'true feeling for rural nature,' which is accurate enough, but perhaps the least of what he could have learned from her.[10] The year *The Emigrants* was published, 1793, was also the year of the twenty-three-year-old Wordsworth's debut with *Descriptive Sketches* and *An Evening Walk*, poems manifestly in search of a style and subject matter. A cursory glance [...] will suggest how charged is Charlotte Smith's poem with features that in a few years were to become identifiably Wordsworth's: in style, the long, sinuous verse paragraphs, the weighted monosyllables, the quick evocation of natural detail; in matter, the absorbing and self-mythicizing voice and the creatures of its contemplation – the aged, the idiots, the female vagrants, the exiled and alienated.

These are figures with which we have been long familiar, in Coleridge's, as well as Wordsworth's, contributions to *Lyrical Ballads*, perhaps less so in Southey's *Botany-Bay* and *English Eclogues*, which are cut from the same bolt. In Southey's hands, in particular, they are instruments of a leveling political program. But their ubiquity, and their continuation, transcend the limited environment in which we now locate them, for they are the legitimate offspring of this first generation of self-reflecting women poets. In the year of her death, 1800, Mary Robinson published her last and best volume of verse, with the firm of Longman's, bearing an advertising sheet that featured their second edition of *Lyrical Ballads*, and poems by Southey and Cottle. But to read the titles of her *Lyrical Tales*, as well as poems not published there, is to recognize more than her affinity with Wordsworth and Coleridge. 'The Alien Boy,' 'All Alone,' 'The Deserted Cottage,' 'The Exile,' 'The Fugitive,' 'The Maniac,' 'The Savage of Aveyron' – these are the displacements of feminine consciousness, the victims of sensibility, mice in the trap. And though we can locate their genesis in the later years of the eighteenth century, they are still discernibly the characteristics of women's poetry throughout the first quarter of the nineteenth century. [...]

As late as Felicia Hemans's *The Forest Sanctuary* of 1825, the poem she is said to have thought her best (and certainly its Spenserian stanzas are of a high finish), we witness a retreat into the savage interior of South America by a father and son – a displacement as evident as it is endemic in poetry by women – escaping the manifold persecutions of European civilization. At the end they are alienated and alone, with such integrity as still carries meaning. Even as both Hemans and Landon moved away from such hardminded realism into the realms of piety and sentimentality, their heroines still regularly perished. Contrary to what one might conventionally expect, in poetry at least, the unhappy ending is the norm of women writers of the Romantic period.

III

The two features of women's poetry we have been examining, an investment in quotidian tones and details and a portrayal of alienated sensibility, are not as isolated as this analysis would make them appear. Often they are present in tandem, with an effect that presages much later poetry and casts an oblique light on our customary expectations of the literature of British Romanticism [...]

The humanitarianism of the Dissenting tradition makes women poets sympathetic to distress and victimization, but the void at the center of sensibility should alert us to a profound awareness among these poets of being themselves dispossessed, figured through details they do not control, uniting an unstructurable longing of sensibility with the hard-earned sense of thingness.

That the threat of a collapse into this void is generally averted is, however, as significant as its presence. Even as we extract patterns from historical retrospect, it is essential to recognize that Smith's sonnets or Taylor's moral essays are the elaboration of a literary formula as much as are the *Lyrical Ballads*. A collapse in such circumstances would have been a contradiction of premises. What saves Charlotte Smith from the inanition she inscribes is quite simply its inscription. Edition after edition of the *Elegiac Sonnets* testified to a success that cannot be undervalued, success within a traditional male preserve. And her experience is paradigmatic. Even where the perspective of the poet seems radically self-denying, it is balanced by the self-confidence of its art. Where isolation seems most acute, there is the knowledge that a community is being built in its stead. The achievement of these women poets was to create literature from perspectives necessarily limited by the hegemony of male values. And that those perspectives should enter the cultural mainstream was, in the large sense, the foremost view they had in mind, even though they could not from their contemporary recognition have anticipated the effacement they suffered from history. Poets, they might well have told us, even if confined to the domestic circle, are still the unacknowledged legislators of the world.

Notes

1 [William Harness], *Blackwood's*, 16 (1824); 162.

2 *Thoughts on the Condition of Women, and on the Injustice of Mental Subordination,* 2nd ed. (London: Longman's, 1799), pp.95–96. The first edition of this work was published under the pseudonymn Anne Frances Randall: although conclusive proof of Mary Robinson's authorship has not been advanced, the attribution is venerable. For the identities of the writers cited, consult *A Dictionary of British and American Women Writers: 1660–1800*, ed. Janet Todd (Totowa, N.J.: Rowman and Allenheld, 1985).

3 *The Poetical Works of Mary E. Robinson* (London: Richard Phillips, 1806), 3: 274–76.

4 This poem was published in the *Morning Post* and reprinted after Robinson's death in an anthology edited by her daughter: *The Wild Wreath*, ed Mary E. Robinson (London: Richard Phillips, 1804), pp.160–62. It was not included in the *Poetical Works* of 1806, presumably on grounds of decorum.

5 *Poems* (London: Cadell and Davies, 1816), p.286.

6 See 'Hannah More's Tracts for the Times: Social Fiction and Female Ideology,' in *Fettered or Free? British Women Novelists 1670–1815*, ed. Mary Anne Schofield and Cecilia Macheski (Athens: Ohio University Press, 1985), pp.264–84.

7 *The Works of Anna Laetitia Barbauld* (London: Longman's, 1825), I: 35–38.

8 *Poems on Various Subjects* (London: G.G.J. and J. Robinson, 1787), p.6.

9 *Elegiac Sonnets*, 6th ed. (London: Cadell and Davies, 1792), p.44.

10 See William Wordsworth, *Poetical Works*, ed. Ernest De Selincourt and Helen Darbishire (Oxford: Clarendon Press, 1952–59), 4: 403.

The oriental renaissance

by Raymond Schwab

From: Schwab, R. (1984) *The Oriental Renaissance: Europe's Rediscovery of India and the East, 1680–1880*, trans. G. Patterson-Black and V. Reinking, Columbia University Press, pp.16–20, 192–197. Endnotes omitted.

Editorial Note: The following extract is translated from the French and this, together with the academic idiom, might make it difficult to read. I hope the following comments will help. In the first section, 'The Dimensions of the Event', Schwab describes a widening of the Eurocentric world-view. Early historians created a kind of mythic history representing the east as a fabulous other world. This view widened after the Renaissance, especially in the eighteenth century as orientalism became a systematic scholarly enquiry into the languages and cultures of the Orient. These scholarly endeavours, Schwab suggests, amounted to a rediscovery of the past, and specifically to the discovery of a common European origin even before the Greeks and Romans. This is why he describes it as the culmination of the Renaissance. Instead of the mythic history and geography of the Orient that had existed up until the Renaissance it became possible to investigate the Orient in newly rational or scientific ways. Schwab then suggests that orientalism is intrinsic to Romanticism and the second section extracted here, 'The Lake School and Politics', is concerned with the relations of literary men such as Macaulay with the British colony in India. It is evident that economic and political factors enabled this to happen with The East India Company an important link. Schwab then traces Indian influences in the work of Southey and other Romantic poets, attaching special importance to the poetry of Coleridge.

The Dimensions of the Event

Only after 1771 does the world become truly round; half the intellectual map is no longer a blank. In other words, this is not a second Renaissance but the first, belatedly reaching its logical culmination. [...] Thrice already had Europe discovered oriental Asia, but each time our 'Mediterranean classicisms' had [...] wanted only to find there 'analogous classicisms.' Here is one of the rare times when the forming of a new atmosphere can be perceived: as a result of certain repeated conjunctions of personnel and resources, a thrust in the unconscious of one or two generations, little by little a widening historical vision expanded the horizon of creative thinkers and allowed a reminting of the current coin of ideas. Henceforth the world would be one where Sanskrit and linguistics, even for those unaware of them, would have changed the images peopling time and space.

From at least the time of Herodotus to perhaps the time of Montaigne, when humanity was discussed it was a family matter inside a hermetic little Mediterranean room. Since then it has become a banality to remind Europe she is a small promontory of Asia. I say 'perhaps' until Montaigne because savages were becoming an inconvenient constraint on his generalizations – but then, they were still 'savages.' The great question facing civilized man for three centuries would be knowing where the savage began and ended, and which of the two events was the worthier. It is a variant on the question of the 'barbarian,' but it reverses the terms of choice – a serious choice in that it involves questions of idolatry and the pagan, notions which themselves are soon subject to revision. These cross-currents greatly stirred the air breathed by Voltaire, Rousseau, Diderot, and after them, Herder and the Romantics. And, dare we say, the debate is not closed yet.

Although their adventures had opened perspectives primarily on war and trade, everyone knows how much we owe to the fifteenth-century navigators. We seldom remember that it was only at the end of the eighteenth century that the orientalists, making use of new channels, brought back a view of humanity different from that of the gold-hunters and the slave merchants. Formerly the only humanity had been the one reported by missionaries and already depicted. When Vasco de Gama landed at Goa, the Zamorin asked him what he was seeking; he answered, 'Christians and spices.' It is not quite two hundred years since the human race ceased to be divided between a center of civilization, great, like a dilated point, and the vast and contemptible unknown. This division was, moreover, contrary to the Christian ideal, which in order to function in the world, and to do so in other guises, had to unite all the unknowns to the knowns *through a common origin*. This extraordinary and decisive reconciliation was, for the first time, brought about by a wholly new work of human genius: *the deciphering of lost writings*. Until that point, humanity had lacked three-quarters of its past, and missionaries and laymen vied in the research that would determine who would plant his flag there.

The 1771 edition of the *Zend Avesta* marks the first approach to an Asian text totally independent of the biblical and classical traditions. The history *of* languages and history *through* languages both begin with this work, which is also, we could say, the beginning of world history. At first only probable, such history became certain and irrevocable when, in 1784, the first Indic scholars began the reading of Sanskrit and published, in 1785, a translation of the *Bhagavad Gita*. From the dawn of time a harvest had been ripening whose hour had come. One would think [...] that the ten centuries following the Gothic invasions worked exclusively to provide the elements needed for a conception of the world. The times were swarming with navigators, scholiasts, collectors, and moralists who equipped themselves with a patchwork image of men from all times and countries, and who unwittingly heralded the census of all humanity from which modern man seeks self-understanding. Now the task that had been glimpsed by Herodotus and Plutarch, and announced by Montaigne and Voltaire, could be undertaken: the comparison of us with everyone else. Here the ancient 'wonders' of lotus-eaters and mermen ended: the final 'fabulous' discovery would be that of human multiplicity.

The millennial multitudes exhumed by the philologists were the forerunners of all the ideas concerning 'the masses.' The growth in communications visibly reduced the size of the world, and would have had much less effect on international relations if the most ancient extremities of the world had not already been united in the universities. Linguistic fundamentals, mechanical invention, and political revolutions all appeared simultaneously, and the whole would have been crippled had any one of these elements been lacking. It was logically inevitable that a civilization believing itself unique would find itself drowned in the sum total of civilizations, just as personal boundaries would be swamped by overflowing mobs and dislocations of the rational. All this together was called Romanticism, and it produced, through its many re-creations of the past, the present that propels us forward. Thus in the end the unprecedented prestige of history summoned from the past the justification – whether racial struggle or class revenge – for all those changes in the poor that are called revolutions. Less than fifty years after his fellow countrymen were astonished that one could be Persian, Anquetil taught them to compare Persian works with Greek ones. Before him only the Latin, Greek, Jewish, and Arab writers spoke reliably of ancient times. The Bible was an aerolite; the whole universe of sacred writings could be held in one hand. Anquetil cast into that universe a suspicion of the untold; he said that 'the common sense of the universe' could no longer be confined between the northern borders of Spain and Denmark, on the one hand, nor between England and the western edge of Turkey on the other.

Wherever oriental studies established themselves as an authentic discipline, they profited from serious and widespread curiosity, and increased it. As I have remarked in my life of Anquetil, 'The Orient was no longer a fantasy of blasé cosmopolitans who turned their gaze toward faraway places; the *Thousand and One Nights* and its imitators were not sufficient to quench the thirst for the exotic, and a nature closer to the pristine was henceforth to be sought in Surat as well as in Tahiti. At the same time, antiquity ceased to be the subject of compilations of conjectures or a pantry of commonplaces. It rose from the earth in the form of restored cities where the shadow of human endeavor could be followed anew. Between the appearance of Bernard de Montfaucon's *Antiquité expliquée et representée en figures* in 1719 and that of Winckelmann's *Thoughts on the Imitation of Greek Works in Painting and Sculpture* in 1755, knowledge acquired through reading was suddenly transformed by knowledge acquired through the handling of actual objects, objects for which an active search had been made. This is the point at which the mania for excavation broke out. In 1753, Robert Wood published *The Ruins of Palmyra, otherwise Tedmor, in the Desert*. In 1757 the expanded edition of *Observations sur les antiquités d'Herculanum* by Charles Cochin and Jérôme Bellicard was published, with great fanfare. Between the two, in 1754, Anquetil left for India. Only in that same year did the Englishman James Stuart and the Frenchman Julian Leroy begin, independently, the methodical exploration of Greece. As early as 1759 Anquetil proposed extending the methods of these scientific expeditions to the other three continents, and it is through him that the mysterious dimensions encompassed by the vagueness of the term "Orient" were repatriated from the empire of hearsay and from the wings of court theater. As the first pickax fell on lavas that Pliny had watched flow, Anquetil bounded to the other end of the ancient world, which was not termed antiquity and scarcely the world.'

After examining a sample of Sanskrit characters sent from Oxford, which no scholar in Europe could read, Anquetil thought to go to India to trace the secret of this unknown writing. This inspiration, this stroke of genius, was 'Columbus' egg' for linguistics. Anquetil left, convinced that he would bring back something to establish scientifically the primacy of the Chosen People and the chronology of the Bible. However, an entirely different faction also kept an eye on him with, as Quinet says, 'a desire to find in the ancient Orient a society to rival the Hebraic one.' What machinery Anquetil would set in motion between these well-ordered armies of the spirit! All notions concerning revelation and civilization would be reexamined. When an age of exoticism outgrows curio-collecting, and the boldness of the laboratories supplements the daring of the libraries, the result is inevitable: although something is always happening, from time to time there is a 'watershed' whose effect can no longer be denied. If history gives to posterity the power to restore coherence and purpose to what was only confusion in the eyes of contemporaries, rarely have the heirs been so able as then to analyze the composition of the air left for them to breathe.

The aged Chateaubriand was disturbed that he could no longer recognize the heaven of his youth. As he stated in *Mémoires d'outre-tombe,* not only had travelers' explorations changed it, but 'history [has] made discoveries reaching back to the dawn of time, and sacred languages have allowed their lost vocabularies to be read.' Among the upheavals created by linguistics – an invention of technicians – we should remember this one: the continent of the Hindus, the Chinese, and the Sumerians regained – with all the grandeur of its metaphysical tradition, which we had rediscovered, and with all the weight of its intellectual seniority, which we had unveiled – the power to question us. Through the authority of its age, Asia suddenly began to seem again an equal in modern controversies. For example, would there have been a Ramakrishna without William Jones or independence for India without Gandhi?

Let us delve further. Sylvain Lévi has remarked austutely: 'The definitive break between the Orient and the Occident dates from the Renaissance. The ancient world is, after all, so narrow that it easily lends itself to a vision of unity.' The Middle Ages still dreamed of a universal monarchy of pope and emperor. Bossuet's *Discours sur l'histoire universelle* in the seventeenth century does not exceed the boundaries of the City of God as Saint Augustine defined them, and wantonly ignores the traditions of India, of Tibet, of China, and of Japan reported by the missionaries. Not since the humanist Renaissance substituted the 'mystique of progress' for that of salvation had the past so helped to mold the future. And this in itself meant nothing until 1749, when Rousseau, provoked by an academic question, discovered and proclaimed that real progress is not ahead of man but behind him. Pascal, referring to Bacon's old comparison of the human species with the human individual, had already declared that the alleged ancients were, in fact, the adolescents of history. But Pascal's inspiration was to add that as both the individual and humanity mature, they turn their backs on this fact. To them the primitive is the ideal human type. We begin by positing with Rousseau that the savage, this unknown man, is the good man. We end by not arguing with Spencer that the primitive man who is man's touchstone is also the Stone Age Man. A hundred percent or zero percent human, he is the same primitive.

These tenets, blossoming in Romanticism, assisted the spread of Indic studies incalculably. And India – this was the legendary land of naked sages! These two qualities had been united by the Greeks in a single word – gymnosophists – that through the centuries had perpetuated an image that was rediscovered intact. The second Renaissance for a large part of its history would be variations on the word 'primitive.' Each time someone touched buried cities and indecipherable texts, he claimed to have uncovered the cradle of humanity, the important thing being to restore its youth to a humanity overwhelmed by the notion of its advanced age (*haute-époque*). Having done this, one can solicit from these rediscovered civilizations – whether we are, like Chateaubriand, faithful or, like Volney, skeptical – arguments to buttress or demolish faith. [...]

The Lake School and Politics

The great period of India in English poetry naturally coincides with the revelations of Calcutta, or followed them soon after. The first British administrators had found out everything they could concerning the local civilizations, disentangling Indic thought from its Islamic overlay; the Indic scholars who rose to answer their call were doubtless hoping for a real universality of culture. This attitude was unable to win over any large number of the isolationists for whom the exchanges between civilizations had to be made in a single direction; the small number who succeeded in fathoming the reality only collided with the bustling mass that trembled at the prospect of losing its beliefs or power.

Until the Great Mutiny of 1857, the East India Company was the principal organ of government. At first the company was favorably inclined toward the local religions; but in the nineteenth century it was to increasingly avoid contact with them. In 1817 Sir Thomas Munro protested racial prejudice. The breach widened to the point of hostilities in the 1830s, an extremely decisive period for English economics and politics, in which industrial vertigo, evangelical revivalism, and social disputes were intertwined. The civil servants imbued with the Victorian spirit, to whom Macaulay must have seemed a dazzling precursor, no longer went to India to gain knowledge of a new world or its mode of existence but to maintain British prestige or complete a useful phase in their careers. The literature written by company employees or their relatives prior to Rudyard Kipling created a new view of India. This phenomenon occurred precisely at the time that the fashion for orientalism which invaded European salons and intellectual reviews was taking shape: this explains why Great Britain was not the home of the Oriental Renaissance. One would have expected to find it there, since India was under British dominion, but that was precisely why it was not.

Indeed, a dispute about colonial administration was emerging, and growing acrimonious, between the Anglicists and the Orientalists, in which the latter term took on a very specific meaning: the debate centered on whether European or Indian education should obtain in the colony. The corollary question of jobs for the natives was also raised. The attention paid to Indic literatures was to be dependent on these mundane disputes. The dispute began over the issue of an annual subsidy of ten thousand pounds which the company, in reviewing its 1813 charter, had seen fit to allot to public instruction. The question was how to provide for the best return on these funds. A little-discussed 'filtration theory' prevailed at the time, but this trickle was drying up. The critical issue was how to establish a system of higher education, since Indic traditions and methods could not be adapted and it was not believed that European ones could be imposed. The two sides clashed primarily in Bengal, stirring up small groups of educated natives who besieged the government. This was certainly most unfortunate for the Orientalists, for they had but a fragile foothold and were without the moral qualities that would enable them to sustain the contest. British historians have gone so far as to hold the movement of Rammohun Roy responsible for the Indian hostility to Hinduism which, between 1820 and 1830, had supposedly encouraged the young English administrators to imagine that they were dealing with 'a decayed society.' In addition, the funeral pyre of widows, the sacrifice of daughters, the marriage of children, the untouchables, the 'regrettable aberrations of Hinduism' came to form the established litany of execrations that soothed the consciences of so many colonialists. It should be noted that Wilson, the intrepid leader of the Orientalists himself, had defended his clients more with ardor than with tenable arguments.

It is important to recognize that native education, religious as well as literary, had degenerated severely. Keshab Chandra Sen, writing about his childhood, described how 'the ancient scriptures, the famous records of numerous Hindu sects, had long been discredited. The Vedas and Upanishads were sealed books. All we knew of the immortal *Mahabharata, Ramayana* or *Bhagavad-Gita* was from execrable translations into popular Bengali, which no respectable young man was supposed to read.' In this period of decline the vernacular literature itself had had nothing for two centuries worthy of the tradition of Tulsi Das or Tukaram. Finally we have seen from Jacquemont's account that a certain indolence prevailed among the British philologists at Calcutta.

The defeat of the Orientalists was achieved through the ill-informed but energetic talents of Macaulay, who could be called the patron saint of English Indophobia, with Kipling as his successor. Even those among their compatriots who did not share in their prejudice admired the zest with which they shouldered it.

> The question before us now is simply whether ... we shall teach languages in which, by universal confession, there are no books on any subject which deserve to be compared to our own; whether, when we can teach European science, we shall teach systems which, by universal confession, whenever they differ from those of Europe, differ for the worse; and whether, when we can patronise sound Philosophy and true History, we shall countenance, at the public expense, medical doctrines, which would disgrace an English farrier, – Astronomy, which would move laughter in girls at an English boarding school, – History, abounding with kings thirty feet high, and reigns thirty thousand years long, – and Geography, made up of seas of treacle and seas of butter.

In all of English literature, perhaps nothing more cavalier, more Pickwickian, has ever been written. This resounding, 'Minute of the 2nd of February 1835, on Indian Education' by Macaulay cut short the eagerness of young people for Indian languages. It lightened the burden of governors set on fortifying the subcontinent without cutting into the budget at home. Bentinck 'as Governor-General should have seriously considered the demolition of the Taj Mahal and the sale of its marble. He "was only diverted because the test auction of materials from the Agra Palace proved unsatisfactory."'

Macaulay was counting on nature to replace Hinduism with Christianity. He suffered some disappointment in this respect – even the Hindus who accepted Anglican culture kept their own religion. As for language, the conqueror declared his own to be official in 1835. Twenty years later it was, nevertheless, necessary to allow education in the native dialect in certain provinces. Outside Bengal, contact with less passive people revived an interest in or indulgence of other ways of being and thinking. But soon the Great Mutiny, and the merciless repression that followed it, destroyed all the pacts and left only malice and misunderstanding.

These various phases are reflected in literary history. The first English poet whom India profoundly inspired was William Jones himself, and it should never be forgotten that he had only slightly acclimatized oriental poetry in adapting it for his compatriots. Goethe clearly pointed this out in his notes to the *Divan*: 'As a far-seeing man, he seeks to connect the unknown to the known, true values to recognized values. ... And it was not only from the archaeological side but also from the patriotic side that he had to endure a good many annoyances: it vexed him to see oriental poetry debased; this is clearly shown in the harshly ironic article *Arabs, Sive de Poësi, Anglorum Dialogues*, condensed into only two pages, which he inserted at the end of his work on the poetry of Asia.' Jones was as famous in England for his original poetry as for his introduction of India. The two aspects of his reputation reinforced one another, and both are present in the hymns he addressed to Hindu divinities celebrating a religion 'Wrapt in eternal solitary shade.' The first German Romantics, Schelling and Novalis among them, were very much taken by these hymns, before they became popular in England. In 1857 Villemain cited and translated another verse from Jones's 'Hymn to Surya' in the *Revue des Deux-Mondes*. In 1828 Quinet stated that this work was remarkable in promoting a passion for Asia among the poets of the Lake School: 'Lake School, Coleridge, Shelley completely Indic, Byron, etc.' How accurate is this?

After reading the copious scholarly notes in which they comment on their own work, one cannot doubt that the poets of the Lake School had read the *Asiatic Researches*. Byron himself, who did much to interest the political opposition and moral nonconformists in the Orient, seems to have read at least the poetical works of Jones. Southey, the author of an 'Indian epic,' *The Curse of Kehama* (1810), referred to Jones by name, displaying a knowledge of the Hindu religion which he drew from the *Bhagavad Gita*, the *Gita Govinda*, the Vedas, and the *Laws of Manu*. He celebrated the descent of the Ganges in the manner of the *Ramayana*, fifteen pages from which he quoted in full. In his first volume of collected poems in 1827 Tennyson was scarcely less explicit.

In 1811 Shelley, who knew Southey's Indic epic and its Persian counterpart, *Thalaba*, plunged into pantheistic visions which were in evidence ten years later. It is true that in his 'Queen Mab' (1813) Shelley could be thought closer to Volney, and that he gathered some lovely oriental names from the old d'Herbelot; furthermore Shelley was more impressed by Jones's poetic side, frequently the Persian poetry, the *Thousand and*

One Nights triumphing over the Vedas – a development with which, after Beckford and Morier, we are quite familiar. But it is Shelley's 'Adonais' (1821) with its open-hearted pantheism which is important to us here. It was no longer a matter of exploiting a setting or extending a vocabulary; a doctrine was sought within a new spiritual climate beyond the games of the imagination. In such writers, as we will see in Wordsworth, the influence was far more than skin deep. It was not just a passing fancy in the history of poetry, as we will see with the Americans. 'Adonais' had spoken with the depth of a soul: 'He hath awakened from the dream of life … The One remains, the many change and pass.' 'He is made one with Nature … He is a portion of the loveliness / Which once he made more lovely.' One can not believe that the echo of Vedanta has not infused new life into a certain concept taken from German metaphysics.

It is exactly the same with Wordsworth:

And I have felt
A presence that disturbs me with the joy
Of elevated thoughts; a sense sublime
Of something far more deeply interfused …
A motion and a spirit, that impels
All thinking things, all objects of all thought,
And rolls through all things.

('Tintern Abbey')

To every natural form, rock, fruit or flower,
Even the loose stones that cover the highway,
I gave a mortal life: I saw them feel,
Or linked them to some feeling; the great mass
Lay bedded in a quickening soul, and all
That I beheld respired with inward meaning.

(*The Prelude*, Book 3)

Our birth is but a sleep and a forgetting;
The Soul that rises with us, our life's Star,
Hath had elsewhere its setting,
And cometh from afar.

('Ode: Intimations of Immortality')

Brook! whose society the Poet seeks …
It seems the Eternal Soul is clothed in thee
With purer robes than those of flesh and blood,
And hath bestowed on thee a safer good;
Unwearied joy, and life without its cares.

('Brook! whose society')

Wordsworth was 'a pantheistic idealist' in the German manner, according to Sarrazin, and like Goethe's and Shelley's his pantheism remained 'essentially moral and providential.' Hindu dogma was slightly distorted by this limitation, but at least it was not merely a plaything.

With Blake, a solitary visionary, we again encounter affinities between occultism, Neoplatonism, and pantheism extending toward fellowship with animals and objects, as well as toward the annihilation of the self. I have not seen any definite contacts with Hindu texts pointed out; yet the accumulation of coincidences among the intellectual fashions which promoted Boehme, Schelling, and the Upanishads simultaneously is striking. The same observations hold true for Coleridge, and the same mixture appears in the work of his brother-in-law Southey. Coleridge's poetry is doubtless one of the great innovations of England, which was not impoverished in this domain. From Byron to Edgar Allan Poe, Coleridge's poetry was wonderfully contagious; and it was no small secret, this bizarre Orient without a country which this poetry brought them. But Coleridge's influence as a religious philosopher was even more widespread and durable. The *Biographia Literaria* is full of instances of the author's contacts with all the mysticisms turned up by the wake of the German Romantics; Boehme and Schelling were again foremost, along with the *Naturphilosophie* born with the new Indic studies. Other names, which at the time shone brilliantly, have faded. India had its place in the works of the Scotsmen Campbell and Thomas Moore. Moore's widely famous *Lallah Rookh,* written in 1817, gave him an international reputation. [...]

The Corsair

by Lord Byron

From: McGann, J.J. (ed.) (1981) *Lord Byron, The Complete Poetical Works*, Vol III, Oxford University Press, pp.156–9, 165–7, 172, 177–80, 181–9, 194–7, 199–204, 207–9, 213–14.

The poem begins with the pirates returning to their island after a successful raid and bringing news that the Turkish Pasha is preparing to attack. Their leader Conrad is described:

Canto I

[...]
That man of loneliness and mystery,
Scarce seen to smile, and seldom heard to sigh;
Whose name appals the fiercest of his crew,   175
And tints each swarthy cheek with sallower hue;
Still sways their souls with that commanding art
That dazzles, leads, yet chills the vulgar heart.
[...]
Unlike the heroes of each ancient race,
Demons in act, but Gods at least in face,
In Conrad's form seems little to admire,   195
Though his dark eye-brow shades a glance of fire;
Robust but not Herculean – to the sight
No giant frame sets forth his common height;
Yet, in the whole, who paused to look again,
Saw more than marks the crowd of vulgar men;   200
They gaze and marvel how – and still confess
That thus it is, but why they cannot guess.
Sun-burnt his cheek, his forehead high and pale
The sable curls in wild profusion veil;
And oft perforce his rising lip reveals   205
The haughtier thought it curbs, but scarce conceals.
Though smooth his voice, and calm his general mien,
Still seems there something he would not have seen:
His features' deepening lines and varying hue
At times attracted, yet perplexed the view,   210
As if within that murkiness of mind
Worked feelings fearful, and yet undefined;
Such might it be – that none could truly tell –
Too close enquiry his stern glance would quell.
There breathe but few whose aspect might defy   215
The full encounter of his searching eye;
He had the skill, when Cunning's gaze would seek
To probe his heart and watch his changing cheek,
At once the observer's purpose to espy,
And on himself roll back his scrutiny,   220
Lest he to Conrad rather should betray
Some secret thought, than drag that chief's to day.
There was a laughing Devil in his sneer,
That raised emotions both of rage and fear;

And where his frown of hatred darkly fell,   225
Hope withering fled – and Mercy sighed farewell!

(10)
Slight are the outward signs of evil thought,
Within – within – 'twas there the spirit wrought!
Love shows all changes – Hate, Ambition, Guile,
Betray no further than the bitter smile;   230
The lip's least curl, the lightest paleness thrown
Along the governed aspect, speak alone
Of deeper passions; and to judge their mien,
He, who would see, must be himself unseen.
Then – with the hurried tread, the upward eye,   235
The clenched hand, the pause of agony,
That listens, starting, lest the step too near
Approach intrusive on that mood of fear:
Then – with each feature working from the heart,
With feelings loosed to strengthen – not depart;   240
That rise – convulse – contend – that freeze, or glow,
Flush in the cheek, or damp upon the brow;
Then – Stranger! if thou canst, and tremblest not,
Behold his soul – the rest that soothes his lot!
Mark – how that lone and blighted bosom sears   245
The scathing thought of execrated years!
Behold – but who hath seen, or e'er shall see,
Man as himself – the secret spirit free?

(11)
Yet was not Conrad thus by Nature sent
To lead the guilty – guilt's worst instrument –   250
His soul was changed, before his deeds had driven
Him forth to war with man and forfeit heaven.
Warped by the world in Disappointment's school,
In words too wise, in conduct *there* a fool;
Too firm to yield, and far too proud to stoop,   255
Doomed by his very virtues for a dupe,
He cursed those virtues as the cause of ill,
And not the traitors who betrayed him still;
Nor deemed that gifts bestowed on better men
Had left him joy, and means to give again.   260
Feared – shunned – belied – ere youth had lost her force,
He hated man too much to feel remorse,
And thought the voice of wrath a sacred call,
To pay the injuries of some on all.
He knew himself a villain – but he deemed   265
The rest no better than the thing he seemed;
And scorned the best as hypocrites who hid
Those deeds the bolder spirit plainly did.
He knew himself detested, but he knew
The hearts that loathed him, crouched and dreaded too.   270
Lone, wild, and strange, he stood alike exempt
From all affection and from all contempt:
His name could sadden, and his acts surprize;
But they that feared him dared not to despise:
Man spurns the worm, but pauses ere he wake   275

304

The slumbering venom of the folded snake:
The first may turn – but not avenge the blow;
The last expires – but leaves no living foe;
Fast to the doomed offender's form it clings,
And he may crush – not conquer – still it stings!   280

Conrad orders the returning pirates to set off again that night. He bids farewell to his wife, Medora:

[...]
'Again – again – and oft again – my love!   450
If there be life below, and hope above,
He will return – but now, the moments bring
The time of parting with redoubled wing:
The why – the where – what boots it now to tell?
Since all must end in that wild word – farewell!   455
Yet would I fain – did time allow – disclose –
Fear not – these are no formidable foes;
And here shall watch a more than wonted guard,
For sudden siege and long defence prepared:
Nor be thou lonely – though thy lord's away,   460
Our matrons and thy handmaids with thee stay;
And this thy comfort – that, when next we meet,
Security shall make repose more sweet:
List! – 'tis the bugle – Juan shrilly blew –
One kiss – one more – another – Oh! Adieu!'   465

She rose – she sprung – she clung to his embrace,
Till his heart heaved beneath her hidden face.
He dared not raise to his that deep-blue eye,
Which downcast drooped in tearless agony.
Her long fair hair lay floating o'er his arms,   470
In all the wildness of dishevelled charms;
Scarce beat that bosom where his image dwelt
So full – *that* feeling seemed almost unfelt!
Hark – peals the thunder of the signal-gun!
It told 'twas sunset – and he cursed that sun.   475
Again – again – that form he madly pressed,
Which mutely clasped, imploringly caressed!
And tottering to the couch his bride he bore,
One moment gazed – as if to gaze no more;
Felt – that for him earth held but her alone,   480
Kissed her cold forehead – turned – is Conrad gone?

(15)
'And is he gone?' – on sudden solitude
How oft that fearful question will intrude?
''Twas but an instant past – and here he stood!
And now' – without the portal's porch she rushed,   485
And then at length her tears in freedom gushed;
Big – bright – and fast, unknown to her they fell;
But still her lips refused to send – 'Farewell!'
For in that word – that fatal word – howe'er
We promise – hope – believe – there breathes despair.   490
O'er every feature of that still, pale face,
Had sorrow fixed what time can ne'er erase:

305

The tender blue of that large loving eye
Grew frozen with its gaze on vacancy,
Till – Oh, how far! – it caught a glimpse of him,   495
And then it flowed – and phrenzied seemed to swim
Through those long, dark, and glistening lashes dewed
With drops of sadness oft to be renewed.
'He's gone!' – against her heart that hand is driven,
Convulsed and quick – then gently raised to heaven;   500
She looked and saw the heaving of the main;
The white sail set – she dared not look again;
But turned with sickening soul within the gate –
'It is no dream – and I am desolate!'

The court of the Pasha Seyd in Coron is described:

Canto II

[...]
High in his hall reclines the turbaned Seyd;
Around – the bearded chiefs he came to lead.   30
Removed the banquet, and the last pilaff –
Forbidden draughts, 'tis said, he dared to quaff,
Though to the rest the sober berry's juice,
The slaves bear round for rigid Moslem's use;
The long Chibouque's dissolving cloud supply,   35
While dance the Almahs to wild minstrelsy.
The rising morn will view the chiefs embark;
But waves are somewhat treacherous in the dark:
And revellers may more securely sleep
On silken couch than o'er the rugged deep;   40
Feast there who can – nor combat till they must,
And less to conquest than to Korans trust;
And yet the numbers crowded in his host
Might warrant more than even the Pacha's boast.

Conrad, disguised as a dervish, Zatanai, admits the pirates. There is a fight
and the court is set ablaze. The pirates enter the harem where Conrad rescues Gulnare, one of the handmaidens:

[...]
Quick at the word – they seized him each a torch,
And fire the dome from minaret to porch.
A stern delight was fixed in Conrad's eye,
But sudden sunk – for on his ear the cry
Of women struck, and like a deadly knell   200
Knocked at that heart unmoved by battle's yell.
'Oh! burst the Haram – wrong not on your lives
One female form – remember – *we* have wives.
On them such outrage Vengeance will repay;
Man is our foe, and such 'tis ours to slay: 205
But still we spared – must spare the weaker prey.
Oh! I forgot – but Heaven will not forgive
If at my word the helpless cease to live;
Follow who will – I go – we yet have time
Our souls to lighten of at least a crime.'   210

[...]
But first, ere came the rallying host to blows,
And rank to rank, and hand to hand oppose,
Gulnare and all her Haram handmaids freed,   255
Safe in the dome of one who held their creed,
By Conrad's mandate safely were bestowed,
And dried those tears for life and fame that flowed:
And when that dark-eyed lady, young Gulnare,
Recalled those thoughts late wandering in despair,   260
Much did she marvel o'er the courtesy
That smoothed his accents, softened in his eye:
'Twas strange – *that* robber thus with gore bedewed,
Seemed gentler then than Seyd in fondest mood.
The Pacha wooed as if he deemed the slave   265
Must seem delighted with the heart he gave;
The Corsair vowed protection, soothed affright,
As if his homage were a woman's right.
'The wish is wrong – nay worse for female – vain:
Yet much I long to view that chief again;   270
If but to thank for, what my fear forgot,
The life – my loving lord remembered not!'

In rescuing Gulnare, Conrad is wounded, captured and imprisoned in a
tower:

[...]
The Leech was sent – but not in mercy – there   310
To note how much the life yet left could bear;
He found enough to load with heaviest chain,
And promise feeling for the wrench of pain:
To-morrow – yea – to-morrow's evening sun
Will sinking see impalement's pangs begun,   315
And rising with the wonted blush of morn
Behold how well or ill those pangs are borne.
Of torments this the longest and the worst,
Which adds all other agony to thirst,
That day by day death still forbears to slake,   320
While famished vultures flit around the stake.
'Oh! water – water!' – smiling Hate denies
The victim's prayer – for if he drinks – he dies.
This was his doom: – the Leech, the guard were gone,
And left proud Conrad fettered and alone.   325

(10)
'Twere vain to paint to what his feelings grew –
It even were doubtful if their victim knew.
There is a war, a chaos of the mind,
When all its elements convulsed – combined –
Lie dark and jarring with perturbed force,   330
And gnashing with impenitent Remorse;
That juggling fiend – who never spake before –
But cries, 'I warned thee!' when the deed is o'er.
Vain voice! the spirit burning but unbent,
May writhe – rebel – the weak alone repent!   335
Even in that lonely hour when most it feels,

And, to itself, all – all that self reveals,
No single passion, and no ruling thought
That leaves the rest as once unseen, unsought;
But the wild prospect when the soul reviews –   340
All rushing through their thousand avenues.
Ambition's dreams expiring, love's regret,
Endangered glory, life itself beset;
The joy untasted, the contempt or hate
'Gainst those who fain would triumph in our fate;   345
The hopeless past, the hasting future driven
Too quickly on to guess if hell or heaven;
Deeds, thoughts, and words, perhaps remembered not
So keenly till that hour, but ne'er forgot;
Things light or lovely in their acted time,   350
But now to stern reflection each a crime;
The withering sense of evil unrevealed,
Not cankering less because the more concealed –
All, in a word, from which all eyes must start,
That opening sepulchre – the naked heart   355
Bares with its buried woes, till Pride awake,
To snatch the mirror from the soul – and break.
Ay – Pride can veil, and courage brave it all,
All – all – before – beyond – the deadliest fall.
Each hath some fear, and he who least betrays,   360
The only hypocrite deserving praise:
Not the loud recreant wretch who boasts and flies;
But he who looks on death – and silent dies.
So steeled by pondering o'er his far career,
He halfway meets him should he menace near!   365

(11)
In the high chamber of his highest tower,
Sate Conrad, fettered in the Pacha's power.
His palace perished in the flame – this fort
Contained at once his captive and his court.
Not much could Conrad of his sentence blame,   370
His foe, if vanquished, had but shared the same:–

Conrad finally sleeps, dreaming of Medora, but is visited by Gulnare. She does not release him but promises to have his life spared. This extract recounts their conversation:

[...]
He slept in calmest seeming – for his breath
Was hushed so deep – Ah! happy if in death!
He slept – Who o'er his placid slumber bends?
His foes are gone – and here he hath no friends;   395
Is it some seraph sent to grant him grace?
No 'tis an earthly form with heavenly face!
Its white arm raised a lamp – yet gently hid,
Lest the ray flash abruptly on the lid
Of that closed eye, which opens but to pain,   400
And once unclosed – but once may close again.
That form, with eye so dark, and cheek so fair,
And auburn waves of gemmed and braided hair;

With shape of fairy lightness – naked foot,
That shines like snow, and falls on earth as mute – 405
Through guards and dunnest night how came it there?
Ah! rather ask what will not woman dare?
Whom youth and pity lead like thee, Gulnare!
She could not sleep – and while the Pacha's rest
In muttering dreams yet saw his pirate-guest, 410
She left his side – his signet ring she bore,
Which oft in sport adorned her hand before –
And with it, scarcely questioned, won her way
Through drowsy guards that must that sign obey.
Worn out with toil, and tired with changing blows, 415
Their eyes had envied Conrad his repose;
And chill and nodding at the turret door,
They stretch their listless limbs, and watch no more:
Just raised their heads to hail the signet-ring,
Nor ask or what or who the sign may bring. 420

(13)
She gazed in wonder, 'Can he calmly sleep,
While other eyes his fall or ravage weep?
And mine in restlessness are wandering here –
What sudden spell hath made this man so dear?
True – 'tis to him my life, and more, I owe, 425
And me and mine he spared from worse than woe:
'Tis late to think – but soft – his slumber breaks –
How heavily he sighs! – he starts – awakes!'

He raised his head – and dazzled with the light,
His eye seemed dubious if it saw aright: 430
He moved his hand – the grating of his chain
Too harshly told him that he lived again.
'What is that form? if not a shape of air,
Methinks, my jailor's face shows wond'rous fair?'

'Pirate! thou know'st me not – but I am one, 435
Grateful for deeds thou hast too rarely done;
Look on me – and remember her, thy hand
Snatched from the flames, and thy more fearful band.
I come through darkness – and I scarce know why –
Yet not to hurt – I would not see thee die.' 440

'If so, kind lady! thine the only eye
That would not here in that gay hope delight:
Theirs is the chance – and let them use their right.
But still I thank their courtesy or thine,
That would confess me at so fair a shrine!' 445

Strange though it seem – yet with extremest grief
Is linked a mirth – it doth not bring relief –
That playfulness of Sorrow ne'er beguiles,
And smiles in bitterness – but still it smiles;
And sometimes with the wisest and the best, 450
Till even the scaffold echoes with their jest!
Yet not the joy to which it seems akin –
It may deceive all hearts, save that within.
Whate'er it was that flashed on Conrad, now

309

A laughing wildness half unbent his brow: 455
And these his accents had a sound of mirth,
As if the last he could enjoy on earth;
Yet 'gainst his nature – for through that short life,
Few thoughts had he to spare from gloom and strife.

(14)
'Corsair! thy doom is named – but I have power 460
To soothe the Pacha in his weaker hour.
Thee would I spare – nay more – would save thee now,
But this – time – hope – nor even thy strength allow;
But all I can, I will: at least, delay
The sentence that remits thee scarce a day. 465
More now were ruin – even thyself were loth
The vain attempt should bring but doom to both.'
'Yes! – loth indeed: – my soul is nerved to all,
Or fall'n too low to fear a further fall:
Tempt not thyself with peril; me with hope, 470
Of flight from foes with whom I could not cope;
Unfit to vanquish – shall I meanly fly,
The one of all my band that would not die?
Yet there is one – to whom my memory clings,
'Till to these eyes her own wild softness springs. 475
My sole resources in the path I trod
Were these – my bark – my sword – my love – my God!
The last I left in youth – he leaves me now –
And Man but works his will to lay me low.
I have no thought to mock his throne with prayer 480
Wrung from the coward crouching of despair;
It is enough – I breathe – and I can bear.
My sword is shaken from the worthless hand
That might have better kept so true a brand;
My bark is sunk or captive – but my love – 485
For her in sooth my voice would mount above:
Oh! she is all that still to earth can bind –
And this will break a heart so more than kind,
And blight a form – till thine appeared, Gulnare!
Mine eye ne'er asked if others were as fair.' 490

'Thou lov'st another then? – but what to me
Is this – 'tis nothing – nothing e'er can be:
But yet – thou lov'st – and – Oh! I envy those
Whose hearts on hearts as faithful can repose,
Who never feel the void – the wandering thought 495
That sighs o'er visions – such as mine hath wrought.'
'Lady – methought thy love was his, for whom
This arm redeemed thee from a fiery tomb.'
'My love stern Seyd's! Oh – No – No – not my love –
Yet much this heart, that strives no more, once strove 500
To meet his passion – but it would not be.
I felt – I feel – love dwells with – with the free.
I am a slave, a favoured slave at best,
To share his splendour, and seem very blest!
Oft must my soul the question undergo, 505
Of – 'Dost thou love?' and burn to answer 'No!'

310

Oh! hard it is that fondness to sustain,
And struggle not to feel averse in vain;
But harder still the heart's recoil to bear,
And hide from one – perhaps another there.   510
He takes the hand I give not – nor withhold –
Its pulse nor checked – nor quickened – calmly cold:
And when resigned, it drops a lifeless weight
From one I never loved enough to hate.
No warmth these lips return by his imprest,   515
And chilled remembrance shudders o'er the rest.
Yes – had I ever proved that passion's zeal,
The change to hatred were at least to feel:
But still – he goes unmourned – returns unsought –
And oft when present – absent from my thought.   520
Or when reflection comes, and come it must –
I fear that henceforth 'twill but bring disgust;
I am his slave – but, in despite of pride,
'Twere worse than bondage to become his bride.
Oh! that this dotage of his breast would cease!   525
Or seek another and give mine release,
But yesterday – I could have said, to peace!
Yes – if unwonted fondness now I feign,
Remember – captive! 'tis to break thy chain.
Repay the life that to thy hand I owe;   530
To give thee back to all endeared below,
Who share such love as I can never know.
Farewell – morn breaks – and I must now away:
'Twill cost me dear – but dread no death to-day!'

(15)
She pressed his fettered fingers to her heart,   535
And bowed her head, and turned her to depart,
And noiseless as a lovely dream is gone.
And was she here? and is he now alone?
What gem hath dropped and sparkles o'er his chain?
The tear most sacred, shed for other's pain,   540
That starts at once – bright – pure – from Pity's mine,
Already polished by the hand divine!

Oh! too convincing – dangerously dear –
In woman's eye the unanswerable tear!
That weapon of her weakness she can wield,   545
To save, subdue – at once her spear and shield:
Avoid it – Virtue ebbs and Wisdom errs,
Too fondly gazing on that grief of hers!
What lost a world, and made a hero fly?
The timid tear in Cleopatra's eye.   550
Yet be the soft triumvir's fault forgiven,
By this – how many lose not earth – but heaven!
Consign their souls to man's eternal foe,
and seal their own to spare some wanton's woe!

In Canto III the survivors return and report what they know to Medora. The poem then moves back to Coron where Gulnare pleads with the Seyd – unsuccessfully – for Conrad's life:

Canto III

[...]
Within the Haram's secret chamber sate
Stern Seyd, still pondering o'er his Captive's fate;
His thoughts on love and hate alternate dwell,
Now with Gulnare, and now in Conrad's cell;
Here at his feet the lovely slave reclined   135
Surveys his brow – would soothe his gloom of mind,
While many an anxious glance her large dark eye
Sends in its idle search for sympathy,
His only bends in seeming o'er his beads,
But inly views his victim as he bleeds.   140

'Pacha! the day is thine; and on thy crest
Sits Triumph – Conrad taken – fall'n the rest!
His doom is fixed – he dies: and well his fate
Was earned – yet much too worthless for thy hate:
Methinks, a short release, for ransom told   145
With all his treasure, not unwisely sold;
Report speaks largely of his pirate-hoard –
Would that of this my Pacha were the Lord!
While baffled, weakened by this fatal fray –
Watched – followed – he were then an easier prey;   150
But once cut off – the remnant of his band
Embark their wealth, and seek a safer strand.'

'Gulnare! – if for each drop of blood a gem
Were offered rich as Stamboul's diadem;
If for each hair of his a massy mine   155
Of virgin ore should supplicating shine;
If all our Arab tales divulge or dream
Of wealth were here – that gold should not redeem!
It had not now redeemed a single hour;
But that I know him fettered, in my power;   160
And, thirsting for revenge, I ponder still
On pangs that longest rack, and latest kill.'

'Nay, Seyd! – I seek not to restrain thy rage,
Too justly moved for mercy to assuage;
My thoughts were only to secure for thee   165
His riches – thus released, he were not free:
Disabled, shorn of half his might and band,
His capture could but wait thy first command.'

'His capture *could*! – and shall I then resign
One day to him – the wretch already mine?   170
Release my foe! – at whose remonstrance? – thine!
Fair suitor! – to thy virtuous gratitude,
That thus repays this Giaour's relenting mood,
Which thee and thine alone of all could spare,
No doubt – regardless if the prize were fair,   175
My thanks and praise alike are due – now hear!

312

I have a counsel for thy gentler ear:
I do mistrust thee, woman! and each word
Of thine stamps truth on all Suspicion heard.
Borne in his arms through fire from yon Serai –   180
Say, wert thou lingering there with him to fly?
Thou need'st not answer – thy confession speaks,
Already reddening on thy guilty cheeks;
Then, lovely dame, bethink thee! and beware:
'Tis not *his* life alone may claim such care!   185
Another word and – nay – I need no more.
Accursed was the moment when he bore
Thee from the flames, which better far – but – no –
I then had mourned thee with a lover's woe –
Now 'tis thy lord that warns – deceitful thing!   190
Know'st thou that I can clip thy wanton wing?
In words alone I am not wont to chafe:
Look to thyself – nor deem thy falsehood safe!'

He rose – and slowly, sternly thence withdrew,
Rage in his eye and threats in his adieu: 195
Ah! little recked that chief of womanhood –
Which frowns ne'er quelled, nor menaces subdued;
And little deemed he what thy heart, Gulnare!
When soft could feel, and when incensed could dare.
His doubts appeared to wrong – nor yet she knew   200
How deep the root from whence compassion grew –
She was a slave – from such may captives claim
A fellow-feeling, differing but in name;
Still half unconscious – heedless of his wrath,
Again she ventured on the dangerous path,   205
Again his rage repelled – until arose
That strife of thought, the source of woman's woes!

Gulnare returns to Conrad and says she will release him if he will kill Pasha
Seyd:

[...]
The midnight passed – and to the massy door   270
A light step came – it paused – it moved once more;
Slow turns the grating bolt and sullen key:
'Tis as his heart foreboded – that fair she!
Whate'er her sins, to him a guardian saint,
And beauteous still as hermit's hope can paint;   275
Yet changed since last within that cell she came,
More pale her cheek, more tremulous her frame:
On him she cast her dark and hurried eye,
Which spoke before her accents – 'thou must die!
Yes, thou must die – there is but one resource,   280
The last – the worst – if torture were not worse.'

'Lady! I look to none – my lips proclaim
What last proclaimed they – Conrad still the same:
Why should'st thou seek an outlaw's life to spare,
And change the sentence I deserve to bear?   285
Well have I earned – nor here alone – the meed
Of Seyd's revenge, by many a lawless deed.'

'Why should I seek? because – Oh! didst thou not
Redeem my life from worse than slavery's lot?
Why should I seek? – hath misery made thee blind 290
To the fond workings of a woman's mind!
And must I say? albeit my heart rebel
With all that woman feels, but should not tell –
Because – despite thy crimes – that heart is moved:
It feared thee – thanked thee – pitied – maddened – loved. 295
Reply not, tell not now thy tale again,
Thou lov'st another – and I love in vain;
Though fond as mine her bosom, form more fair,
I rush through peril which she would not dare.
If that thy heart to hers were truly dear, 300
Were I thine own – thou wert not lonely here:
An outlaw's spouse – and leave her lord to roam!
What hath such gentle dame to do with home?
But speak not now – o'er thine and o'er my head
Hangs the keen sabre by a single thread; 305
If thou hast courage still, and would'st be free,
Receive this poignard – rise – and follow me!'

'Ay – in my chains! my steps will gently tread,
With these adornments, o'er each slumbering head!
Thou hast forgot – is this a garb for flight? 310
Or is that instrument more fit for fight?'

'Misdoubting Corsair! I have gained the guard,
Ripe for revolt, and greedy for reward.
A single word of mine removes that chain:
Without some aid how here could I remain? 315
Well, since we met, hath sped my busy time,
If in aught evil, for thy sake the crime:
The crime – 'tis none to punish those of Seyd.
That hated tyrant, Conrad – he must bleed!
I see thee shudder – but my soul is changed – 320
Wronged – spurned – reviled – and it shall be avenged –
Accused of what till now my heart disdained –
Too faithful, though to bitter bondage chained.
Yes, smile! – but he had little cause to sneer,
I was not treacherous then – nor thou too dear: 325
But he has said it – and the jealous well,
Those tyrants, teasing, tempting to rebel,
Deserve the fate their fretting lips foretell.
I never loved – he bought me – somewhat high –
Since with me came a heart he could not buy. 330
I was a slave unmurmuring; he hath said,
But for his rescue I with thee had fled.
'Twas false thou know'st – but let such augurs rue,
Their words are omens Insult renders true.
Nor was thy respite granted to my prayer; 335
This fleeting grace was only to prepare
New torments for thy life, and my despair.
Mine too he threatens; but his dotage still
Would fain reserve me for his lordly will:
When wearier of these fleeting charms and me, 340

314

There yawns the sack – and yonder rolls the sea!
What, am I then a toy for dotard's play,
To wear but till the gilding frets away?
I saw thee – loved thee – owe thee all – would save,
If but to shew how grateful is a slave.   345
But had he not thus menaced fame and life,
(And well he keeps his oaths pronounced in strife)
I still had saved thee – but the Pacha spared.
Now I am all thine own – for all prepared:
Thou lov'st me not – nor know'st – or but the worst.   350
Alas! this love – that hatred are the first –
Oh! could'st thou prove my truth, thou would'st not start,
Nor fear the fire that lights an Eastern heart,
'Tis now the beacon of thy safety – now
It points within the port a Mainote prow: 355
But in one chamber, where our path must lead,
There sleeps – he must not wake – the oppressor Seyd!'

'Gulnare – Gulnare – I never felt till now
My abject fortune, withered fame so low:
Seyd is mine enemy: had swept my band   360
From earth with ruthless but with open hand,
And therefore came I, in my bark of war,
To smite the smiter with the scimitar;
Such is my weapon – not the secret knife –
Who spares a woman's seeks not slumber's life.   365
Thine saved I gladly, Lady, not for this –
Let me not deem that mercy shewn amiss.
Now fare thee well – more peace be with thy breast!
Night wears apace – my last of earthly rest!'

'Rest! Rest! by sunrise must thy sinews shake,   370
And thy limbs writhe around the ready stake.
I heard the order – saw – I will not see –
If thou wilt perish, I will fall with thee.
My life – my love – my hatred – all below
Are on this cast – Corsair! 'tis but a blow!   375
Without it flight were idle – how evade
His sure pursuit? my wrongs too unrepaid,
My youth disgraced – the long, long wasted years,
One blow shall cancel with our future fears;
But since the dagger suits thee less than brand,   380
I'll try the firmness of a female hand.
The guards are gained – one moment all were o'er –
Corsair! we meet in safety or no more;
If errs my feeble hand, the morning cloud
Will hover o'er thy scaffold, and my shroud.'   385

After Conrad's refusal, Gulnare herself kills Pasha Seyd. Conrad sees the
blood on her cheek:

        [...]
        He had seen battle – he had brooded lone
        O'er promised pangs to sentenced guilt foreshown;
        He had been tempted – chastened – and the chain   420

315

Yet on his arms might ever there remain:
But ne'er from strife – captivity – remorse –
From all his feelings in their inmost force –
So thrilled – so shuddered every creeping vein,
As now they froze before that purple stain.   425
That spot of blood, that light but guilty streak,
Had banished all the beauty from her cheek!
Blood he had viewed – could view unmoved – but then
It flowed in combat, or was shed by men!

The two make their escape and eventually meet Conrad's former crew
under the command of Anselmo:

[...]
These greetings o'er, the feelings that o'erflow,
Yet grieve to win him back without a blow;
They sailed prepared for vengeance – had they known
A woman's hand secured that deed her own,
She were their queen – less scrupulous are they   510
Than haughty Conrad how they win their way.
With many an asking smile, and wondering stare,
They whisper round, and gaze upon Gulnare;
And her, at once above – beneath her sex,
Whom blood appalled not, their regards perplex.   515
To Conrad turns her faint imploring eye,
She drops her veil, and stands in silence by;
Her arms are meekly folded on that breast,
Which – Conrad safe – to fate resigned the rest.
Though worse than phrenzy could that bosom fill,   520
Extreme in love or hate, in good or ill,
The worst of crimes had left her woman still!

(17)
This Conrad marked, and felt – ah! could he less?
Hate of that deed – but grief for her distress;
What she has done no tears can wash away,   525
And heaven must punish on its angry day:
But – it was done: he knew, whate'er her guilt,
For him that poignard smote, that blood was spilt;
And he was free! – and she for him had given
Her all on earth, and more than all in heaven!   530
And now he turned him to that dark-eyed slave
Whose brow was bowed beneath the glance he gave,
Who now seemed changed and humble: – faint and meek,
But varying oft the colour of her cheek
To deeper shades of paleness – all its red   535
That fearful spot which stained it from the dead!
He took that hand – it trembled – now too late –
So soft in love – so wildly nerved in hate;
He clasped that hand – it trembled – and his own
had lost its firmness, and his voice its tone.   540
'Gulnare!' – but she replied not – 'dear Gulnare!'
She raised her eye – her only answer there –
At once she sought and sunk in his embrace:
If he had driven her from that resting place,

316

His had been more or less than mortal heart, 545
But – good or ill – it bade her not depart.
Perchance, but for the bodings of his breast,
His latest virtue then had joined the rest.
Yet even Medora might forgive the kiss
That asked from form so fair no more than this, 550
The first, the last that Frailty stole from Faith –
To lips where Love had lavished all his breath,
To lips – whose broken sighs such fragrance fling,
As he had fanned them freshly with his wing!

On their return however Medora, believing Conrad to have been killed, has herself died of grief, and Conrad sets off again, alone:

[…]
His heart was formed for softness – warped to wrong;
Betrayed too early, and beguiled too long;
Each feeling pure – as falls the dropping dew
Within the grot; like that had hardened too; 665
Less clear, perchance, its earthly trials passed,
But sunk, and chilled, and petrified at last.
Yet tempests wear, and lightning cleaves the rock;
If such his heart, so shattered it the shock.
There grew one flower beneath its rugged brow, 670
Though dark the shade – it sheltered, – saved till now.
The thunder came – that bolt hath blasted both,
The Granite's firmness, and the Lily's growth:
The gentle plant hath left no leaf to tell
Its tale, but shrunk and withered where it fell, 675
And of its cold protector, blacken round
But shivered fragments on the barren ground!

(24)
'Tis morn – to venture on his lonely hour
Few dare; though now Anselmo sought his tower.
He was not there – nor seen along the shore; 680
Ere night, alarmed, their isle is traversed o'er:
Another morn – another bids them seek,
And shout his name till echo waxeth weak;
Mount – grotto – cavern – valley searched in vain,
They find on shore a sea-boat's broken chain: 685
Their hope revives – they follow o'er the main.
'Tis idle all – moons roll on moons away,
And Conrad comes not – came not since that day:
Nor trace, nor tidings of his doom declare
Where lives his grief, or perished his despair! 690
Long mourned his band whom none could mourn beside;
And fair the monument they gave his bride:
For him they raise not the recording stone –
His death yet dubious, deeds too widely known;
He left a Corsair's name to other times, 695
Linked with one virtue, and a thousand crimes.

317

The uncanny

by Sigmund Freud

From: Strachey, J. (trans.) (1955) *The Complete Psychological Works of Sigmund Freud, Volume XVII (1917–1919): An Infantile Neurosis and Other Works*, The Hogarth Press, pp.227–233, 249–252.

[Of the 'uncanny' it has been said] 'In telling a story, one of the most successful devices for easily creating uncanny effects is to leave the reader in uncertainty whether a particular figure in the story is a human being or an automaton, and to do it in such a way that his attention is not focused directly upon his uncertainty, so that he may not be led to go into the matter and clear it up immediately. That, as we have said, would quickly dissipate the peculiar emotional effect of the thing. E. T. A. Hoffmann has repeatedly employed this psychological artifice with success in his fantastic narratives.'

This observation, undoubtedly a correct one, refers primarily to the story of 'The Sand-Man' in Hoffmann's *Nachtstücken*,[1] which contains the original of Olympia, the doll that appears in the first act of Offenbach's opera, *Tales of Hoffmann.* But I cannot think – and I hope most readers of the story will agree with me – that the theme of the doll Olympia, who is to all appearances a living being, is by any means the only, or indeed the most important, element that must be held responsible for the quite unparalleled atmosphere of uncanniness evoked by the story. Nor is this atmosphere heightened by the fact that the author himself treats the episode of Olympia with a faint touch of satire and uses it to poke fun at the young man's idealization of his mistress. The main theme of the story is, on the contrary, something different, something which gives it its name, and which is always re-introduced at critical moments: it is the theme of the 'Sand-Man' who tears out children's eyes.

This fantastic tale opens with the childhood recollections of the student Nathaniel. In spite of his present happiness, he cannot banish the memories associated with the mysterious and terrifying death of his beloved father. On certain evenings his mother used to send the children to bed early, warning them that 'the Sand-Man was coming'; and, sure enough, Nathaniel would not fail to hear the heavy tread of a visitor, with whom his father would then be occupied for the evening. When questioned about the Sand-Man, his mother, it is true, denied that such a person existed except as a figure of speech; but his nurse could give him more definite information: 'He's a wicked man who comes when children won't go to bed, and throws handfuls of sand in their eyes so that they jump out of their heads all bleeding. Then he puts the eyes in a sack and carries them off to the half-moon to feed his children. They sit up there in their nest, and their beaks are hooked like owls' beaks, and they use them to peck up naughty boys' and girls' eyes with.'

Although little Nathaniel was sensible and old enough not to credit the figure of the Sand-Man with such gruesome attributes, yet the dread of him became fixed in his heart. He determined to find out what the Sand-Man looked like; and one evening, when the Sand-Man was expected again, he hid in his father's study. He recognized the visitor as the lawyer Coppelius, a repulsive person whom the children were frightened of when he occasionally came to a meal; and he now identified this Coppelius with the dreaded Sand-Man. As regards the rest of the scene, Hoffmann already leaves us in doubt whether what we are witnessing is the first delirium of the panic-stricken boy, or a succession of events which are to be regarded in the story as being real. His father and the guest are at work at a brazier with glowing flames. The little eavesdropper hears Coppelius call out: 'Eyes here! Eyes here!' and betrays himself by screaming aloud. Coppelius seizes him and is on the point of dropping bits of red-hot coal from the fire into his eyes, and then of throwing them into the brazier, but his father begs him off and saves his eyes. After this the boy falls into a deep swoon; and a long illness brings his experience to an end. Those who decide in favour of the rationalistic interpretation of the Sand-Man will not fail to recognize in the child's phantasy the persisting influence of his nurse's story. The bits of sand that are to be thrown into the child's eyes turn into bits of red-hot coal from the flames; and in both cases they are intended to make his eyes jump out. In the course of another visit of the Sand-Man's, a year later, his father is killed in his study by an explosion. The lawyer Coppelius disappears from the place without leaving a trace behind.

Nathaniel, now a student, believes that he has recognized this phantom of horror from his childhood in an itinerant optician, an Italian called Giuseppe Coppola, who at his university town, offers him weather-glasses for sale. When Nathaniel refuses, the man goes on: 'Not weather-glasses? not weather-glasses? also got fine eyes, fine eyes!' The student's terror is allayed when he finds that the proffered eyes are only harmless spectacles, and he buys a pocket spy-glass from Coppola. With its aid he looks across into Professor Spalanzani's house opposite and there spies Spalanzani's beautiful, but strangely silent and motionless daughter, Olympia. He soon falls in love with her so violently that, because of her, he quite forgets the clever and sensible girl to whom he is betrothed. But Olympia is an automaton whose clock-work has been made by Spalanzani, and whose eyes have been put in by Coppola, the Sand-Man. The student surprises the two Masters quarrelling over their handiwork. The optician carries off the wooden eyeless doll; and the mechanician, Spalanzani, picks up Olympia's bleeding eyes from the ground and throws them at Nathaniel's breast, saying that Coppola had stolen them from the student. Nathaniel succumbs to a fresh attack of madness, and in his delirium his recollection of his father's death is mingled with this new experience. 'Hurry up! hurry up! ring of fire!' he cries. 'Spin about, ring of fire – Hurrah! Hurry up, wooden doll! lovely wooden doll, spin about –.' He then falls upon the professor, Olympia's 'father', and tries to strangle him.

Rallying from a long and serious illness, Nathaniel seems at last to have recovered. He intends to marry his betrothed, with whom he has become reconciled. One day he and she are walking through the city market-place, over which the high tower of the Town Hall throws its huge shadow. On the girl's suggestion, they climb the tower, leaving her brother, who is walking with them, down below. From the top, Clara's attention is drawn to a curious object moving along the street. Nathaniel looks at this thing through Coppola's spy-glass, which he finds in his pocket, and falls into a new attack of madness. Shouting 'Spin about, wooden doll!' he tries to throw the girl into the gulf below. Her brother, brought to her side by her cries, rescues her and hastens down with her to safety. On the tower above, the madman rushes round, shrieking 'Ring of fire, spin about!' – and we know the origin of the words. Among the people who begin to gather below there comes forward the figure of the lawyer Coppelius, who has suddenly returned. We may suppose that it was his approach, seen through the spy-glass, which threw Nathaniel into his fit of madness. As the onlookers prepare to go up and overpower the madman, Coppelius laughs and says: 'Wait a bit; he'll come down of himself.' Nathaniel suddenly stands still, catches sight of Coppelius, and with a wild shriek 'Yes! "Fine eyes – fine eyes"!' flings himself over the parapet. While he lies on the paving-stones with a shattered skull the Sand-Man vanishes in the throng.

This short summary leaves no doubt, I think, that the feeling of something uncanny is directly attached to the figure of the Sand-Man, that is, to the idea of being robbed of one's eyes, and that Jentsch's point of an intellectual uncertainty has nothing to do with the effect. Uncertainty whether an object is living or inanimate, which admittedly applied to the doll Olympia, is quite irrelevant in connection with this other, more striking instance of uncanniness. It is true that the writer creates a kind of uncertainty in us in the beginning by not letting us know, no doubt purposely, whether he is taking us into the real world or into a purely fantastic one of his own creation. He has, of course, a right to do either; and if he chooses to stage his action in a world peopled with spirits, demons and ghosts, as Shakespeare does in *Hamlet*, in *Macbeth* and, in a different sense, in *The Tempest* and *A Midsummer-Night's Dream*, we must bow to his decision and treat his setting as though it were real for as long as we put ourselves into his hands. But this uncertainty disappears in the course of Hoffmann's story, and we perceive that he intends to make us, too, look through the demon optician's spectacles or spy-glass – perhaps, indeed, that the author in his very own person once peered through such an instrument. For the conclusion of the story makes it quite clear that Coppola the optician really *is* the lawyer Coppelius[2] and also, therefore, the Sand-Man.

There is no question therefore, of any intellectual uncertainty here: we know now that we are not supposed to be looking on at the products of a madman's imagination, behind which we, with the superiority of rational minds, are able to detect the sober truth; and yet this knowledge does not lessen the impression of uncanniness in the least degree. The theory of intellectual uncertainty is thus incapable of explaining that impression.

We know from psycho-analytic experience, however, that the fear of damaging or losing one's eyes is a terrible one in children. Many adults retain their apprehensiveness in this respect, and no physical injury is so much dreaded by them as an injury to the eye. We are accustomed to say, too, that we will treasure a thing as the apple of our eye. A study of dreams, phantasies and myths has taught us that anxiety about one's eyes, the fear of going blind, is often enough a substitute for the dread of being castrated. The self-blinding of the mythical criminal, Oedipus, was simply a mitigated form of the punishment of castration – the only punishment that was adequate for him by the *lex talionis*. We may try on rationalistic grounds to deny that fears about the eye are derived from the fear of castration, and may argue that it is very natural that so precious an organ as the eye should be guarded by a proportionate dread. Indeed, we might go further and say that the fear of castration itself contains no other significance and no deeper secret than a justifiable dread of this rational kind. But this view does not account adequately for the substitutive relation between the eye and the male organ which is seen to exist in dreams and myths and phantasies; nor can it dispel the impression that the threat of being castrated in especial excites a peculiarly violent and obscure emotion, and that this emotion is what first gives the idea of losing other organs its intense colouring. All further doubts are removed when we learn the details of their 'castration complex' from the analysis of neurotic patients, and realize its immense importance in their mental life.

Moreover, I would not recommend any opponent of the psycho-analytic view to select this particular story of the Sand-Man with which to support his argument that anxiety about the eyes has nothing to do with the castration complex. For why does Hoffmann bring the anxiety about eyes into such intimate connection with the father's death? And why does the Sand-Man always appear as a disturber of love? He separates the unfortunate Nathaniel from his betrothed and from her brother, his best friend; he destroys the second object of his love, Olympia, the lovely doll; and he drives him into suicide at the moment when he has won back his Clara and is about to be happily united to her. Elements in the story like these, and many others, seem arbitrary and meaningless so long as we deny all connection between fears about the eye and castration; but they become intelligible as soon as we replace the Sand-Man by the dreaded father at whose hands castration is expected.[3]

We shall venture, therefore, to refer the uncanny effect of the Sand-Man to the anxiety belonging to the castration complex of childhood. But having reached the idea that we can make an infantile factor such as this responsible for feelings of uncanniness, we are encouraged to see whether we can apply it to other instances of the uncanny. We find in the story of the Sand-Man the other theme on which Jentsch lays stress, of a doll which appears to be alive. Jentsch believes that a particularly favourable condition for awakening uncanny feelings is created when there is intellectual uncertainty whether an object is alive or not, and when an inanimate object becomes too much like an animate one. Now, dolls are of course rather closely connected with childhood life. We remember that in their early games children do not distinguish at all sharply between living and inanimate objects, and that they are especially fond of treating their dolls like live people. In fact, I have occasionally heard a woman patient declare that even at the age of eight she had still been convinced that her dolls would be certain to come to life if she were to look at them in a particular, extremely concentrated, way. So that here, too, it is not difficult to discover a factor from childhood. But, curiously enough, while the Sand-Man story deals with the arousing of an early childhood fear, the idea of a 'living doll' excites no fear at all; children have no fear of their dolls coming to life, they may even desire it. The source of uncanny feelings would not, therefore, be an infantile fear in this case, but rather an infantile wish or even merely an infantile belief. There seems to be a contradiction here; but perhaps it is only a complication, which may be helpful to us later on.

321

Hoffmann is the unrivalled master of the uncanny in literature. [...]

Our conclusion could then be stated thus: an uncanny experience occurs either when infantile complexes which have been repressed are once more revived by some impression, or when primitive beliefs which have been surmounted seem once more to be confirmed. Finally, we must not let our predilection for smooth solutions and lucid exposition blind us to the fact that these two classes of uncanny experience are not always sharply distinguishable. When we consider that primitive beliefs are most intimately connected with infantile complexes, and are, in fact, based on them, we shall not be greatly astonished to find that the distinction is often a hazy one.

The uncanny as it is depicted in *literature*, in stories and imaginative productions, merits in truth a separate discussion. Above all, it is a much more fertile province than the uncanny in real life, for it contains the whole of the latter and something more besides, something that cannot be found in real life. The contrast between what has been repressed and what has been surmounted cannot be transposed on to the uncanny in fiction without profound modification; for the realm of phantasy depends for its effect on the fact that its content is not submitted to reality-testing. The somewhat paradoxical result is that *in the first place a great deal that is not uncanny in fiction would be so if it happened in real life; and in the second place that there are many more means of creating uncanny effects in fiction than there are in real life.*

The imaginative writer has this licence among many others, that he can select his world of representation so that it either coincides with the realities we are familiar with or departs from them in what particulars he pleases. We accept his ruling in every case. In fairy tales, for instance, the world of reality is left behind from the very start, and the animistic system of beliefs is frankly adopted. Wish-fulfilments, secret powers, omnipotence of thoughts, animation of inanimate objects, all the elements so common in fairy stories, can exert no uncanny influence here; for, as we have learnt, that feeling cannot arise unless there is a conflict of judgement as to whether things which have been 'surmounted' and are regarded as incredible may not, after all, be possible; and this problem is eliminated from the outset by the postulates of the world of fairy tales. Thus we see that fairy stories, which have furnished us with most of the contradictions to our hypothesis of the uncanny, confirm the first part of our proposition – that in the realm of fiction many things are not uncanny which would be so if they happened in real life. In the case of these stories there are other contributory factors, which we shall briefly touch upon later.

The creative writer can also choose a setting which though less imaginary than the world of fairy tales, does yet differ from the real world by admitting superior spiritual beings such as daemonic spirits or ghosts of the dead. So long as they remain within their setting of poetic reality, such figures lose any uncanniness which they might possess. The souls in Dante's *Inferno*, or the supernatural apparitions in Shakespeare's *Hamlet, Macbeth* or *Julius Caesar,* may be gloomy and terrible enough, but they are no more really uncanny than Homer's jovial world of gods. We adapt our judgement to the imaginary reality imposed on us by the writer, and regard souls, spirits and ghosts as though their existence had the same validity as our own has in material reality. In this case too we avoid all trace of the uncanny.

The situation is altered as soon as the writer pretends to move in the world of common reality. In this case he accepts as well all the conditions operating to produce uncanny feelings in real life; and everything that would have an uncanny effect in reality has it in his story. But in this case he can even increase his effect and multiply it far beyond what could happen in reality, by bringing about events which never or very rarely happen in fact. In doing this he is in a sense betraying us to the superstitiousness which we have ostensibly surmounted; he deceives us by promising to give us the sober truth, and then after all overstepping it. We react to his inventions as we would have reacted to real experiences; by the time we have seen through his trick it is already too late and the author has achieved his object. But it must be added that his success is not unalloyed. We retain a feeling of dissatisfaction, a kind of grudge against the attempted deceit. I have noticed this particularly after reading Schnitzler's *Die Weissagung* [*The Prophecy*] and similar stories which flirt with the supernatural. However, the writer has one more means which he can use in order to avoid our recalcitrance and at the same time to improve his chances of success. He can keep us in the dark for a long time about the precise nature of the presuppositions on which the world he writes about is based, or he can cunningly and ingeniously avoid any definite information on the point to the last. Speaking generally, however, we find a confirmation of the second part of our proposition – that fiction presents more opportunities for creating uncanny feelings than are possible in real life.

Strictly speaking, all these complications relate only to that class of the uncanny which proceeds from forms of thought that have been surmounted. The class which proceeds from repressed complexes is more resistant and remains as powerful in fiction as in real experience, subject to one exception. [...] The uncanny belonging to the first class – that proceeding from forms of thought that have been surmounted – retains its character not only in experience but in fiction as well, so long as the setting is one of material reality; but where it is given an arbitrary and artificial setting in fiction, it is apt to lose that character.

We have clearly not exhausted the possibilities of poetic licence and the privileges enjoyed by story-writers in evoking or in excluding an uncanny feeling. In the main we adopt an unvarying passive attitude towards real experience and are subject to the influence of our physical environment. But the story-teller has a *peculiarly* directive power over us; by means of the moods he can put us into, he is able to guide the current of our emotions, to dam it up in one direction and make it flow in another, and he often obtains a great variety of effects from the same material. All this is nothing new, and has doubtless long since been fully taken into account by students of aesthetics. We have drifted into this field of research half involuntarily, through the temptation to explain certain instances which contradicted our theory of the causes of the uncanny. Accordingly we will now return to the examination of a few of those instances.

We have already asked why it is that the severed hand in the story of the treasure of Rhampsinitus has no uncanny effect in the way that the severed hand has in Hauff's story. The question seems to have gained in importance now that we have recognized that the class of the uncanny which proceeds from repressed complexes is the more resistant of the two. The answer is easy. In the Herodotus story our thoughts are concentrated much more on the superior cunning of the master-thief than on the feelings of the princess. The princess may very well have had an uncanny feeling, indeed she very probably fell into a swoon; but *we* have no such sensations, for we put ourselves in the thief's place, not in hers. In Nestroy's farce, *Der Zerrissene* [*The Torn Man*], another means is used to avoid any impression of the uncanny in the scene in which the fleeing man, convinced that he is a murderer, lifts up one trapdoor after another and each time sees what he takes to be the ghost of his victim rising up out of it. He calls out in despair, 'But I've only killed *one* man. Why this ghastly multiplication?' We know what went before this scene and do not share his error, so what must be uncanny to him has an irresistibly comic effect on us. Even a 'real' ghost, as in Oscar Wilde's *Canterville Ghost*, loses all power of at least arousing *gruesome* feelings in us as soon as the author begins to amuse himself by being ironical about it and allows liberties to be taken with it. Thus we see how independent emotional effects can be of the actual subject-matter in the world of fiction. In fairy stories feelings of fear – including therefore uncanny feelings – are ruled out altogether. We understand this, and that is why we ignore any opportunities we find in them for developing such feelings.

Concerning the factors of silence, solitude and darkness, we can only say that they are actually elements in the production of the infantile anxiety from which the majority of human beings have never become quite free. This problem has been discussed from a psycho-analytic point of view elsewhere.

Notes

1   Hoffmann's *Sämtliche Werke*, Grisebach Edition, 3. [A translation of 'The Sand-Man' is included in *Eight Tales of Hoffmann*, translated by J. M. Cohen, London, Pan Books, 1952.]

2   Frau Dr. Rank has pointed out the association of the name with '*coppella*' = crucible, connecting it with the chemical operations that caused the father's death; and also with '*coppo*' = eye-socket. [Except in the first (1919) edition this footnote was attached, it seems erroneously, to the first occurrence of the name Coppelius on this page.]

3   In fact, Hoffmann's imaginative treatment of his material has not made such wild confusion of its elements that we cannot reconstruct their original arrangement. In the story of Nathaniel's childhood, the figures of his father and Coppelius represent the two opposites into which the father-imago is split by his ambivalence; whereas the one threatens to blind him – that is, to castrate him –, the other, the 'good' father, intercedes for his sight. The part of the complex which is most strongly repressed, the death-wish against the 'bad' father, finds expression in the death of the 'good' father, and Coppelius is made answerable for it. This pair of fathers is represented later, in his student days, by Professor Spalanzani and Coppola the optician. The Professor is in himself a member of the father-series, and Coppola is recognized as identical with Coppelius the lawyer. Just as they used before to work together over the secret brazier, so now they have jointly created the doll Olympia; the Professor is even called the father of Olympia. This double

occurrence of activity in common betrays them as divisions of the father-imago: both the mechanician and the optician were the father of Nathaniel (and of Olympia as well). In the frightening scene in childhood, Coppelius, after sparing Nathaniel's eyes, had screwed off his arms and legs as an experiment; that is, he had worked on him as a mechanician would on a doll. This singular feature, which seems quite outside the picture of the Sand-Man, introduces a new castration equivalent; but it also points to the inner identity of Coppelius with his later counterpart, Spalanzani the mechanician, and prepares us for the interpretation of Olympia. This automatic doll can be nothing else than a materialization of Nathaniel's feminine attitude towards his father in his infancy. Her fathers, Spalanzani and Coppola, are, after all, nothing but new editions, reincarnations of Nathaniel's pair of fathers. Spalanzani's otherwise incomprehensible statement that the optician has stolen Nathaniel's eyes, so as to set them in the doll, now becomes significant as supplying evidence of the identity of Olympia and Nathaniel. Olympia is, as it were, a dissociated complex of Nathaniel's which confronts him as a person, and Nathaniel's enslavement to this complex is expressed in his senseless obsessive love for Olympia. We may with justice call love of this kind narcissistic, and we can understand why someone who has fallen victim to it should relinquish the real, external object of his love. The psychological truth of the situation in which the young man, fixated upon his father by his castration complex, becomes incapable of loving a woman, is amply proved by numerous analyses of patients whose story, though less fantastic, is hardly less tragic than that of the student Nathaniel.

Hoffmann was the child of an unhappy marriage. When he was three years old, his father left his small family, and was never united to them again. According to Grisebach, in his biographical introduction to Hoffmann's works, the writer's relation to his father was always a most sensitive subject with him.

The concept of Romanticism in literary history

by René Wellek

From: Wellek, R. (1963) *Concepts of Criticism*, ed. S.G. Nichols Jr., Yale University Press, pp.160–161, 178–193, 195–7. Footnotes edited and renumbered from the original.

If we examine the characteristics of the actual literature which called itself or was called 'romantic' all over the continent, we find throughout Europe the same conceptions of poetry and of the workings and nature of poetic imagination, the same conception of nature and its relation to man, and basically the same poetic style, with a use of imagery, symbolism, and myth which is clearly distinct from that of eighteenth-century neoclassicism. This conclusion might be strengthened or modified by attention to other frequently discussed elements: subjectivism, mediaevalism, folklore, etc. But the following three criteria should be particularly convincing, since each is central for one aspect of the practice of literature: imagination for the view of poetry, nature for the view of the world, and symbol and myth for poetic style [...]

The great poets of the English romantic movement constitute a fairly coherent group, with the same view of poetry and the same conception of imagination, the same view of nature and mind. They share also a poetic style, a use of imagery, symbolism, and myth, which is quite distinct from anything that had been practiced by the eighteenth century, and which was felt by their contemporaries to be obscure and almost unintelligible.

The affinity of the concepts of imagination among the English romantic poets scarcely needs demonstration. Blake considers all nature to be 'imagination itself.' Our highest aim is:

> To see a World in a Grain of Sand:
> And a Heaven in a Wild Flower,
> Hold Infinity in the palm of your hand
> And Eternity in an hour.[1]

Thus imagination is not merely the power of visualization, somewhere in between sense and reason, which it had been to Aristotle or Addison, nor even the inventive power of the poet, which by Hume and many other eighteenth-century theorists was conceived of as a 'combination of innate sensibility, the power of association, and the faculty of conception,'[2] but a creative power by which the mind 'gains insight into reality, reads nature as a symbol of something behind or within nature not ordinarily perceived.'[3] Thus imagination is the basis of Blake's rejection of the mechanistic world picture, the basis of an idealistic epistemology –

> The Sun's Light when he unfolds it
> Depends on the Organ that beholds it;[4]

and, of course, the basis of an aesthetics, the justification of art and his own peculiar kind of art. This conception of imagination sufficiently justifies the necessity of myth and of metaphor and symbol as its vehicle.

The concept of the imagination in Wordsworth is fundamentally the same, though Wordsworth draws more heavily on eighteenth-century theories and compromises with naturalism. Still, [...] imagination is for him 'creative,' an insight into the nature of reality and hence the basic justification of art. The poet becomes a living soul who 'sees into the life of things.' Imagination is thus an organ of knowledge which transforms objects, sees through them, even if they are only the 'meanest flower' or the humble ass, an idiot boy, or simply a child: 'mighty prophet, seer blest.'

The whole of the *Prelude* is a history of the poet's imagination which, in a central passage of the last book, is called

> Another name for absolute power
> And clearest insight, amplitude of mind,
> And Reason in her most exalted mood.[5]

In a letter to Landor, Wordsworth tells him that 'in poetry it is the imaginative only, i.e. that which is conversant or turns upon Infinity, that powerfully affects me.' 'All great poets are in this view powerful Religionists.'[6]

It is hardly necessary to explain what a central role the imagination plays in Coleridge's theory and practice. There is a book by I.A. Richards, *Coleridge on Imagination,* and recently R.P. Warren has carefully related the theory to the *Rime of the Ancient Mariner.*[7] The key passage in *Biographia Literaria* on primary and secondary imagination is too well known to need quoting. It is Schellingian in its formulation – on the whole, Coleridge's theory is closely dependent on the Germans. His term for 'imagination,' the 'esemplastic power,' is a translation of 'Einbildungskraft,' based on a fanciful etymology of the German.[8] But, when Coleridge ignores his technical jargon, as in the ode *Dejection* (1802), he still speaks of the 'shaping spirit of the imagination,' of imagination as a 'dim analogue of creation, not all that we *believe,* but all that we can *conceive* of creation.'[9] If Coleridge had not known the Germans, he would have been able to expound a neo-Platonic theory, just as Shelley did in his *Defense of Poetry.*

Shelley's *Defense of Poetry* is almost identical, in general conception, with Coleridge's theory. Imagination is the 'principle of synthesis.' Poetry may be defined as the 'expression of the imagination.' A poet 'participates in the eternal, the infinite, and the one.' Poetry lifts the veil from the 'hidden beauty of the world, and makes familiar objects be as if they were not familiar.' 'Poetry redeems from decay the visitations of the divinity in man.' To Shelley imagination is creative, and the poet's imagination is an instrument of knowledge of the real. Shelley, more sharply than any other English poet with the exception of Blake, states that the poetic moment is the moment of vision; that the words are but a 'feeble shadow,' that the mind in composition is a 'fading coal.'[10] In Shelley we find the most radical divorce between the poetic faculty and will and consciousness.

The affinities and fundamental identities of Keats' views are obvious, though Keats (under the influence of Hazlitt) has more of the sensationalist vocabulary than either Coleridge or Shelley. But he also says: 'What the imagination seizes as Beauty must be Truth whether it existed before or not.'[11] Clarence D. Thorpe, in analyzing all of Keats' relevant scattered pronouncements, concludes: 'Such is the power of creative imagination, a seeing, reconciling, combining force that seizes the old, penetrates beneath its surface, disengages the truth slumbering there, and, building afresh, bodies forth anew a reconstructed universe in fair forms of artistic power and beauty.'[12] This could be a summary of the theories of imagination of all the romantic poets.

Clearly, such a theory implies a theory of reality and, especially, of nature. There are individual differences among the great romantic poets concerning the conception of nature. But all of them share a common objection to the mechanistic universe of the eighteenth century – even though Wordsworth admires Newton and accepts him, at least in the orthodox interpretation. All romantic poets conceived of nature as an organic whole, on the analogue of man rather than a concourse of atoms – a nature that is not divorced from aesthetic values, which are just as real (or rather more real) than the abstractions of science.

Blake stands somewhat apart. He violently objects to the eighteenth-century cosmology, personified by Newton.

> May God us keep
> From Single Vision and Newton's sleep.[13]

Blake's writings are also full of condemnations of Locke and Bacon, atomism, deism, natural religion, and so forth. But he does not share the romantic deification of nature; he comments expressly on Wordsworth's preface to the *Excursion*: 'You shall not bring me down to believe such fitting and fitted.'[14] To Blake nature is everywhere fallen. It fell with man; the fall of man and the creation of the physical world were the same event. In the Golden Age to come, nature will (with man) be restored to her pristine glory. Man and nature are, in Blake, not only continuous, but emblematic of each other:

> Each grain of Sand,
> Every Stone on the Land,
> Each rock and each hill,
> Each fountain and rill,
> Each herb and each tree,
> Mountain, hill, earth, and sea,
> Cloud, Meteor, and Star
> Are Men Seen Afar.[15]

In *Milton* especially, nature appears as man's body turned inside out. The ridges of mountains across the world are Albion's fractured spine. Nothing exists outside Albion; sun, moon, stars, the center of the earth, and the depth of the sea were all within his mind and body. Time even is a pulsation of the artery, and space a globule of blood. The crabbed symbolism, the strident tone have kept these later poems from being widely read; but the books by Damon, Percival, Schorer, and Frye[16] have shown the subtlety and coherence of Blake's speculations which set him in the great tradition of *Naturphilosophie* as it comes down from Plato's *Timaeus* to Paracelsus, Böhme, and Swedenborg.

In Wordsworth's conception of nature there is a shift from something like animistic pantheism to a conception reconcilable with traditional Christianity. Nature is animated, alive, filled with God or the Spirit of the World; it is mysteriously present, it gives a discipline of fear and ministry of plea-

328

sure. Nature is also a language, a system of symbols. The rocks, the crags, the streams on Simplon Pass

> Were all like workings of one mind, the features
> Of the same face, blossoms upon one tree;
> Characters of the great Apocalypse
> The types and symbols of Eternity.[17]

We would misunderstand idealistic epistemology if we questioned the 'objectivity' which Wordworth ascribes to these conceptions. It is a dialectical relation, not a mere subjectivist imposition, in spite of such passages as

> ... from thyself it comes, that thou must give,
> Else never canst receive.[18]

The mind must collaborate and it is its very nature that it should be so.

> ... my voice proclaims
> How exquisitely the individual Mind
> (And the progressive powers perhaps no less
> Of the whole species) to the external World
> Is fitted: – and how exquisitely, too ...
> The external world is fitted to the Mind;
> And the creation (by no lower name
> Can it be called) which they with blended might
> Accomplish.[19]

The ancestry of these ideas in Cudworth, Shaftesbury, Berkeley, and others is obvious; there are certain poetic anticipations in Akenside and Collins; but, in Wordsworth, a natural philosophy, a metaphysical concept of nature, enters poetry and finds a highly individual expression – the brooding presence of the hills, of the firm, eternal forms of nature, combined with a vivid sense of the almost dreamlike unreality of the world.

The general concept of nature he shares with his friend Coleridge. We could easily match all the fundamental concepts of Wordsworth in Coleridge; probably their phrasing is due to the influence of Coleridge, who early was a student of the Cambridge Platonists and of Berkeley.

> The one Life within us and abroad ...
> And what if all of animated nature ...
> Plastic and vast, one intellectual breeze.
> At once the Soul of each, and God of all ...

the 'eternal language, which thy God utters. ...' 'Symbolical, one mighty alphabet,' and the conception of subject-object relation:

> We receive but what we give
> And in our life alone does Nature live![20]

– these are quotations from the early poetry. The later Coleridge developed an elaborate philosophy of nature which leans heavily on Schelling's and Steffens' *Naturphilosophie*. Nature is consistently interpreted by analogy with the progress of man to self-consciousness, and Coleridge indulges in all the contemporary speculative chemistry and physics (electricity, magnetism) to buttress a position which is near to vitalism or panpsychism.

Echoes of this contemporary science also permeate Shelley's conceptions and even images. There are many allusions in his poetry to chemical, electrical, and magnetic theories – to theories expounded by Erasmus Darwin and Humphrey Davy. But, in general terms, Shelley mainly echoes Wordsworth and Coleridge on the 'spirit of nature.' There is the same concept of the vitality of nature, its continuity with man, its emblematic language. There is also the concept of the cooperation and interrelation of subject and object, as in the beginning of *Mont Blanc*:

> The everlasting universe of things
> Flows through the mind, and rolls its rapid waves,
> Now dark – now glittering – now reflecting gloom –
> Now lending splendor, where from secret springs
> The source of human thought its tribute brings
> Of waters, – with a sound but half its own.

This seems to say: There is nothing outside the mind of man, but the receptive function of the stream of consciousness is very much larger than the tiny active principle in the mind.

> My own, my human mind, which passively
> Now renders and receives fast influencings,
> Holding an unremitting interchange
> With the clear universe of things around.

Here we have, in spite of the stress on the passivity of the mind, a clear conception of a give and take, of an interchange between its creative and purely receptive principles. Shelley conceives of nature as one phenomenal flux; he sings of clouds, wind, and water rather than, like Wordsworth, of the mountains or the 'soul of lonely places.' But he does not, of course, stop with nature, but seeks the higher unity behind it:

> Life, like a dome of many-colored glass,
> Stains the white radiance of Eternity.[21]

In the highest ecstasy, all individuality and particularity are abolished by the great harmony of the world. But in Shelley, in contrast to Blake or Wordsworth who calmly look into the life of things, the ideal itself dissolves; his voice falters; the highest exaltation becomes a total loss of personality, an instrument of death and annihilation.

In Keats, the romantic conception of nature occurs, but only in attenuated form, though it would be hard to deny the poet of *Endymion* or the 'Ode to a Nightingale' an intimate relation to nature and to the nature mythology of the ancients. *Hyperion* (1820) obscurely hints at an optimistic evolutionism, as in the speech of Oceanos to his fellow Titans:

> We fall by course of Nature's law, not force ...
>   As thou wast not the first of powers
> So art thou not the last ...
> So on our heels a fresh perfection treads.
>   ... for 'tis the eternal law
> That first in beauty should be first in might.[22]

But Keats, possibly because he was a student of medicine, was least affected by the romantic conception of nature.

This conception occurs, though only fitfully, in Byron, who does *not* share the romantic conception of imagination. It is present especially in the third canto of *Childe Harold* (1818), written in Geneva when Shelley was his constant companion:

> I live not in myself, but I become
> Portion of that around me; and to me
> High mountains are a feeling.

Byron mentions:

> ... the feeling infinite, so felt
> In solitude where we are least alone;
> A truth which through our being then doth melt
> And purifies from self.[23]

But generally Byron is rather a deist who believes in the Newtonian world machine and constantly contrasts man's passion and unhappiness with the serene and indifferent beauty of nature. Byron knows the horror of man's isolation, the terrors of the empty spaces, and does not share the fundamental rejection of the eighteenth-century cosmology nor the feeling of continuity and basic at-homeness in the universe of the great romantic poets.

This conception of the nature of poetic imagination and of the universe has obvious consequences for poetic practice. All the great romantic poets are mythopoeic, are symbolists whose practice must be understood in terms of their attempt to give a total mythic interpretation of the world to which the poet holds the key. The contemporaries of Blake began this revival of mythic poetry – which can be seen even in their interest in Spenser, in *Midsummer Night's Dream* and *The Tempest*, in the devils and witches of Burns, in the interest of Collins in Highland superstitions and their value for the poet, in the pseudo-Norse mythology of Gray, and in the antiquarian researches of Jacob Bryant and Edward Davies. But the first English poet to create a new mythology on a grand scale was Blake.

Blake's mythology is neither classical nor Christian, though it incorporates many Biblical and Miltonic elements. It draws vaguely on some Celtic (Druidical) mythology or rather names, but essentially it is an original (possibly a too original) creation which tries to give both a cosmogony and an apocalypse: a philosophy of history, a psychology, and (as has been recently stressed) a vision of politics and morals. Even the simplest of the *Songs of Innocence* and *Songs of Experience* are permeated by Blake's symbols. His last poems, such as *Jerusalem*, require an effort of interpretation which may not be commensurate to the aesthetic rewards we get; but Northrop Frye has certainly shown convincingly that Blake was an extraordinarily original thinker who had ideas on cycles of culture, metaphysical theories of time, speculations about the universal diffusion throughout primitive society of archetypal myths and rituals which may be frequently confused and dilettantish, but which should not prove incomprehensible to an age which has acclaimed Toynbee, Dunne on time, and has developed modern anthropology.

Wordsworth, at first sight, is the romantic poet farthest removed from symbolism and mythology. [...] But Wordsworth does stress imagery in his theory and is by no means indifferent to mythology. He plays an important part in the new interest in Greek mythology interpreted in terms of animism. There is the sonnet, 'The World Is too Much with Us,' and there is a passage in the fourth book of the *Excursion* (1814) which celebrates the dim inklings of immortality that the Greek sacrificing a lock in a stream may have had. There is the later turning to classical mythology, 'Laodamia' and the 'Ode to Lycoris,' poems which Wordsworth defended also for their material 'which may ally itself with real sentiment.'

But, most important, his poetry is not without pervading symbols. Cleanth Brooks has shown convincingly how the 'Ode: Intimations of Immortality' is based on a double, contradictory metaphor of light and how even the sonnet 'Upon Westminster Bridge' conceals an all-pervasive figure.[24] *The White Doe of Rylstone* may be really allegorical, in an almost medieval sense (the doe is like an animal in a bestiary), but even this late piece shows Wordsworth's endeavor to go beyond the anecdotal or the descriptive, beyond the naming and analyzing of emotions and states of mind.

In Coleridge a theory of symbolism is central; the artist discourses to us by symbols, and nature is a symbolic language. The distinction between symbol and allegory is, in Coleridge, related to that between imagination and fancy (which, in some ways, can be described as a theory of imagery), genius and talent, reason and understanding. In a late discussion he says that an allegory is but a translation of abstract notions into a picture language, which is itself nothing but an abstraction from objects of sense. On the other hand, a symbol is characterized by a translucence of the special in the individual, or of the general in the special, or of the universal in the general; above all, a symbol is characterized by the translucence of the eternal through and in the temporal. The faculty of symbols is the imagination. Coleridge condemned classical as distinct from Christian mythology in many early pronouncements; but later he became interested in a symbolically reinterpreted Greek mythology and wrote a queer piece 'On the *Prometheus* of Aeschylus' (1825), which is closely dependent on Schelling's treatise, *Über die Gottheiten von Samothrace* (1815).[25]

The early great poetry of Coleridge is certainly symbolic throughout. R.P. Warren has recently given an interpretation of the *Ancient Mariner*, which may go too far in detail, but is convincing in the general thesis – the whole poem implies a concept of 'sacramentalism,' of the holiness of nature and all natural beings, and is organized on symbols of moonlight and sunlight, wind and rain.

That Shelley is a symbolist and mythologist needs no argument. Not only is Shelley's poetry metaphorical through and through, but he aspires to create a new myth of the redemption of the earth which uses classical materials very freely, e.g. in *Prometheus Unbound* (1820), in the 'Witch of Atlas,' and in *Adonais* (1821). This last poem can be easily misinterpreted if it is seen merely as a pastoral elegy in the tradition of Bion and Moschus. Through Shelley's poetry runs a fairly consistent system of recurrent symbols: the eagle and the serpent (which has Gnostic antecedents), temples, towers, the boat, the stream, the cave, and, of course, the veil, the cupola of stained glass, and the white radiance of eternity.

Death is the veil which those who live call life:
They sleep and it is lifted.[26]

In Shelley the ecstasy takes on a hectic, falsetto tone, the voice breaks at the highest points; he swoons, 'I faint, I fail!' 'I fall upon the thorns of life! I bleed.'[27] Shelley would like us to transcend the boundaries of individuality, to be absorbed into some nirvana. This craving for unity explains also one pervading characteristic of his style; synaesthesia and the fusing of the spheres of the different senses in Shelley is paralleled in his rapid transitions and fusions of the emotions, from pleasure to pain, from sorrow to joy.

Keats is a mythologist, too. *Endymion* and *Hyperion* are eloquent witnesses. There is in Keats the recurrent symbolism of moon and sleep, temple and nightingale. The great odes are not merely a series of pictures, but symbolic constructions in which the poet tries to state the conflict of artist and society, time and eternity.

Byron also [...] can be interpreted in these terms: *Manfred* (1817), *Cain, Heaven and Earth*, and even *Sardanapalus* (1821). The great poets are not alone in their time. Southey wrote his epics, *Thalaba, Madoc* (1805), *The Curse of Kehama* (1810), on mythological themes from ancient Wales and India. Thomas Moore gained fame with the Oriental pseudo-splendor of *Lalla Rookh* (1817), Mrs. Tighe's *Psyche* influenced Keats. Finally, in 1821, Carlyle published *Sartor Resartus*, with its philosophy of clothes, and in which a whole chapter is called 'Symbolism.' Whatever the level of penetration, there is a widespread return to the mythic conception of poetry which had been all but forgotten in the eighteenth century. Pope at most could conceive of burlesque machines such as the sylphs in the *Rape of the Lock* or the grandiose, semiserious last yawn of Night at the conclusion of the *Dunciad*.

It could be argued that these romantic attitudes, beliefs, and techniques were confined to a small group of great poets and that, on the whole, the England of the early nineteenth century shared many points of view with the Age of Reason. One may grant that the English romantic movement was never as self-conscious or, possibly, as radical as the German or French movements, that eighteenth-century attitudes were far more influential and widespread than on the continent, e.g. in philosophy where utilitarianism and Scottish common-sense philosophy held sway, and that the English romantic theory of poetry is a curious amalgamation of sensualism and associationism, inherited from the eighteenth century and the new or old Platonic idealism. The only major writer who propounded a coherent 'idealistic' system was Coleridge, and his 'system' or plan for a system was largely an importation from Germany. But there is a good deal of evidence among the minor writers also that the intellectual atmosphere was changing in England. Some of the minor proponents of Kant, such as the curious jeweler, Thomas Wirgman, may be cited. There was much romantic science, biology, and chemistry in England, of which we know very little today. If we examine the literary ideas and scholarship of the time, we can trace the changes which occurred somewhat earlier on the continent. The romantic conception of folklore can be found, e.g. in the remarkable preface to the second edition of Thomas Warton's *History of English Poetry*, by

Richard Price (1824); Price knew the Schlegels, the brothers Grimm, and even Creuzer's *Symbolik*. In 1827 William Motherwell, the first faithful editor of the Scottish ballads, spoke of popular poetry as 'that body of poetry which has inwoven itself with the feelings and passions of the people, and which shadows forth as it were an actual embodiment of their Universal mind, and its intellectual and moral tendencies.'[28] Much research in minor writers and periodicals would be needed to substantiate this fully, but enough evidence has been produced to show that England also underwent the change of intellectual atmosphere which was general in Europe. [...]

My conclusion concerning the unity of the romantic movement may be distressingly orthodox and even conventional. [...] On the whole, political criteria seem grossly overrated as a basis for judging a man's basic view of the world and artistic allegiance.

I do not, of course, deny differences between the various romantic movements, differences of emphasis and distribution of elements, differences in the pace of development, in the individualities of the great writers. I am perfectly aware that the three groups of ideas I have selected have their historical ancestry before the Enlightenment and in under-currents during the eighteenth century. The view of an organic nature descends from neo-Platonism through Giordano Bruno, Böhme, the Cambridge Platonists, and some passages in Shaftesbury. The view of imagination as creative and of poetry as prophecy has a similar ancestry. A symbolist, and even mythic, conception of poetry is frequent in history, e.g. in the baroque age with its emblematic art, its view of nature as hieroglyphics which man and especially the poet is destined to read. In a sense, romanticism is the revival of something old, but it is a revival with a difference; these ideas were translated into terms acceptable to men who had undergone the experience of the Enlightenment. It may be difficult to distinguish clearly between a romantic and a baroque symbol, the romantic and the Böhmean view of nature and imagination. But for our problem we need only know that there is a difference between the symbol in Pope and in Shelley. This can be described; the change from the type of imagery and symbolism used by Pope to that used by Shelley is an empirical fact of history. It seems difficult to deny that we are confronted with substantially the same fact in noting the difference between Lessing and Novalis or Voltaire and Victor Hugo.

Lovejoy has argued that the 'new ideas of the period were in large part heterogeneous, logically independent and sometimes essentially antithetic to one another in their implications'.[29] If we look back on our argument it will be obvious that this view must be mistaken. There is, on the contrary, a profound coherence and mutual implication between the romantic views of nature, imagination, and symbol. Without such a view of nature we could not believe in the significance of symbol and myth. Without symbol and myth the poet would lack the tools for the insight into reality which he claimed, and without such an epistemology, which believes in the creativity of the human mind, there would not be a living nature and a true symbolism. We may not accept this view of the world for ourselves – few of us can accept it literally today – but we should grant that it is coherent and integrated and, as I hope to have shown, all-pervasive in Europe. [...]

Notes

1 'Auguries of Innocence,' *Poetry and Prose of William Blake*, ed. Geoffrey Keynes (New York, 1927), p.118.

2 Walter J. Bate's description in *From Classic to Romantic* (Cambridge, Mass., 1946), p.113.

3 I.A. Richards, *Coleridge on Imagination* (London, 1935), p.145.

4 'For the Sexes: The Gates of Paradise,' *Blake*, p.752.

5 *Prelude* (1850 version), XIV, 190 ff. In the 1805 version this passage is in Book XIII, line 168 ff.

6 Jan. 21, 1824. In *Letters: Later Years*, ed. E. de Selincourt (Oxford), *1*, 134–35.

7 *The Rime of the Ancient Mariner: With an Essay by Robert Penn Warren* (New York, 1946).

8 'Einbildungskraft' is interpreted by Coleridge as 'In-eins-Bildung.' But the prefix 'ein' has nothing to do with 'in-eins.'

9 Jan. 15, 1804. In *Letters*, ed. E. H. Coleridge, *2* (London, 1890), 450.

10 Shelley's *Literary and Philosophical Criticism*, ed. J. Shawcross (London, 1909), pp.131, 155, 153.

11 Letter to B. Bailey, Nov. 22, 1817, in *Letters*, ed. M. B. Forman (4th ed. London, 1952), p.67.

12 *The Mind of John Keats* (Oxford, 1926), p.126.

13 Letter to T. Butts, Nov. 22, 1802, *Blake*, p.1068.

14 Ibid., p.1026 (written in 1826).

15 Letter to T. Butts, Oct. 2, 1800, ibid., 1052.

16 S. Foster Damon, *William Blake* (Boston, 1924); William C. Percival, *William Blake's 'Circle of Destiny'* (New York, 1938); Mark Schorer, *William Blake* (New York, 1946); Northrop Frye, *Fearful Symmetry: A Study of William Blake* (Princeton, 1947).

17 *Prelude* (1850 version), VI, 636 ff. In the 1805 version this is Book VI, line 568 ff.

18 Ibid., XII, 276–77. In the 1805 version this is at XI, 332 ff.

19 Preface to *Excursion. Poetical Works*, ed. E. de Selincourt and H. Darbishire (Oxford, 1949), 5, 5.

20 From 'The Eolian Harp,' 'Frost at Midnight,' 'The Destiny of Nations,' and 'Dejection,' *The Poems*, ed. E.H. Coleridge (Oxford, 1912), pp.101–02, 132, 242, 365.

21 *Adonais*, lines 462–63.

22 Book II, lines 181–90, 189, 212, 228–29.

23 *Childe Harold*, canto III, stanzas 72, 90.

24 *The Well Wrought Urn* (New York, 1947).

25 *The Statesman's Manual*, in *Complete Works*, ed. Shedd, *I* (New York, 1853), 437–38.

26 *Prometheus Unbound*, III, scene 3, lines 113–14.

27 'The Indian Serenade,' 'Ode to the West Wind.'

28 *Minstrelsy: Ancient and Modern* (Glasgow, 1827), p.v.

29 'The Meaning of Romanticism for the Historian of Ideas,' *Journal of the History of Ideas, 2* (1941), 261.

Bibliography

Abrams, M.H. (1953) *The Mirror and the Lamp: Romantic Theory and the Critical Tradition*, Oxford University Press.

Abrams, M.H. (ed.) (1993) *The Norton Anthology of English Literature*, 2 vols, W.W. Norton.

Adburgham, A. (1972) *Women in Print: Writing Women and Women's Magazines from the Restoration to the Accession of Victoria*, Allen and Unwin.

Allott, M. (ed.) (1970) *Keats: The Complete Poems*, Longman.

Althusser, L. (1984) 'Ideology and ideological state apparatuses: notes towards an investigation' in *Essays on Ideology*, Verso (first published in French in 1970).

Austen, J. (1990 edn) *Northanger Abbey*, edited by J. Davie, Oxford University Press (first published 1818).

Austen, J. (1990 edn) *Pride and Prejudice*, edited by J. Kinsley, Oxford University Press (first published 1813).

Barbauld, A. *see* McCarthy, W. and Kraft, E.

Barron, G. (1987) 'Prison or pleasure dome: images of enclosure in Romantic literature', unpublished MA dissertation, University of London.

Barton, A. (1992) *Byron: Don Juan*, Landmarks of World Literature series, Cambridge University Press.

Beer, J. (ed.) (1993 edn) *Poems of S.T. Coleridge*, Dent (first published 1963).

Bennett, J. (1795 edn) *Letters to a Young Lady*, 2 vols, T. Cadell Junior and W. Davies.

Bentley, G.E. (ed.) (1978) *William Blake's Writings*, 2 vols, Clarendon Press.

Beutin, W., et al. (1993) *A History of German Literature*, translated by C. Krojzl, Routledge.

Blake, W. *see* Bentley, G.E.; Erdman, D.V.

Bromwich, D. (ed.) (1987) *Romantic Critical Essays*, Cambridge University Press.

Burke, E. (1968 edn) *Reflections on the Revolution in France*, edited by C.C. O'Brien, Penguin (first published 1790).

Burke, E. (1987 edn) *A Philosophical Enquiry into the Origin of Our Ideas of the Sublime and the Beautiful*, edited by J.T. Boulton, Basil Blackwell (first published 1757–59).

Burney, F. (1982 edn) *Evelina*, edited by E.A. Bloom, Oxford University Press (first published 1778).

Byron, G.G. *see* Barton, A.; Marchand, L.A.; McGann, J.J. (1980–93); Page, F.

Carey, J. (ed.) (1971) *Milton: Complete Shorter Poems*, Longman.

Carter, A. (1992) *Expletives Deleted: Selected Writings*, Chatto and Windus.

Chase, C. (ed.) (1993) *Romanticism*, Longman.

Christensen, J. (1993) *Lord Byron's Strength: Romantic Writing and Commercial Society*, Johns Hopkins University Press.

Clare, J. *see* Robinson, E. and Powell, D.

Cohen, J. (ed.) (1951) *Tales From Hoffmann*, The Bodley Head.

Coleridge, S.T. *see* Beer, J.; Griggs, E.L.; White, R.J.

Colley, L. (1992) *Britons: Forging the Nation 1707–1837*, Yale University Press.

Cook, J. (1993) 'Paul de Man and imaginative consolation' in N. Wood (ed.) *The Prelude*, Theory in Practice Series, Open University Press.

Countess Blessington (1969 edn) *Conversations of Lord Byron*, edited by E.J. Lovell, Princeton University Press.

Curran, S. (1988) 'Romantic poetry: the "I" altered' in A.K. Mellor (ed.) *Romanticism and Feminism*, Indiana University Press.

de Quincey, T. (1971 edn) *Confessions of an English Opium Eater*, edited by G. Lindop, Penguin (first published 1821).

de Selincourt, E. (ed.) (1967) *The Letters of William and Dorothy Wordsworth*, Oxford University Press.

Dickens, C. (1994 edn) *Great Expectations*, edited by M. Cardwell and K. Flint, Oxford University Press (first published 1860–61).

Dyer, D. (1977) *The Stories of Kleist: A Critical Study*, Duckworth.

Edgeworth, M. (1993 edn) *Letters for Literary Ladies*, edited by C. Connolly, Dent (first published 1795).

Edgeworth, M. (1993 edn) *Belinda*, edited by E.N. Chuilleanain, Dent (first published 1801).

Eliot, G. (1994 edn) *Middlemarch*, edited by R. Ashton, Penguin (first published 1871–2).

Erdman, D.V. (ed.) (1982) *The Complete Poetry and Prose of William Blake*, Anchor Press/Doubleday.

Foot, M. and Kramnick, I. (eds) (1987) *The Thomas Paine Reader*, Penguin (first published ?).

Fordyce, J. (1796 edn) *Sermons to Young Women*, vol.1, Oxford (first published 1765).

Forman, M.B. (ed.) (1931) *The Letters of John Keats*, 2 vols, Oxford University Press.

Franklin, C. (1993) 'Juan's sea changes: class, race, and gender in Byron's *Don Juan*' in N. Wood (ed.) *Don Juan*, Theory in Practice Series, Open University Press, pp.56–89.

Freud, S. *see* Strachey, J.

Gildea, R. (1987) *Barricades and Borders: Europe 1800–1914*, Oxford University Press.

Gilfillan, G. (1847) 'Female authors, no.1 – Mrs. Hemans', *Tait's Edinburgh Magazine*, 14, pp.359–63.

Gilfillan, G. (1847) 'Female authors, no.2 – Mrs. Elizabeth Barrett Browning', *Tait's Edinburgh Magazine*, 14, pp.620–25.

Gillman, J. (1838) *Life of S.T. Coleridge*, London.

Goethe, J.W. von (1989 edn) *The Sorrows of Young Werther*, translated by M. Hulse, Penguin (first published 1774).

Griggs, E.L. (ed.) (1956) *Collected Letters of Samuel Taylor Coleridge, Volume I: 1785–1800*, Clarendon Press.

Hamilton, P. (1987) *Wordsworth*, Harvester New Readings, Harvester.

Hartman, G. (1964) *Wordsworth's Poetry, 1787–1814*, Yale University Press.

Homans, M. (1980) *Women Writers and Poetic Identity: Dorothy Wordsworth, Emily Brontë, and Emily Dickinson*, Princeton University Press.

Hutchinson, T. (ed.) (1970) *Shelley: Poetical Works*, rev. G.M. Matthews, Oxford University Press.

Ibsen, H. (1992 edn) *A Doll's House*, anonymous undated English translation from around 1900, Dover.

Ingpen, R. and Peck, W.E. (eds) (1926–30) *The Complete Works of Percy Bysshe Shelley* (The Julian Edition), 10 vols, Ernest Benn.

James, C.L.R. (1980) *Black Jacobins*, Alison and Busby.

Janowitz, A. (1984) 'Shelley's monument to Ozymandias', *Philological Quarterly*, 63, pp.477–91.

Jones, F. (ed.) (1964) *Collected Letters of P.B. Shelley*, vol.1, Oxford University Press.

Jones, V. (ed.) (1990) *Women in the Eighteenth Century: Constructions of Femininity*, Routledge.

Jones, W. (1799) *Works of Sir William Jones*, vol.5, London.

Keats, J. *see* Allot, M.; Forman, M.B.

Kelly, G. (1989) *English Fiction of the Romantic Period 1788–1830*, Longman.

Kelly, G. (1993) *Women, Writing and Revolution 1790–1827*, Clarendon Press.

Ketcham, C.H. (ed.) (1989) *Shorter Poems, 1807–1820, by William Wordsworth*, The Cornell Wordsworth, Cornell University Press.

Klancher, J.P. (1987) *The Making of English Reading Audiences, 1790–1832*, University of Wisconsin Press.

Knowles, J. (1831) *The Life and Writings of Henry Fuseli*, London.

Landon, L.E. (L.E.L.) (1835) 'On the characteristics of Mrs. Hemans's writing', *New Monthly Magazine*, 44, pp.425–33.

Leask, N. (1992) *British Romantic Writers and the East: Anxieties of Empire*, Cambridge University Press.

Leighton, A. (1992) *Victorian Women Poets: Writing Against the Heart*, Harvester.

Levin, S. (1987) *Dorothy Wordsworth and Romanticism*, Rutgers.

Levinson, M. (1988) *Keats's Life of Allegory: The Origins of a Style*, Basil Blackwell.

Lockhart, J.G. (1840) 'Modern English poetesses', *Quarterly Review*, 66, pp.374–418.

Lonsdale, D. (ed.) (1989) *Eighteenth-Century Women Poets: An Oxford Anthology*, Oxford University Press.

Lonsdale, R. (ed.) (1989) *Eighteenth Century Women Poets*, Oxford University Press.

Lovell, T. (1987) *Consuming Fiction*, Verso.

MacQueen, J. (1970) *Allegory*, Methuen.

Marchand, L.A. (ed.) (1973–82) *Byron's Letters and Journals*, 12 vols, John Murray.

Mason, M. (ed.) (1992) *Lyrical Ballads*, Longman Annotated Texts.

McCarthy, W. and Kraft, E. (eds) (1994) *The Poems of Anna Letitia Barbauld*, University of Georgia Press.

McGann, J.J. (ed.) (1980–1993) *Lord Byron: The Complete Poetical Works*, 7 vols, Clarendon Press.

McGann, J.J. (1983) *The Romantic Ideology: A Critical Investigation*, University of Chicago Press.

McGann, J.J. (1985) 'Keats and the historical method in literary criticism', 'The Book of Byron and the Book of a World' and 'The Ancient Mariner: the meaning of the meanings' in *The Beauty of Inflections: Literary Investigations in Historical Method and Theory*, Clarendon Press.

McGann, J.J. (ed.) (1992) *The New Oxford Book of Romantic Period Verse*, Oxford University Press.

Mellor, A.K. (1980) *English Romantic Irony*, Harvard University Press.

Mellor, A.K. (1993) *Romanticism and Gender*, Routledge.

Milton, J. (1971 edn) *Paradise Lost*, edited by A. Fowler, Longman (first published 1667); *see also* Carey, J.

Moorman, M. (ed.) (1971) *Journal of Dorothy Wordsworth*, Oxford.

More, H. (1801) *Works*, vols 7–8, London.

Nemoianu, V. (1984) *The Taming of Romanticism: European Literature and the Age of Biedermeier*, Harvard University Press.

Page, F. (ed.) (1970) *Lord Byron, Poetical Works*, Oxford University Press.

Paglia, C. (1991) *Sexual Personae: Art and Decadence from Nefertiti to Emily Dickinson*, Penguin.

Paine, T. (1791) *Rights of Man*, J. Johnson; *see also* Foot, M. and Kramnick, I.

Reed, M.L. (ed.) (1991) *The Thirteen-Book Prelude*, The Cornell Wordsworth, Cornell University Press.

Reiman, D.H. (ed.) (1972) *The Romantics Reviewed: Contemporary Reviews of British Romantic Writers, Part B, Byron and Regency Society Poets, vol. I, Annual Review – British Review*, Garland.

Rivers, I. (1979) *Classical and Christian Ideas in English Renaissance Poetry*, Allen and Unwin.

Robinson, E. and Powell, D. (eds) (1984) *The Later Poems of John Clare*, 2 vols, Clarendon Press.

Ross, M.B. (1989) *The Contours of Masculine Desire: Romanticism and the Rise of Women's Poetry*, Oxford University Press.

Rutherford, A. (ed.) (1970) *Byron: The Critical Heritage*, Routledge and Kegan Paul.

Said, E. (1978) *Orientalism*, Penguin.

Sales, R. (1983) 'Lord Byron's speaking part' in *English Literature in History 1780–1830: Pastoral and Politics*, Hutchinson, pp.204–31.

Schwab, R. (1984) *The Oriental Renaissance: Europe's Rediscovery of India and the East, 1680–1880*, translated by G.P. Black and V. Reinking, Columbia University Press.

Shelley, M. (1994 edn) *Frankenstein: The 1818 Text*, edited and introduced by M. Butler, Oxford University Press.

Shelley, P.B. *see* Ingpen, R. and Peck, W.E.; Jones, F.; Webb, T.; Hutchinson, T.

Simpson, D. (1986) 'Reading Blake and Derrida – our Caesars neither prais'd nor buried' in N. Hilton and T.A. Vogler (eds) *Unnam'd Forms: Blake and Textuality*, University of California Press, pp.11–25.

Spivak, G. (1988) 'Can the subaltern speak?' in C. Nelson and L. Grossberg (eds) *Marxism and the Interpretation of Culture*, Macmillan.

St Clair, W. (1989) *The Godwins and the Shelleys: The Biography of a Family*, Faber and Faber.

Sterne, L. (1967 edn) *The Life and Opinions of Tristram Shandy, Gentleman*, edited by G. Petrie, Penguin (first published 1759–67).

Stillinger, J. (1971) *The Hoodwinking of Madeline and Other Essays on Keats's Poems*, University of Illinois Press.

Strachey, J. (trans.) (1955) *The Complete Psychological Works of Sigmund Freud*, vol. XVII (1917–1919) *An Infantile Neurosis and Other Works*, The Hogarth Press.

Taylor, R. (trans.) (1985) *Six German Romantic Tales*, Angel Books.

Thompson, E.P. (1968) *The Making of the English Working Class*, Penguin.

Thorslev, P.L. (1962) *The Byronic Hero: Types and Prototypes*, University of Minnesota Press.

Todd, J. (1989) *The Sign of Angellica: Women, Writing and Fiction, 1660–1800*, Virago.

Todd, J. and Butler, M. (eds) (1989) *The Works of Mary Wollstonecraft*, vol.5, Pickering and Chatto (first published 1759–97).

Turner, C. (1992) *Living by the Pen: Women Writers in the Eighteenth Century*, Routledge.

Webb, T. (ed.) (1995) *Percy Bysshe Shelley: Poems and Prose*, Everyman.

Wellek, R. (1963) *Concepts of Criticism*, edited by S.G. Nichols Jr, Yale University Press.

White, R.J. (ed.) (1972) *Collected Works of Samuel Taylor Coleridge, vol.6 Lay Sermons*, Routledge and Kegan Paul.

Williams, R. (1958) *Culture and Society, 1780–1950*, Chatto and Windus.

Williams, R. (1976) *Keywords: A Vocabulary of Culture and Society*, Fontana (revised and expanded 1983, Flamingo/Fontana).

Wollstonecraft, M. (1975 edn) *A Vindication of the Rights of Woman*, edited by M. Kramnick, Pelican (first published 1792); *see also* Todd, J. and Butler, M.

Wordsworth, D. *see* de Selincourt, E.; Moorman, M.

Wordsworth, J., Abrams, M.H. and Gill, S. (eds) (1979) *The Prelude, 1799, 1805, 1850*, W. W. Norton.

Wordsworth, W. *see* de Selincourt, E.; Hartman, G.; Ketcham, C.H.; Mason, M.; Reed, M.L.; Wordsworth, J. *et al.*

Wu, D. (ed.) (1994) *Romanticism: An Anthology*, Blackwell.

Acknowledgements

Grateful acknowledgement is made to the following sources for permission to reproduce material in this book:

Curran, S. (1988) 'Romantic poetry: the "I" altered' in Mellor, A.K. (ed.) *Romanticism and Feminism*, Indiana University Press; Schwab, R. (1950) in Patterson-Black, G. and Reinking, V. (trans) *The Oriental Renaissance, Europe's Rediscovery of India and the East, 1680–1880*, copyright 1950 by Editions Payot, Paris. English language translation copyright © 1984 by Columbia University Press. All rights reserved; Wellek, R. (1963) *Concepts of Criticism*, Yale University Press, copyright © 1963 by Yale University. All rights reserved; Freud, S. (1955) 'The "Uncanny"' in Strachey, J. (ed. and trans.) *The Standard Edition of the Complete Psychological Works of Sigmund Freud*, seventh edition, translation and editorial matter © The Institute of Psycho-Analysis and Mrs Alix Strachey 1955, by permission of Sigmund Freud Copyrights, The Institute of Psycho-Analysis and the Hogarth Press; Williams, R. (1958) *Culture and Society 1780–1950*, Chatto and Windus.

Index

war and restoration in Europe
257–8
women as readers 108
Middlemarch see Eliot, George
Milton, John 11, 68
and allegory 205, 213, 215,
216–17
and Byron's *Don Juan* 167,
170, 172
Paradise Lost 39, 57–8, 65, 67,
213
and *The Book of Urizen* 104
compared with *The Prelude*
117, 122, 123–4, 126,
131
and women poets 188, 189,
190
Paradise Regained 65, 135
Romanticism and 271
Samson Agonistes 122
mimetic view of art 77–8
Mirror and the Lamp see Abrams,
M.H.
Missionary see Morgan, Lady
Sydney
'Modern English Poetesses' see
Lockhart, John Gibson
Monks and the Giants see
'Whistlecraft' (John Hookham
Frere)
Moore, Thomas 162, 229, 236,
302, 333
Moorman, *Journal of Dorothy
Wordsworth* 21–2
More, Hannah 95, 100, 165, 188,
202, 281, 282
'The Bad Bargain' 286
and *Don Juan* 177
and sensibility 186–7
*Strictures on the Modern
System of Female Education*
99, 192
Morgan, Lady Sydney, *The
Missionary* 234
motherhood, and women writers
55, 56
mothers, women represented as
97, 98, 102
mountain passages, in *The
Prelude* 123–8
'Mouse's Petition' see Barbauld,
Anna Laetitia
Murray, John 167

myth
and allegory 209, 213
and the concept of
Romanticism 269, 270, 271,
331–3
myths of origin 39, 44
in 'A Poison Tree' 39, 44

Naked Lunch see Burroughs,
William
Napoleon Bonaparte 9, 50–1, 72, 96
and Byron 164
and ideology 272
and 'Ozymandias' 53–4
and Wordsworth's *Prelude*
134–5, 136
Napoleonic wars 9, 47–8, 50–1,
96, 133, 227
and imperialism 235
and the middle class in Europe
257–8
narrative
dialogic 158
framed 223
literature, story and plot in
209–10
poetry 27, 115
in *The Prelude* 115–18
romantic verse 139–59
irony in 144, 149
'La Belle Dame Sans Merci'
141–6
satire on 139–40
narrator
in 'Anecdote for Fathers' 27–8
in *Don Juan* 171, 172, 175,
178, 179
in *Frankenstein* 58
in 'La Belle Dame Sans Merci'
144
in 'Ozymandias' 52
nationalist movements in Europe
49, 258, 264
nature
and allegory 225
in *Childe Harold's Pilgrimage*
163, 164
and the concept of
Romanticism 269, 270, 271,
328–31
in 'Nurse's Song' 34–5
and Orientalism 229

and the poet's imagination 78
in *The Rime of the Ancyent
Marinere* 206–7, 208
in Romantic poetry 6, 23–5
in Shelley's poetry 68, 157
and women 200–2
in Wordsworth's poetry 34–5,
50, 52, 54, 68, 69, 120, 156
The Prelude 120–2, 125–8,
137
'Tintern Abbey' 118
'New Historicism' 15
New Monthly Magazine 194–5
'Night at Sea' see Landor, Letitia
Elizabeth (L.E.L.)
Northanger Abbey see Austen,
Jane
Norton, Caroline 199
novels
Gothic 139, 141, 143, 238
women reading 93, 94, 107–8
and women writers 59–60, 95,
109–13

ocean, in *Childe Harold's
Pilgrimage* 163
'On Gusto' see Hazlitt, William
'On a Lady's Writing' see
Barbauld, Anna Laetitia
'On the Present State of the Art,
and the Causes which check its
Progress' see Fuseli, Henry
opium
and Coleridge 227, 228, 229,
230, 231
*Confessions of an English
Opium Eater* 230, 242–7
trade 242–3, 245
Oriental Renaissance see Schwab,
Raymond
Orientalism 227–49, 271
Coleridge and 227–32
imperialism and 235–6, 247
'oriental renaissance' 233–4,
235, 247, 294–302
Othello see Shakespeare, William
Otway, Thomas 185, 187
'Ozymandias' see Shelley, Percy
Bysshe

Paine, Thomas 23, 25, 47
The Rights of Man 10, 20, 43,
61